DEATH JR.

GARY WHITTA
&
TED NAIFEH

IMAGE COMICS, INC.

ERIK LARSEN - PUBLISHER
TODD McFARLANE - PRESIDENT
MARC SILVESTRI - CEO
JIM VALENTINO - VICE-PRESIDENT

ERIC STEPHENSON - EXECUTIVE DIRECTOR
JIM DEMONAKOS - PR & MARKETING COORDINATOR
MIA MACHATTON - ACCOUNTS MANAGER
LAURENN McCUBBIN - ART DIRECTOR
ALLEN HUI - PRODUCTION ARTIST
JOE KEATINGE - TRAFFIC MANAGER
JONATHAN CHAN - PRODUCTION ASSISTANT
DREW GILL - PRODUCTION ASSISTANT
TRACI HUI - ADMINISTRATIVE ASSISTANT

WWW.IMAGECOMICS.COM

DEATH, JR., VOL 1. Second Printing. 2005. Published by Image Comics, Inc., Office of publication: 1942 University Avenue, Suite 305, Berkeley, California 94704. Copyright © 2005 Backbone Entertainment. Originally published in single magazine form as DEATH, JR. #1-3. All rights reserved. DEATH, JR.™ (including all prominent characters featured in this issue), its logo and all character likenesses are trademarks of Backbone Entertainment unless otherwise noted. Image Comics® is a trademark of Image Comics, Inc. All rights reserved. No part of this publication may be reproduced or transmitted, in any form or by any means (except for short excerpts for review purposes) without the express written permission of Image Comics, Inc. All names, characters, events and locales in this publication are entirely fictional. Any resemblance to actual persons (living or dead), events or places, without satiric intent, is coincidental. PRINTED IN CANADA.

WRITTEN BY
GARY WHITTA

&

ILLUSTRATED BY
TED NAIFEH

EDITED BY TERRI SELTING
PRODUCED BY NICOLE TANNER

BACKBONE ENTERTAINMENT

COVER ART BY MIKE MIGNOLA

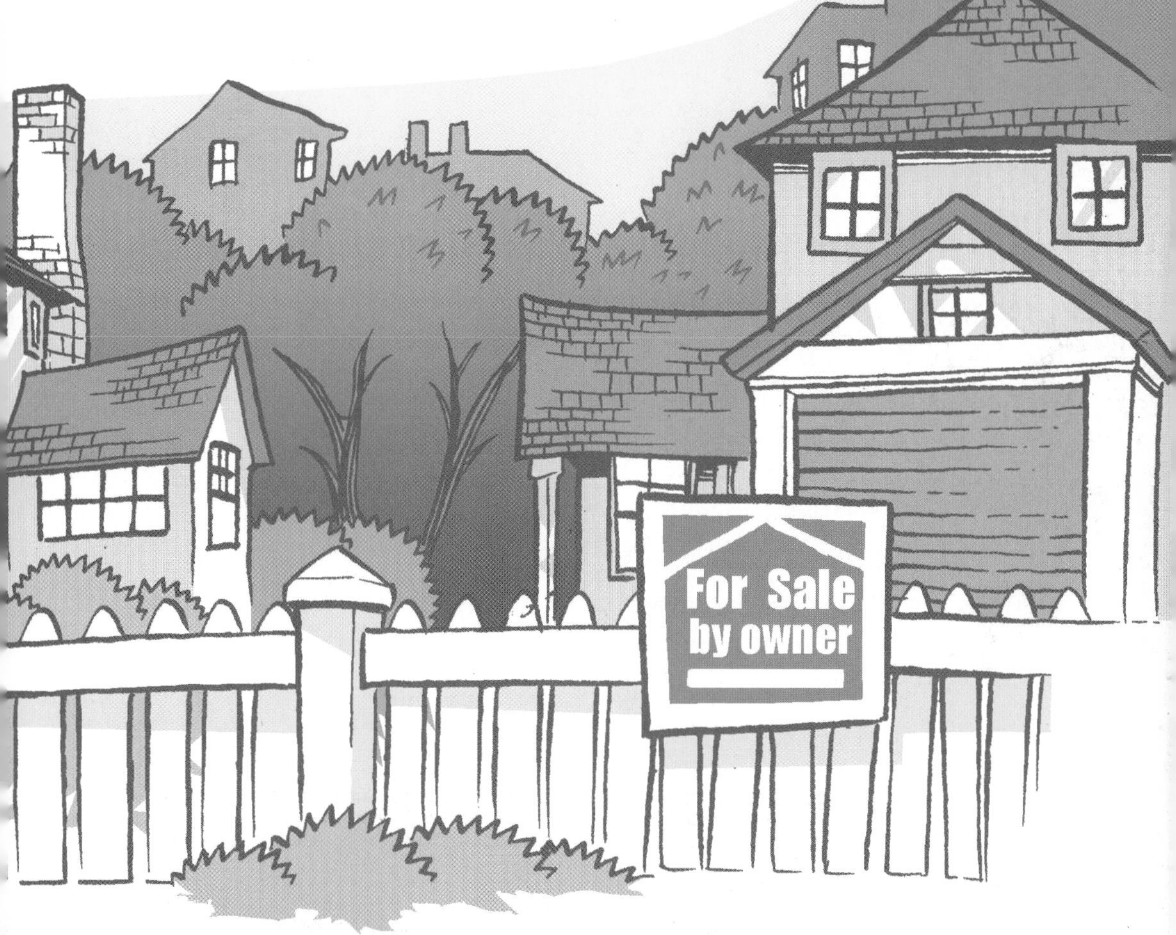
For Sale
by owner

VOL. 1 COVER BY SACH STEFFEL
VOL. 2 COVER BY RHODE MONTIJO
LETTERS BY TED NAIFEH AND TRISTAN CRANE
COLOR BY TED NAIFEH AND CRAIG PHILLIPS
VOL. 3 COVER BY STEVE PURCELL

SPECIAL THANKS TO MIKE MIKA, CHRIS CHARLA, ANDREW AYRE, JON GOLDMAN AND MARK LOUGHRIDGE.

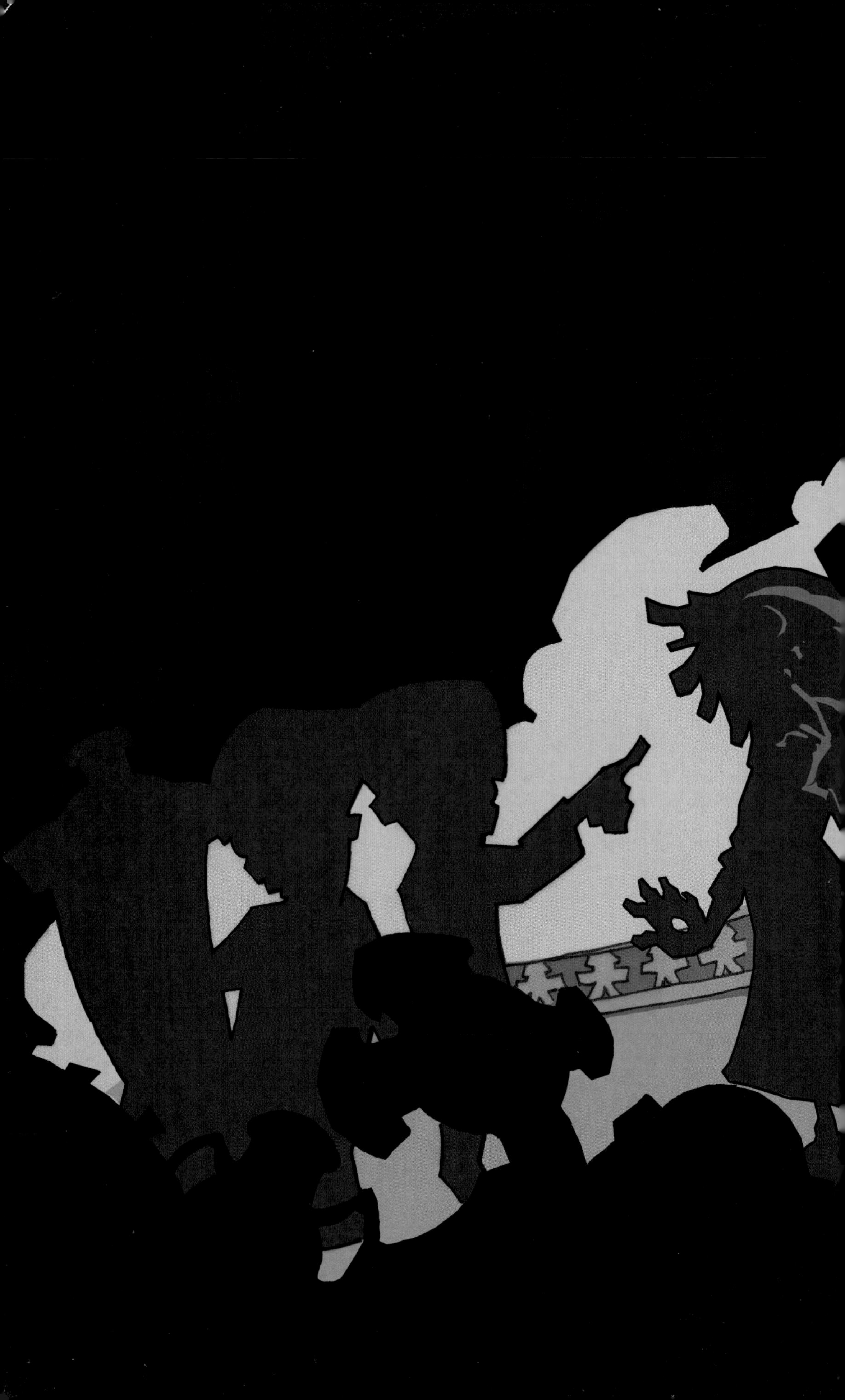

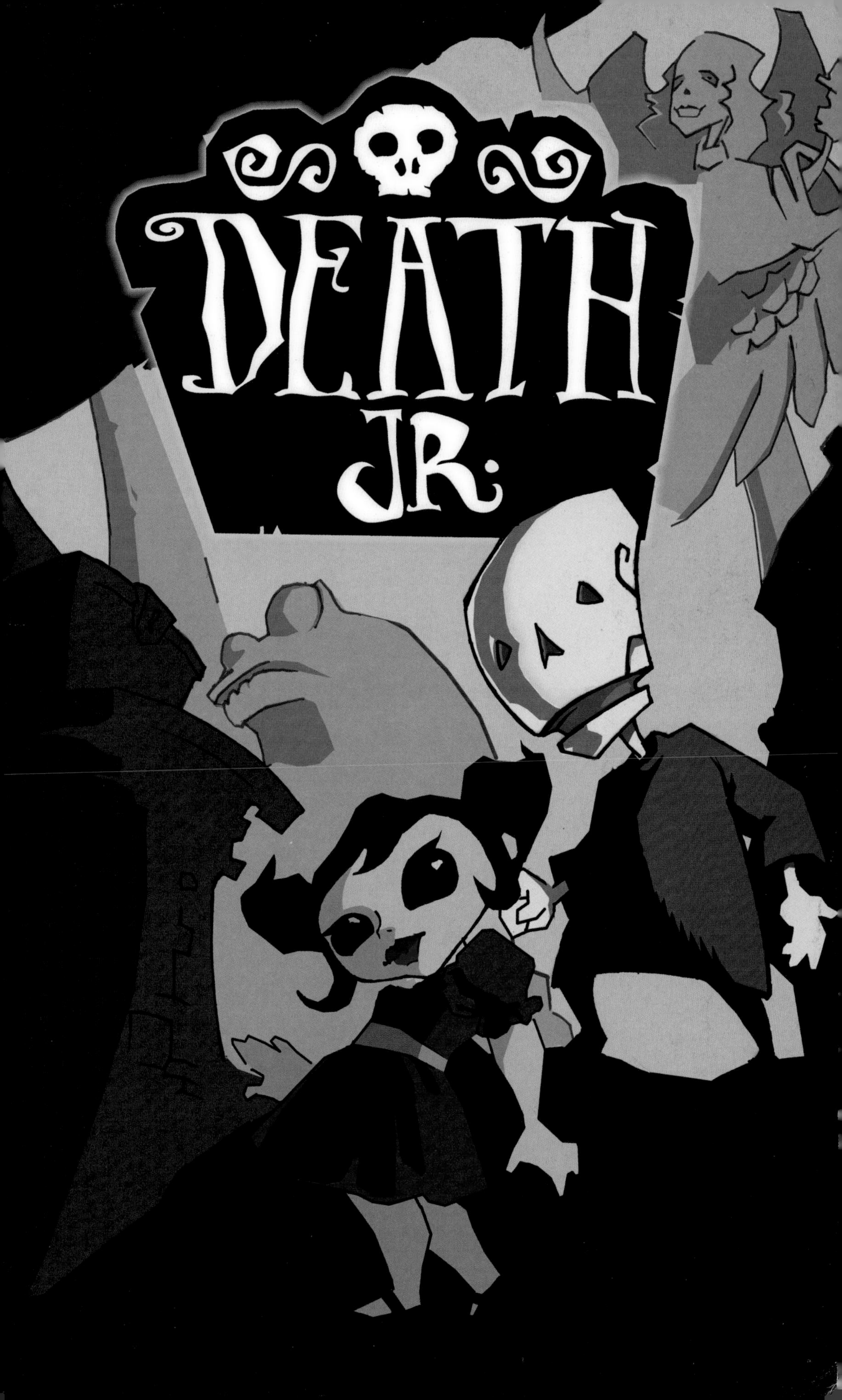
DEATH
JR.

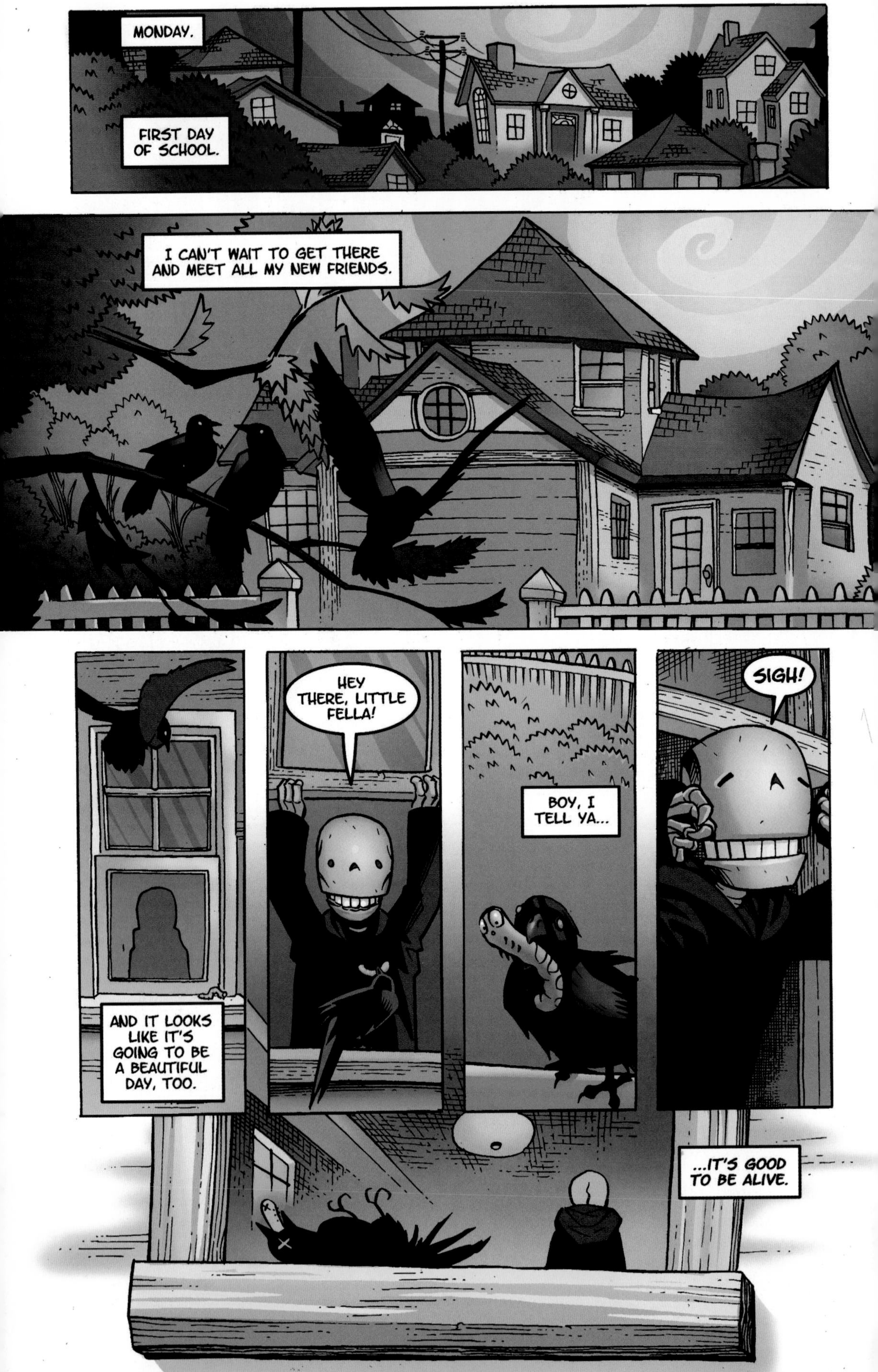
MONDAY.
FIRST DAY OF SCHOOL.
I CAN'T WAIT TO GET THERE AND MEET ALL MY NEW FRIENDS.
AND IT LOOKS LIKE IT'S GOING TO BE A BEAUTIFUL DAY, TOO.
HEY THERE, LITTLE FELLA!
BOY, I TELL YA...
SIGH!
...IT'S GOOD TO BE ALIVE.

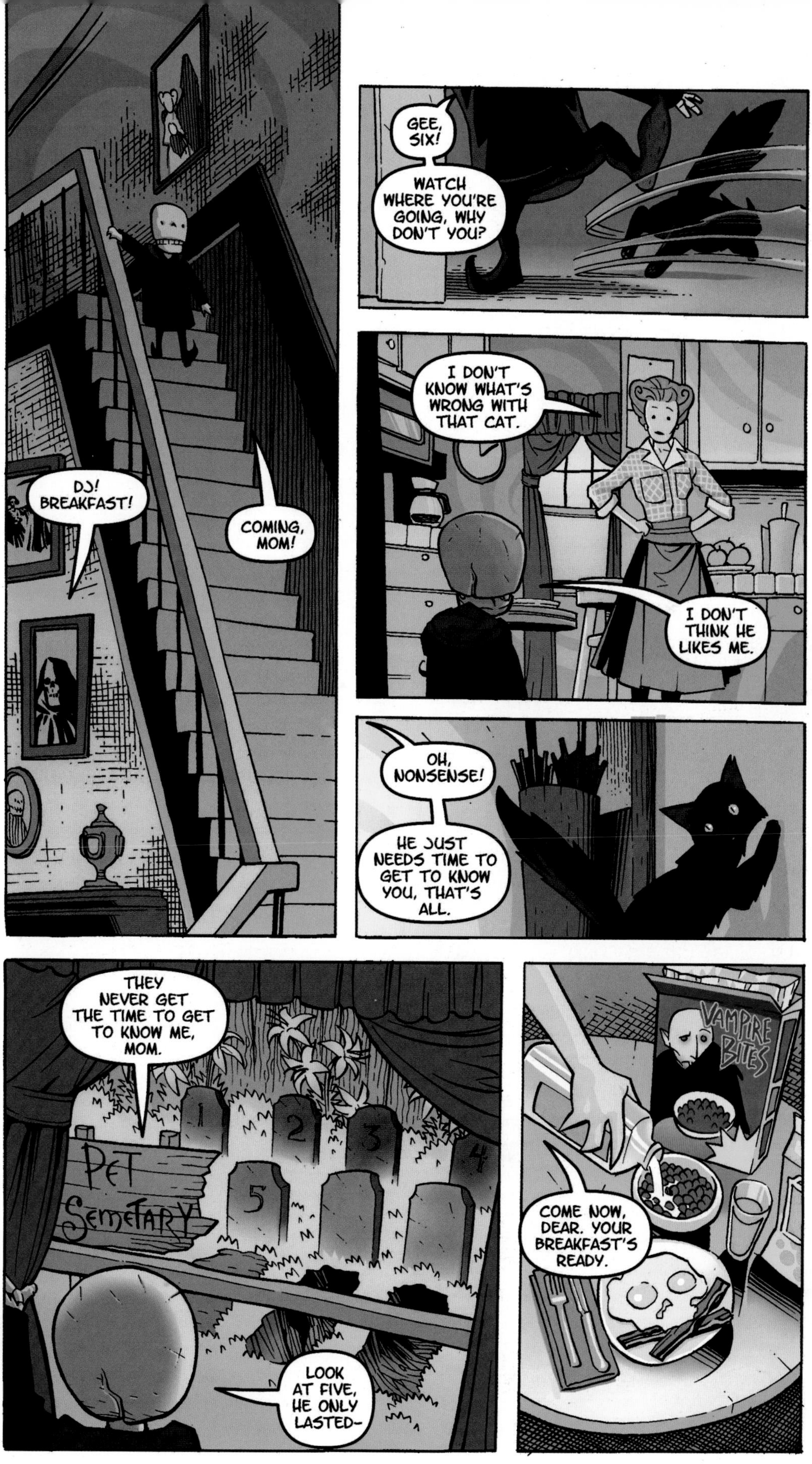
DJ! BREAKFAST!
COMING, MOM!
GEE, SIX!
WATCH WHERE YOU'RE GOING, WHY DON'T YOU?
I DON'T KNOW WHAT'S WRONG WITH THAT CAT.
I DON'T THINK HE LIKES ME.
OH, NONSENSE!
HE JUST NEEDS TIME TO GET TO KNOW YOU, THAT'S ALL.
THEY NEVER GET THE TIME TO GET TO KNOW ME, MOM.
PET SEMETARY
1
2
3
4
5
LOOK AT FIVE, HE ONLY LASTED-
VAMPIRE BITES
COME NOW, DEAR. YOUR BREAKFAST'S READY.

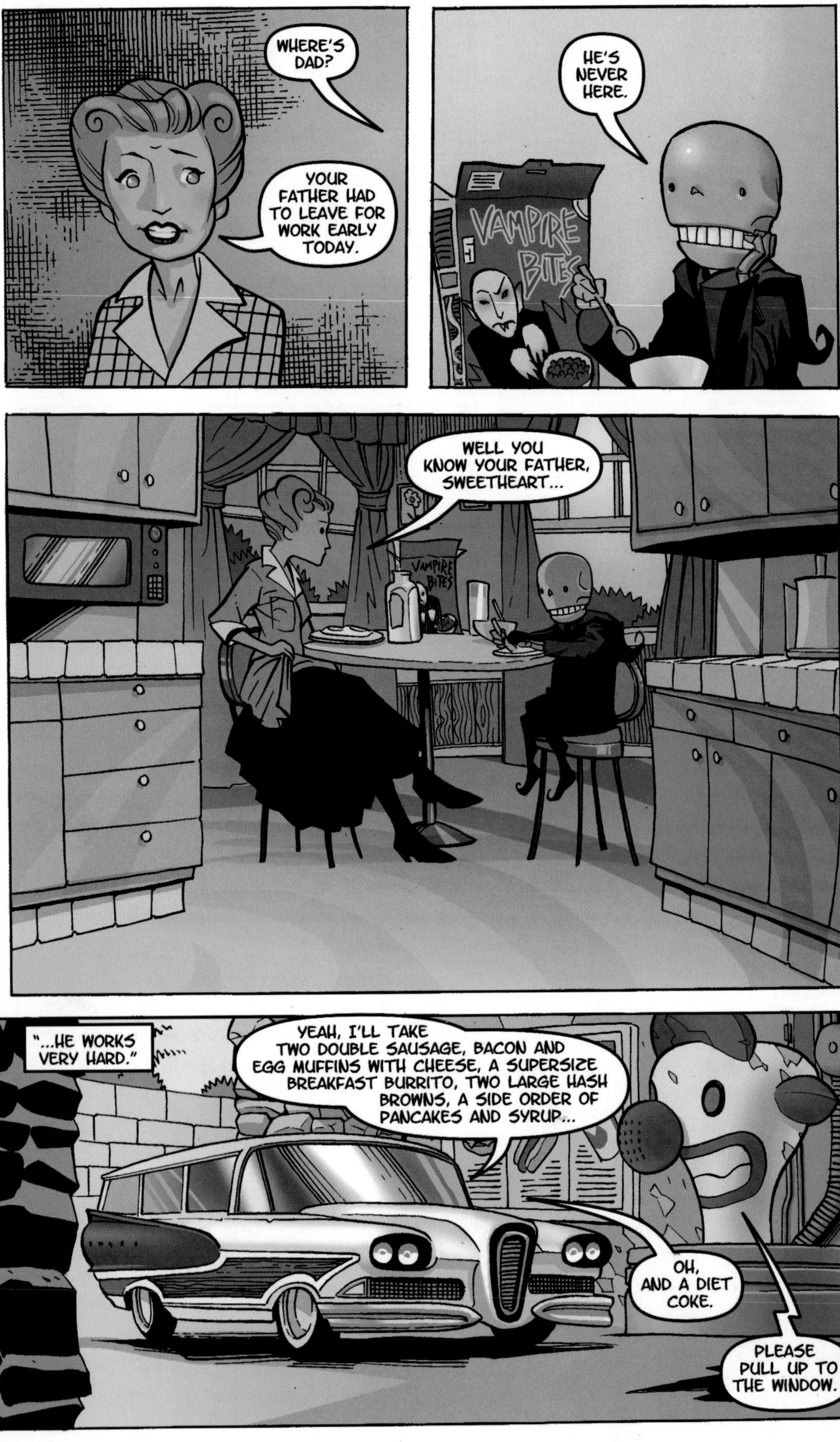
WHERE'S DAD?
YOUR FATHER HAD TO LEAVE FOR WORK EARLY TODAY.
HE'S NEVER HERE.
VAMPIRE BITES
WELL YOU KNOW YOUR FATHER, SWEETHEART...
"...HE WORKS VERY HARD."
YEAH, I'LL TAKE TWO DOUBLE SAUSAGE, BACON AND EGG MUFFINS WITH CHEESE, A SUPERSIZE BREAKFAST BURRITO, TWO LARGE HASH BROWNS, A SIDE ORDER OF PANCAKES AND SYRUP...
OH, AND A DIET COKE.
PLEASE PULL UP TO THE WINDOW.

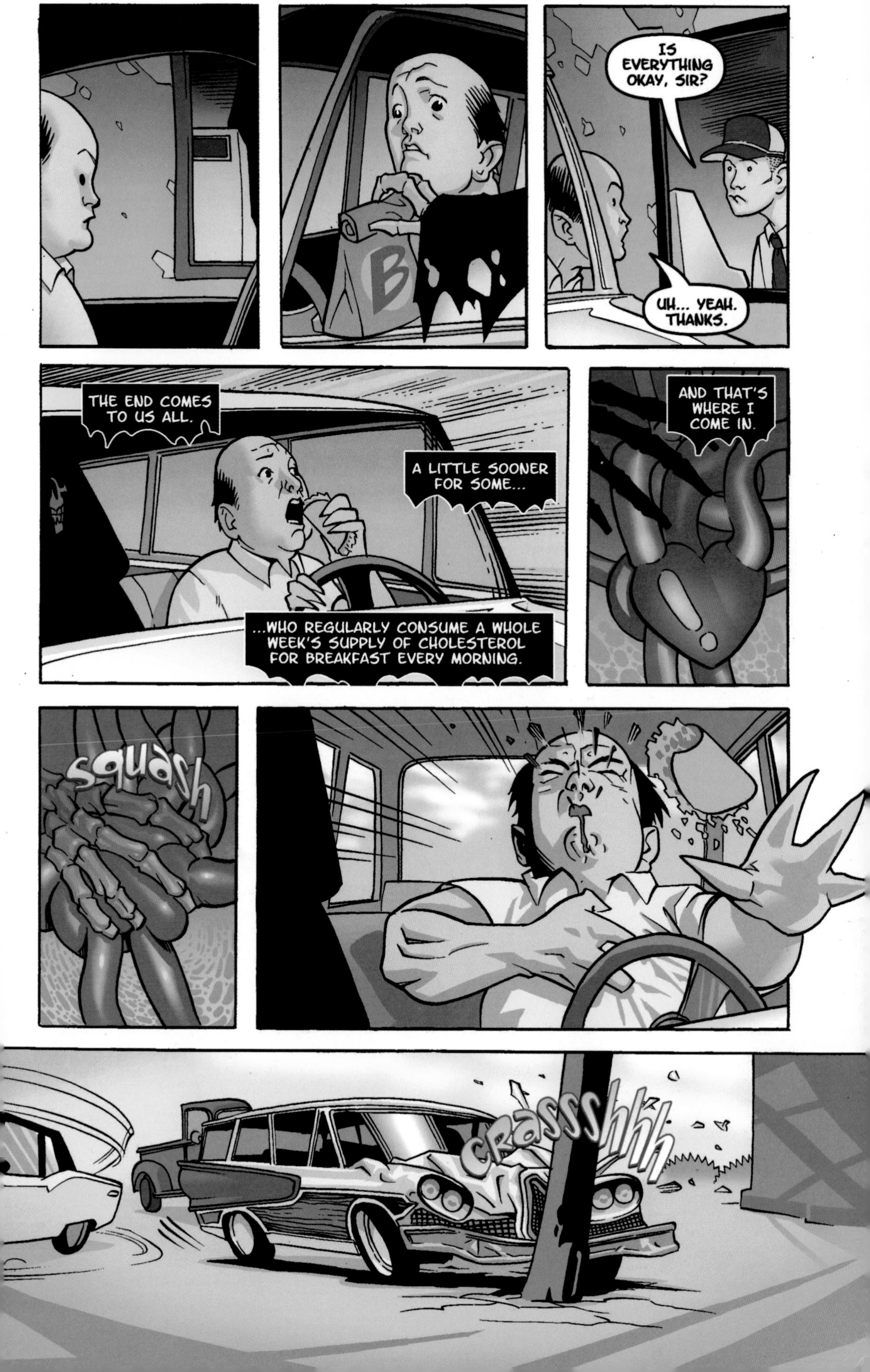
IS EVERYTHING OKAY, SIR?
UH... YEAH. THANKS.
THE END COMES TO US ALL.
A LITTLE SOONER FOR SOME...
...WHO REGULARLY CONSUME A WHOLE WEEK'S SUPPLY OF CHOLESTEROL FOR BREAKFAST EVERY MORNING.
AND THAT'S WHERE I COME IN.
squash
CRASSSHHH

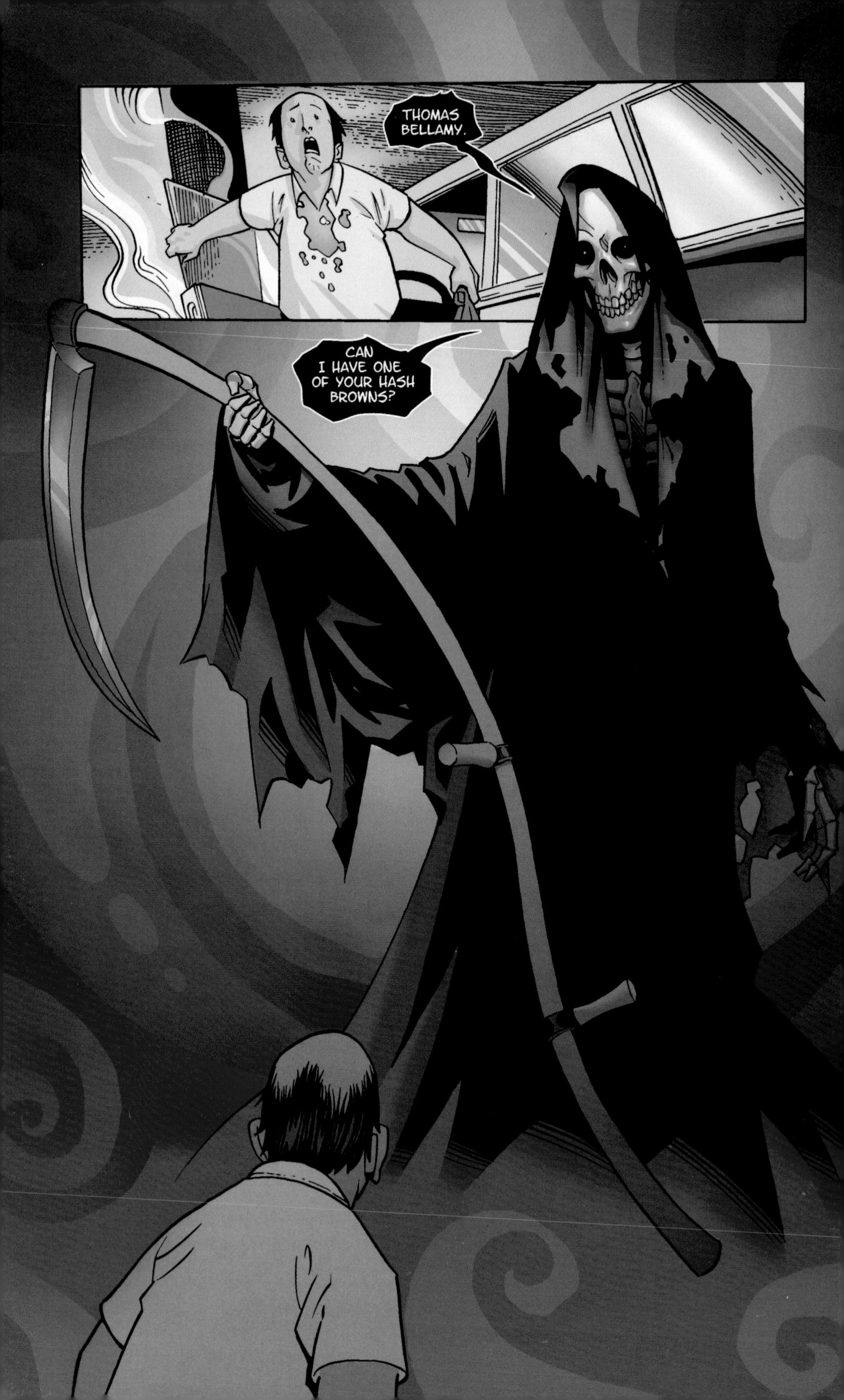
THOMAS BELLAMY.
CAN I HAVE ONE OF YOUR HASH BROWNS?

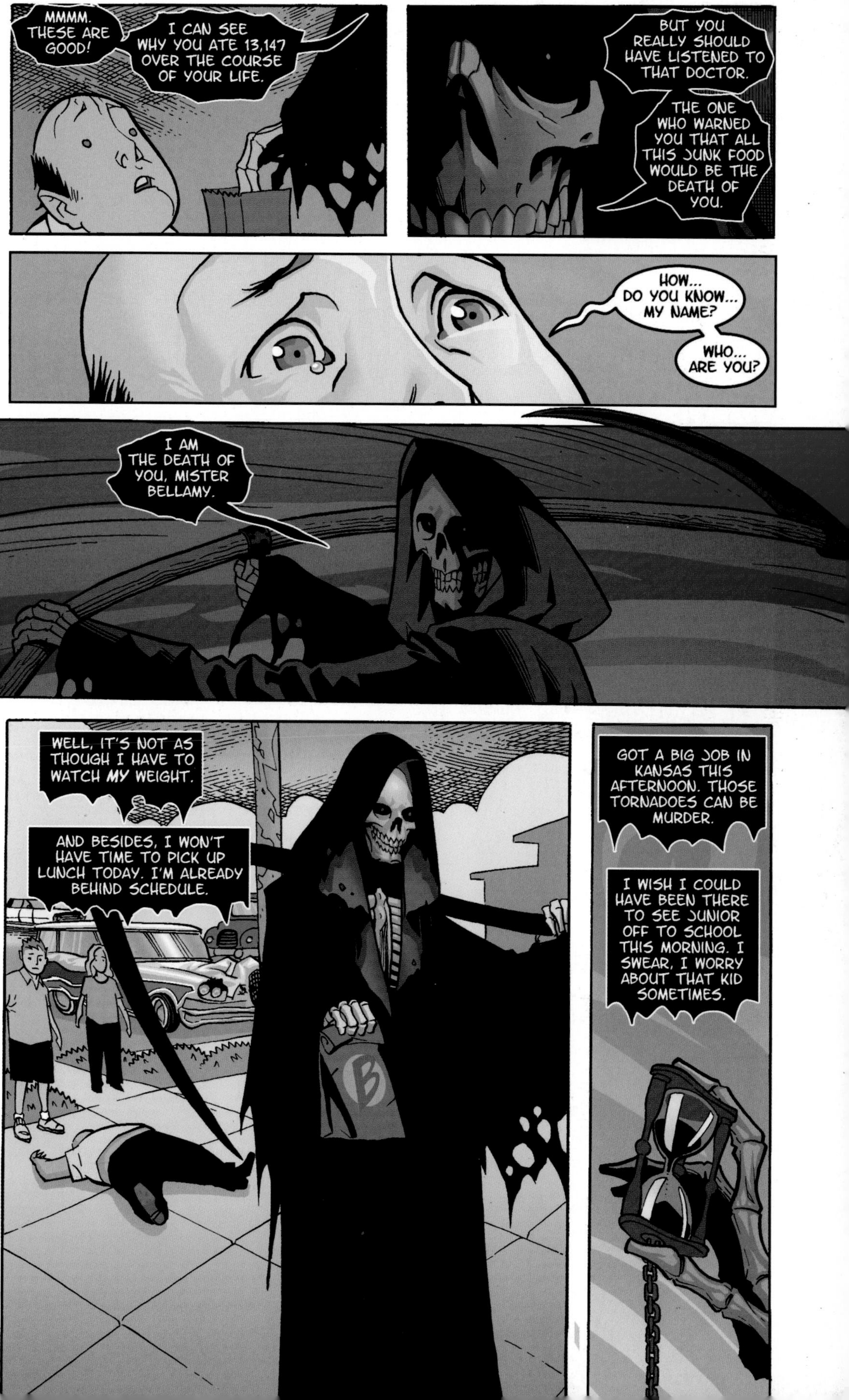
MMMM. THESE ARE GOOD!
I CAN SEE WHY YOU ATE 13,147 OVER THE COURSE OF YOUR LIFE.
BUT YOU REALLY SHOULD HAVE LISTENED TO THAT DOCTOR.
THE ONE WHO WARNED YOU THAT ALL THIS JUNK FOOD WOULD BE THE DEATH OF YOU.
HOW... DO YOU KNOW... MY NAME?
WHO... ARE YOU?
I AM THE DEATH OF YOU, MISTER BELLAMY.
WELL, IT'S NOT AS THOUGH I HAVE TO WATCH *MY* WEIGHT.
AND BESIDES, I WON'T HAVE TIME TO PICK UP LUNCH TODAY. I'M ALREADY BEHIND SCHEDULE.
GOT A BIG JOB IN KANSAS THIS AFTERNOON. THOSE TORNADOES CAN BE MURDER.
I WISH I COULD HAVE BEEN THERE TO SEE JUNIOR OFF TO SCHOOL THIS MORNING. I SWEAR, I WORRY ABOUT THAT KID SOMETIMES.

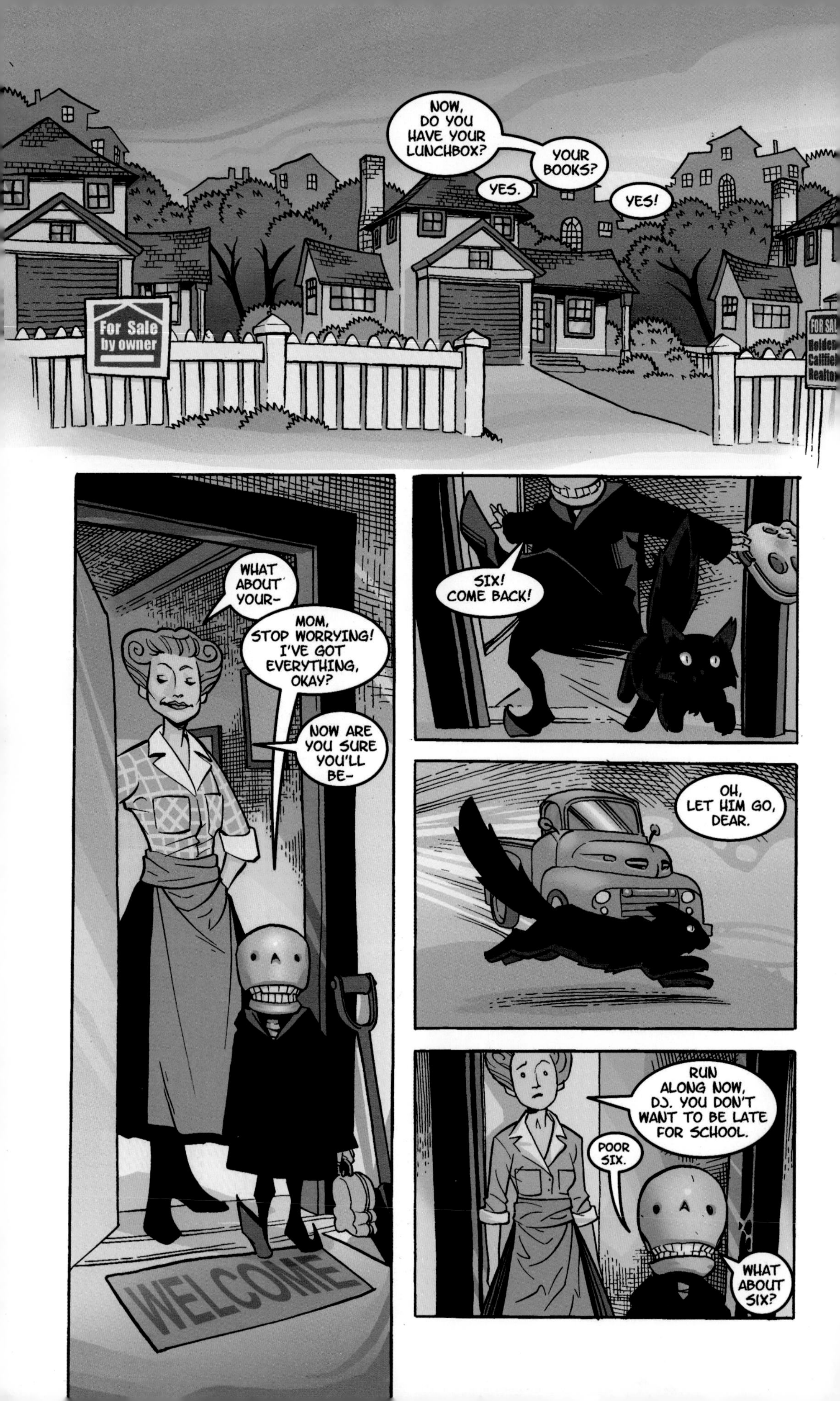

For Sale by owner
NOW, DO YOU HAVE YOUR LUNCHBOX?
YES.
YOUR BOOKS?
YES!
WHAT ABOUT YOUR-
MOM, STOP WORRYING! I'VE GOT EVERYTHING, OKAY?
NOW ARE YOU SURE YOU'LL BE-
WELCOME
SIX! COME BACK!
OH, LET HIM GO, DEAR.
RUN ALONG NOW, DJ. YOU DON'T WANT TO BE LATE FOR SCHOOL.
POOR SIX.
WHAT ABOUT SIX?

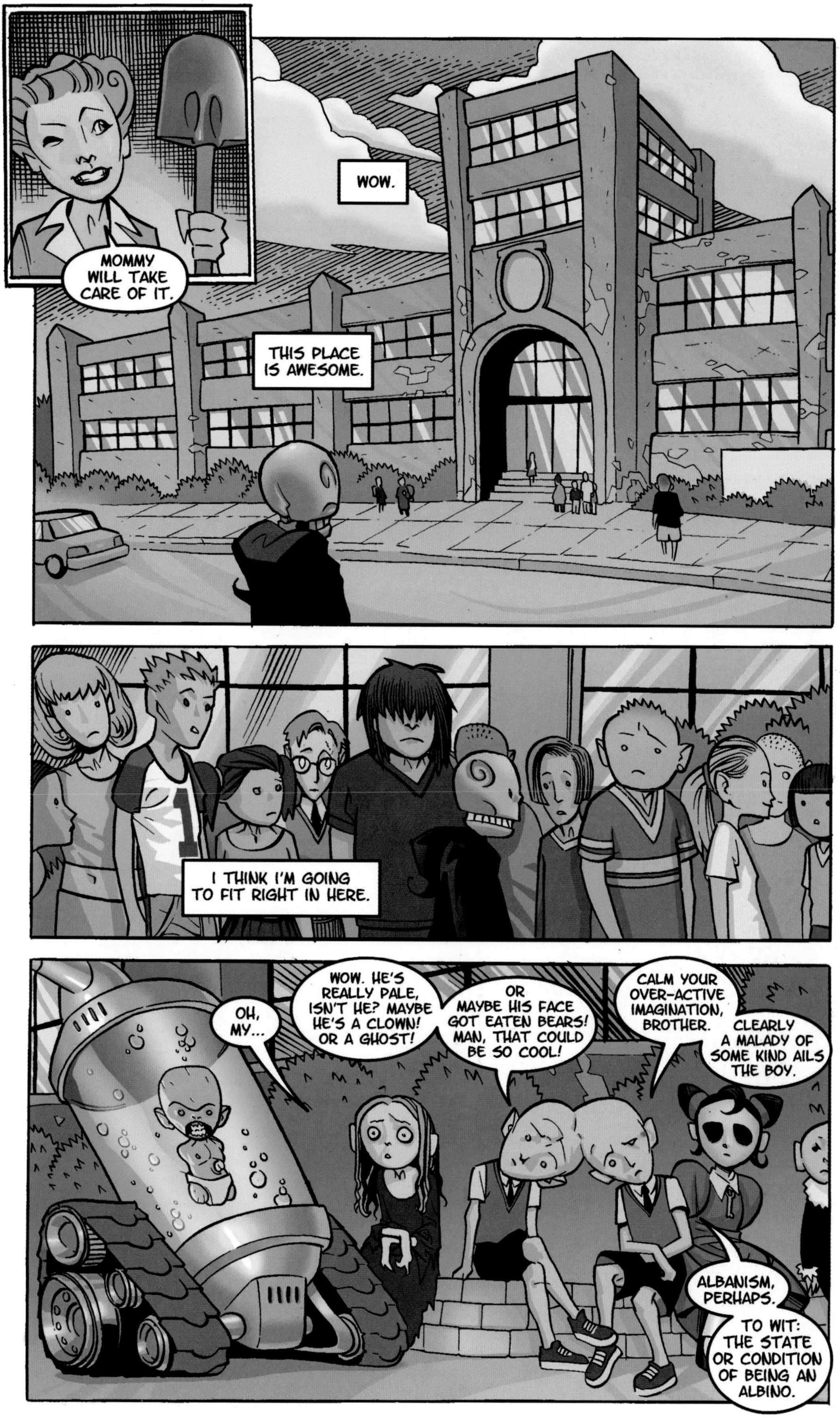
MOMMY WILL TAKE CARE OF IT.
WOW.
THIS PLACE IS AWESOME.
I THINK I'M GOING TO FIT RIGHT IN HERE.
OH, MY...
WOW. HE'S REALLY PALE, ISN'T HE? MAYBE HE'S A CLOWN! OR A GHOST!
OR MAYBE HIS FACE GOT EATEN BEARS! MAN, THAT COULD BE SO COOL!
CALM YOUR OVER-ACTIVE IMAGINATION, BROTHER.
CLEARLY A MALADY OF SOME KIND AILS THE BOY.
ALBANISM, PERHAPS.
TO WIT: THE STATE OR CONDITION OF BEING AN ALBINO.

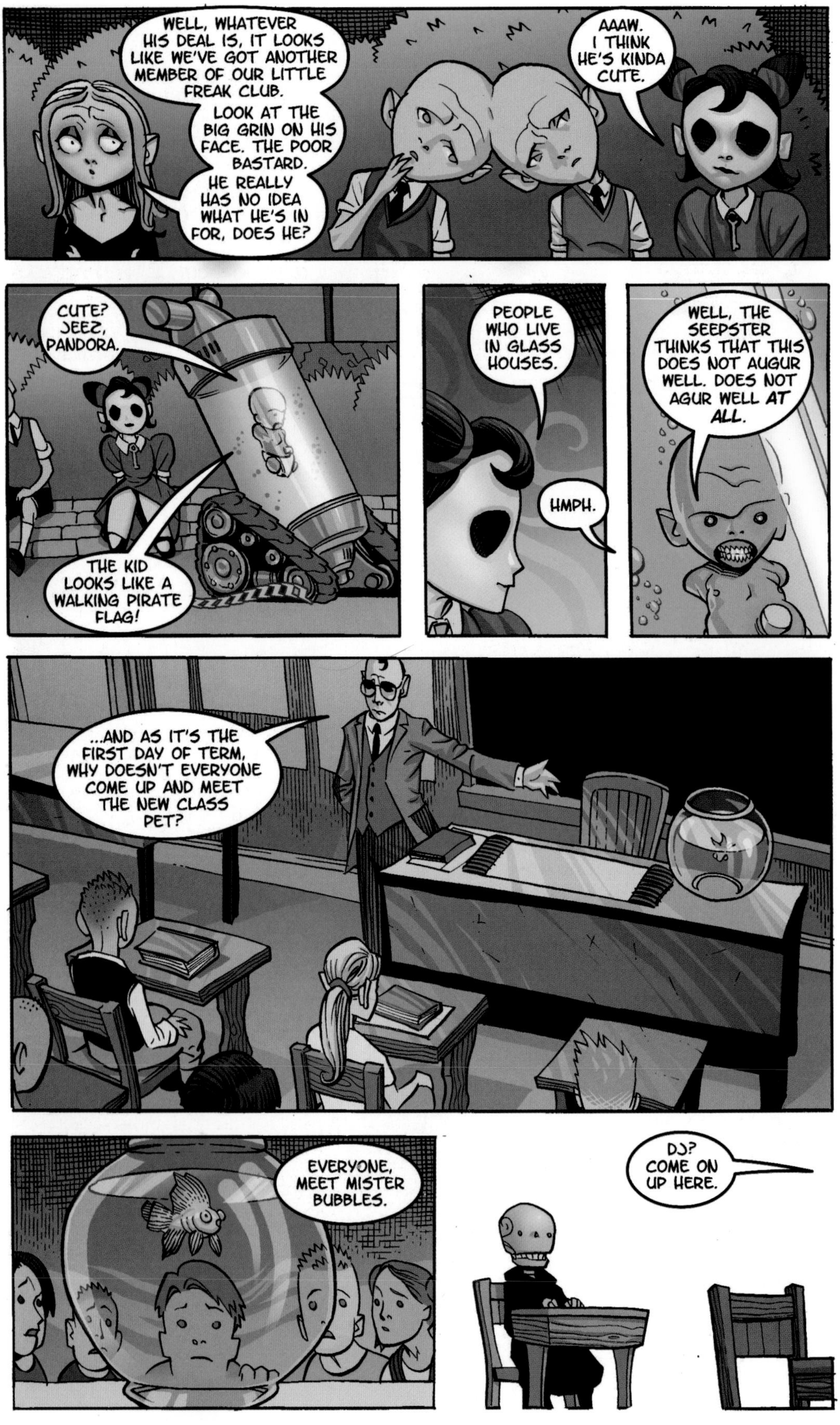
WELL, WHATEVER HIS DEAL IS, IT LOOKS LIKE WE'VE GOT ANOTHER MEMBER OF OUR LITTLE FREAK CLUB.
LOOK AT THE BIG GRIN ON HIS FACE. THE POOR BASTARD.
HE REALLY HAS NO IDEA WHAT HE'S IN FOR, DOES HE?
AAAW. I THINK HE'S KINDA CUTE.
CUTE? JEEZ, PANDORA.
THE KID LOOKS LIKE A WALKING PIRATE FLAG!
PEOPLE WHO LIVE IN GLASS HOUSES.
HMPH.
WELL, THE SEEPSTER THINKS THAT THIS DOES NOT AUGUR WELL. DOES NOT AGUR WELL AT ALL.
...AND AS IT'S THE FIRST DAY OF TERM, WHY DOESN'T EVERYONE COME UP AND MEET THE NEW CLASS PET?
EVERYONE, MEET MISTER BUBBLES.
DJ? COME ON UP HERE.

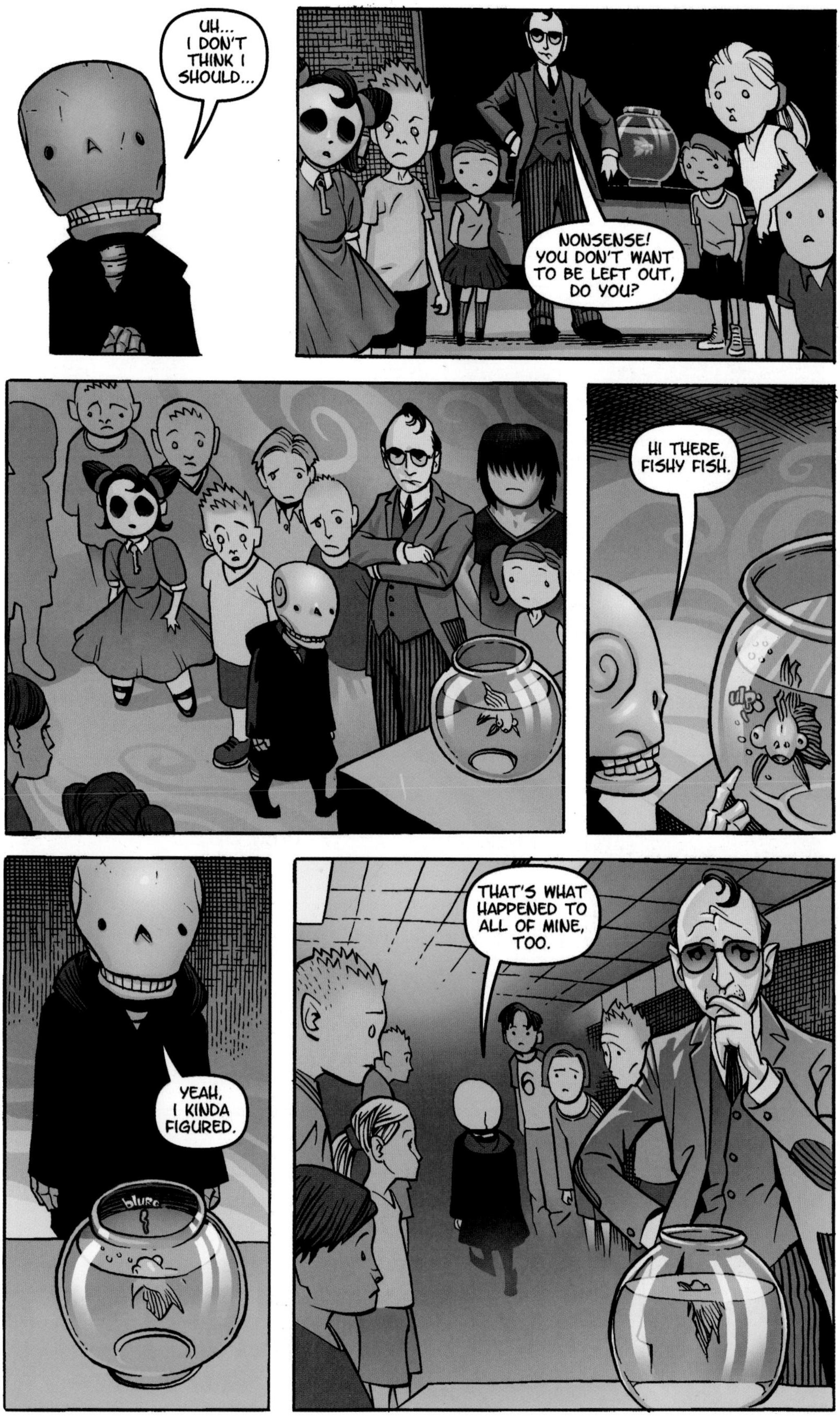
UH... I DON'T THINK I SHOULD...
NONSENSE! YOU DON'T WANT TO BE LEFT OUT, DO YOU?
HI THERE, FISHY FISH.
YEAH, I KINDA FIGURED.
THAT'S WHAT HAPPENED TO ALL OF MINE, TOO.

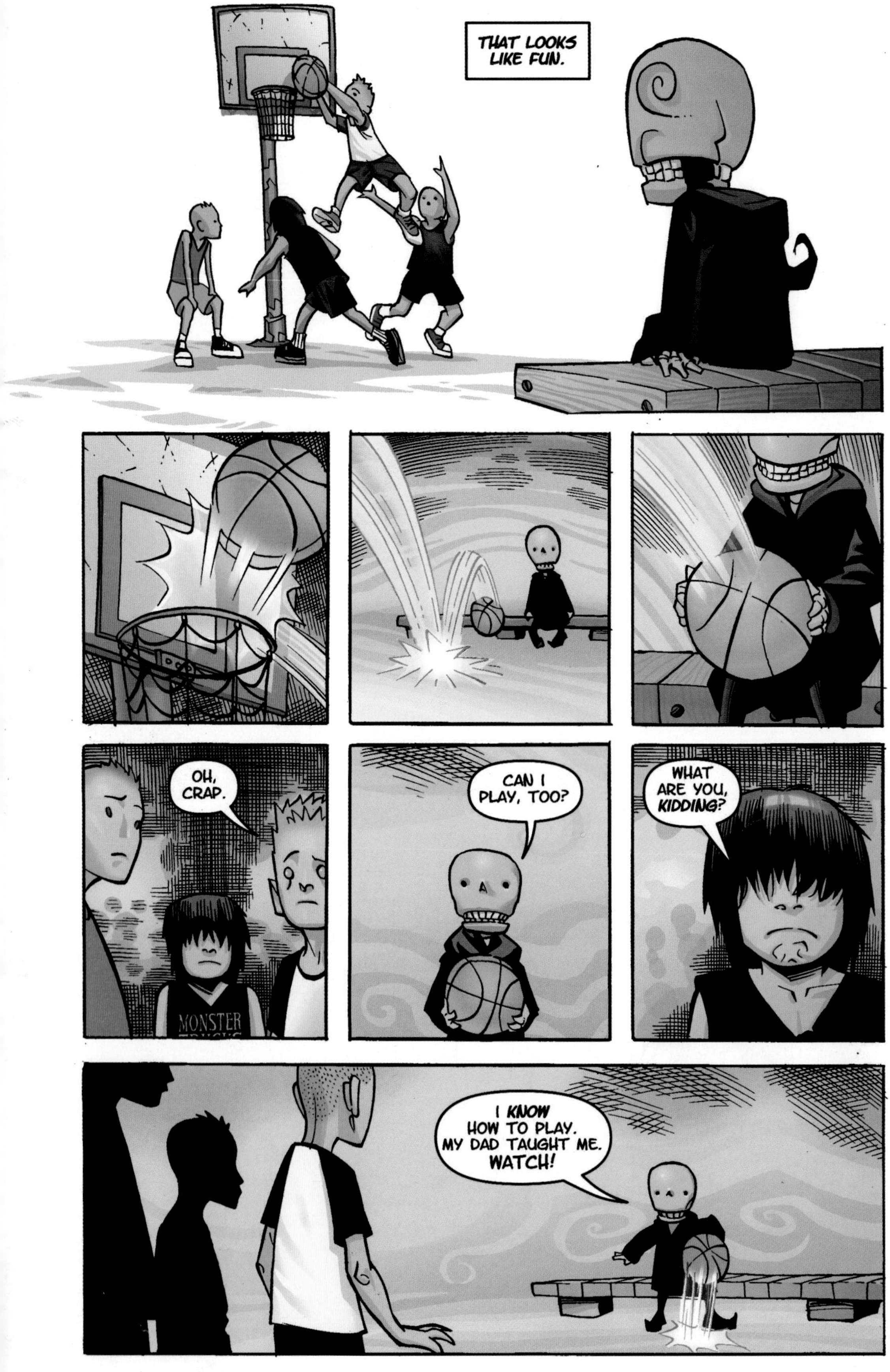
THAT LOOKS LIKE FUN.
OH, CRAP.
MONSTER
CAN I PLAY, TOO?
WHAT ARE YOU, KIDDING?
I KNOW HOW TO PLAY. MY DAD TAUGHT ME. WATCH!

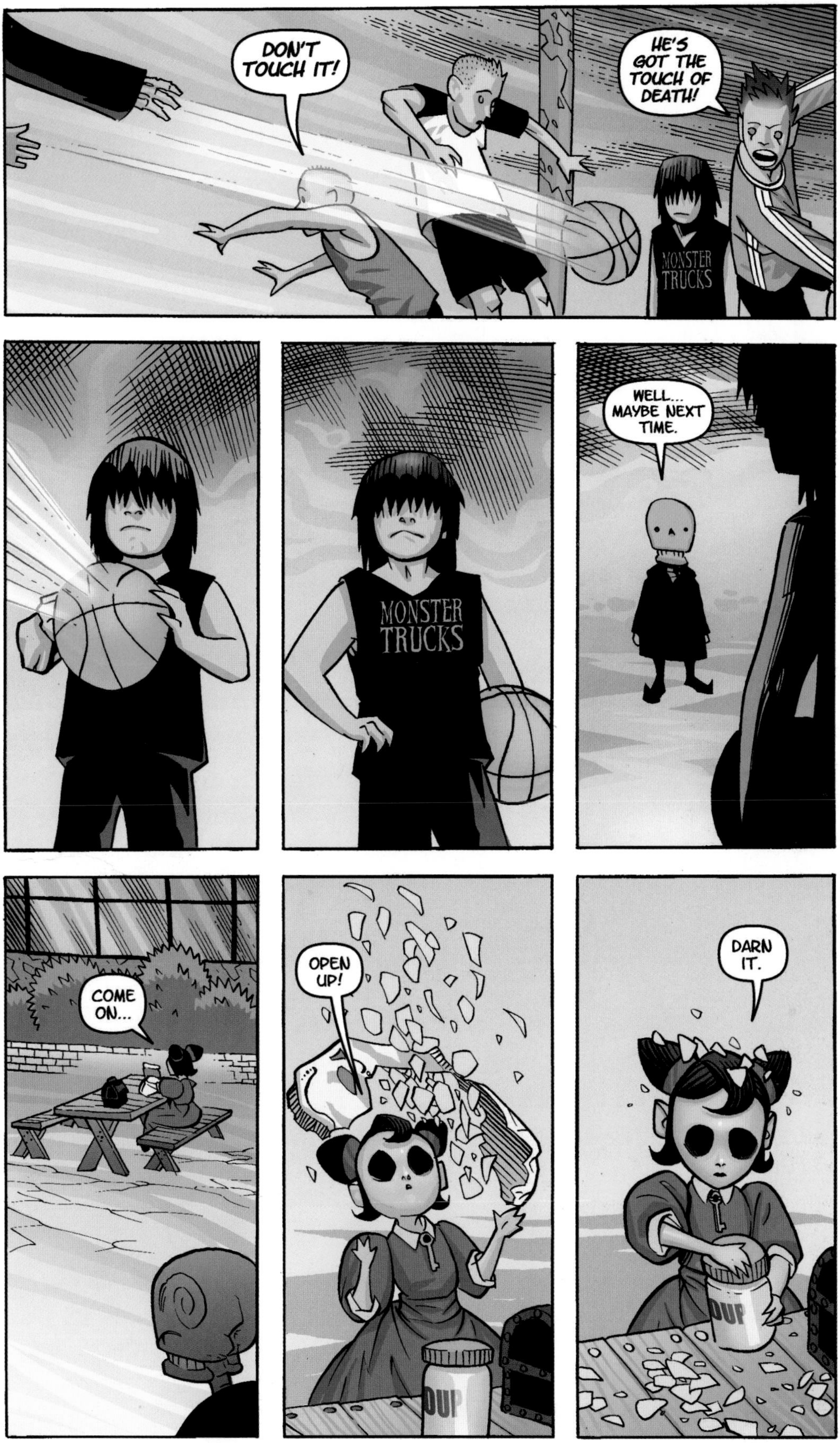
DON'T TOUCH IT!
HE'S GOT THE TOUCH OF DEATH!
MONSTER TRUCKS
MONSTER TRUCKS
MONSTER TRUCKS
WELL... MAYBE NEXT TIME.
COME ON...
OPEN UP!
OUP
DARN IT.
OUP

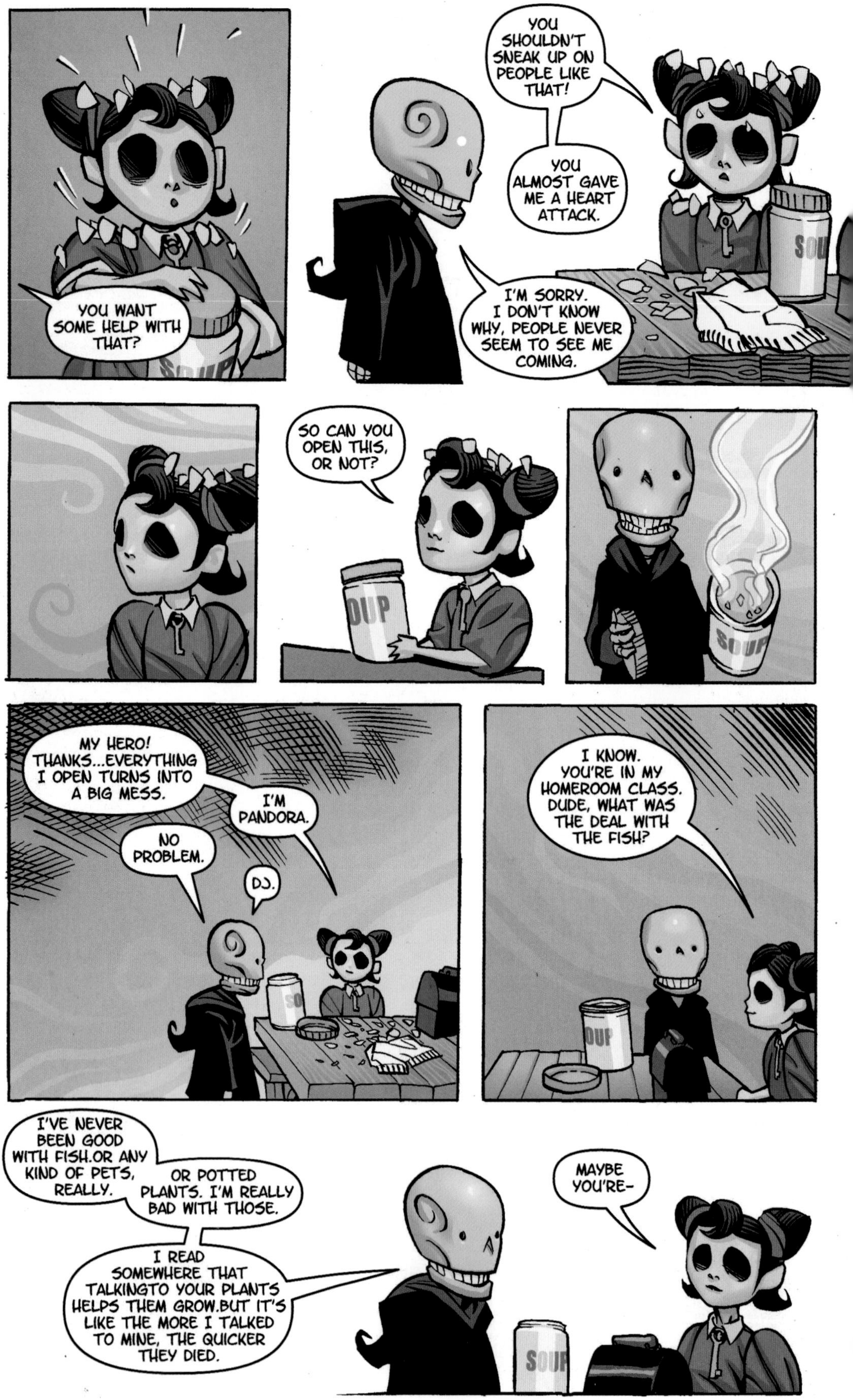
YOU WANT SOME HELP WITH THAT?
YOU SHOULDN'T SNEAK UP ON PEOPLE LIKE THAT!
YOU ALMOST GAVE ME A HEART ATTACK.
I'M SORRY. I DON'T KNOW WHY, PEOPLE NEVER SEEM TO SEE ME COMING.
SOUP
SO CAN YOU OPEN THIS, OR NOT?
SOUP
SOUP
MY HERO! THANKS...EVERYTHING I OPEN TURNS INTO A BIG MESS.
I'M PANDORA.
NO PROBLEM.
DJ.
I KNOW. YOU'RE IN MY HOMEROOM CLASS. DUDE, WHAT WAS THE DEAL WITH THE FISH?
I'VE NEVER BEEN GOOD WITH FISH.OR ANY KIND OF PETS, REALLY.
OR POTTED PLANTS. I'M REALLY BAD WITH THOSE.
I READ SOMEWHERE THAT TALKINGTO YOUR PLANTS HELPS THEM GROW.BUT IT'S LIKE THE MORE I TALKED TO MINE, THE QUICKER THEY DIED.
MAYBE YOU'RE-
SOUP

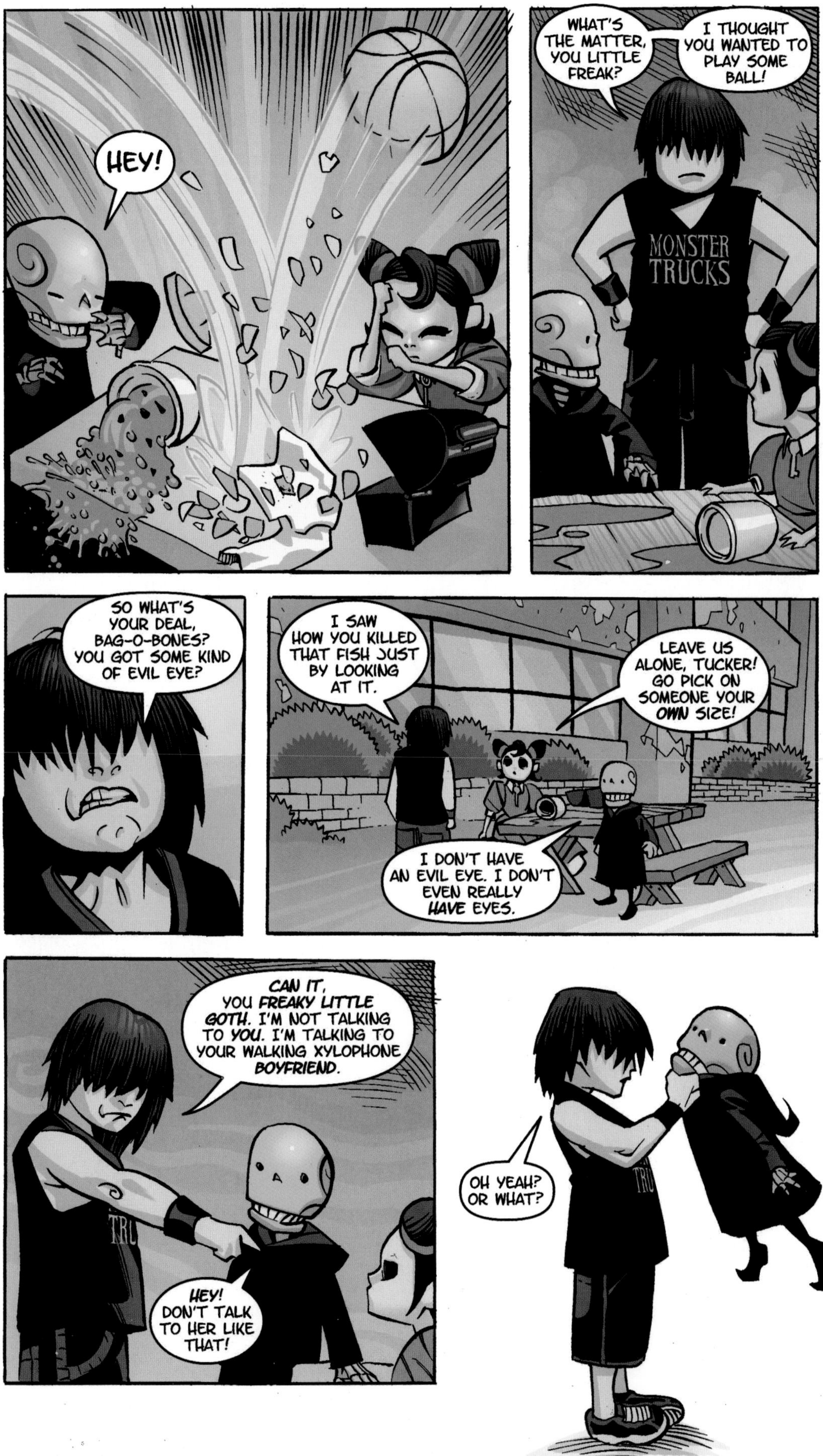
HEY!
WHAT'S THE MATTER, YOU LITTLE FREAK?
I THOUGHT YOU WANTED TO PLAY SOME BALL!
MONSTER TRUCKS
SO WHAT'S YOUR DEAL, BAG-O-BONES? YOU GOT SOME KIND OF EVIL EYE?
I SAW HOW YOU KILLED THAT FISH JUST BY LOOKING AT IT.
LEAVE US ALONE, TUCKER! GO PICK ON SOMEONE YOUR OWN SIZE!
I DON'T HAVE AN EVIL EYE. I DON'T EVEN REALLY HAVE EYES.
CAN IT, YOU FREAKY LITTLE GOTH. I'M NOT TALKING TO YOU. I'M TALKING TO YOUR WALKING XYLOPHONE BOYFRIEND.
HEY! DON'T TALK TO HER LIKE THAT!
OH YEAH? OR WHAT?

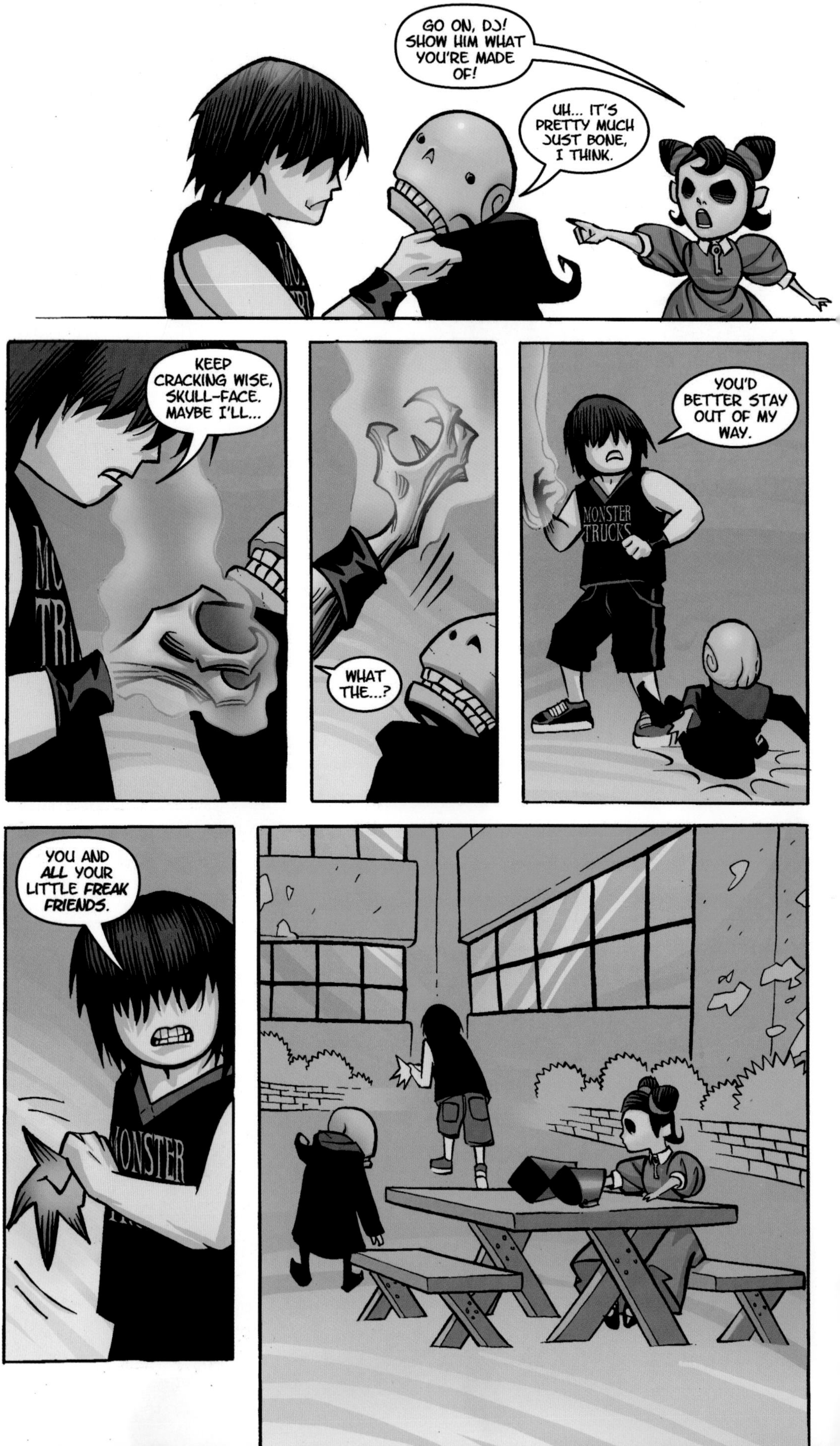
GO ON, DJ! SHOW HIM WHAT YOU'RE MADE OF!
UH... IT'S PRETTY MUCH JUST BONE, I THINK.
KEEP CRACKING WISE, SKULL-FACE. MAYBE I'LL...
WHAT THE...?
YOU'D BETTER STAY OUT OF MY WAY.
MONSTER TRUCKS
YOU AND ALL YOUR LITTLE FREAK FRIENDS.
MONSTER

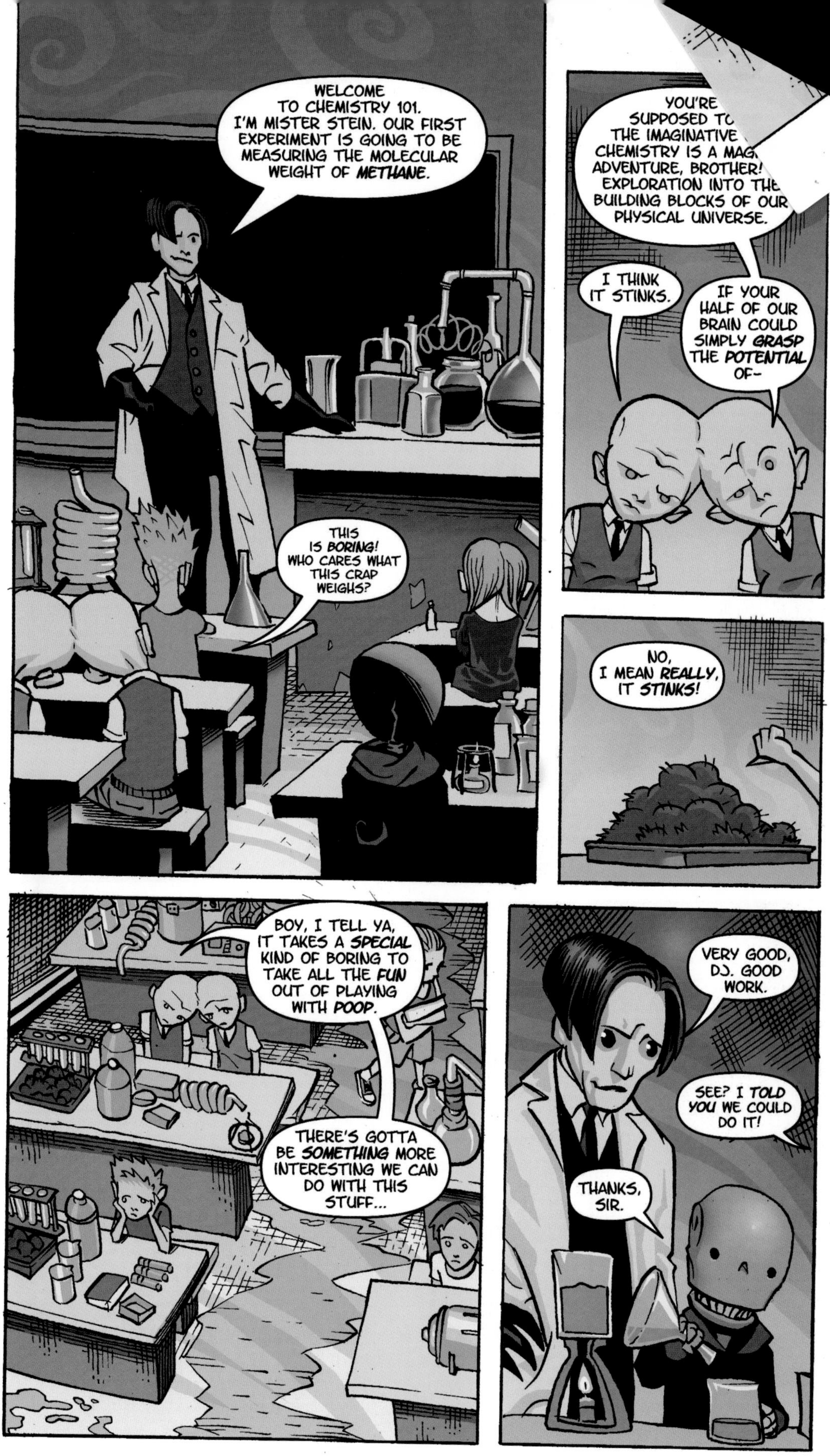

WELCOME TO CHEMISTRY 101. I'M MISTER STEIN. OUR FIRST EXPERIMENT IS GOING TO BE MEASURING THE MOLECULAR WEIGHT OF METHANE.
THIS IS BORING! WHO CARES WHAT THIS CRAP WEIGHS?
YOU'RE SUPPOSED TO THE IMAGINATIVE CHEMISTRY IS A MAG ADVENTURE, BROTHER! EXPLORATION INTO THE BUILDING BLOCKS OF OUR PHYSICAL UNIVERSE.
I THINK IT STINKS.
IF YOUR HALF OF OUR BRAIN COULD SIMPLY GRASP THE POTENTIAL OF-
NO, I MEAN REALLY, IT STINKS!
BOY, I TELL YA, IT TAKES A SPECIAL KIND OF BORING TO TAKE ALL THE FUN OUT OF PLAYING WITH POOP.
THERE'S GOTTA BE SOMETHING MORE INTERESTING WE CAN DO WITH THIS STUFF...
VERY GOOD, DJ. GOOD WORK.
SEE? I TOLD YOU WE COULD DO IT!
THANKS, SIR.

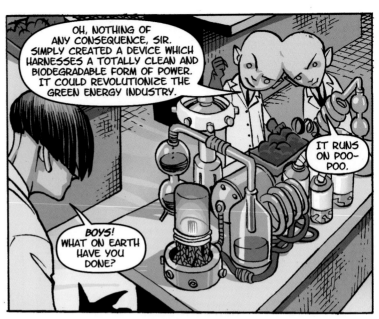

EUREKA! I DO BELIEVE WE MAY TRULY HAVE HIT UPON SOMETHING.

WHAT THE...

OH, NOTHING OF ANY CONSEQUENCE, SIR. SIMPLY CREATED A DEVICE WHICH HARNESSES A TOTALLY CLEAN AND BIODEGRADABLE FORM OF POWER. IT COULD REVOLUTIONIZE THE GREEN ENERGY INDUSTRY.

IT RUNS ON POO-POO.

BOYS! WHAT ON EARTH HAVE YOU DONE?

HOW... HOW DID YOU DO THIS?

I THINK UP THE IDEAS, HE FIGURES OUT HOW TO MAKE 'EM WORK.

OBSERVE!

WELL BOYS, I'D SAY IT'S A SAFE BET YOU ALREADY HAVE A HEAD START ON THIS YEAR'S SCIENCE FAIR.

WE DIDN'T BUILD AN OFF SWITCH INTO THE ORIGINAL SCHEMATIC. DAMMIT, I ALWAYS OVERLOOK SOMETHING!

UH-OH.

WHAT'S WRONG?

BUT WE REALLY SHOULD STICK TO THE CURRICULUM, SO IF YOU COULD JUST SHUT THAT THING OFF FOR NOW...

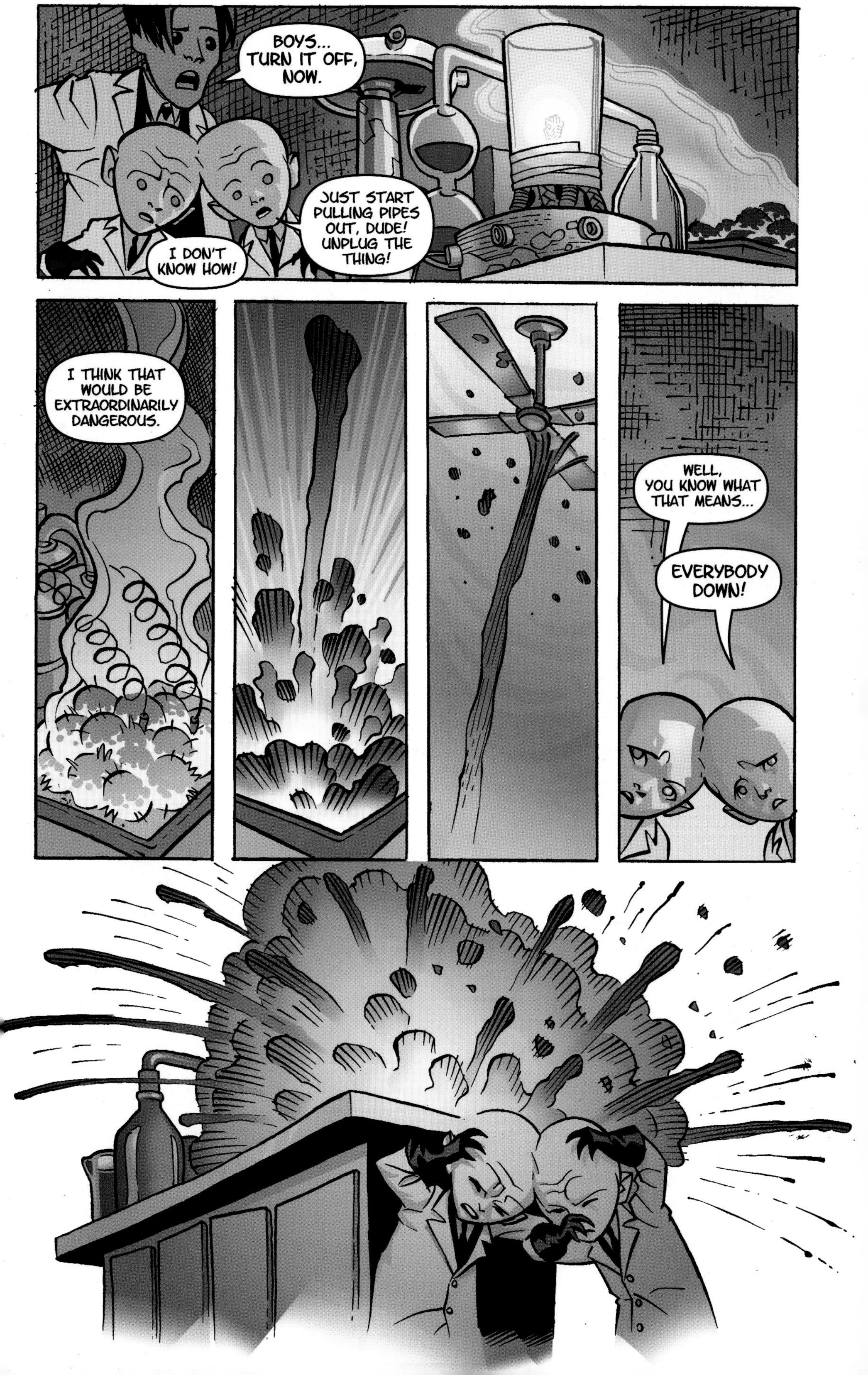
BOYS... TURN IT OFF, NOW.
I DON'T KNOW HOW!
JUST START PULLING PIPES OUT, DUDE! UNPLUG THE THING!
I THINK THAT WOULD BE EXTRAORDINARILY DANGEROUS.
WELL, YOU KNOW WHAT THAT MEANS...
EVERYBODY DOWN!

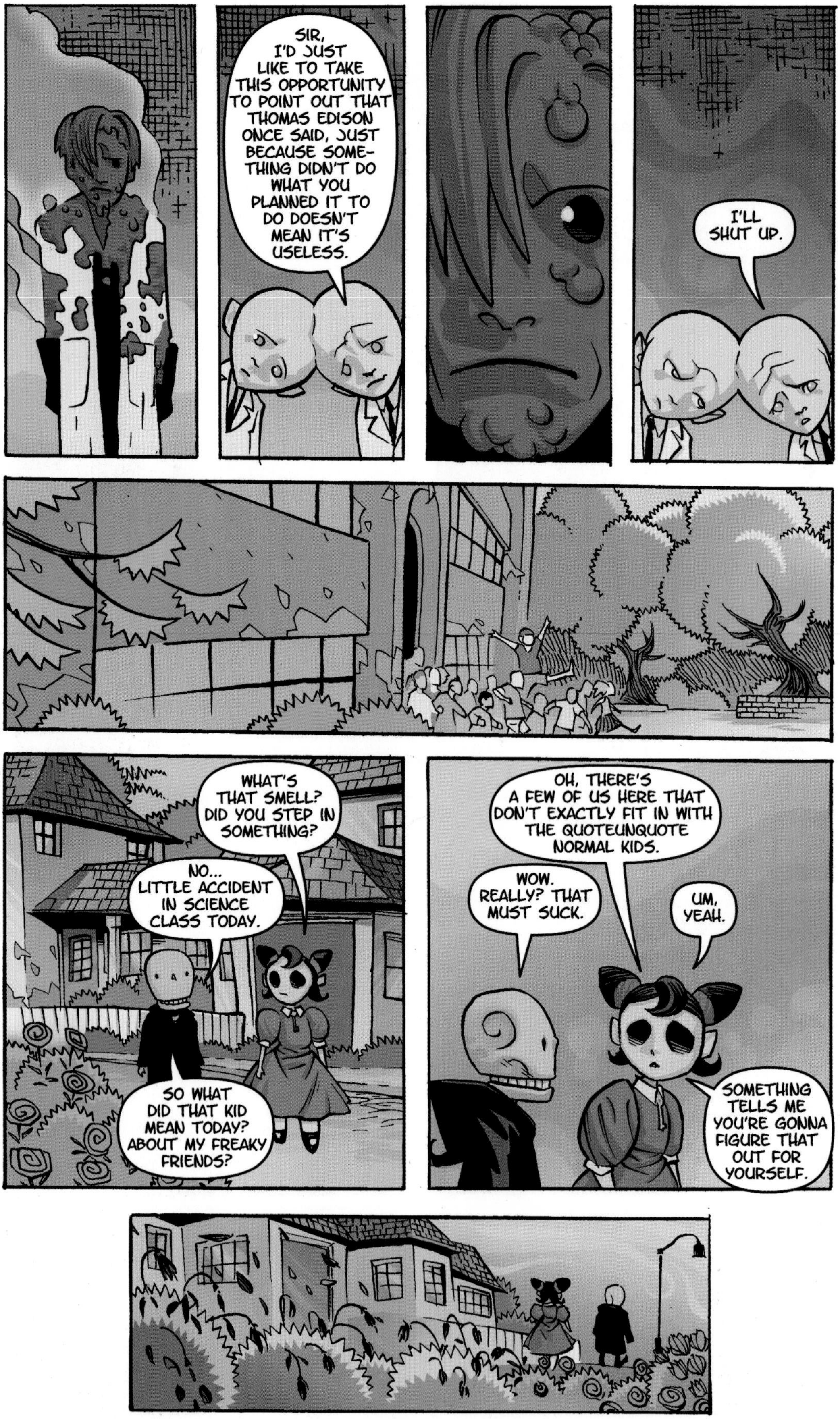
SIR, I'D JUST LIKE TO TAKE THIS OPPORTUNITY TO POINT OUT THAT THOMAS EDISON ONCE SAID, JUST BECAUSE SOME-THING DIDN'T DO WHAT YOU PLANNED IT TO DO DOESN'T MEAN IT'S USELESS.
I'LL SHUT UP.
WHAT'S THAT SMELL? DID YOU STEP IN SOMETHING?
NO... LITTLE ACCIDENT IN SCIENCE CLASS TODAY.
SO WHAT DID THAT KID MEAN TODAY? ABOUT MY FREAKY FRIENDS?
OH, THERE'S A FEW OF US HERE THAT DON'T EXACTLY FIT IN WITH THE QUOTEUNQUOTE NORMAL KIDS.
WOW. REALLY? THAT MUST SUCK.
UM, YEAH.
SOMETHING TELLS ME YOU'RE GONNA FIGURE THAT OUT FOR YOURSELF.

THIS IS WHERE YOU LIVE?

YEAH. YOU LIKE IT?

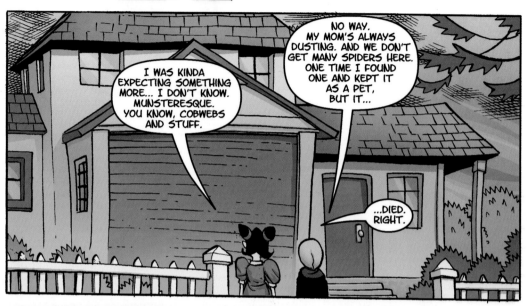

I WAS KINDA EXPECTING SOMETHING MORE... I DON'T KNOW. MUNSTERESQUE. YOU KNOW, COBWEBS AND STUFF.

NO WAY. MY MOM'S ALWAYS DUSTING. AND WE DON'T GET MANY SPIDERS HERE. ONE TIME I FOUND ONE AND KEPT IT AS A PET, BUT IT...

...DIED. RIGHT.

HEY, SEVEN! HOW ARE YA, BUDDY? YOU'RE LOOKING GOOD AS NEW!

DO TRY TO BE CAREFUL THIS TIME, DEAR. THE POOR THING ONLY HAS THREE LIVES LEFT.

OH, AND WHO'S THIS? HAVE YOU BROUGHT A FRIEND HOME FROM SCHOOL?

I KNOW, MOM!

MOM, THIS IS PANDORA. PANDORA, THIS IS MOM. WE WERE JUST GONNA GO–

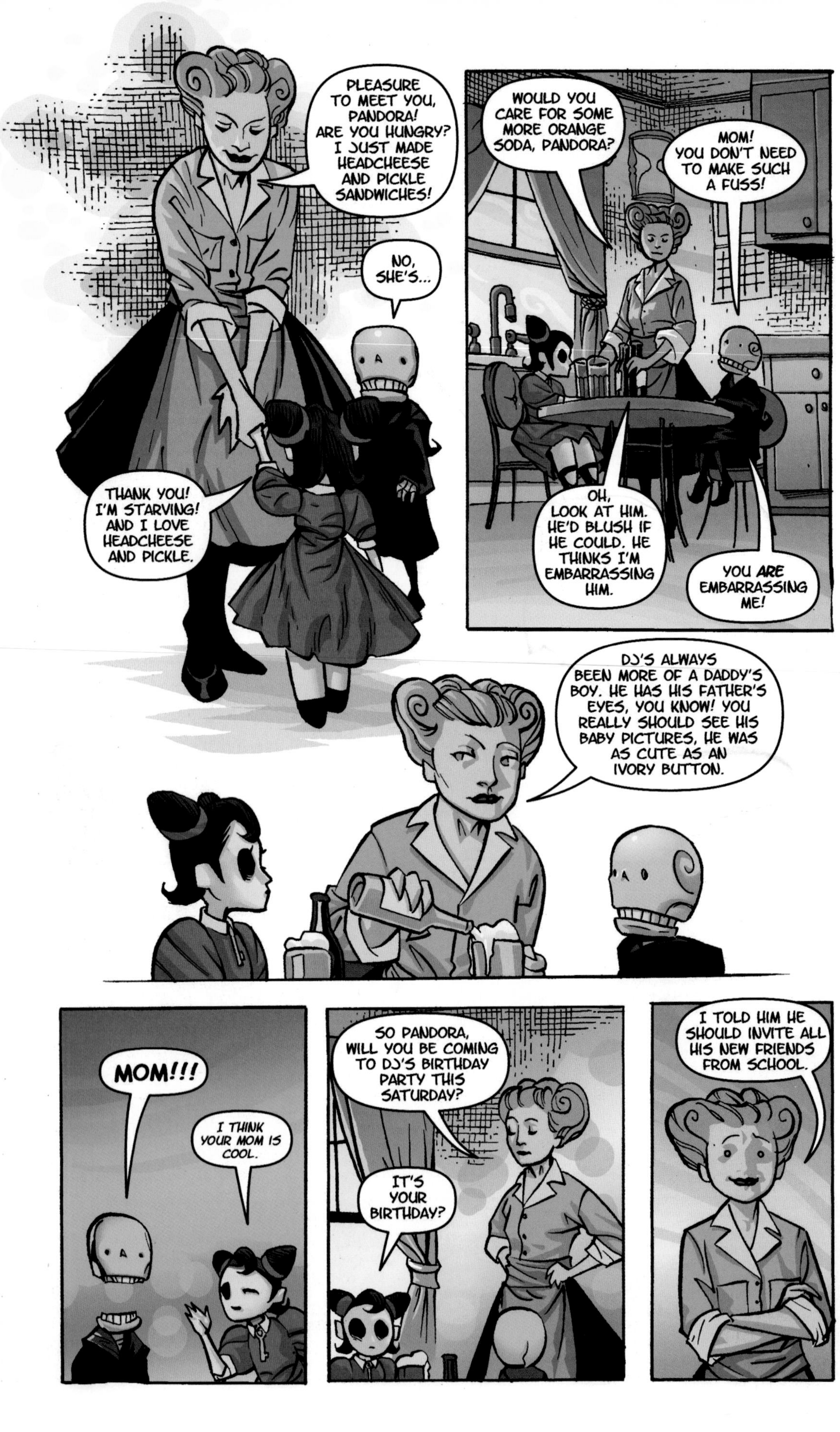
PLEASURE TO MEET YOU, PANDORA! ARE YOU HUNGRY? I JUST MADE HEADCHEESE AND PICKLE SANDWICHES!
NO, SHE'S...
THANK YOU! I'M STARVING! AND I LOVE HEADCHEESE AND PICKLE.
WOULD YOU CARE FOR SOME MORE ORANGE SODA, PANDORA?
MOM! YOU DON'T NEED TO MAKE SUCH A FUSS!
OH, LOOK AT HIM. HE'D BLUSH IF HE COULD. HE THINKS I'M EMBARRASSING HIM.
YOU ARE EMBARRASSING ME!
DJ'S ALWAYS BEEN MORE OF A DADDY'S BOY. HE HAS HIS FATHER'S EYES, YOU KNOW! YOU REALLY SHOULD SEE HIS BABY PICTURES, HE WAS AS CUTE AS AN IVORY BUTTON.
MOM!!!
I THINK YOUR MOM IS COOL.
SO PANDORA, WILL YOU BE COMING TO DJ'S BIRTHDAY PARTY THIS SATURDAY?
IT'S YOUR BIRTHDAY?
I TOLD HIM HE SHOULD INVITE ALL HIS NEW FRIENDS FROM SCHOOL.

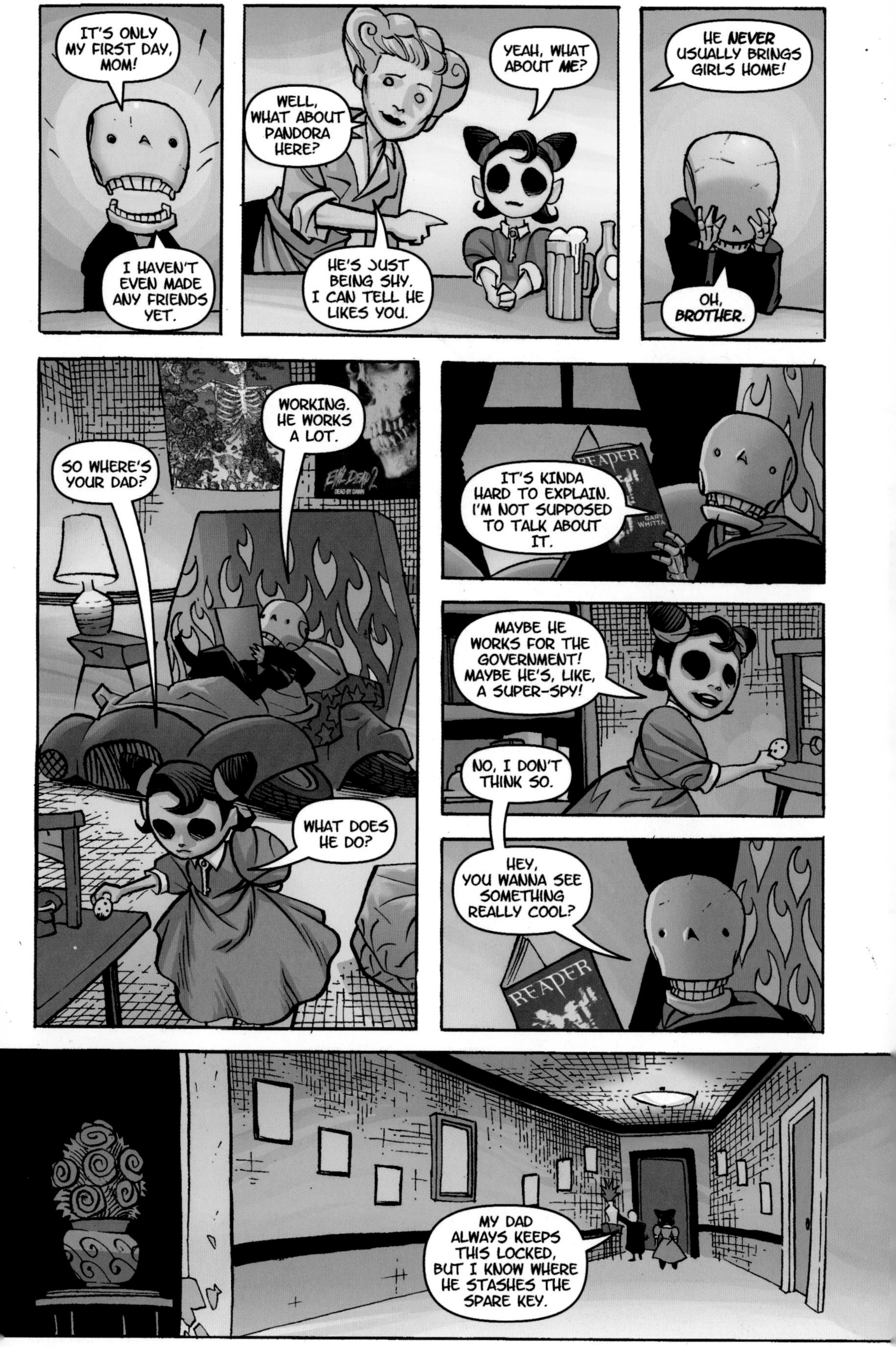
IT'S ONLY MY FIRST DAY, MOM!
I HAVEN'T EVEN MADE ANY FRIENDS YET.
WELL, WHAT ABOUT PANDORA HERE?
YEAH, WHAT ABOUT ME?
HE'S JUST BEING SHY. I CAN TELL HE LIKES YOU.
HE NEVER USUALLY BRINGS GIRLS HOME!
OH, BROTHER.
SO WHERE'S YOUR DAD?
WORKING. HE WORKS A LOT.
EVIL DEAD 2
DEAD BY DAWN
WHAT DOES HE DO?
READER
GARY WHITTA
IT'S KINDA HARD TO EXPLAIN. I'M NOT SUPPOSED TO TALK ABOUT IT.
MAYBE HE WORKS FOR THE GOVERNMENT! MAYBE HE'S, LIKE, A SUPER-SPY!
NO, I DON'T THINK SO.
HEY, YOU WANNA SEE SOMETHING REALLY COOL?
READER
MY DAD ALWAYS KEEPS THIS LOCKED, BUT I KNOW WHERE HE STASHES THE SPARE KEY.

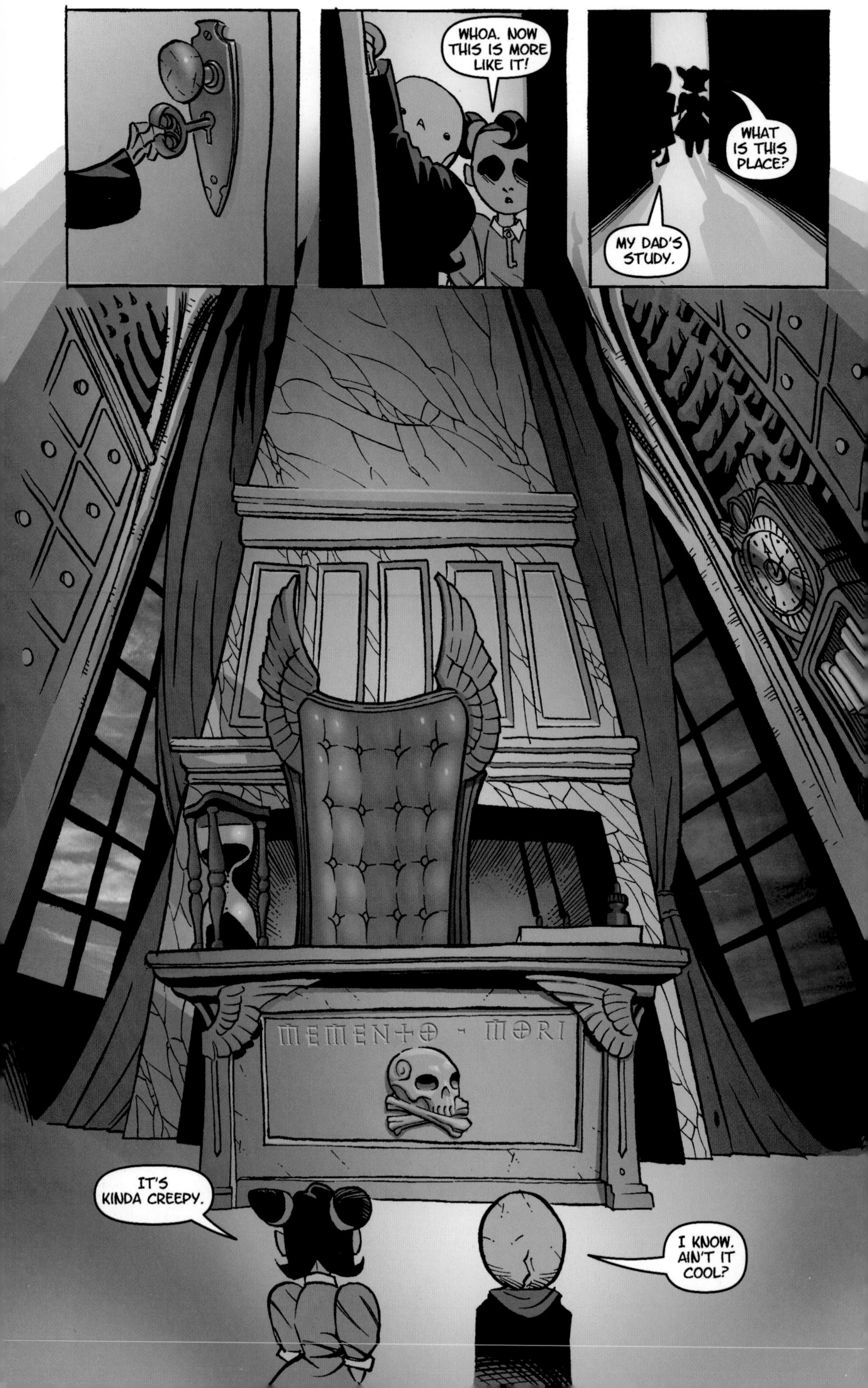
WHOA. NOW THIS IS MORE LIKE IT!
WHAT IS THIS PLACE?
MY DAD'S STUDY.
MEMENTO MORI
IT'S KINDA CREEPY.
I KNOW. AIN'T IT COOL?

ISN'T IT GROOVY?

IT'S AMAZING! THE CRAFTSMAN-SHIP IS JUST BEAUTIFUL!

TOTALLY!

IT'S SO POLISHED, LIKE A MIRROR. I CAN SEE MY REFLECTION IN IT!

I REALLY WANT TO TRY IT OUT.

ME TOO! THOSE HINGES LOOK SOOO WELL OILED. I BET THAT DOOR JUST SLIDES OPEN LIKE A DREAM.

OH YEAH, AND...

WAIT A MINUTE. WHAT?

THE CABINET. IT'S A WORK OF ART!

I'M NOT TALKING ABOUT THE CABINET! I'M TALKING ABOUT WHAT'S INSIDE IT!

OH. SORRY. I JUST KINDA HAVE A THING FOR CABINETS. AND CHESTS.

AND CASKETS, TRUNKS, CRATES, CARTONS...

ALL KINDS OF BOXES, I GUESS.

SO... WHAT IS IT, EXACTLY?

DUH! IT'S A SCYTHE! YOU USE IT FOR REAPING CROPS AND STUFF.

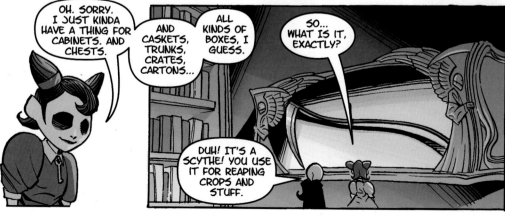

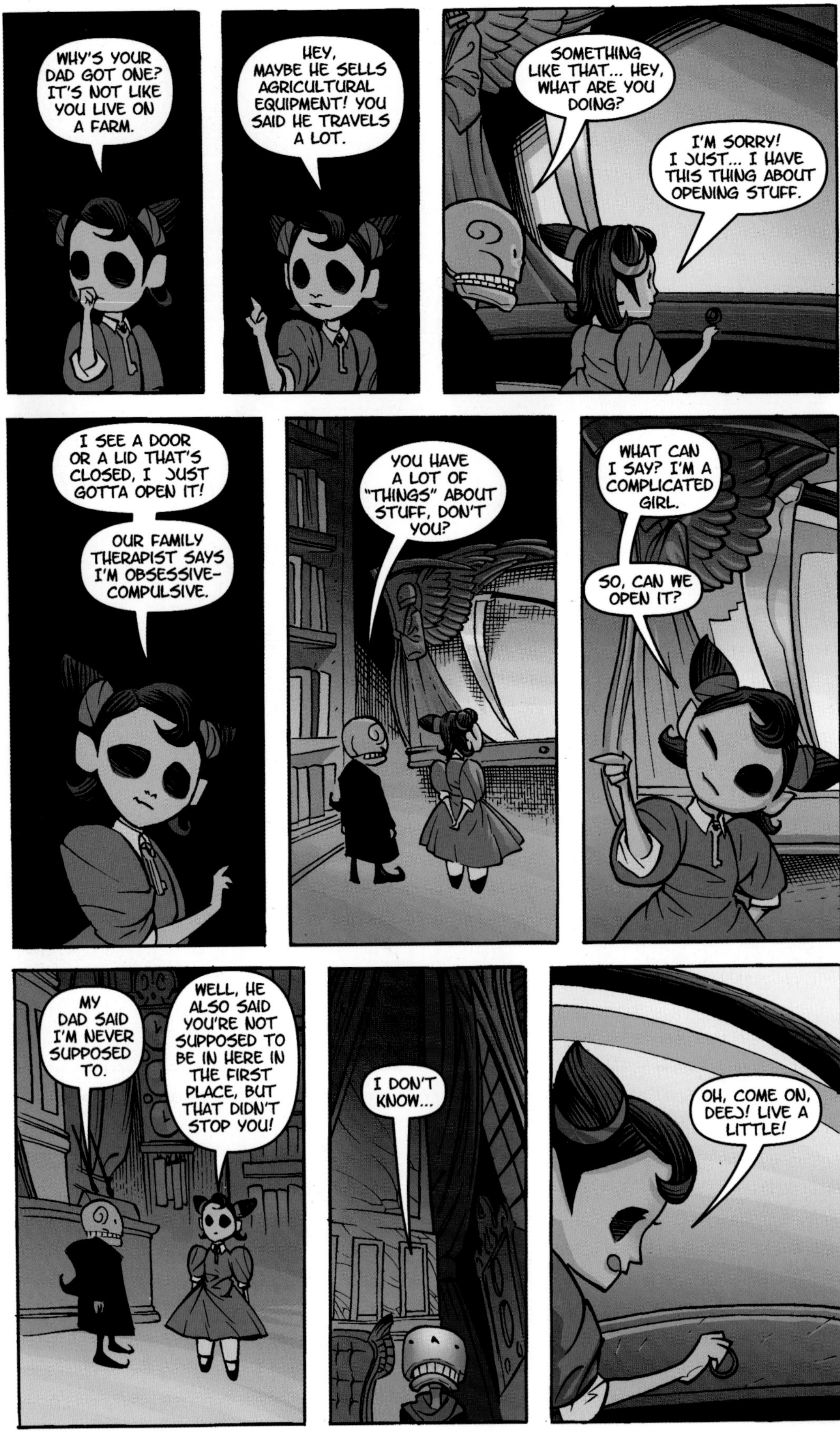
WHY'S YOUR DAD GOT ONE? IT'S NOT LIKE YOU LIVE ON A FARM.
HEY, MAYBE HE SELLS AGRICULTURAL EQUIPMENT! YOU SAID HE TRAVELS A LOT.
SOMETHING LIKE THAT... HEY, WHAT ARE YOU DOING?
I'M SORRY! I JUST... I HAVE THIS THING ABOUT OPENING STUFF.
I SEE A DOOR OR A LID THAT'S CLOSED, I JUST GOTTA OPEN IT!
OUR FAMILY THERAPIST SAYS I'M OBSESSIVE-COMPULSIVE.
YOU HAVE A LOT OF "THINGS" ABOUT STUFF, DON'T YOU?
WHAT CAN I SAY? I'M A COMPLICATED GIRL.
SO, CAN WE OPEN IT?
MY DAD SAID I'M NEVER SUPPOSED TO.
WELL, HE ALSO SAID YOU'RE NOT SUPPOSED TO BE IN HERE IN THE FIRST PLACE, BUT THAT DIDN'T STOP YOU!
I DON'T KNOW...
OH, COME ON, DEEJ! LIVE A LITTLE!

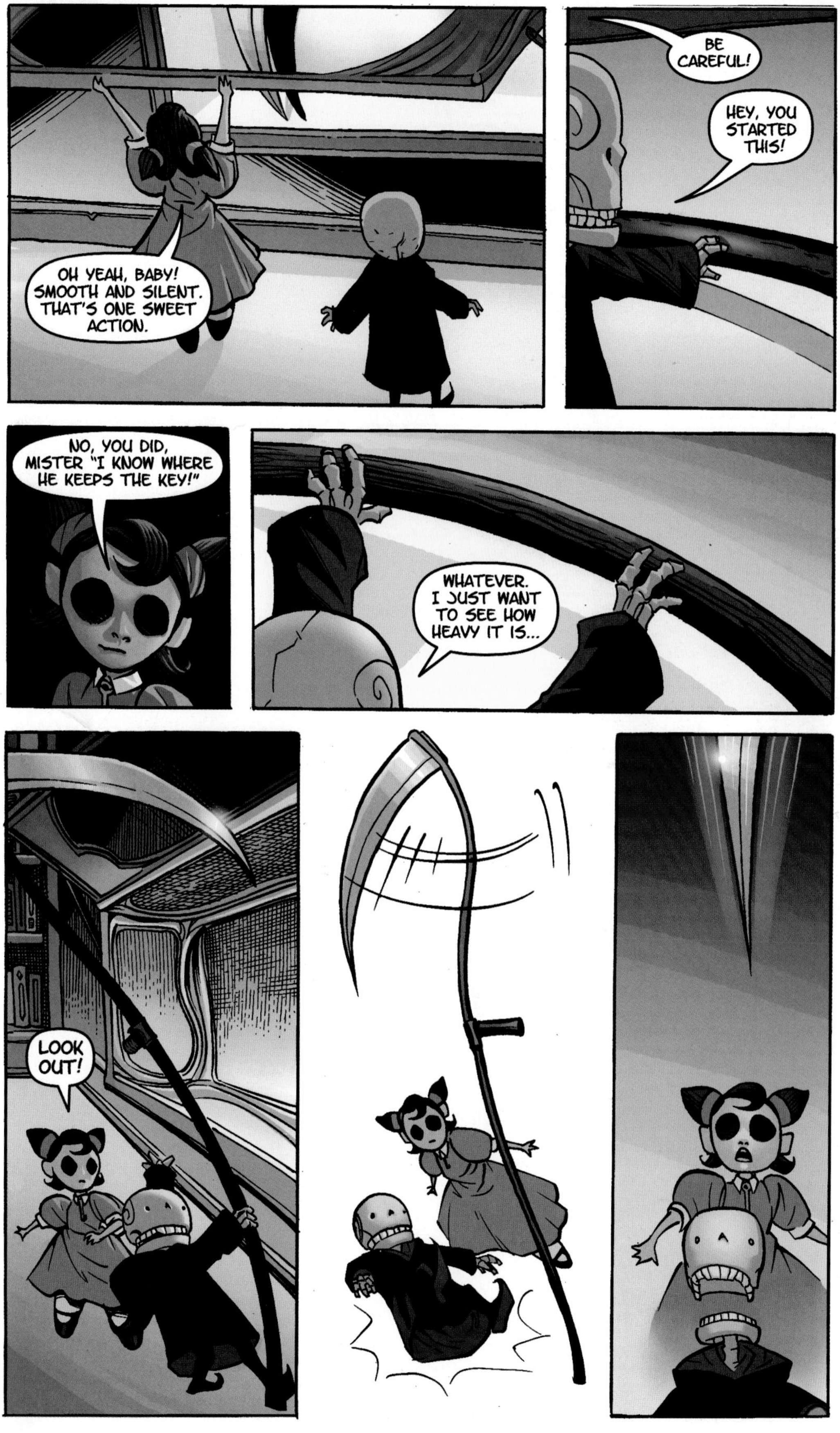
OH YEAH, BABY! SMOOTH AND SILENT. THAT'S ONE SWEET ACTION.
BE CAREFUL!
HEY, YOU STARTED THIS!
NO, YOU DID, MISTER "I KNOW WHERE HE KEEPS THE KEY!"
WHATEVER. I JUST WANT TO SEE HOW HEAVY IT IS...
LOOK OUT!

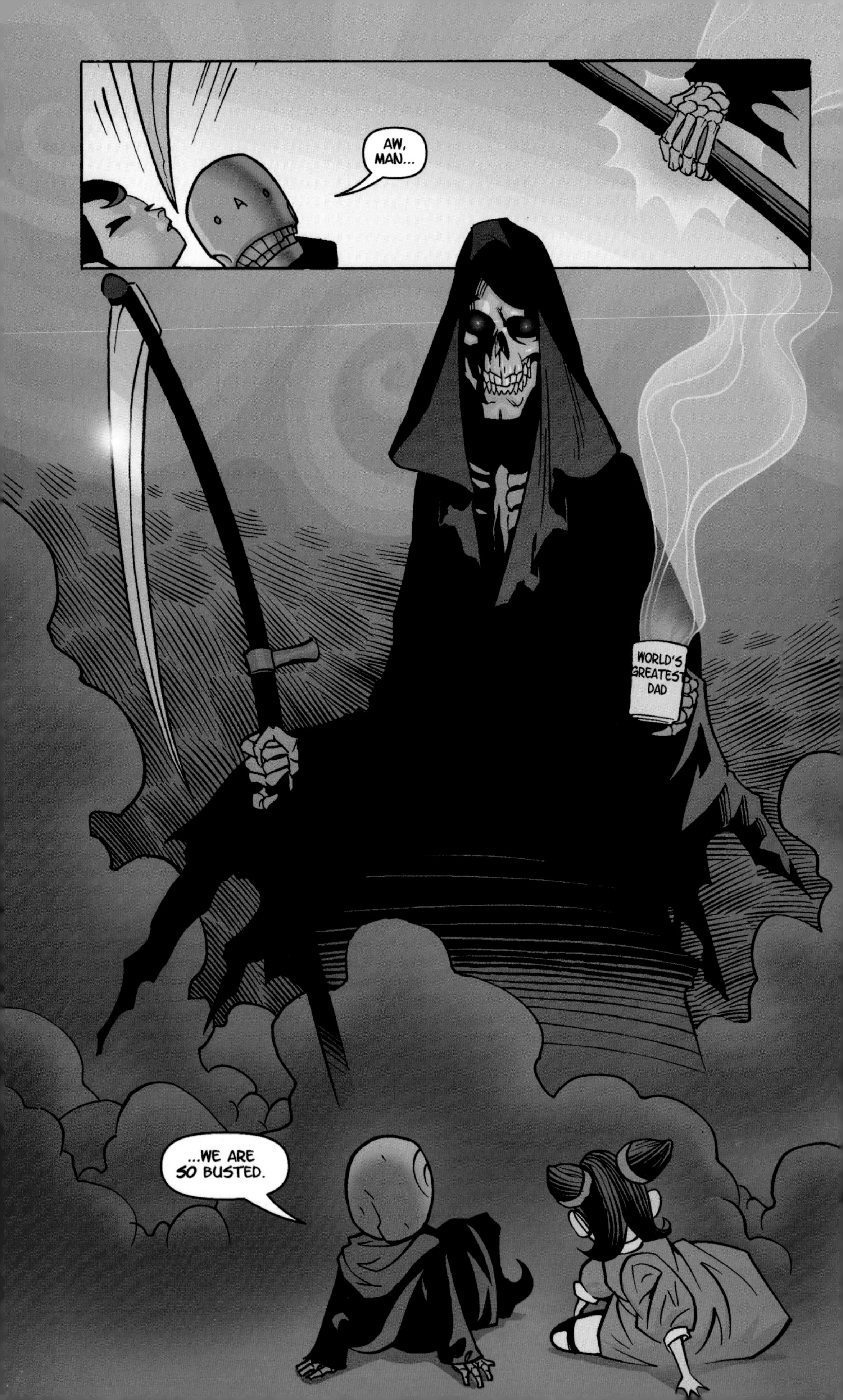
AW, MAN...
WORLD'S GREATEST DAD
...WE ARE SO BUSTED.

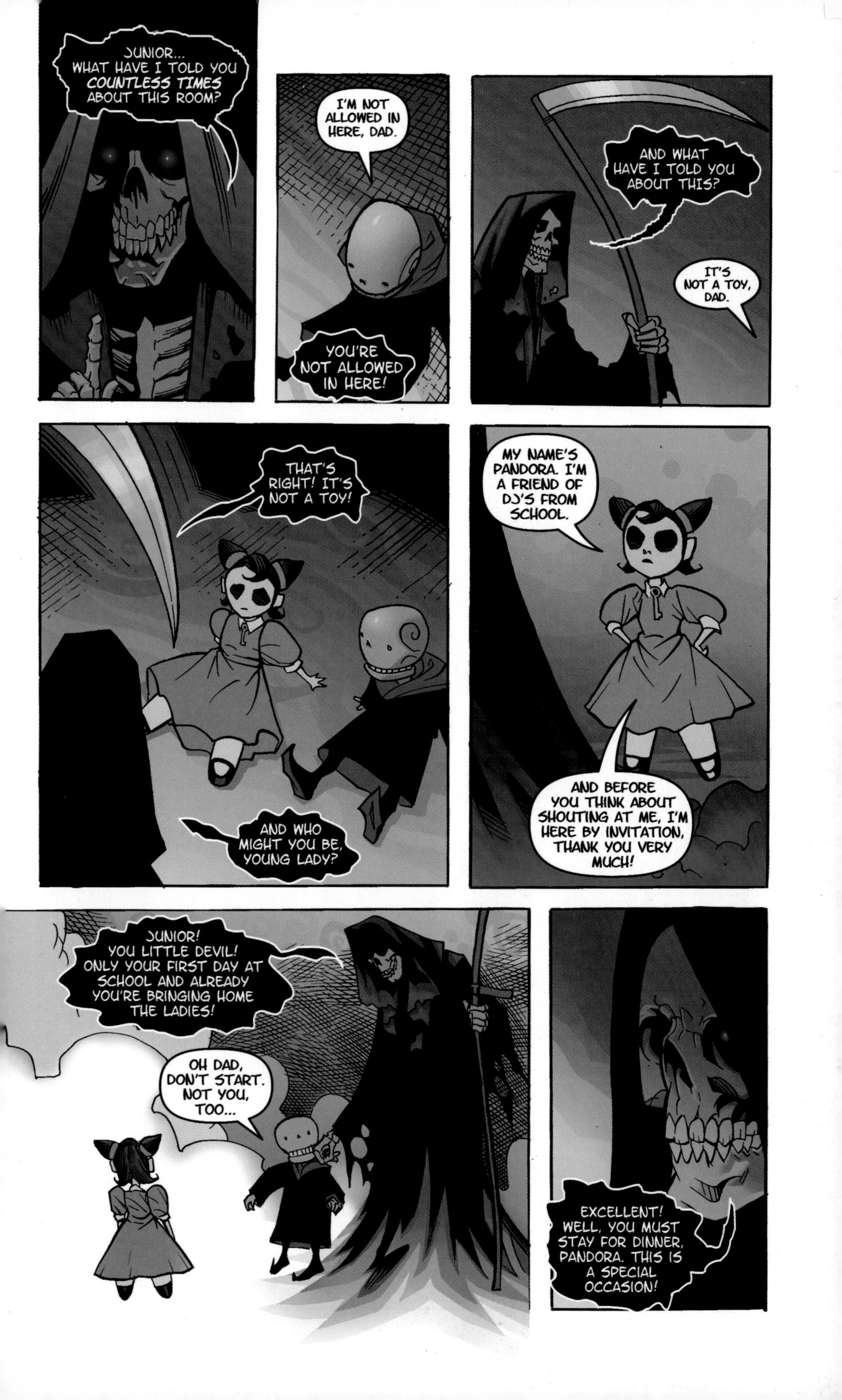

JUNIOR... WHAT HAVE I TOLD YOU COUNTLESS TIMES ABOUT THIS ROOM?
I'M NOT ALLOWED IN HERE, DAD.
YOU'RE NOT ALLOWED IN HERE!
AND WHAT HAVE I TOLD YOU ABOUT THIS?
IT'S NOT A TOY, DAD.
THAT'S RIGHT! IT'S NOT A TOY!
AND WHO MIGHT YOU BE, YOUNG LADY?
MY NAME'S PANDORA. I'M A FRIEND OF DJ'S FROM SCHOOL.
AND BEFORE YOU THINK ABOUT SHOUTING AT ME, I'M HERE BY INVITATION, THANK YOU VERY MUCH!
JUNIOR! YOU LITTLE DEVIL! ONLY YOUR FIRST DAY AT SCHOOL AND ALREADY YOU'RE BRINGING HOME THE LADIES!
OH DAD, DON'T START. NOT YOU, TOO...
EXCELLENT! WELL, YOU MUST STAY FOR DINNER, PANDORA. THIS IS A SPECIAL OCCASION!

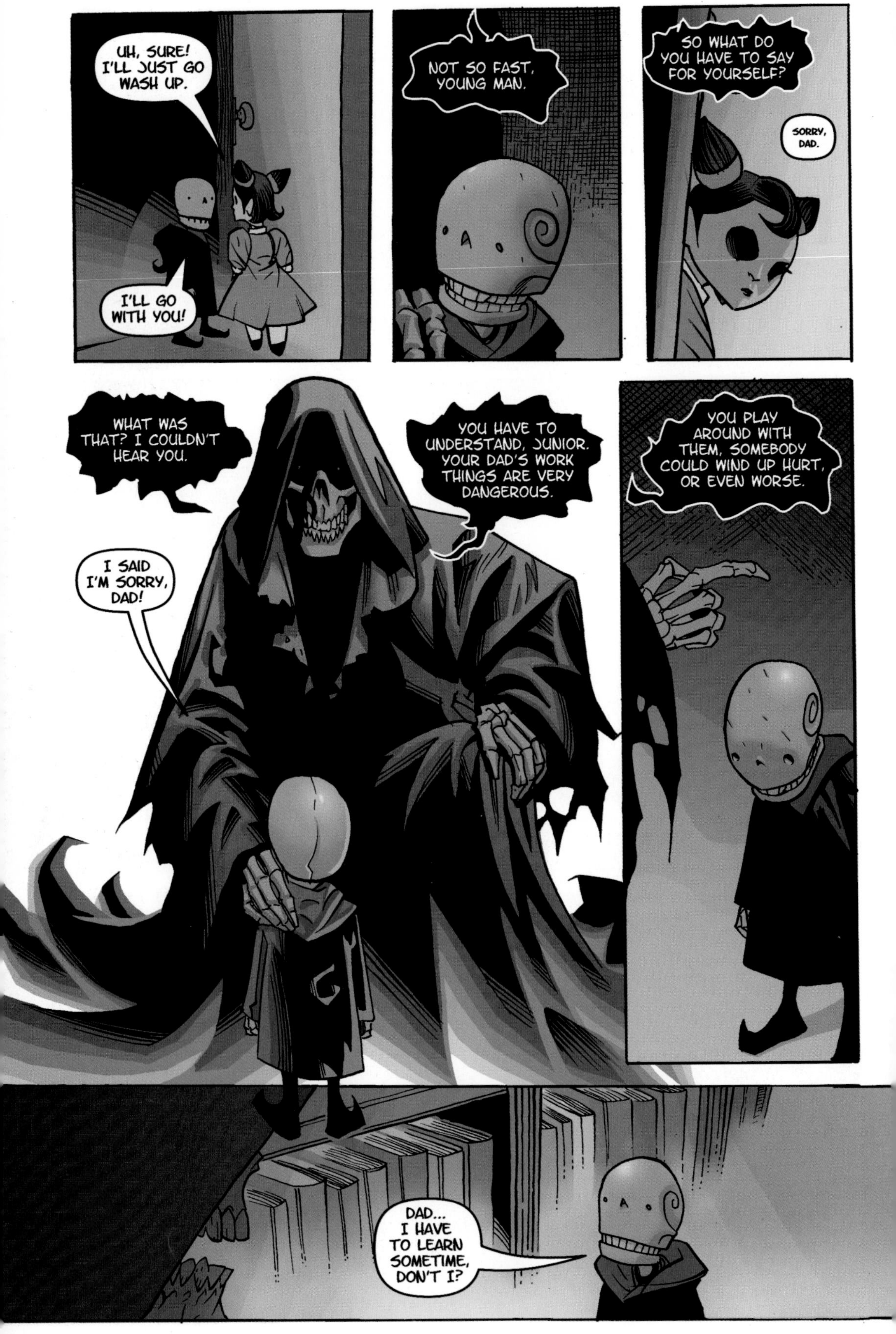
UH, SURE! I'LL JUST GO WASH UP.
I'LL GO WITH YOU!
NOT SO FAST, YOUNG MAN.
SO WHAT DO YOU HAVE TO SAY FOR YOURSELF?
SORRY, DAD.
WHAT WAS THAT? I COULDN'T HEAR YOU.
I SAID I'M SORRY, DAD!
YOU HAVE TO UNDERSTAND, JUNIOR. YOUR DAD'S WORK THINGS ARE VERY DANGEROUS.
YOU PLAY AROUND WITH THEM, SOMEBODY COULD WIND UP HURT, OR EVEN WORSE.
DAD... I HAVE TO LEARN SOMETIME, DON'T I?

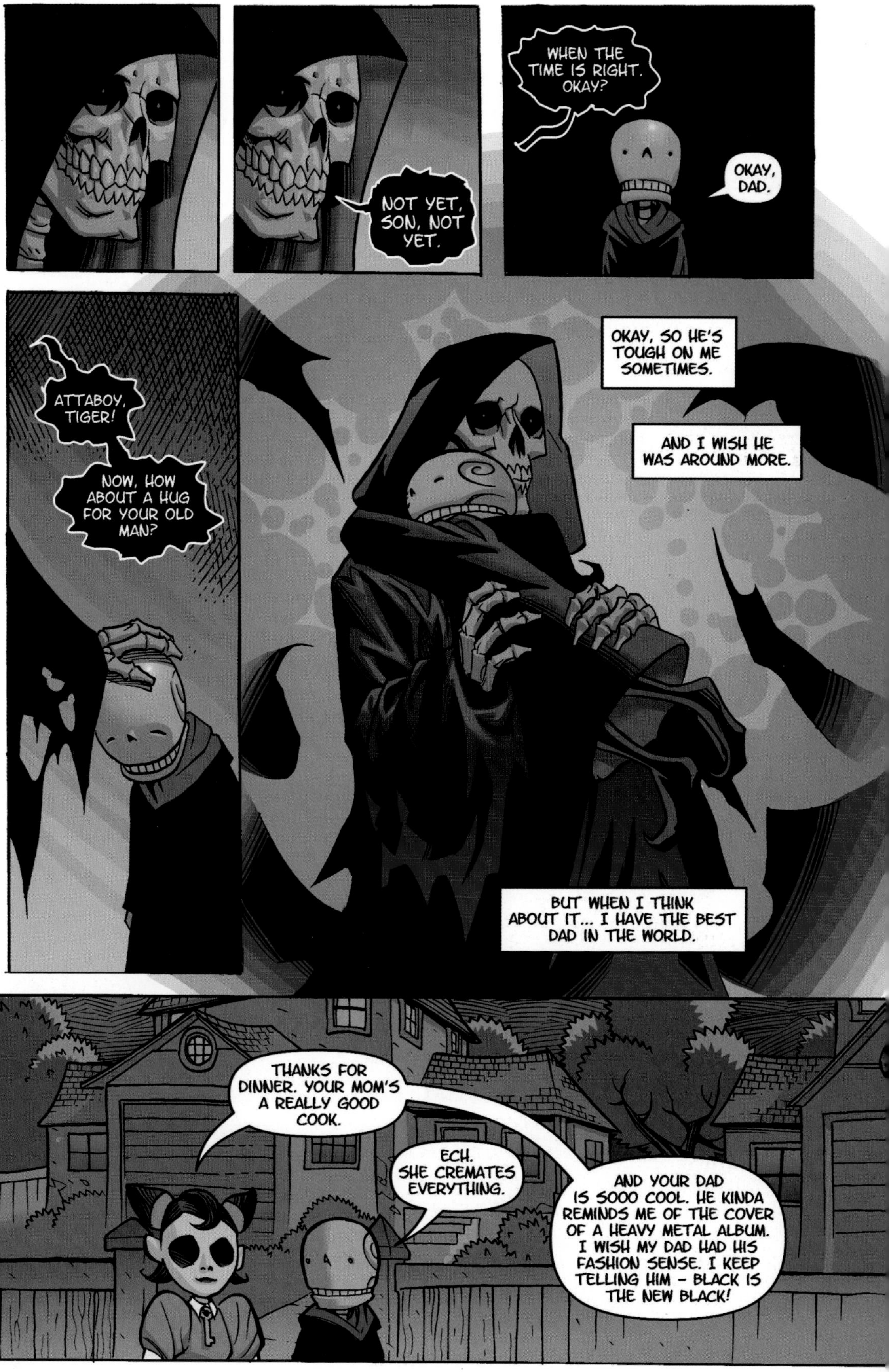
NOT YET, SON, NOT YET.
WHEN THE TIME IS RIGHT. OKAY?
OKAY, DAD.
ATTABOY, TIGER!
NOW, HOW ABOUT A HUG FOR YOUR OLD MAN?
OKAY, SO HE'S TOUGH ON ME SOMETIMES.
AND I WISH HE WAS AROUND MORE.
BUT WHEN I THINK ABOUT IT... I HAVE THE BEST DAD IN THE WORLD.
THANKS FOR DINNER. YOUR MOM'S A REALLY GOOD COOK.
ECH. SHE CREMATES EVERYTHING.
AND YOUR DAD IS SOOO COOL. HE KINDA REMINDS ME OF THE COVER OF A HEAVY METAL ALBUM. I WISH MY DAD HAD HIS FASHION SENSE. I KEEP TELLING HIM - BLACK IS THE NEW BLACK!

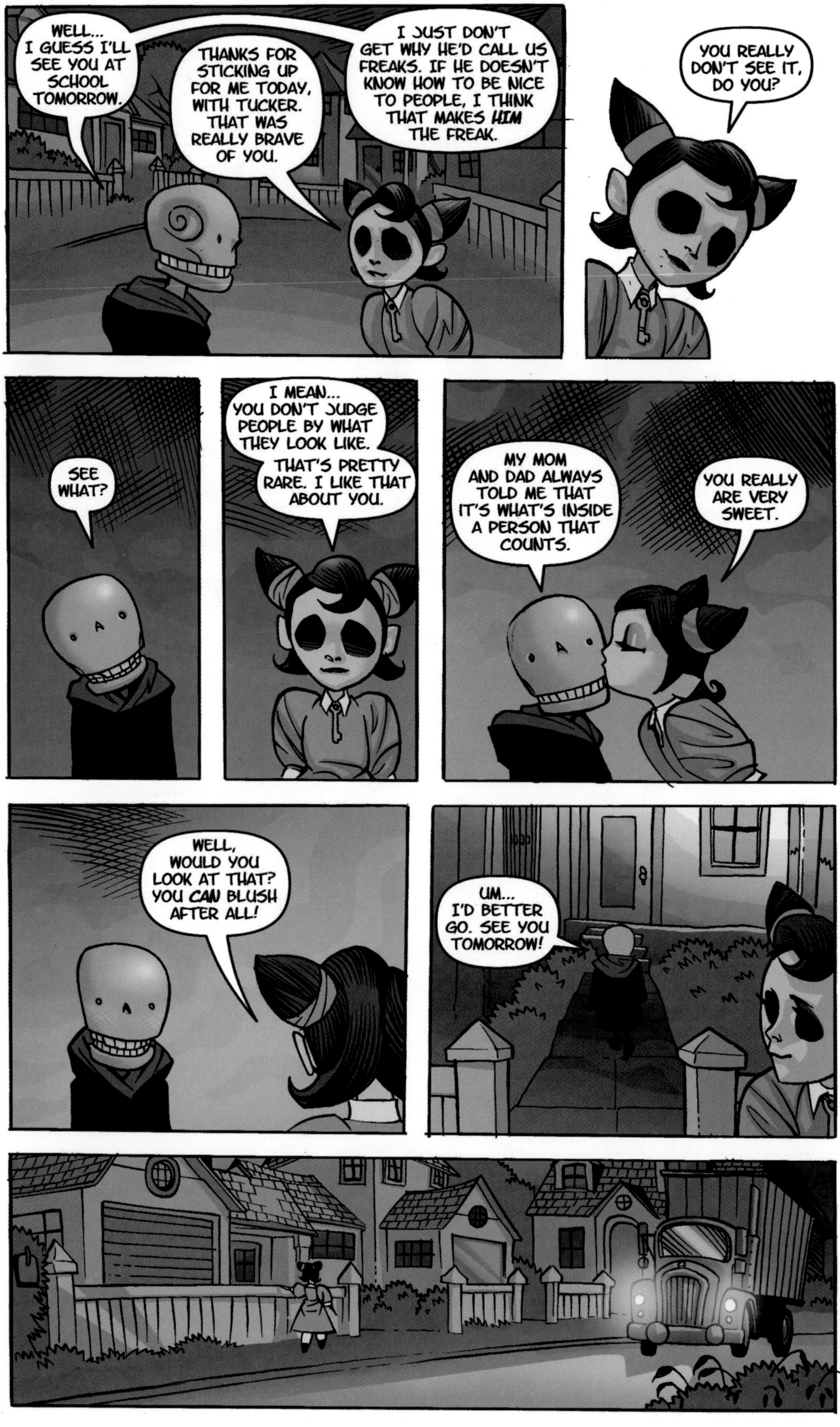
WELL... I GUESS I'LL SEE YOU AT SCHOOL TOMORROW.
THANKS FOR STICKING UP FOR ME TODAY, WITH TUCKER. THAT WAS REALLY BRAVE OF YOU.
I JUST DON'T GET WHY HE'D CALL US FREAKS. IF HE DOESN'T KNOW HOW TO BE NICE TO PEOPLE, I THINK THAT MAKES HIM THE FREAK.
YOU REALLY DON'T SEE IT, DO YOU?
SEE WHAT?
I MEAN... YOU DON'T JUDGE PEOPLE BY WHAT THEY LOOK LIKE.
THAT'S PRETTY RARE. I LIKE THAT ABOUT YOU.
MY MOM AND DAD ALWAYS TOLD ME THAT IT'S WHAT'S INSIDE A PERSON THAT COUNTS.
YOU REALLY ARE VERY SWEET.
WELL, WOULD YOU LOOK AT THAT? YOU CAN BLUSH AFTER ALL!
UM... I'D BETTER GO. SEE YOU TOMORROW!

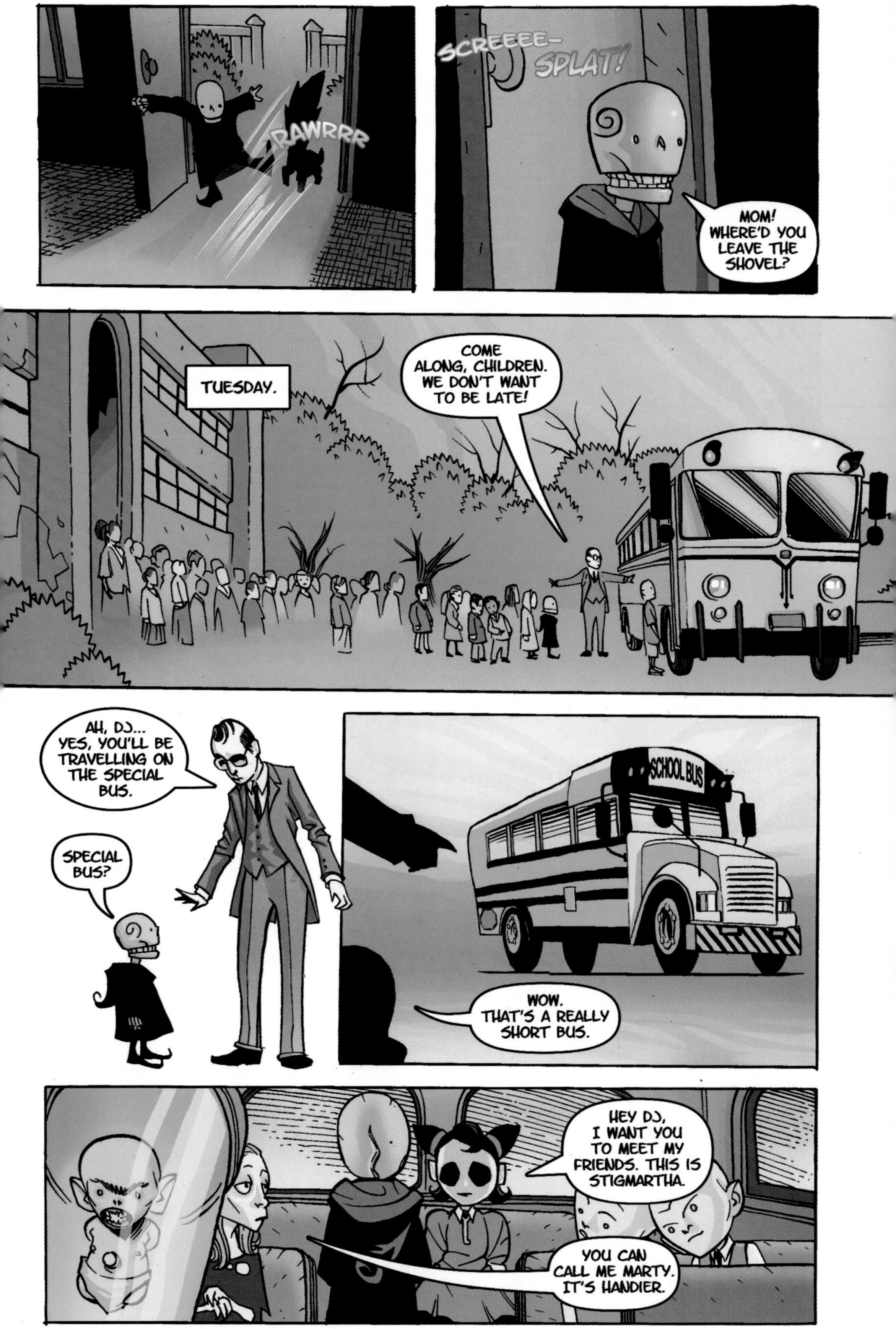

RAWRRR
SCREEEEE-
SPLAT!
MOM! WHERE'D YOU LEAVE THE SHOVEL?
TUESDAY.
COME ALONG, CHILDREN. WE DON'T WANT TO BE LATE!
AH, DJ... YES, YOU'LL BE TRAVELLING ON THE SPECIAL BUS.
SPECIAL BUS?
SCHOOL BUS
WOW. THAT'S A REALLY SHORT BUS.
HEY DJ, I WANT YOU TO MEET MY FRIENDS. THIS IS STIGMARTHA.
YOU CAN CALL ME MARTY. IT'S HANDIER.

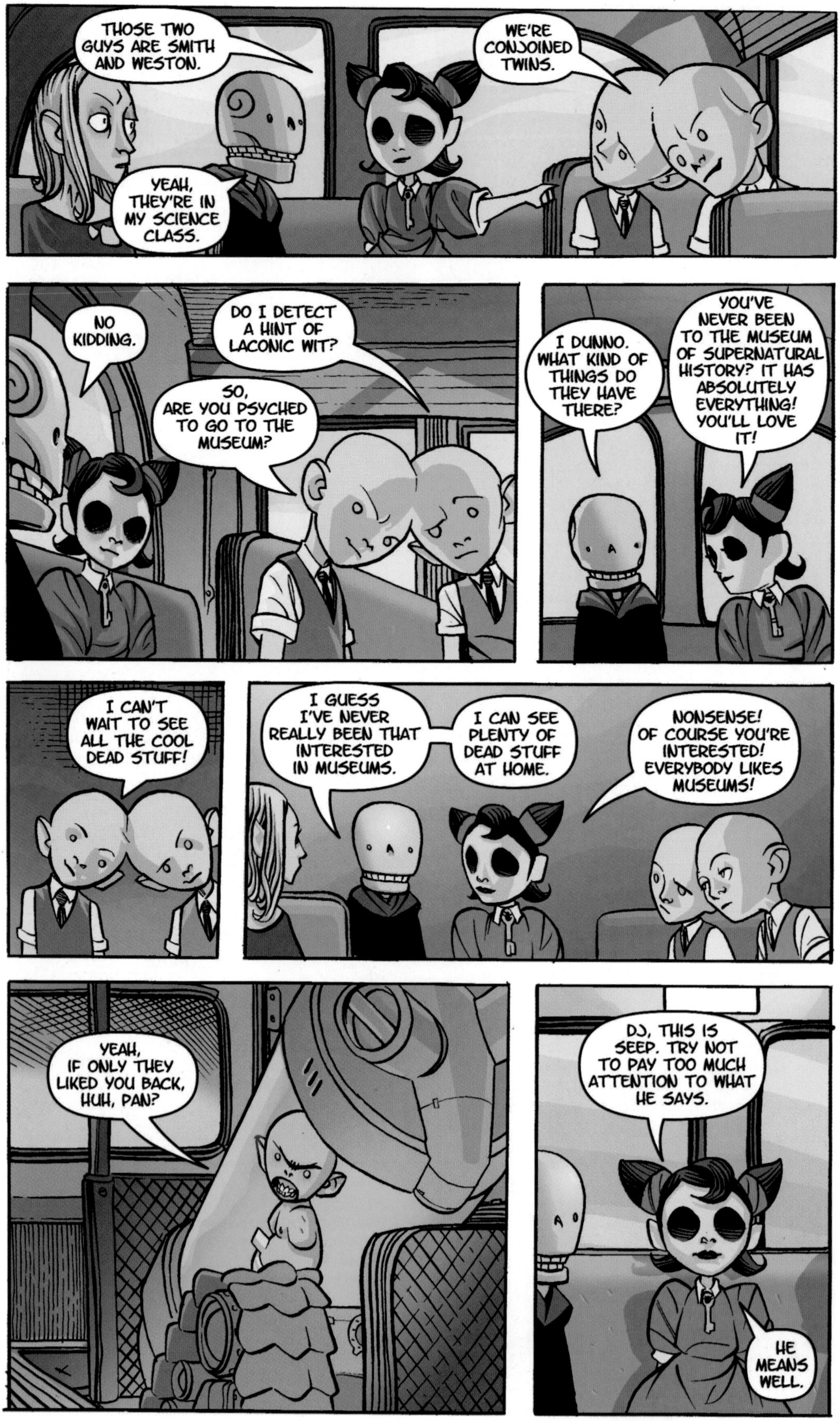
THOSE TWO GUYS ARE SMITH AND WESTON.
WE'RE CONJOINED TWINS.
YEAH, THEY'RE IN MY SCIENCE CLASS.
NO KIDDING.
DO I DETECT A HINT OF LACONIC WIT?
SO, ARE YOU PSYCHED TO GO TO THE MUSEUM?
I DUNNO. WHAT KIND OF THINGS DO THEY HAVE THERE?
YOU'VE NEVER BEEN TO THE MUSEUM OF SUPERNATURAL HISTORY? IT HAS ABSOLUTELY EVERYTHING! YOU'LL LOVE IT!
I CAN'T WAIT TO SEE ALL THE COOL DEAD STUFF!
I GUESS I'VE NEVER REALLY BEEN THAT INTERESTED IN MUSEUMS.
I CAN SEE PLENTY OF DEAD STUFF AT HOME.
NONSENSE! OF COURSE YOU'RE INTERESTED! EVERYBODY LIKES MUSEUMS!
YEAH, IF ONLY THEY LIKED YOU BACK, HUH, PAN?
DJ, THIS IS SEEP. TRY NOT TO PAY TOO MUCH ATTENTION TO WHAT HE SAYS.
HE MEANS WELL.

HEY, TRY LIVING IN A PICKLE JAR YOUR WHOLE LIFE AND SEE WHAT IT DOES FOR *YOUR* ATTITUDE!

MUSEUMS DON'T LIKE YOU?

I TOLD YOU, PAY NO ATTENTION TO HIM! IT WAS NOTHING!

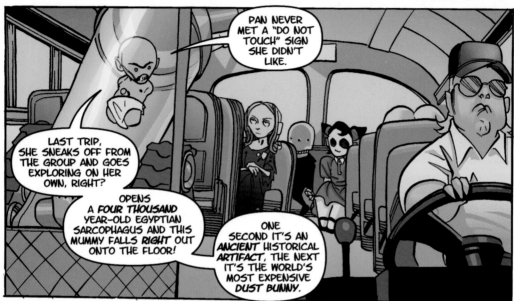

PAN NEVER MET A "DO NOT TOUCH" SIGN SHE DIDN'T LIKE.

LAST TRIP, SHE SNEAKS OFF FROM THE GROUP AND GOES EXPLORING ON HER OWN, RIGHT?

OPENS A *FOUR THOUSAND* YEAR-OLD EGYPTIAN SARCOPHAGUS AND THIS MUMMY FALLS *RIGHT* OUT ONTO THE FLOOR!

ONE SECOND IT'S AN *ANCIENT HISTORICAL ARTIFACT,* THE NEXT IT'S THE WORLD'S MOST EXPENSIVE *DUST BUNNY.*

WELL, I THINK IT'S COOL WE GET TO RIDE THERE ON OUR OWN BUS!

THE OTHER KIDS MUST BE REALLY JEALOUS.

METHINKS THE BOY HAS YET TO GRASP THE TRUE NATURE OF THE EUPHEMISTICALLY-MONIKERED "SPECIAL" BUS ON WHICH WE ARE ASSEMBLED.

UH... YEAH, RIGHT.

DJ, THIS IS THE SHORT BUS. WE'RE NOT RIDING IT AS SOME KIND OF SPECIAL TREAT. IT'S WHERE THEY PUT THE KIDS THEY THINK ARE A LITTLE...

ABERRANT? ABNORMAL?

ANOMALOUS? DEVIANT?

MUTANT? HETEROMORPHIC? PRETERNATURAL?

FREAKY!

WHAT DO YOU MEAN?

HELLO? DO THOSE EYE SOCKETS OF YOURS NOT WORK?

IN CASE IT ESCAPED YOUR ATTENTION, NONE OF US HERE ARE EXACTLY NORMAL.

SMITH AND WESTON OVER THERE, THEY GOT ONE BIG BRAIN BETWEEN THE TWO OF 'EM. LITERALLY.

MARTY BLEEDS FROM HER HANDS WHEN SHE'S NERVOUS... WHICH JUST MAKES HER EVEN MORE NERVOUS.

PANDORA'S JUST, WELL, WEIRD.

AND ME, I'M FLOATING IN A PICKLE JAR!

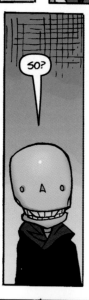

SO?

SO... YOU DON'T THINK THERE'S ANYTHING A LITTLE STRANGE ABOUT ANY OF THAT?

ABOUT YOU?

LIKE WHAT?

LIKE WHAT? YOU'RE A SKULL!

YOUR FACE LOOKS LIKE IT SHOULD BE ON A BOTTLE OF POISON!

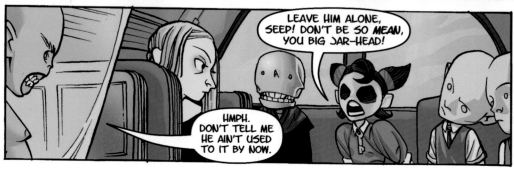

LEAVE HIM ALONE, SEEP! DON'T BE SO MEAN, YOU BIG JAR-HEAD!

HMPH. DON'T TELL ME HE AIN'T USED TO IT BY NOW.

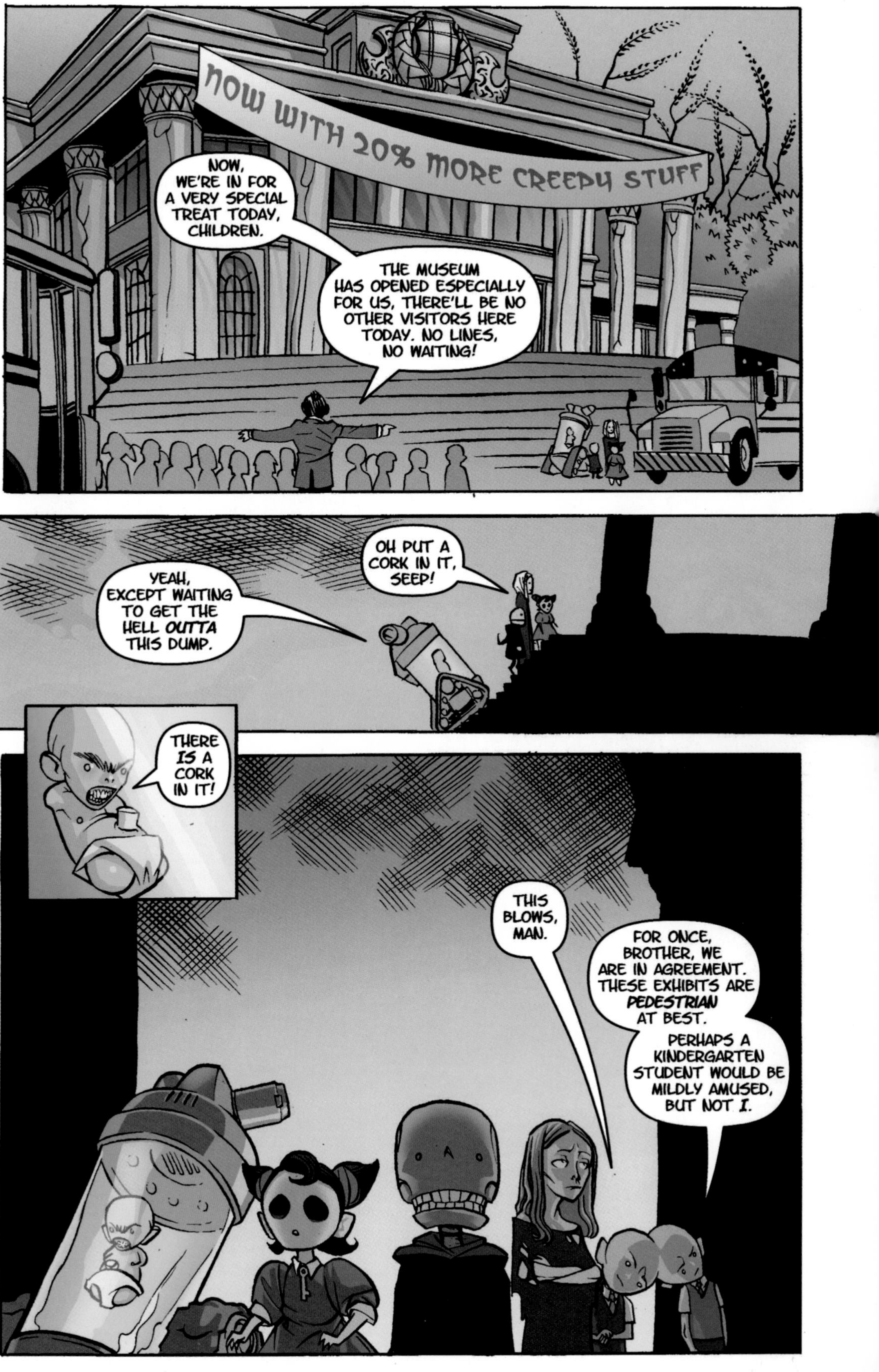
NOW WITH 20% MORE CREEPY STUFF
NOW, WE'RE IN FOR A VERY SPECIAL TREAT TODAY, CHILDREN.
THE MUSEUM HAS OPENED ESPECIALLY FOR US, THERE'LL BE NO OTHER VISITORS HERE TODAY. NO LINES, NO WAITING!
YEAH, EXCEPT WAITING TO GET THE HELL *OUTTA* THIS DUMP.
OH PUT A CORK IN IT, SEEP!
THERE *IS* A CORK IN IT!
THIS BLOWS, MAN.
FOR ONCE, BROTHER, WE ARE IN AGREEMENT. THESE EXHIBITS ARE *PEDESTRIAN* AT BEST.
PERHAPS A KINDERGARTEN STUDENT WOULD BE MILDLY AMUSED, BUT NOT *I*.

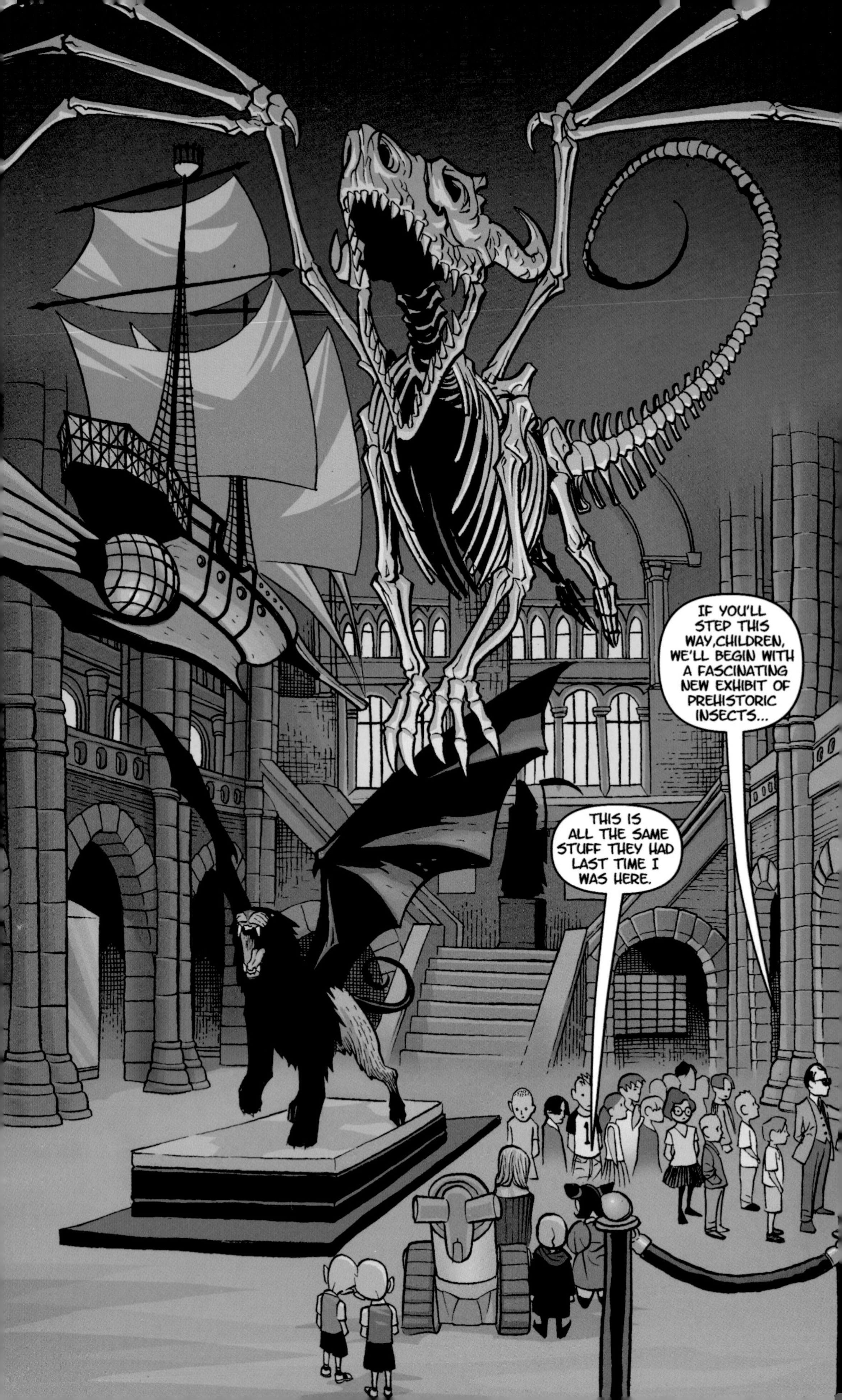
IF YOU'LL STEP THIS WAY,CHILDREN, WE'LL BEGIN WITH A FASCINATING NEW EXHIBIT OF PREHISTORIC INSECTS...
THIS IS ALL THE SAME STUFF THEY HAD LAST TIME I WAS HERE.

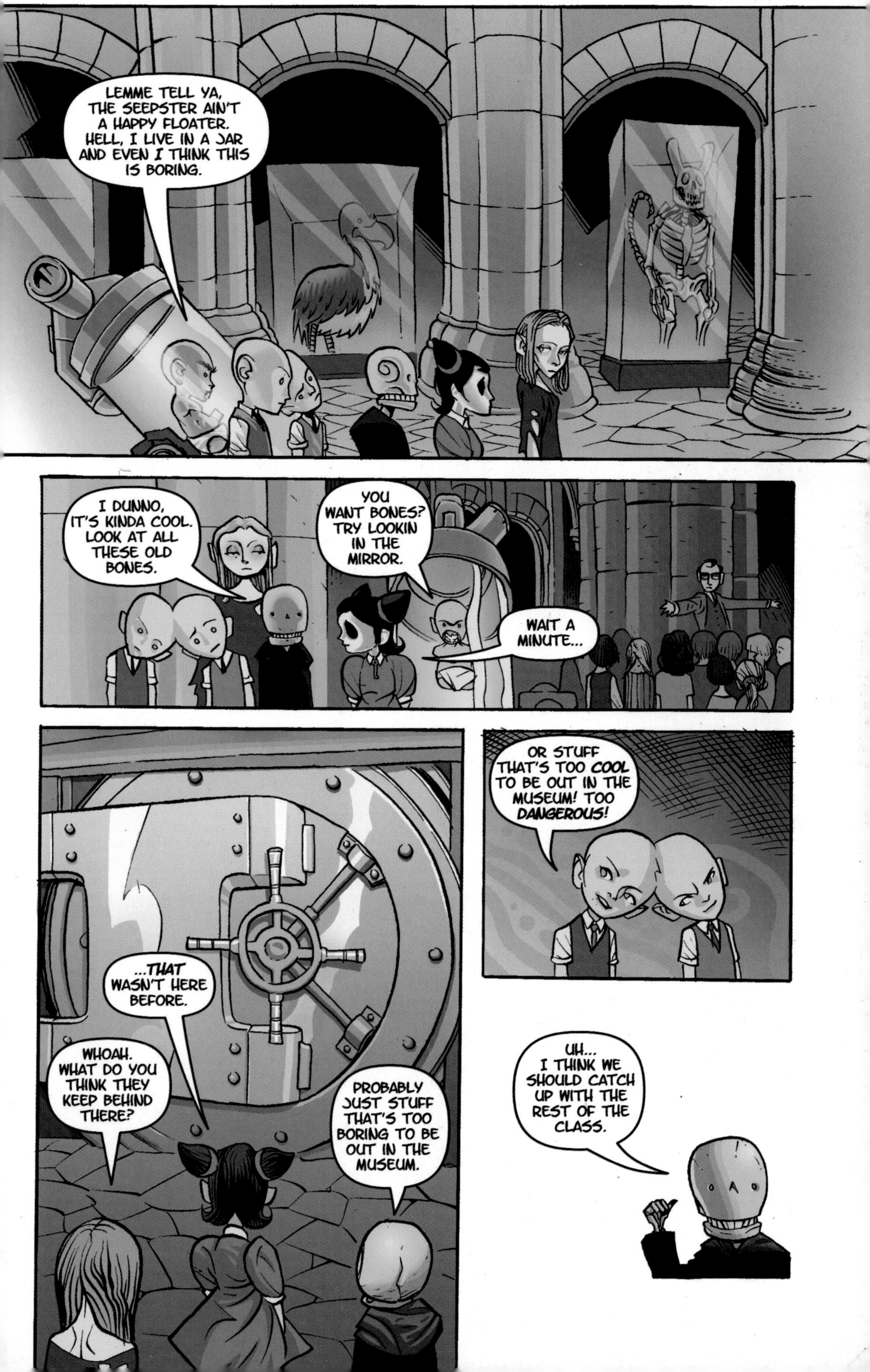
LEMME TELL YA, THE SEEPSTER AIN'T A HAPPY FLOATER. HELL, I LIVE IN A JAR AND EVEN I THINK THIS IS BORING.
I DUNNO, IT'S KINDA COOL. LOOK AT ALL THESE OLD BONES.
YOU WANT BONES? TRY LOOKIN IN THE MIRROR.
WAIT A MINUTE...
...THAT WASN'T HERE BEFORE.
WHOAH. WHAT DO YOU THINK THEY KEEP BEHIND THERE?
PROBABLY JUST STUFF THAT'S TOO BORING TO BE OUT IN THE MUSEUM.
OR STUFF THAT'S TOO COOL TO BE OUT IN THE MUSEUM! TOO DANGEROUS!
UH... I THINK WE SHOULD CATCH UP WITH THE REST OF THE CLASS.

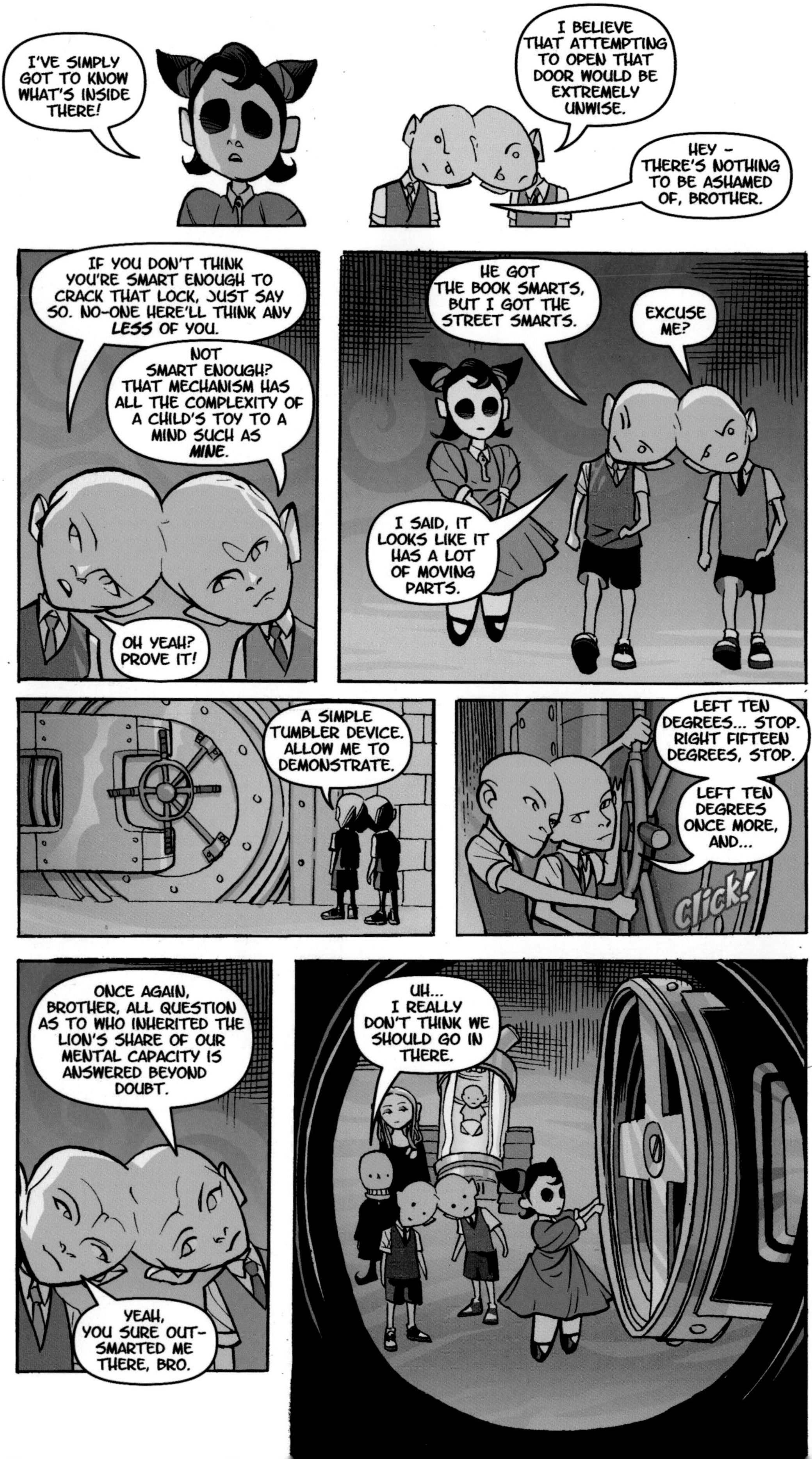
I'VE SIMPLY GOT TO KNOW WHAT'S INSIDE THERE!
I BELIEVE THAT ATTEMPTING TO OPEN THAT DOOR WOULD BE EXTREMELY UNWISE.
HEY - THERE'S NOTHING TO BE ASHAMED OF, BROTHER.
IF YOU DON'T THINK YOU'RE SMART ENOUGH TO CRACK THAT LOCK, JUST SAY SO. NO-ONE HERE'LL THINK ANY LESS OF YOU.
NOT SMART ENOUGH? THAT MECHANISM HAS ALL THE COMPLEXITY OF A CHILD'S TOY TO A MIND SUCH AS MINE.
OH YEAH? PROVE IT!
HE GOT THE BOOK SMARTS, BUT I GOT THE STREET SMARTS.
EXCUSE ME?
I SAID, IT LOOKS LIKE IT HAS A LOT OF MOVING PARTS.
A SIMPLE TUMBLER DEVICE. ALLOW ME TO DEMONSTRATE.
LEFT TEN DEGREES... STOP. RIGHT FIFTEEN DEGREES, STOP.
LEFT TEN DEGREES ONCE MORE, AND...
click!
ONCE AGAIN, BROTHER, ALL QUESTION AS TO WHO INHERITED THE LION'S SHARE OF OUR MENTAL CAPACITY IS ANSWERED BEYOND DOUBT.
YEAH, YOU SURE OUT-SMARTED ME THERE, BRO.
UH... I REALLY DON'T THINK WE SHOULD GO IN THERE.

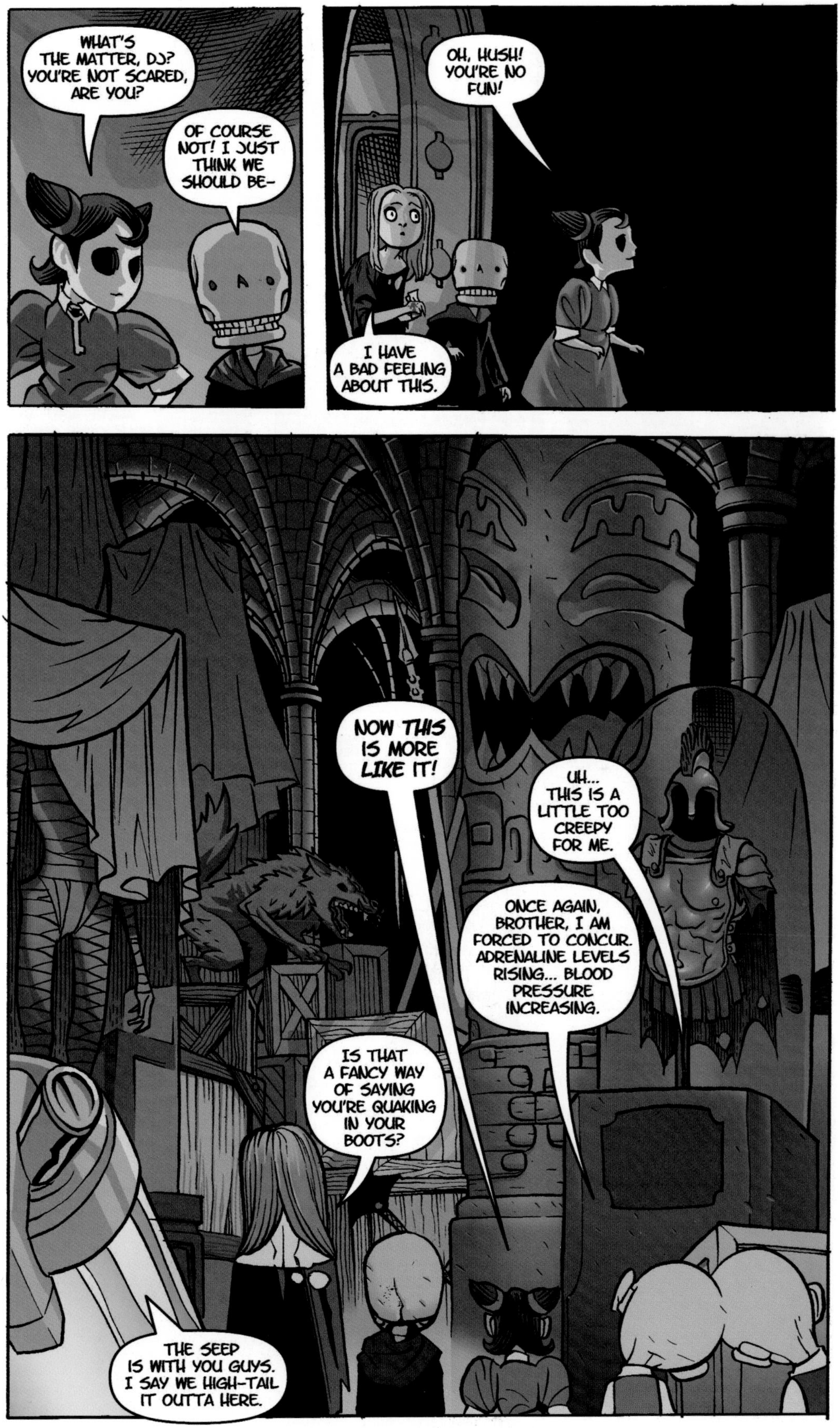
WHAT'S THE MATTER, DJ? YOU'RE NOT SCARED, ARE YOU?
OF COURSE NOT! I JUST THINK WE SHOULD BE-
OH, HUSH! YOU'RE NO FUN!
I HAVE A BAD FEELING ABOUT THIS.
NOW *THIS* IS MORE *LIKE* IT!
UH... THIS IS A LITTLE TOO CREEPY FOR ME.
ONCE AGAIN, BROTHER, I AM FORCED TO CONCUR. ADRENALINE LEVELS RISING... BLOOD PRESSURE INCREASING.
IS THAT A FANCY WAY OF SAYING YOU'RE QUAKING IN YOUR BOOTS?
THE SEEP IS WITH YOU GUYS. I SAY WE HIGH-TAIL IT OUTTA HERE.

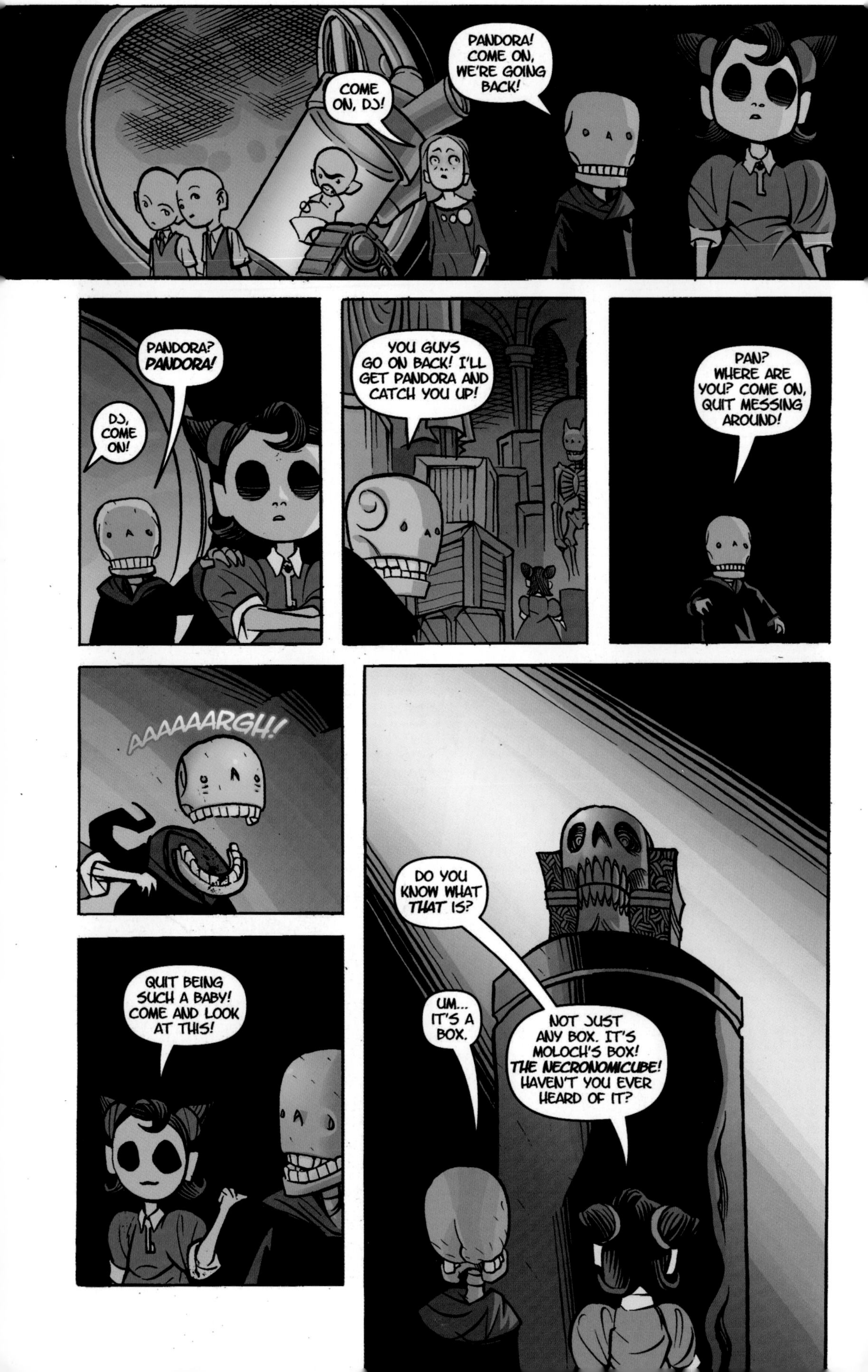
COME ON, DJ!
PANDORA! COME ON, WE'RE GOING BACK!
DJ, COME ON!
PANDORA? **PANDORA!**
YOU GUYS GO ON BACK! I'LL GET PANDORA AND CATCH YOU UP!
PAN? WHERE ARE YOU? COME ON, QUIT MESSING AROUND!
AAAAAARGH!
QUIT BEING SUCH A BABY! COME AND LOOK AT THIS!
DO YOU KNOW WHAT *THAT* IS?
UM... IT'S A BOX.
NOT JUST ANY BOX. IT'S MOLOCH'S BOX! ***THE NECRONOMICUBE!*** HAVEN'T YOU EVER HEARD OF IT?

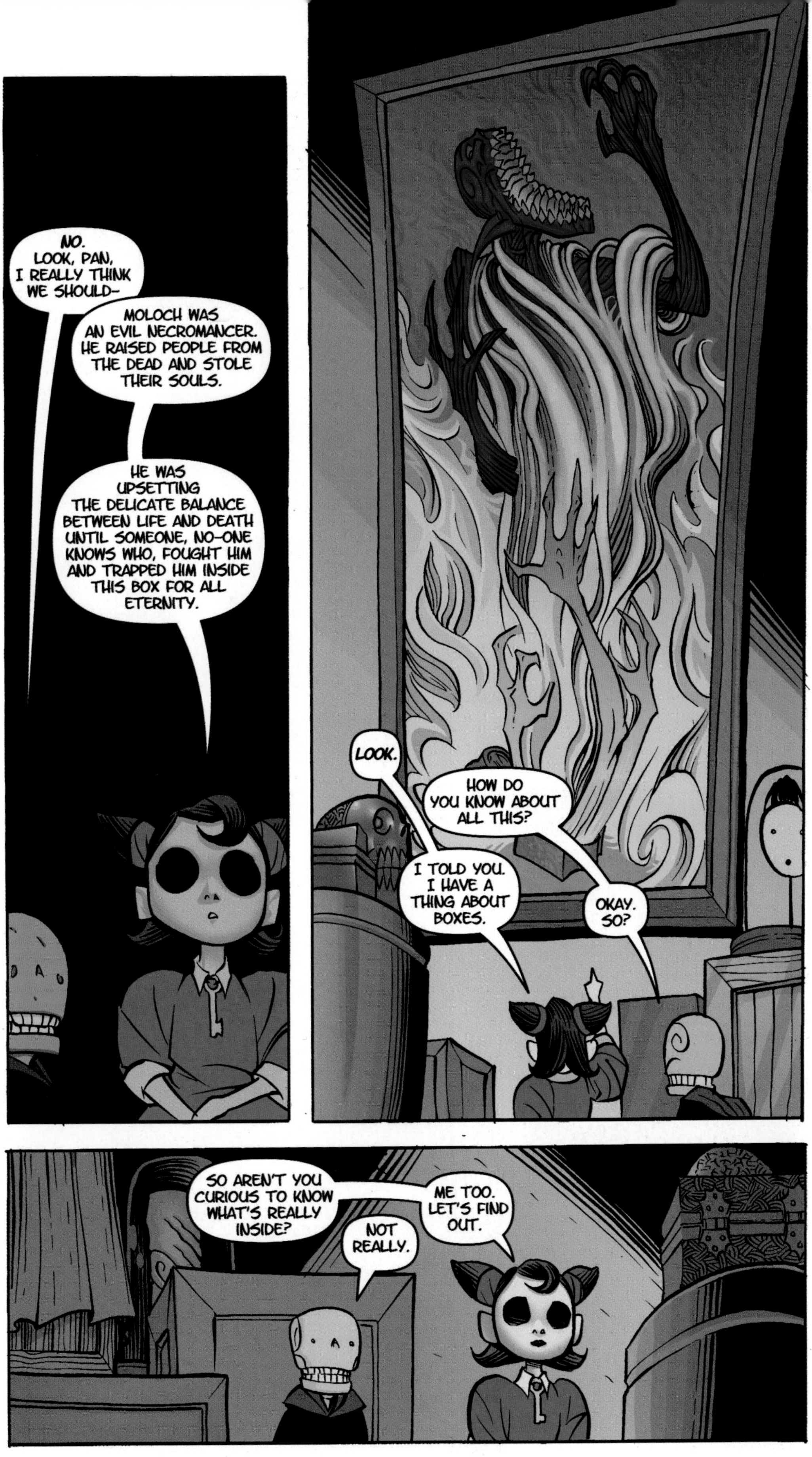
NO. LOOK, PAN, I REALLY THINK WE SHOULD–
MOLOCH WAS AN EVIL NECROMANCER. HE RAISED PEOPLE FROM THE DEAD AND STOLE THEIR SOULS.
HE WAS UPSETTING THE DELICATE BALANCE BETWEEN LIFE AND DEATH UNTIL SOMEONE, NO-ONE KNOWS WHO, FOUGHT HIM AND TRAPPED HIM INSIDE THIS BOX FOR ALL ETERNITY.
LOOK.
HOW DO YOU KNOW ABOUT ALL THIS?
I TOLD YOU. I HAVE A THING ABOUT BOXES.
OKAY. SO?
SO AREN'T YOU CURIOUS TO KNOW WHAT'S REALLY INSIDE?
NOT REALLY.
ME TOO. LET'S FIND OUT.

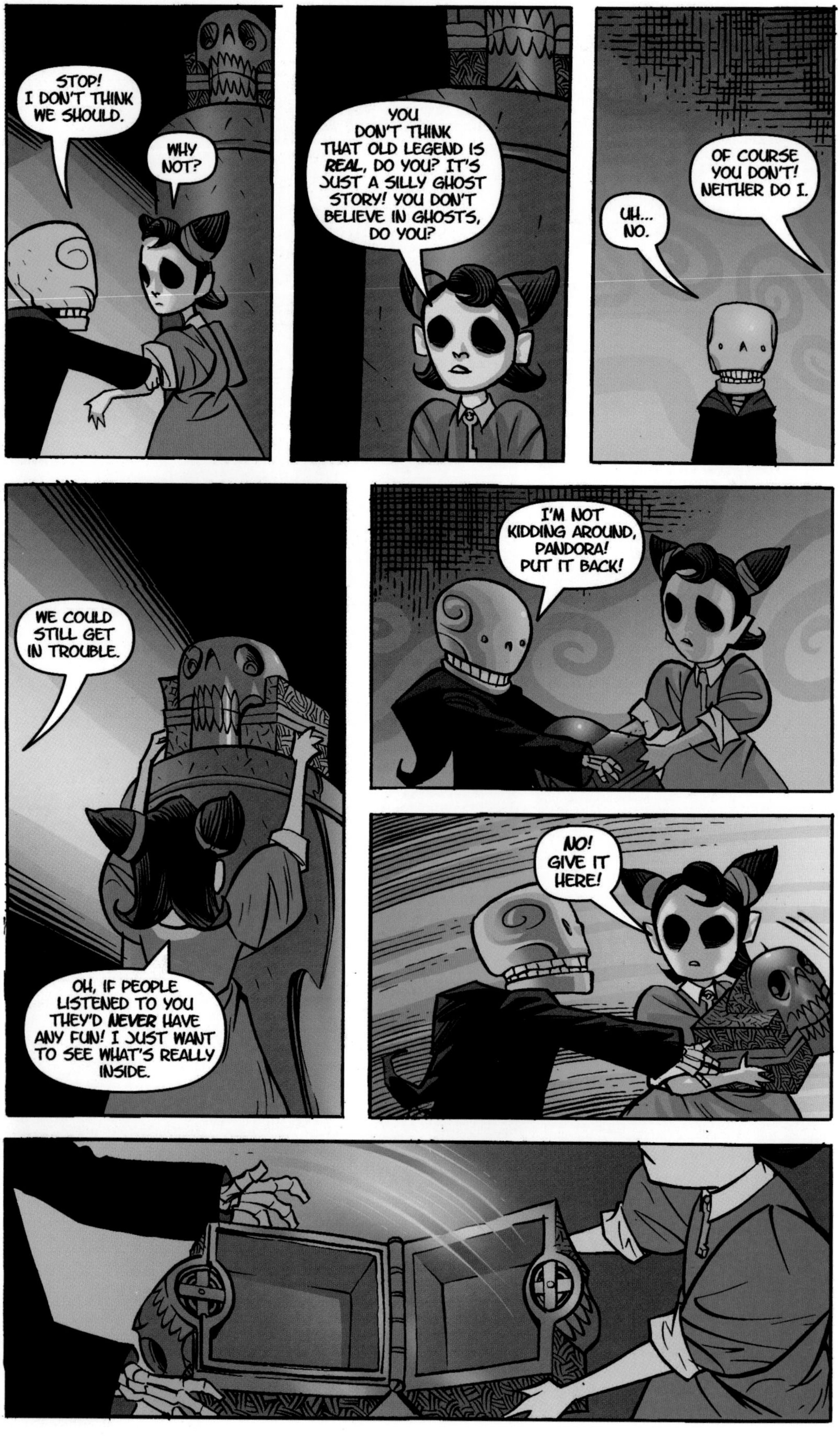

STOP! I DON'T THINK WE SHOULD.
WHY NOT?
YOU DON'T THINK THAT OLD LEGEND IS REAL, DO YOU? IT'S JUST A SILLY GHOST STORY! YOU DON'T BELIEVE IN GHOSTS, DO YOU?
OF COURSE YOU DON'T! NEITHER DO I.
UH... NO.
WE COULD STILL GET IN TROUBLE.
OH, IF PEOPLE LISTENED TO YOU THEY'D NEVER HAVE ANY FUN! I JUST WANT TO SEE WHAT'S REALLY INSIDE.
I'M NOT KIDDING AROUND, PANDORA! PUT IT BACK!
NO! GIVE IT HERE!

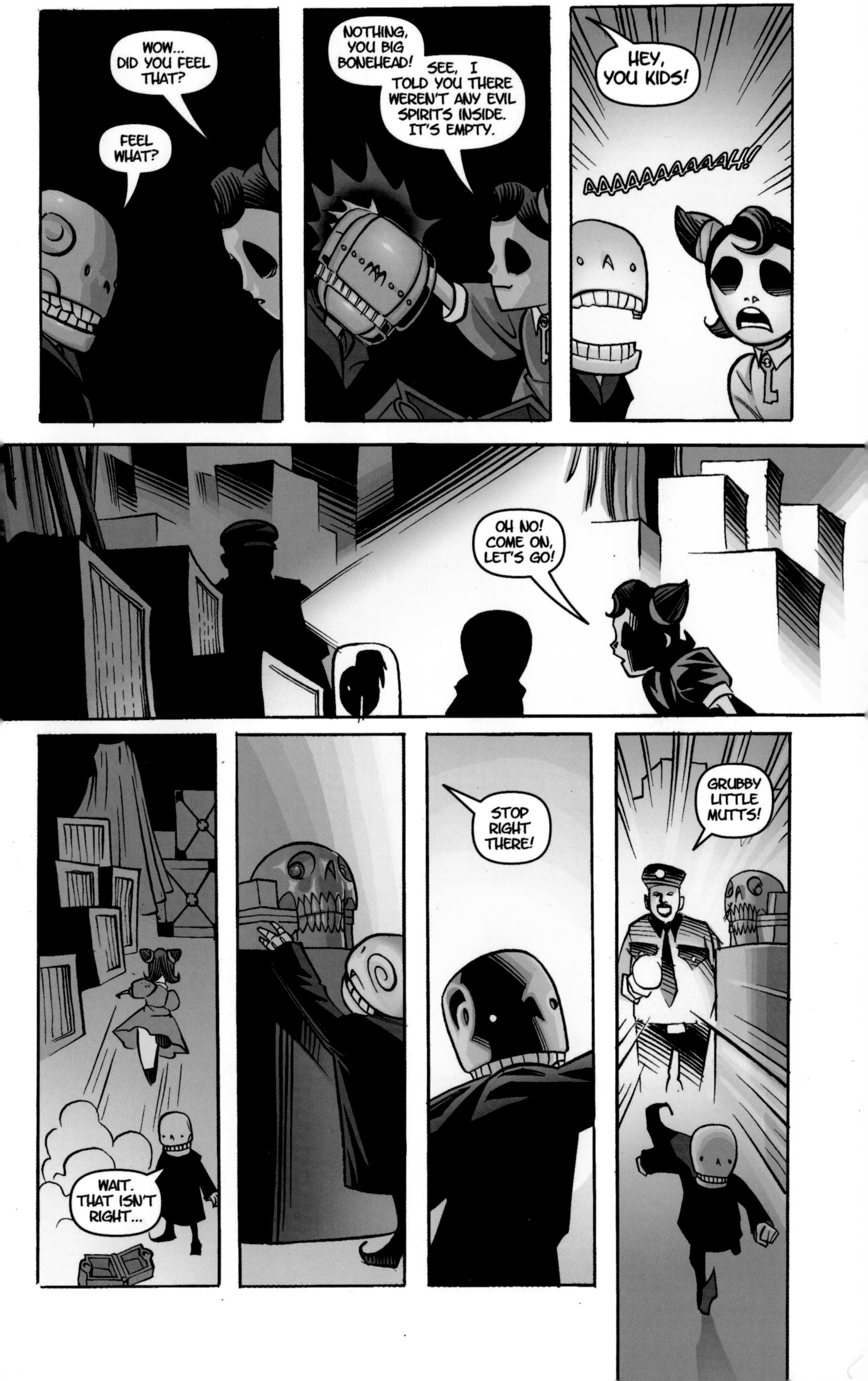
WOW... DID YOU FEEL THAT?
FEEL WHAT?
NOTHING, YOU BIG BONEHEAD!
SEE, I TOLD YOU THERE WEREN'T ANY EVIL SPIRITS INSIDE. IT'S EMPTY.
HEY, YOU KIDS!
AAAAAAAAAAAH!!
OH NO! COME ON, LET'S GO!
WAIT. THAT ISN'T RIGHT...
STOP RIGHT THERE!
GRUBBY LITTLE MUTTS!

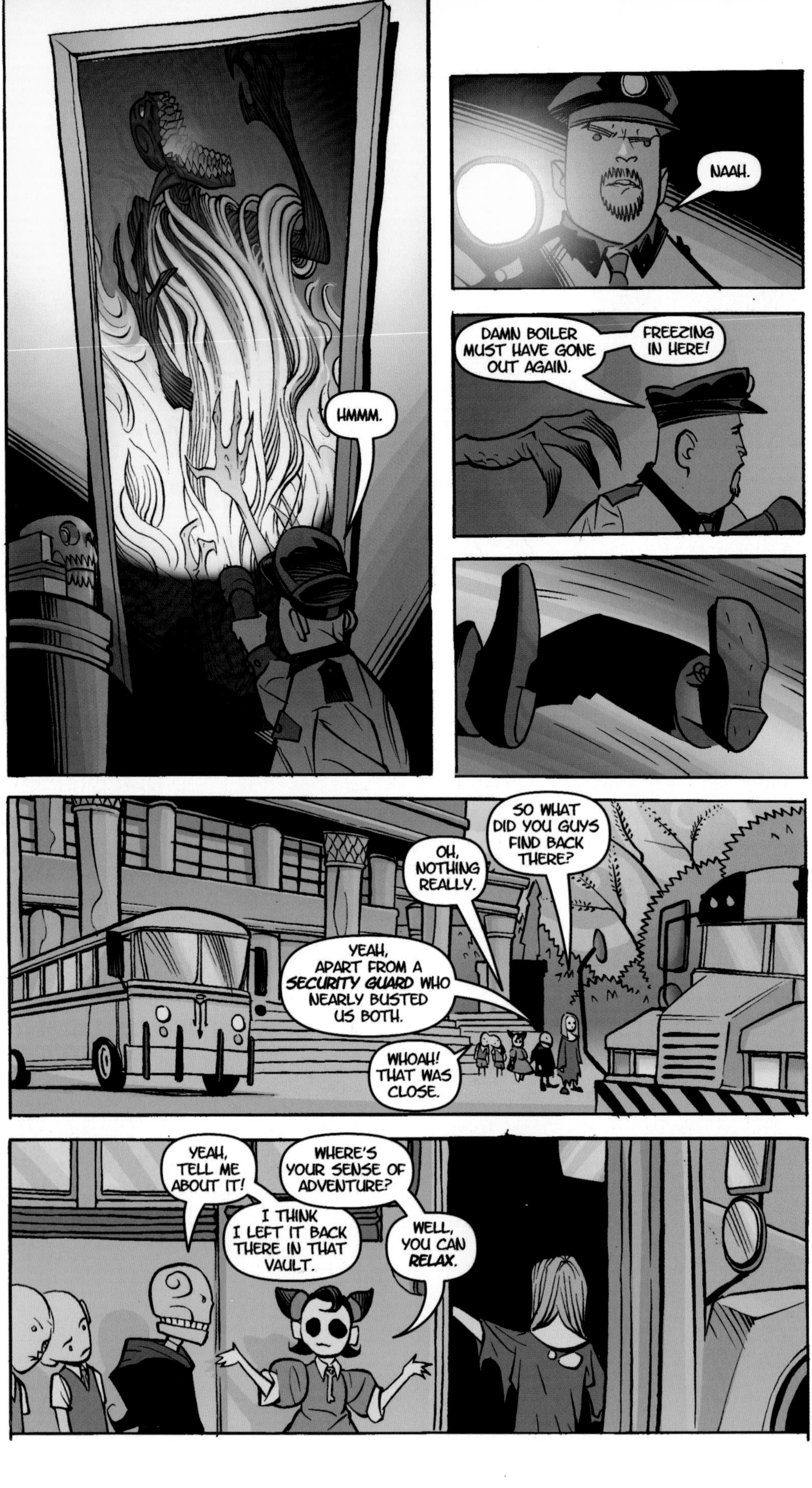
HMMM.
NAAH.
DAMN BOILER MUST HAVE GONE OUT AGAIN.
FREEZING IN HERE!
SO WHAT DID YOU GUYS FIND BACK THERE?
OH, NOTHING REALLY.
YEAH, APART FROM A SECURITY GUARD WHO NEARLY BUSTED US BOTH.
WHOAH! THAT WAS CLOSE.
YEAH, TELL ME ABOUT IT!
WHERE'S YOUR SENSE OF ADVENTURE?
I THINK I LEFT IT BACK THERE IN THAT VAULT.
WELL, YOU CAN RELAX.

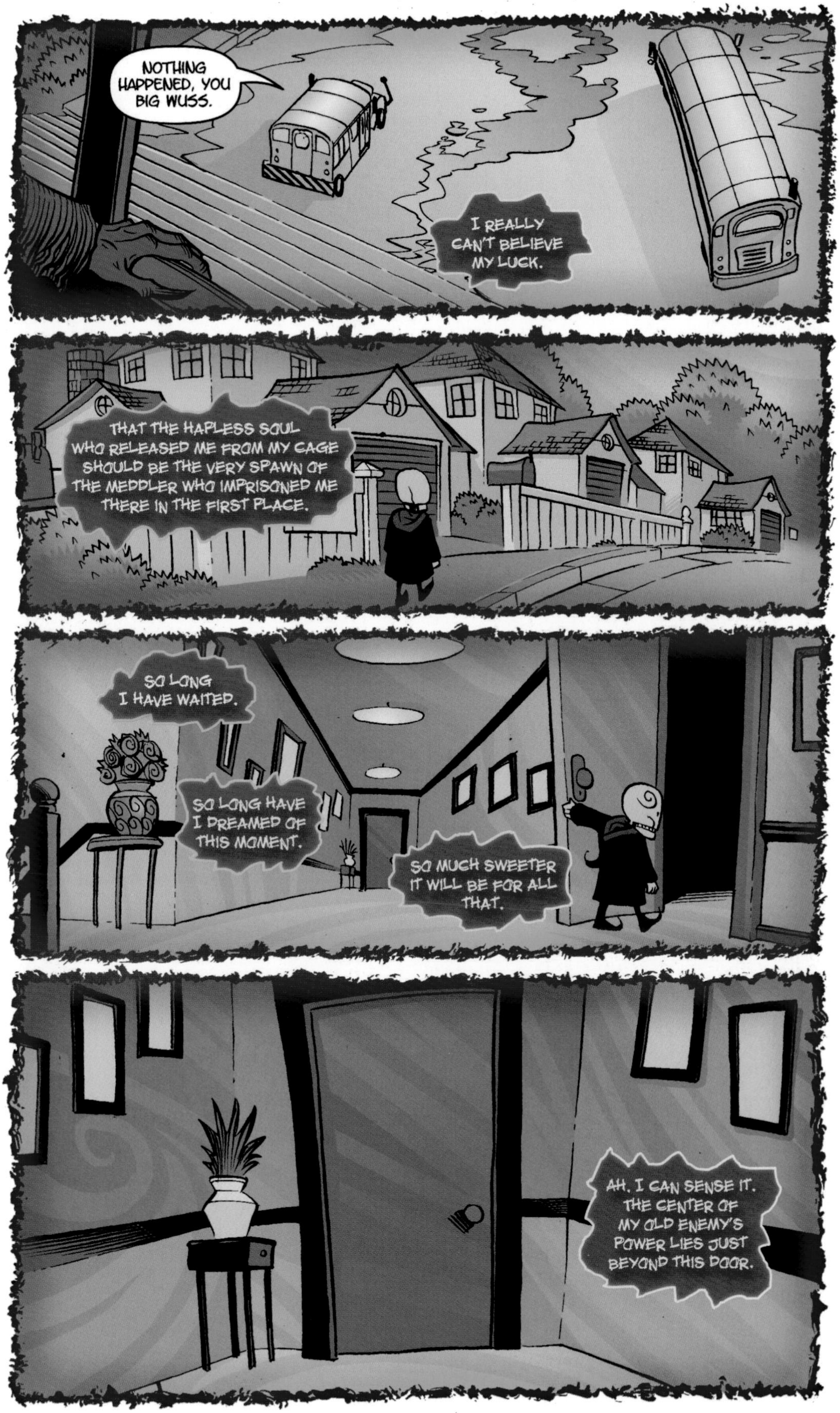
NOTHING HAPPENED, YOU BIG WUSS.
I REALLY CAN'T BELIEVE MY LUCK.
THAT THE HAPLESS SOUL WHO RELEASED ME FROM MY CAGE SHOULD BE THE VERY SPAWN OF THE MEDDLER WHO IMPRISONED ME THERE IN THE FIRST PLACE.
SO LONG I HAVE WAITED.
SO LONG HAVE I DREAMED OF THIS MOMENT.
SO MUCH SWEETER IT WILL BE FOR ALL THAT.
AH. I CAN SENSE IT. THE CENTER OF MY OLD ENEMY'S POWER LIES JUST BEYOND THIS DOOR.

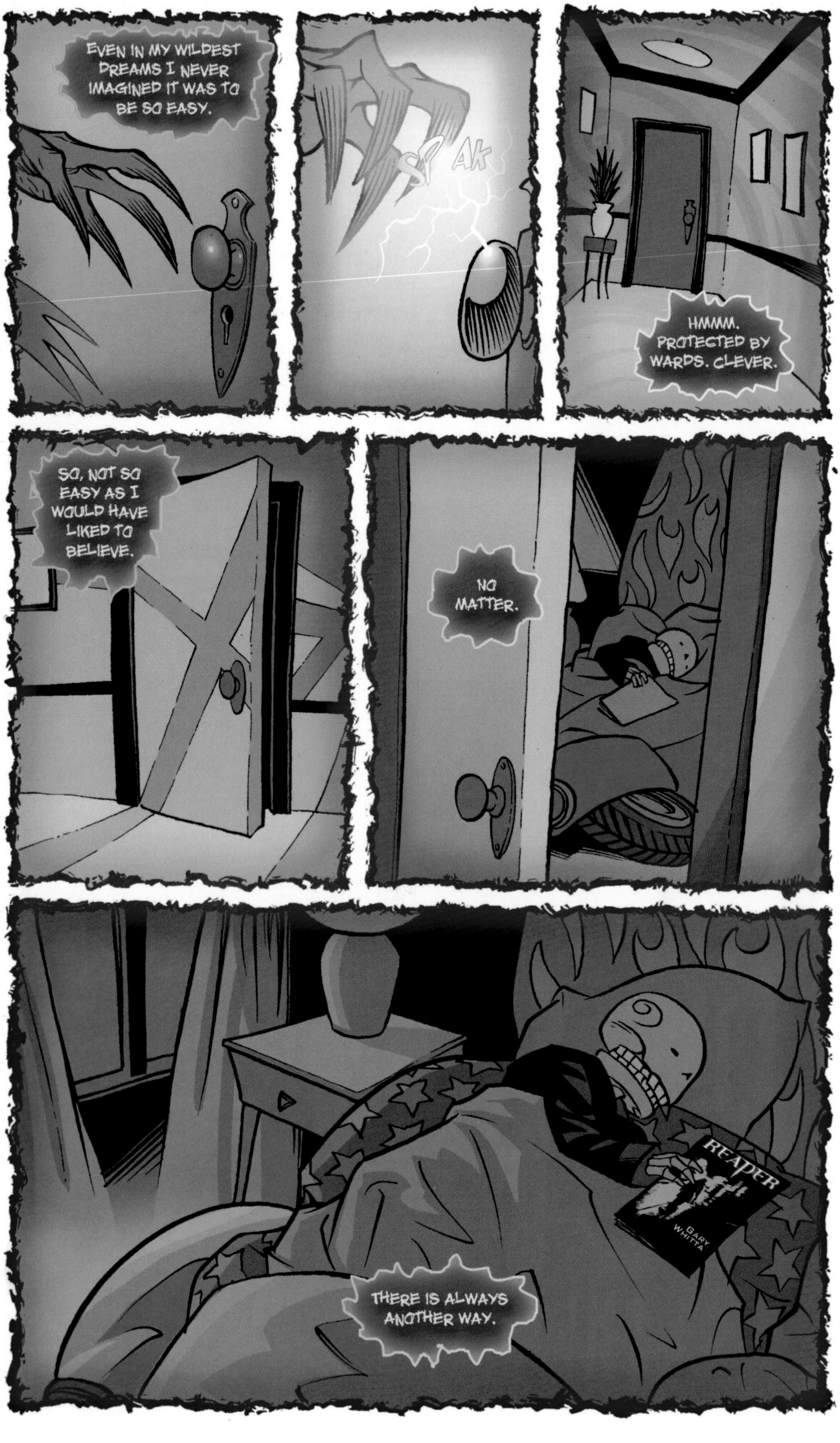

EVEN IN MY WILDEST DREAMS I NEVER IMAGINED IT WAS TO BE SO EASY.
SPAK
HMMM. PROTECTED BY WARDS. CLEVER.
SO, NOT SO EASY AS I WOULD HAVE LIKED TO BELIEVE.
NO MATTER.
READER
GARY WHITTA
THERE IS ALWAYS ANOTHER WAY.

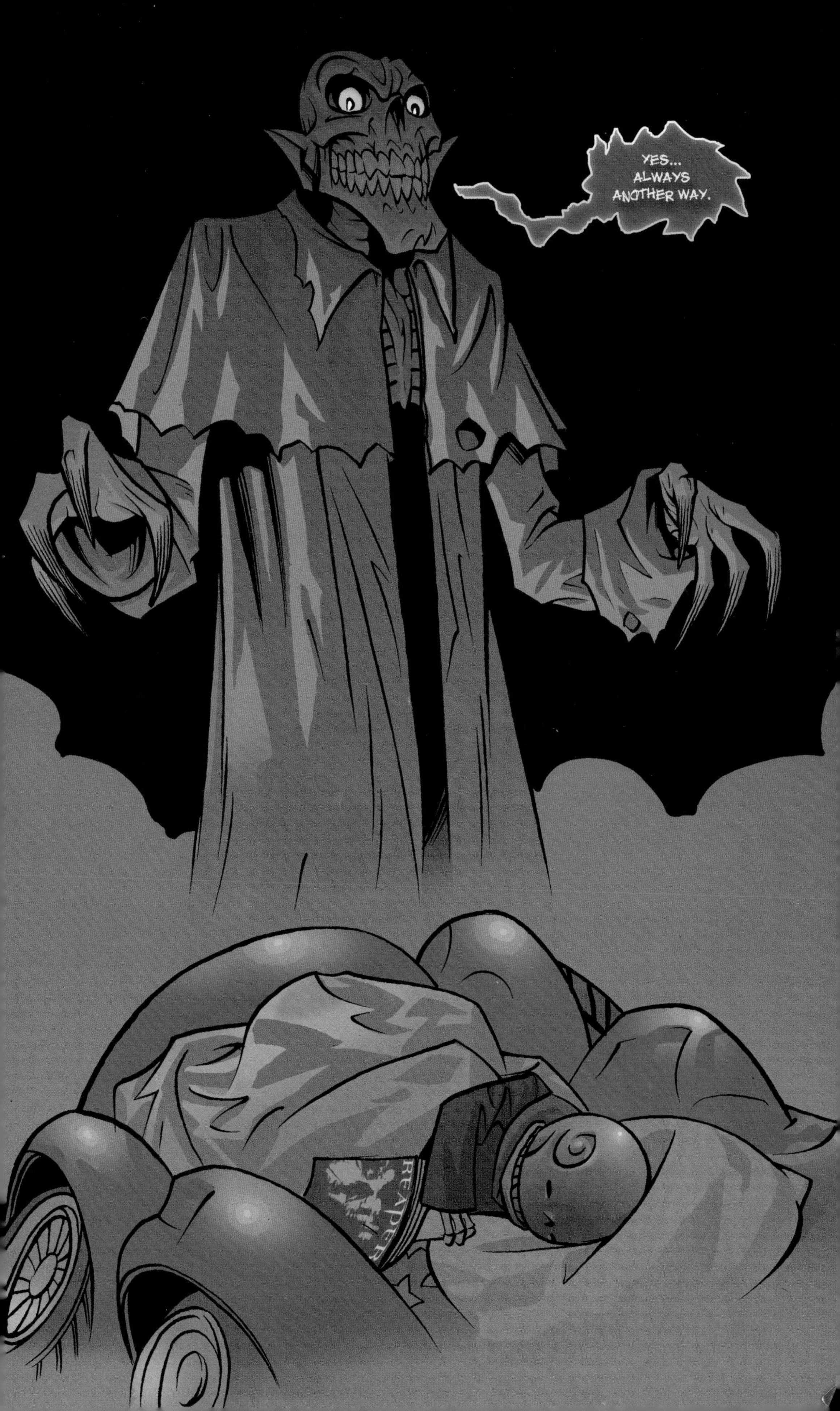
YES... ALWAYS ANOTHER WAY.
REAPER

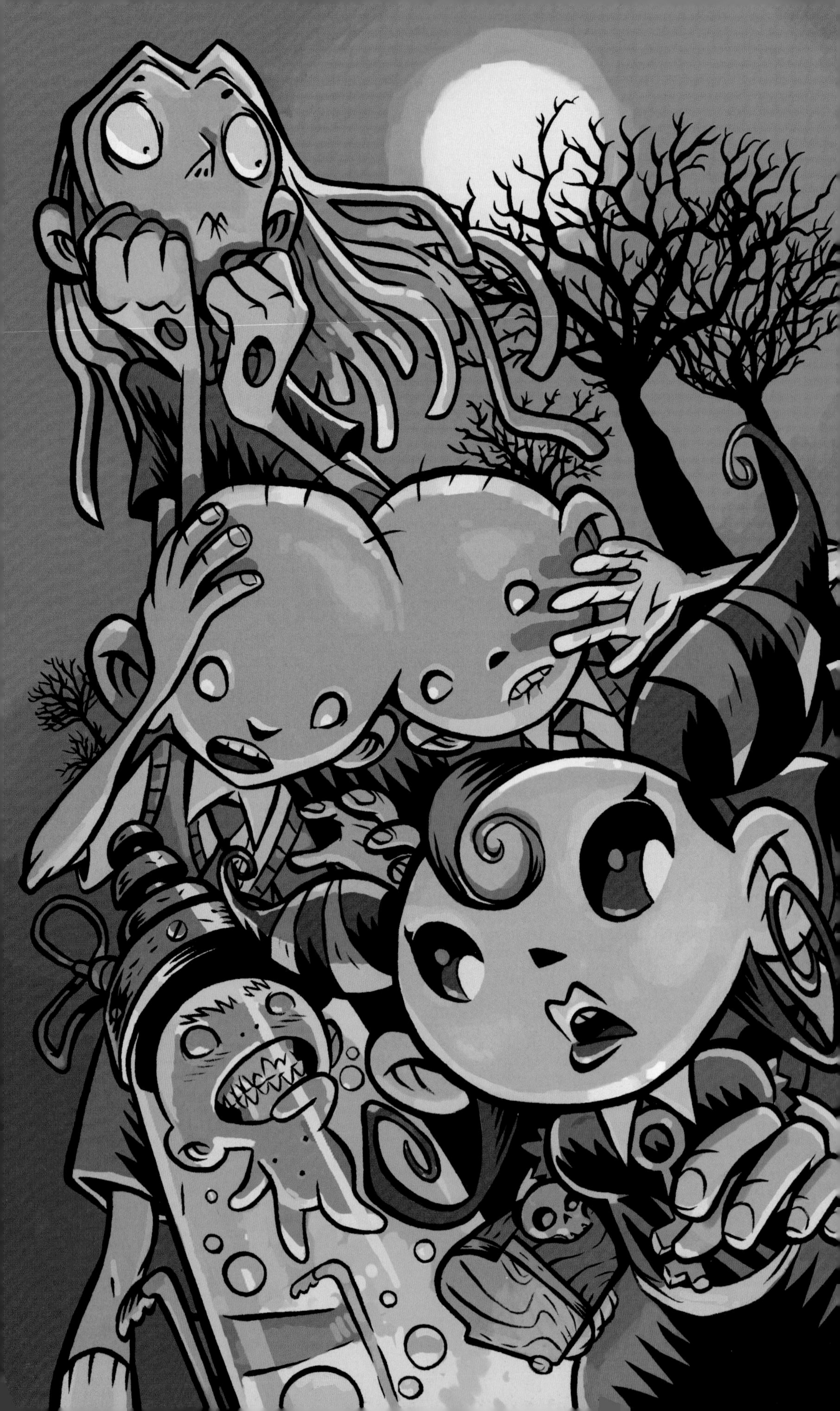

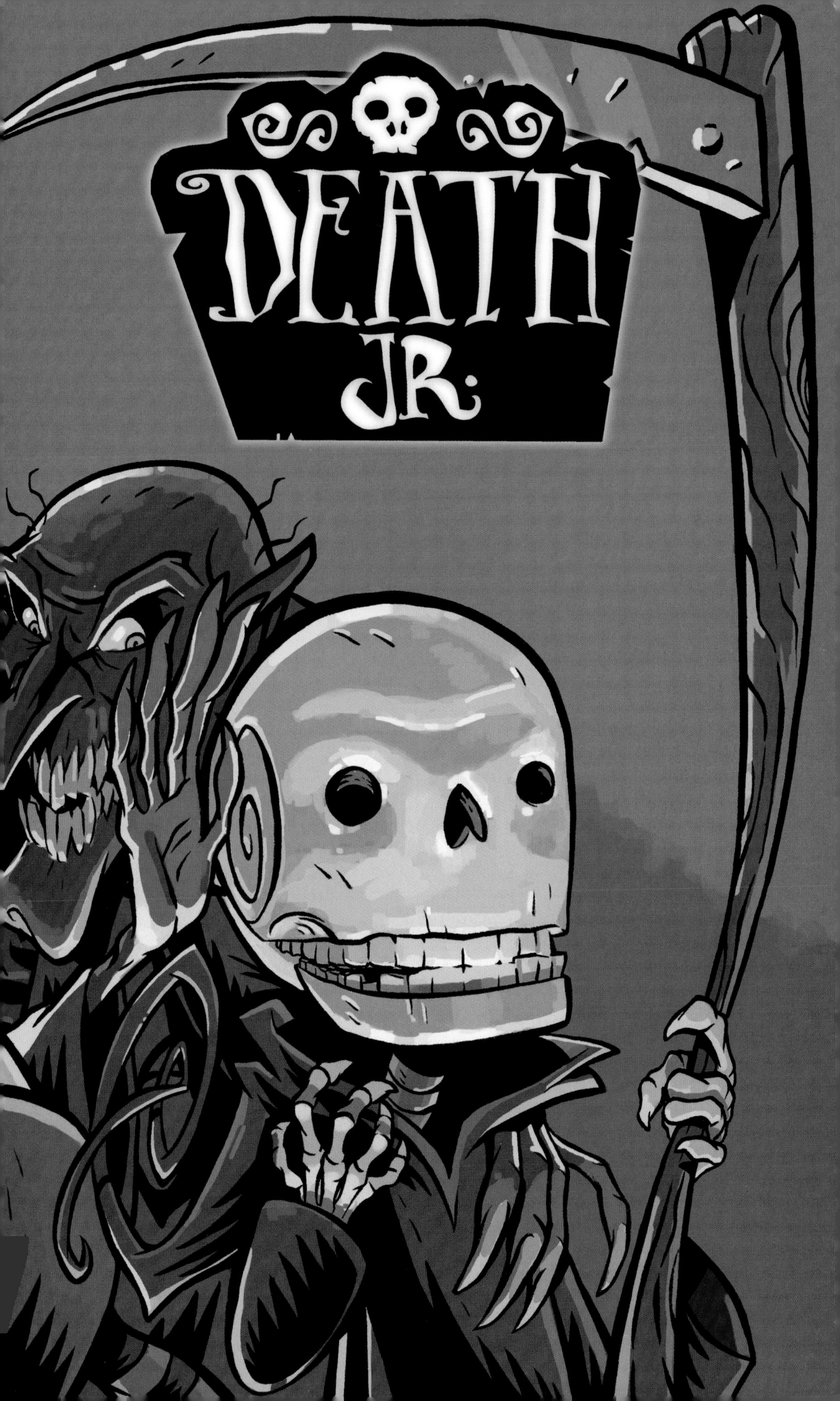
DEATH
JR.

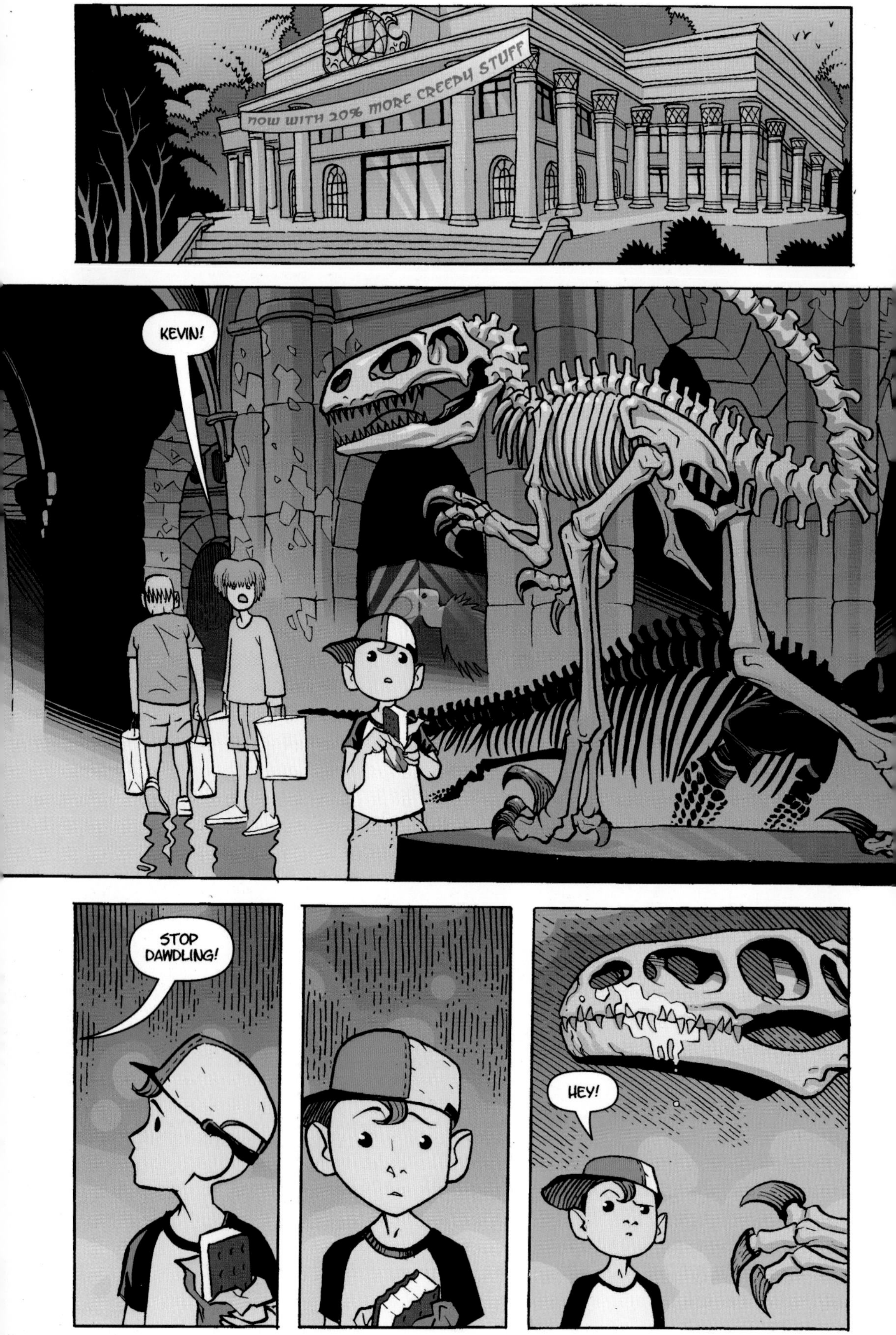
NOW WITH 20% MORE CREEPY STUFF
KEVIN!
STOP DAWDLING!
HEY!

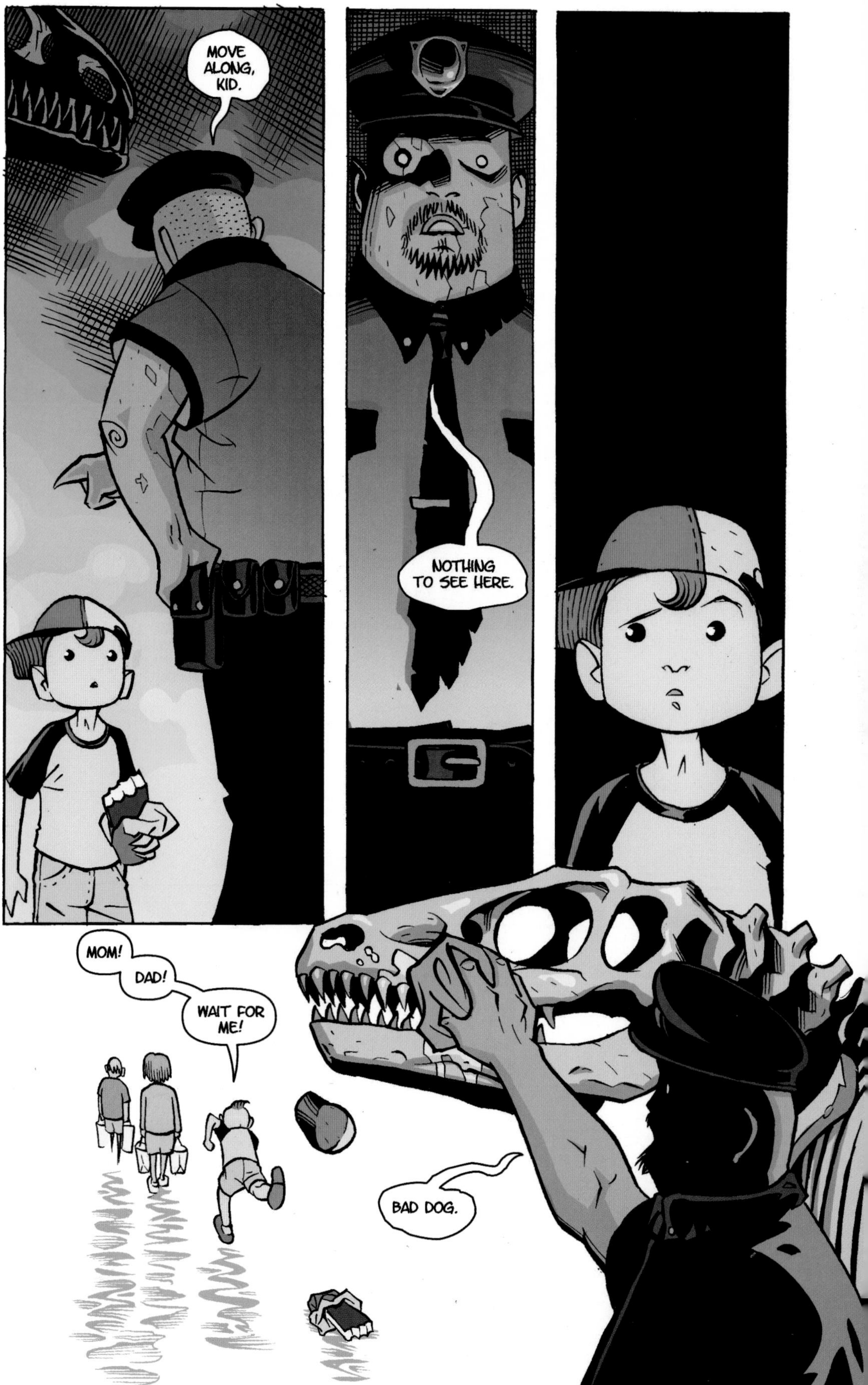
MOVE ALONG, KID.
NOTHING TO SEE HERE.
MOM!
DAD!
WAIT FOR ME!
BAD DOG.

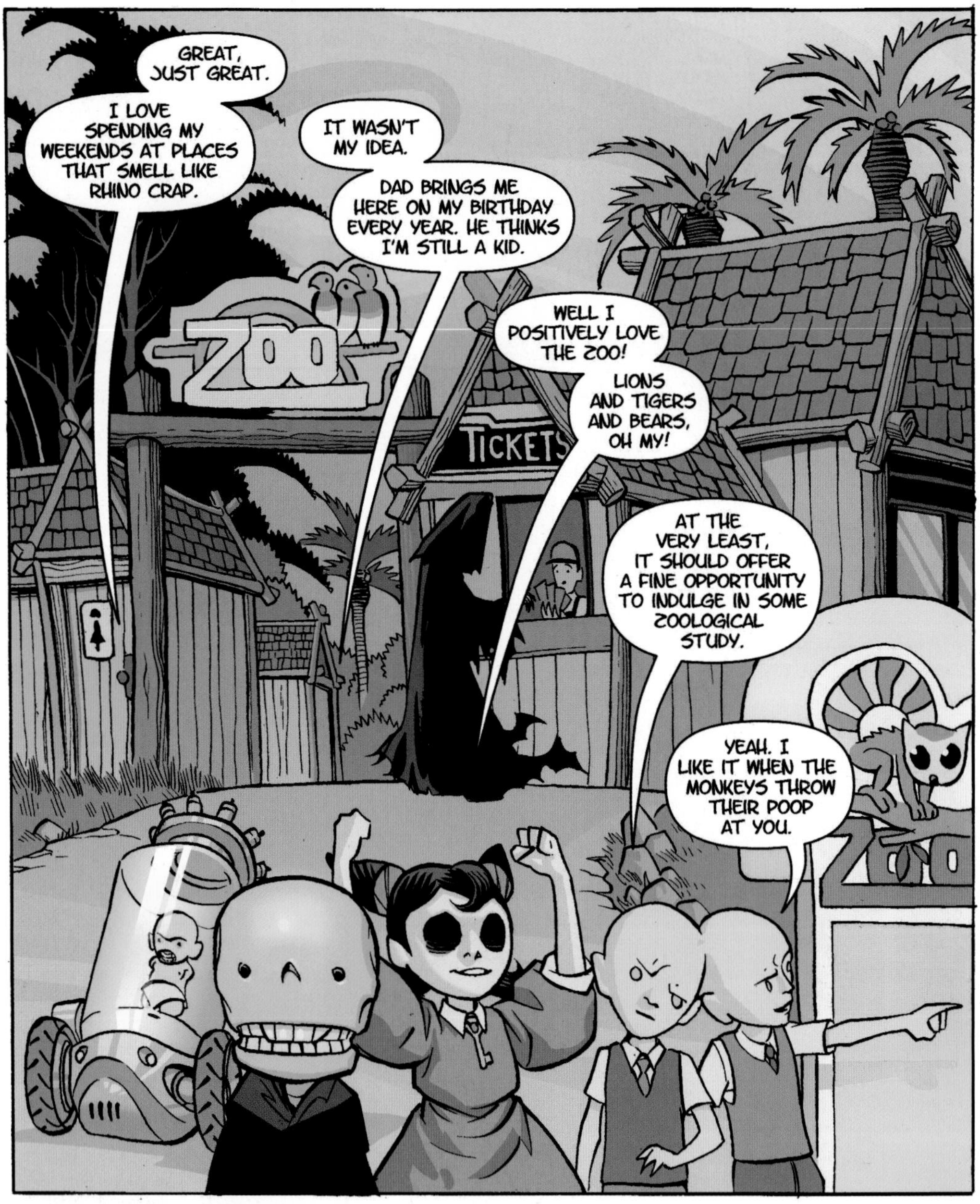
GREAT, JUST GREAT.
I LOVE SPENDING MY WEEKENDS AT PLACES THAT SMELL LIKE RHINO CRAP.
IT WASN'T MY IDEA.
DAD BRINGS ME HERE ON MY BIRTHDAY EVERY YEAR. HE THINKS I'M STILL A KID.
ZOO
TICKETS
WELL I POSITIVELY LOVE THE ZOO!
LIONS AND TIGERS AND BEARS, OH MY!
AT THE VERY LEAST, IT SHOULD OFFER A FINE OPPORTUNITY TO INDULGE IN SOME ZOOLOGICAL STUDY.
YEAH. I LIKE IT WHEN THE MONKEYS THROW THEIR POOP AT YOU.

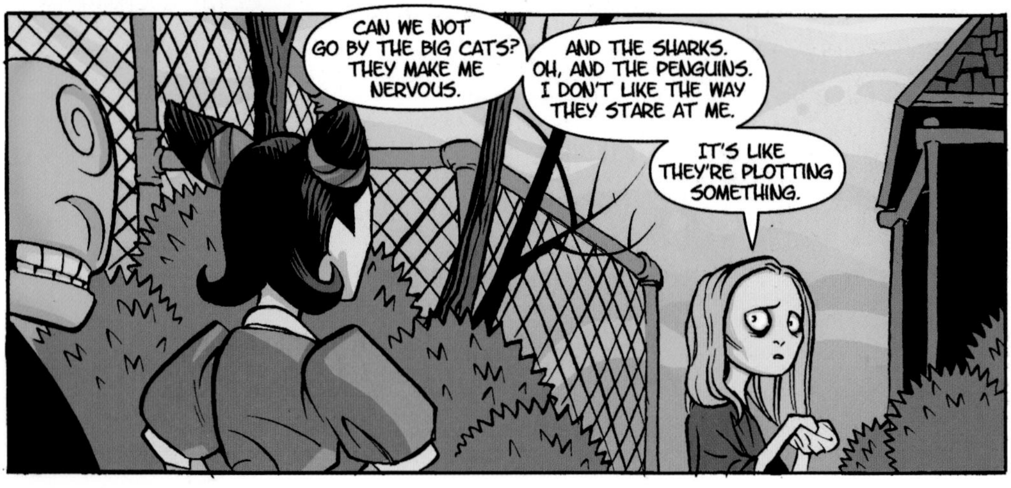
CAN WE NOT GO BY THE BIG CATS? THEY MAKE ME NERVOUS.
AND THE SHARKS. OH, AND THE PENGUINS. I DON'T LIKE THE WAY THEY STARE AT ME.
IT'S LIKE THEY'RE PLOTTING SOMETHING.

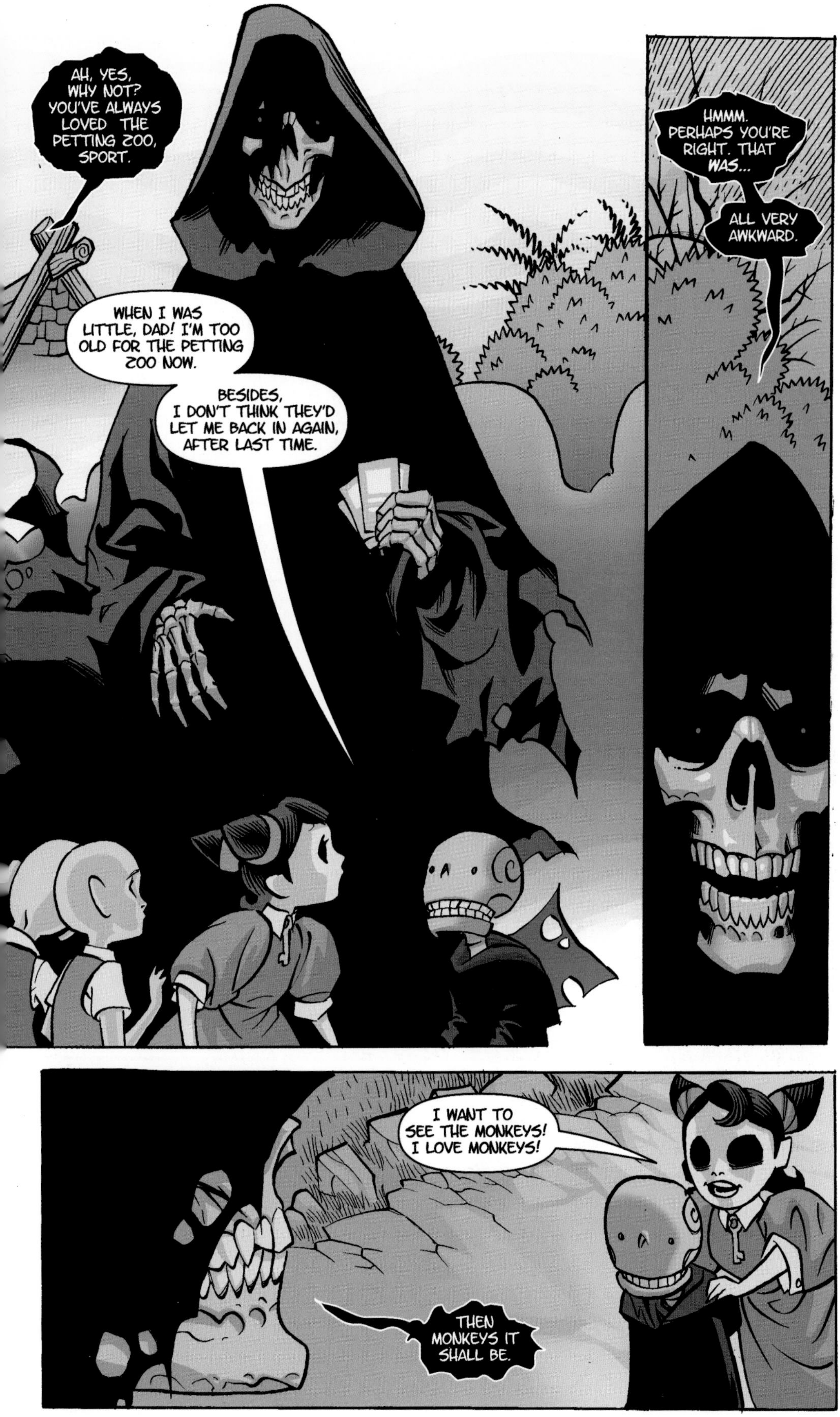
AH, YES, WHY NOT? YOU'VE ALWAYS LOVED THE PETTING ZOO, SPORT.
WHEN I WAS LITTLE, DAD! I'M TOO OLD FOR THE PETTING ZOO NOW.
BESIDES, I DON'T THINK THEY'D LET ME BACK IN AGAIN, AFTER LAST TIME.
HMMM. PERHAPS YOU'RE RIGHT. THAT WAS...
ALL VERY AWKWARD.
I WANT TO SEE THE MONKEYS! I LOVE MONKEYS!
THEN MONKEYS IT SHALL BE.

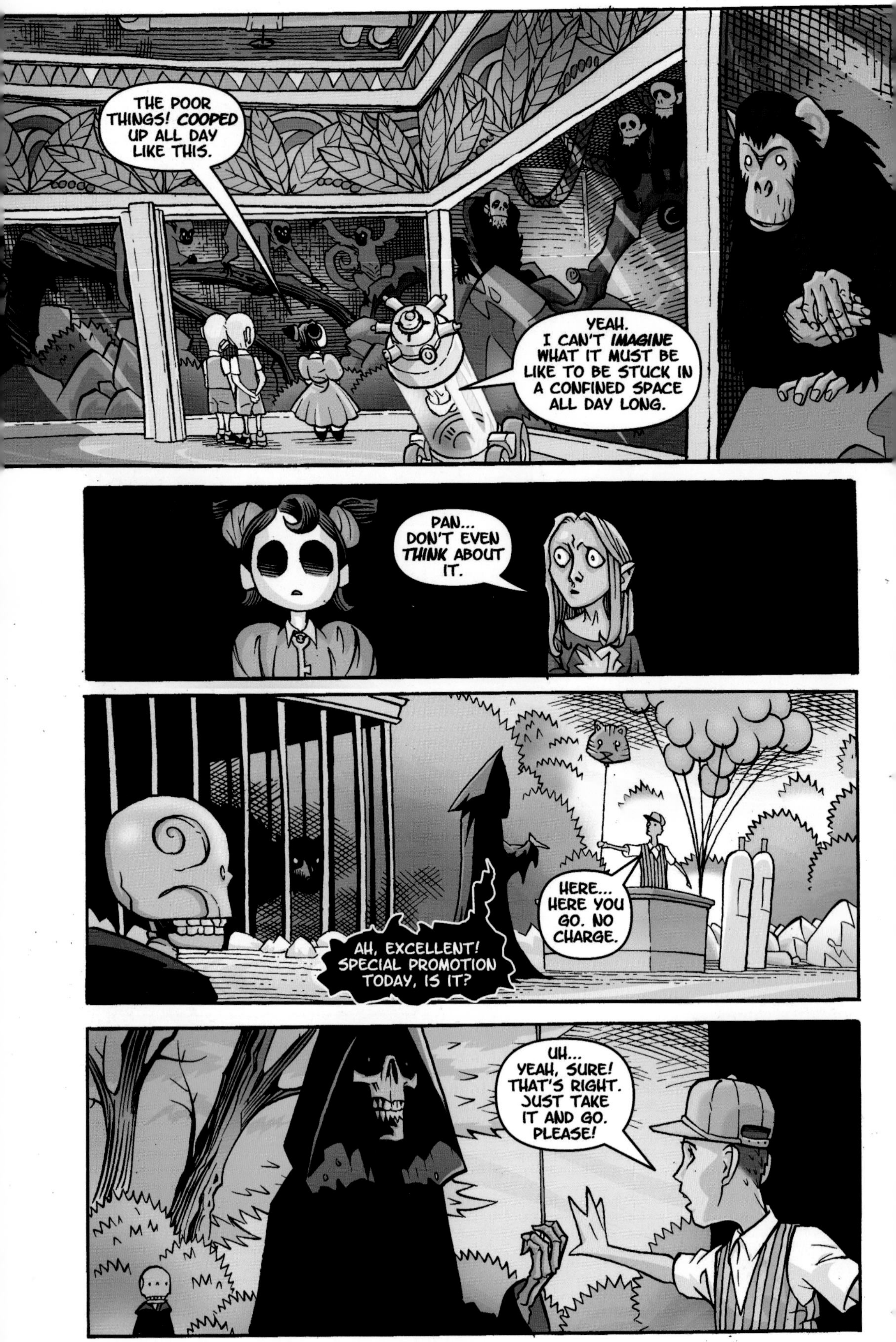
THE POOR THINGS! COOPED UP ALL DAY LIKE THIS.
YEAH. I CAN'T IMAGINE WHAT IT MUST BE LIKE TO BE STUCK IN A CONFINED SPACE ALL DAY LONG.
PAN... DON'T EVEN THINK ABOUT IT.
HERE... HERE YOU GO. NO CHARGE.
AH, EXCELLENT! SPECIAL PROMOTION TODAY, IS IT?
UH... YEAH, SURE! THAT'S RIGHT. JUST TAKE IT AND GO. PLEASE!

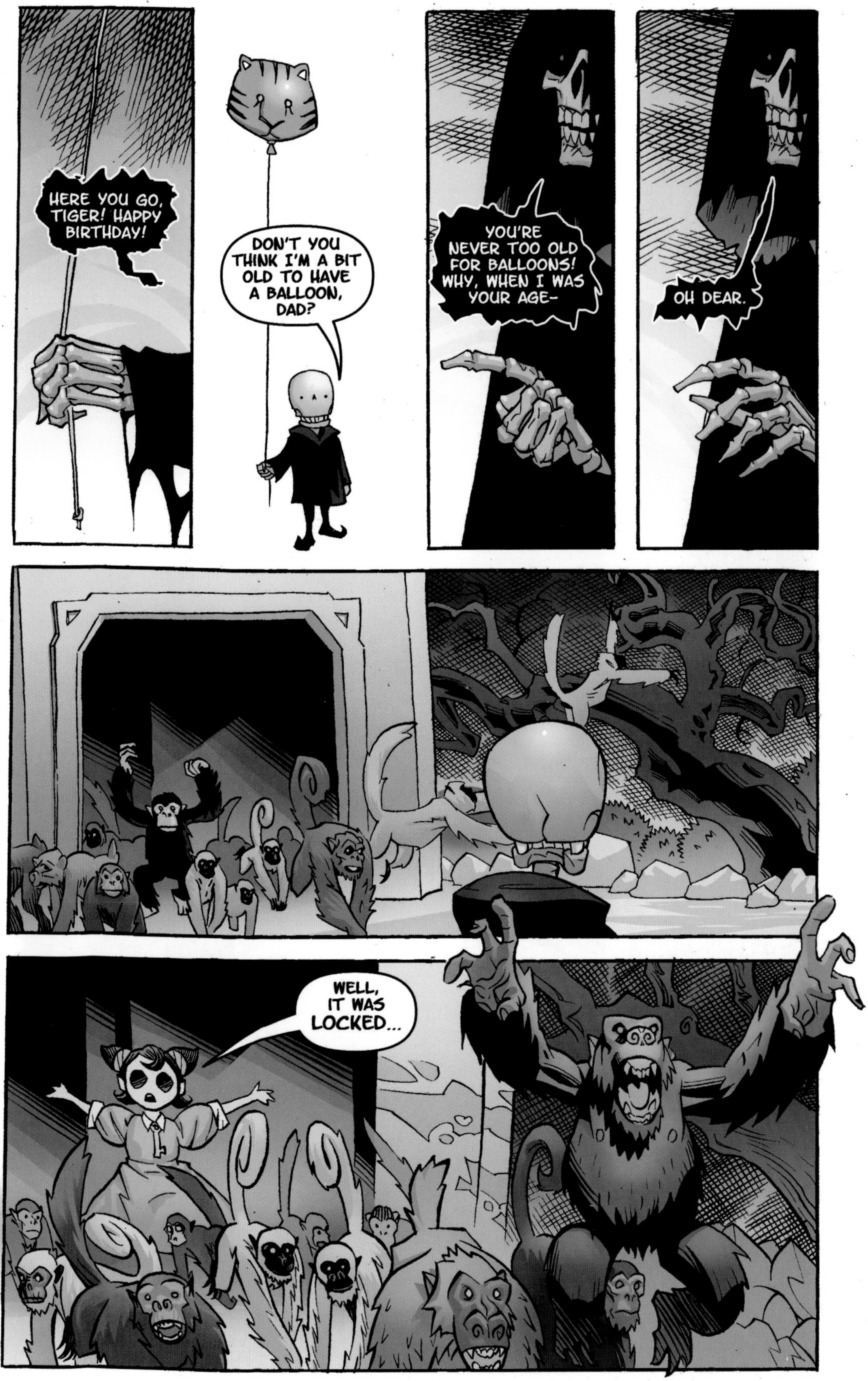
HERE YOU GO, TIGER! HAPPY BIRTHDAY!
DON'T YOU THINK I'M A BIT OLD TO HAVE A BALLOON, DAD?
YOU'RE NEVER TOO OLD FOR BALLOONS! WHY, WHEN I WAS YOUR AGE-
OH DEAR.
WELL, IT WAS LOCKED...

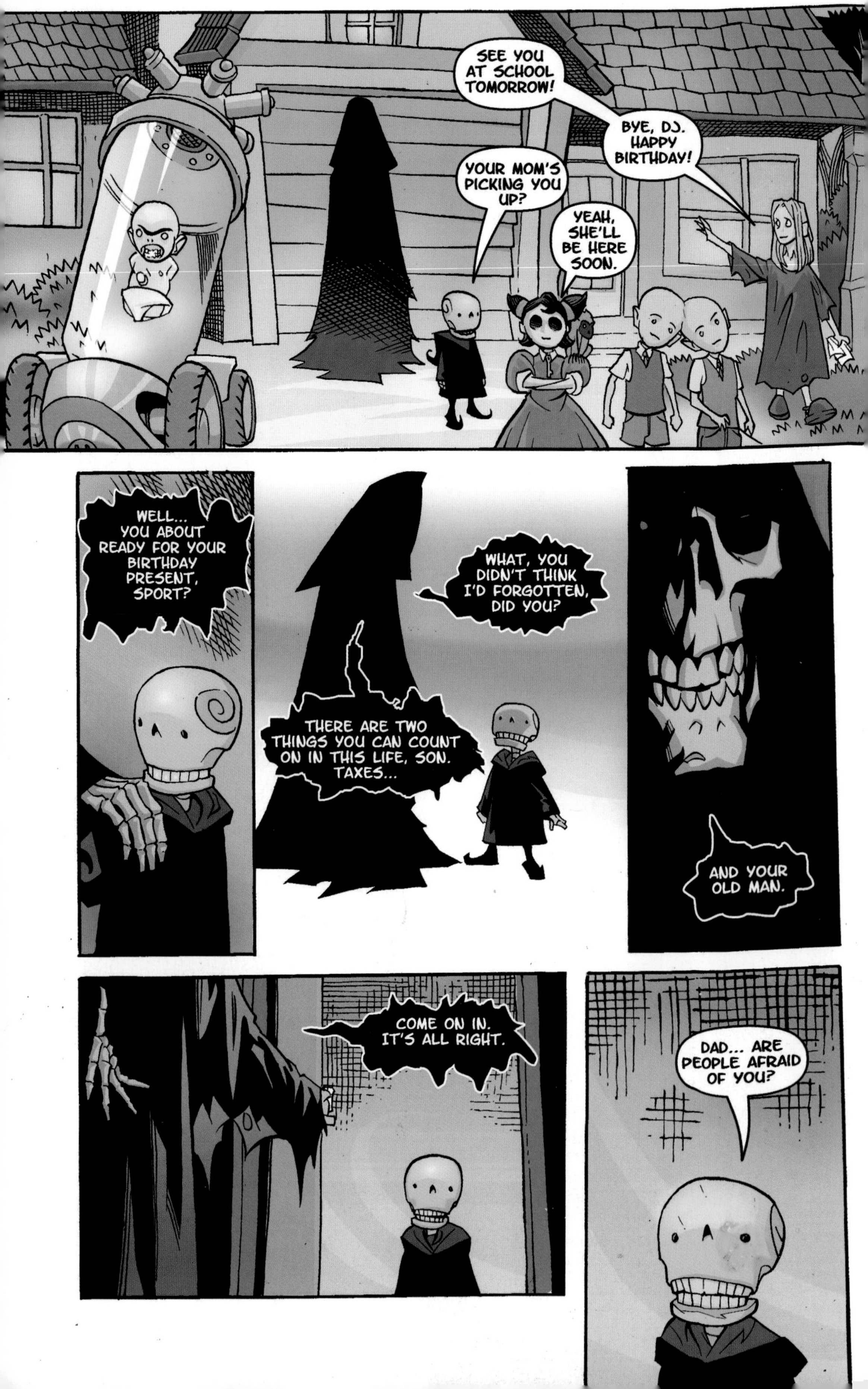
SEE YOU AT SCHOOL TOMORROW!
BYE, DJ. HAPPY BIRTHDAY!
YOUR MOM'S PICKING YOU UP?
YEAH, SHE'LL BE HERE SOON.
WELL... YOU ABOUT READY FOR YOUR BIRTHDAY PRESENT, SPORT?
WHAT, YOU DIDN'T THINK I'D FORGOTTEN, DID YOU?
THERE ARE TWO THINGS YOU CAN COUNT ON IN THIS LIFE, SON. TAXES...
AND YOUR OLD MAN.
COME ON IN. IT'S ALL RIGHT.
DAD... ARE PEOPLE AFRAID OF YOU?

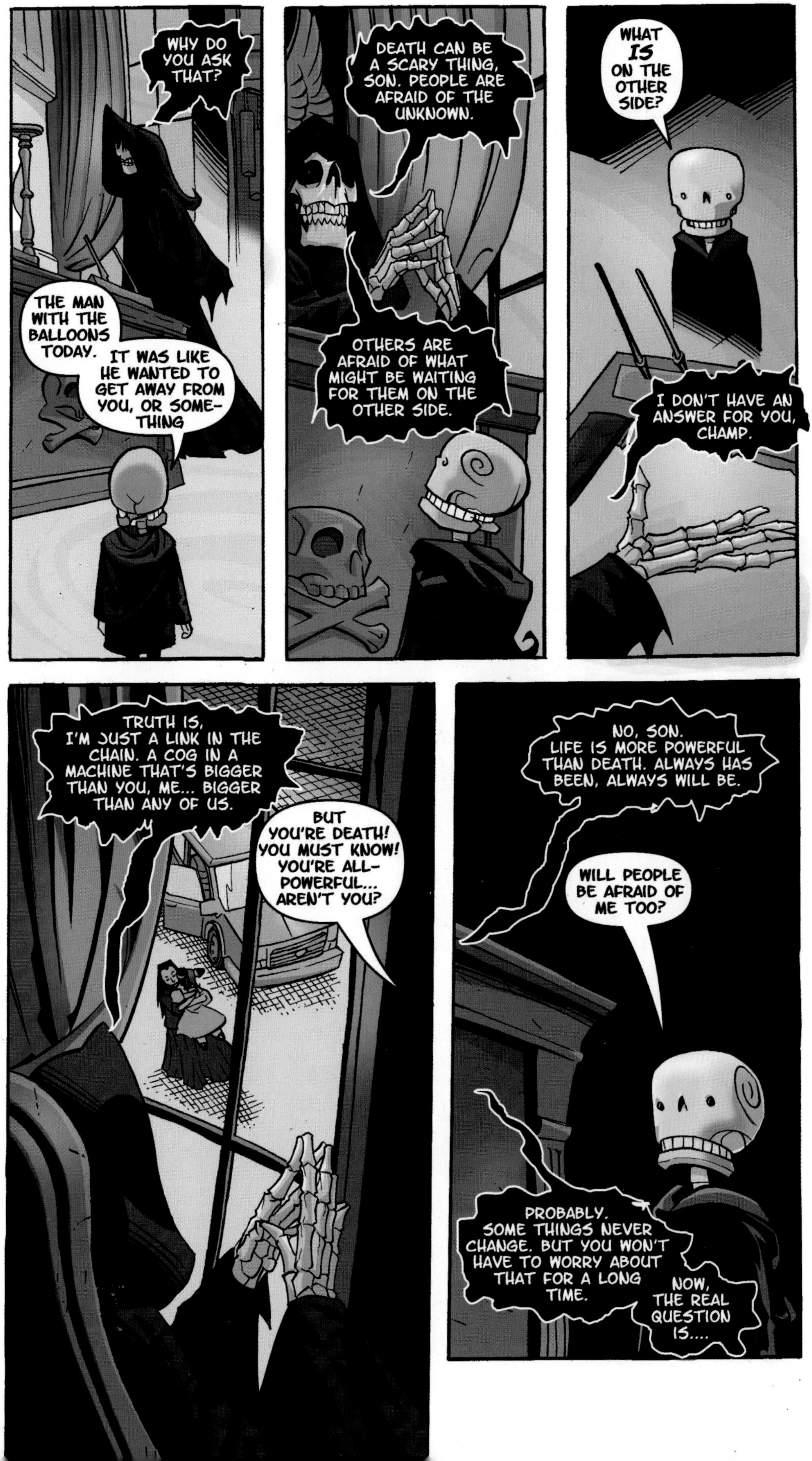
WHY DO YOU ASK THAT?
THE MAN WITH THE BALLOONS TODAY.
IT WAS LIKE HE WANTED TO GET AWAY FROM YOU, OR SOME-THING
DEATH CAN BE A SCARY THING, SON. PEOPLE ARE AFRAID OF THE UNKNOWN.
OTHERS ARE AFRAID OF WHAT MIGHT BE WAITING FOR THEM ON THE OTHER SIDE.
WHAT *IS* ON THE OTHER SIDE?
I DON'T HAVE AN ANSWER FOR YOU, CHAMP.
TRUTH IS, I'M JUST A LINK IN THE CHAIN. A COG IN A MACHINE THAT'S BIGGER THAN YOU, ME... BIGGER THAN ANY OF US.
BUT YOU'RE DEATH! YOU MUST KNOW! YOU'RE ALL-POWERFUL... AREN'T YOU?
NO, SON. LIFE IS MORE POWERFUL THAN DEATH. ALWAYS HAS BEEN, ALWAYS WILL BE.
WILL PEOPLE BE AFRAID OF ME TOO?
PROBABLY. SOME THINGS NEVER CHANGE. BUT YOU WON'T HAVE TO WORRY ABOUT THAT FOR A LONG TIME.
NOW, THE REAL QUESTION IS....

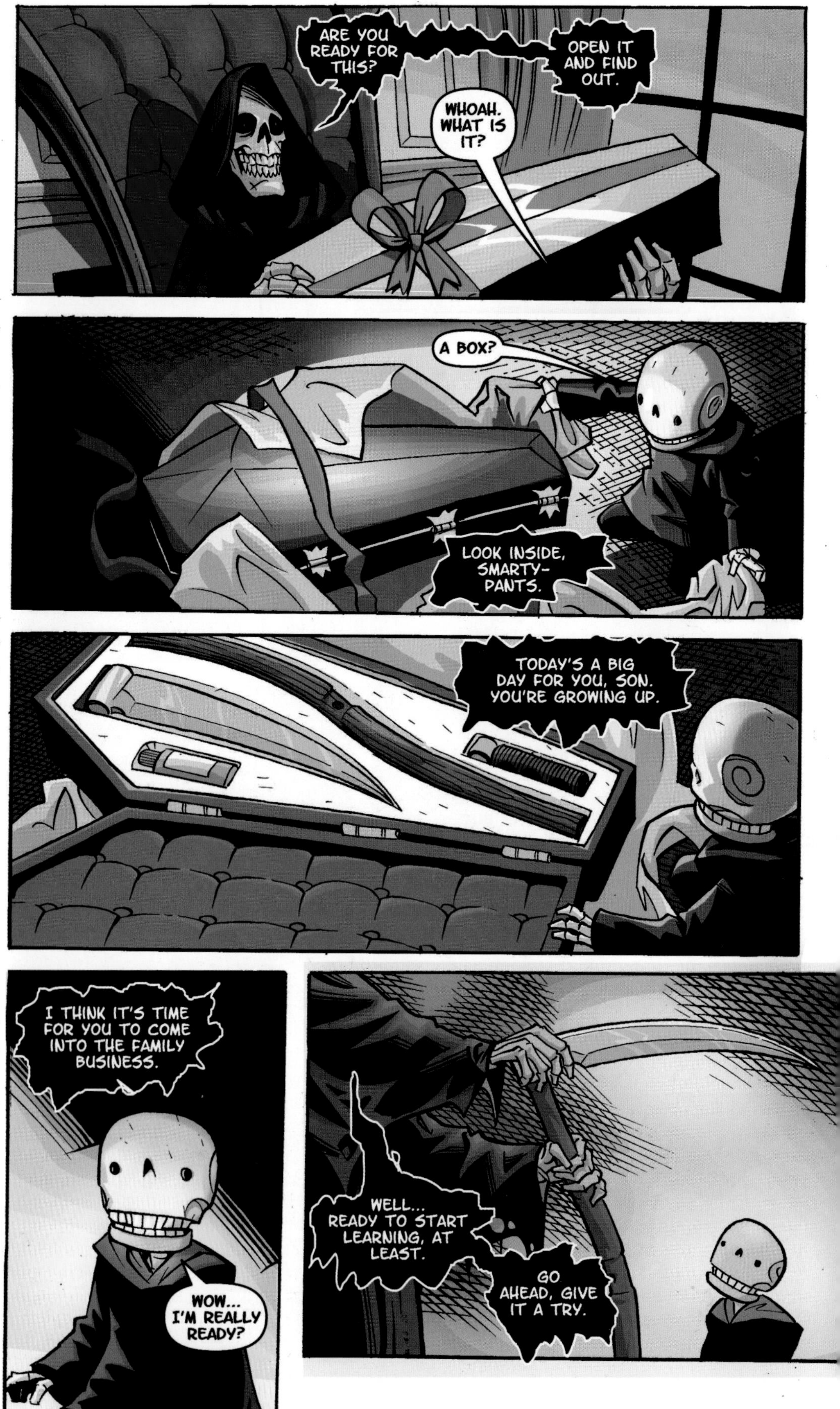
ARE YOU READY FOR THIS?
OPEN IT AND FIND OUT.
WHOAH. WHAT IS IT?
A BOX?
LOOK INSIDE, SMARTY-PANTS.
TODAY'S A BIG DAY FOR YOU, SON. YOU'RE GROWING UP.
I THINK IT'S TIME FOR YOU TO COME INTO THE FAMILY BUSINESS.
WOW... I'M REALLY READY?
WELL... READY TO START LEARNING, AT LEAST.
GO AHEAD, GIVE IT A TRY.

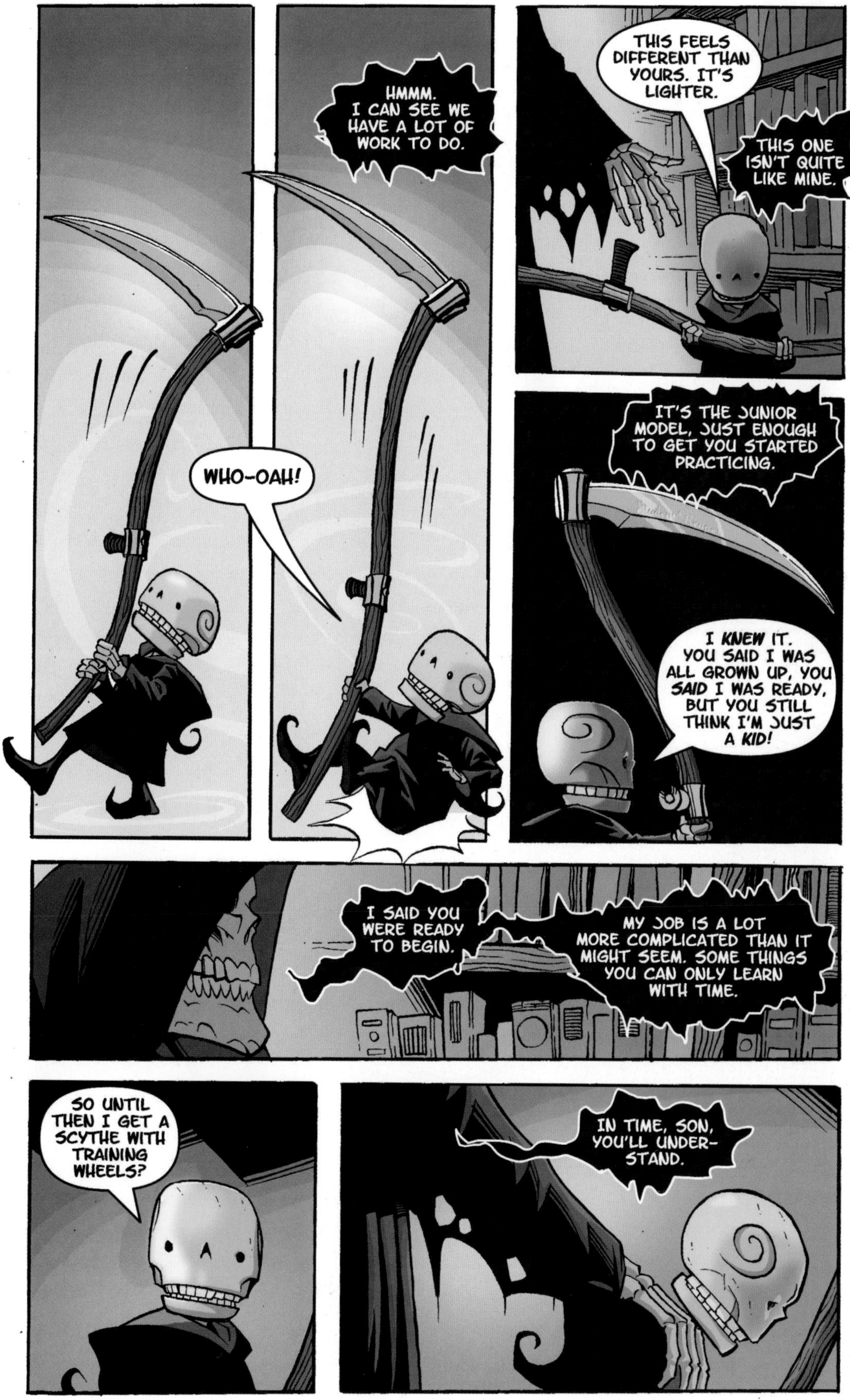

WHO-OAH!
HMMM. I CAN SEE WE HAVE A LOT OF WORK TO DO.
THIS FEELS DIFFERENT THAN YOURS. IT'S LIGHTER.
THIS ONE ISN'T QUITE LIKE MINE.
IT'S THE JUNIOR MODEL, JUST ENOUGH TO GET YOU STARTED PRACTICING.
I KNEW IT. YOU SAID I WAS ALL GROWN UP, YOU SAID I WAS READY, BUT YOU STILL THINK I'M JUST A KID!
I SAID YOU WERE READY TO BEGIN.
MY JOB IS A LOT MORE COMPLICATED THAN IT MIGHT SEEM. SOME THINGS YOU CAN ONLY LEARN WITH TIME.
SO UNTIL THEN I GET A SCYTHE WITH TRAINING WHEELS?
IN TIME, SON, YOU'LL UNDER-STAND.

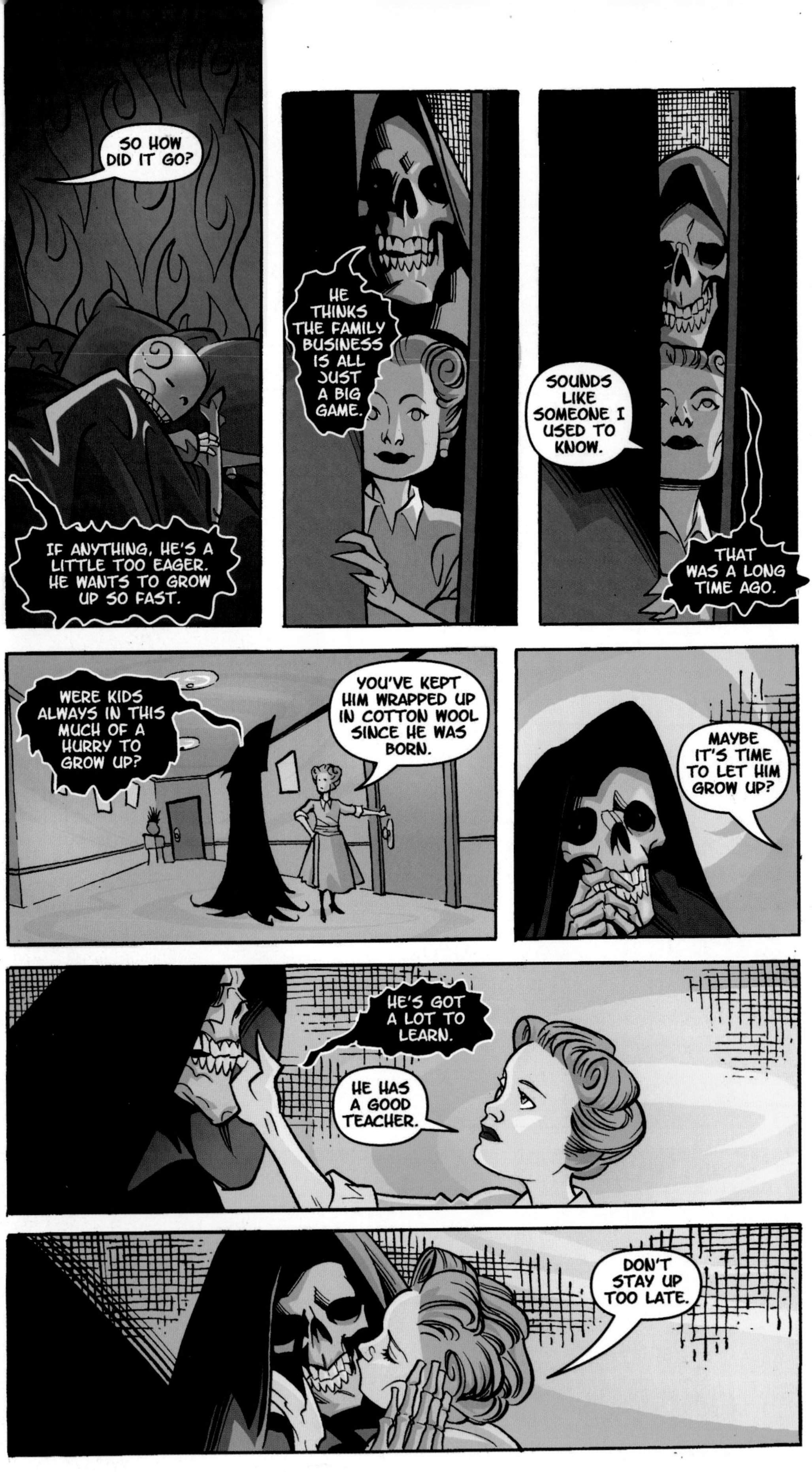
SO HOW DID IT GO?
IF ANYTHING, HE'S A LITTLE TOO EAGER. HE WANTS TO GROW UP SO FAST.
HE THINKS THE FAMILY BUSINESS IS ALL JUST A BIG GAME.
SOUNDS LIKE SOMEONE I USED TO KNOW.
THAT WAS A LONG TIME AGO.
WERE KIDS ALWAYS IN THIS MUCH OF A HURRY TO GROW UP?
YOU'VE KEPT HIM WRAPPED UP IN COTTON WOOL SINCE HE WAS BORN.
MAYBE IT'S TIME TO LET HIM GROW UP?
HE'S GOT A LOT TO LEARN.
HE HAS A GOOD TEACHER.
DON'T STAY UP TOO LATE.

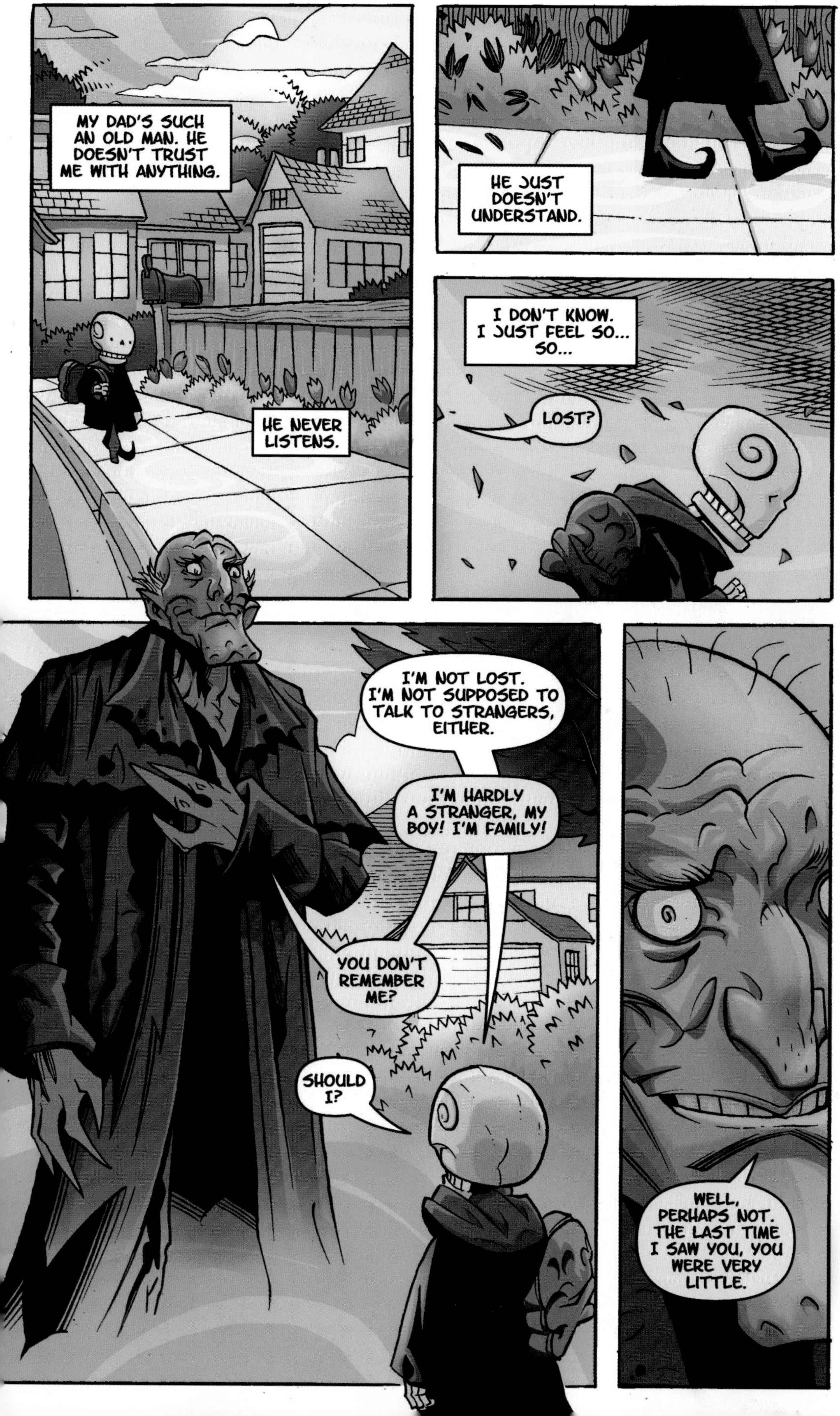

MY DAD'S SUCH AN OLD MAN. HE DOESN'T TRUST ME WITH ANYTHING.
HE NEVER LISTENS.
HE JUST DOESN'T UNDERSTAND.
I DON'T KNOW. I JUST FEEL SO... SO...
LOST?
I'M NOT LOST. I'M NOT SUPPOSED TO TALK TO STRANGERS, EITHER.
I'M HARDLY A STRANGER, MY BOY! I'M FAMILY!
YOU DON'T REMEMBER ME?
SHOULD I?
WELL, PERHAPS NOT. THE LAST TIME I SAW YOU, YOU WERE VERY LITTLE.

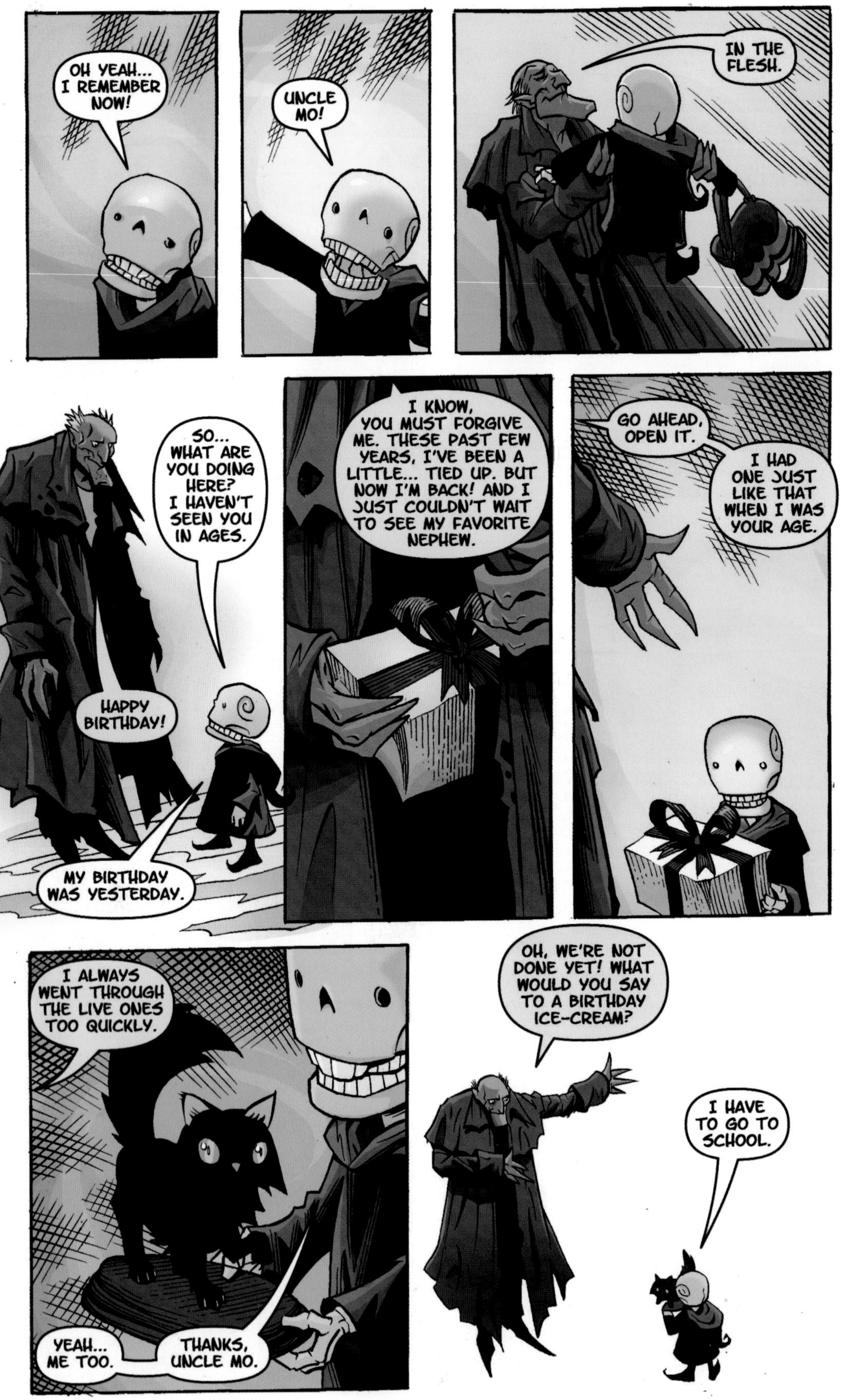
OH YEAH... I REMEMBER NOW!
UNCLE MO!
IN THE FLESH.
SO... WHAT ARE YOU DOING HERE? I HAVEN'T SEEN YOU IN AGES.
HAPPY BIRTHDAY!
MY BIRTHDAY WAS YESTERDAY.
I KNOW, YOU MUST FORGIVE ME. THESE PAST FEW YEARS, I'VE BEEN A LITTLE... TIED UP. BUT NOW I'M BACK! AND I JUST COULDN'T WAIT TO SEE MY FAVORITE NEPHEW.
GO AHEAD, OPEN IT.
I HAD ONE JUST LIKE THAT WHEN I WAS YOUR AGE.
I ALWAYS WENT THROUGH THE LIVE ONES TOO QUICKLY.
THANKS, UNCLE MO.
YEAH... ME TOO.
OH, WE'RE NOT DONE YET! WHAT WOULD YOU SAY TO A BIRTHDAY ICE-CREAM?
I HAVE TO GO TO SCHOOL.

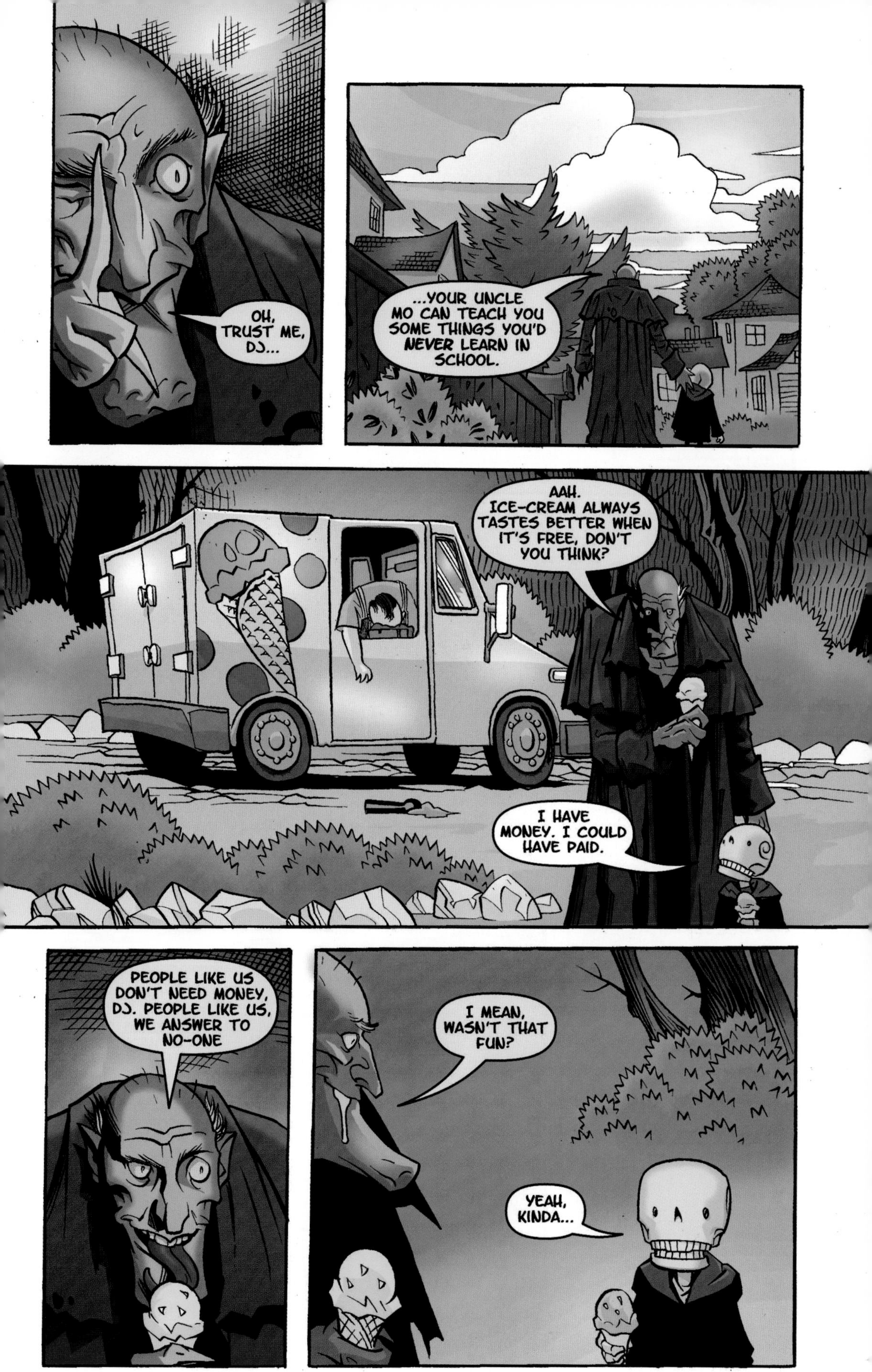
OH, TRUST ME, DJ...
...YOUR UNCLE MO CAN TEACH YOU SOME THINGS YOU'D NEVER LEARN IN SCHOOL.
AAH. ICE-CREAM ALWAYS TASTES BETTER WHEN IT'S FREE, DON'T YOU THINK?
I HAVE MONEY. I COULD HAVE PAID.
PEOPLE LIKE US DON'T NEED MONEY, DJ. PEOPLE LIKE US, WE ANSWER TO NO-ONE
I MEAN, WASN'T THAT FUN?
YEAH, KINDA...

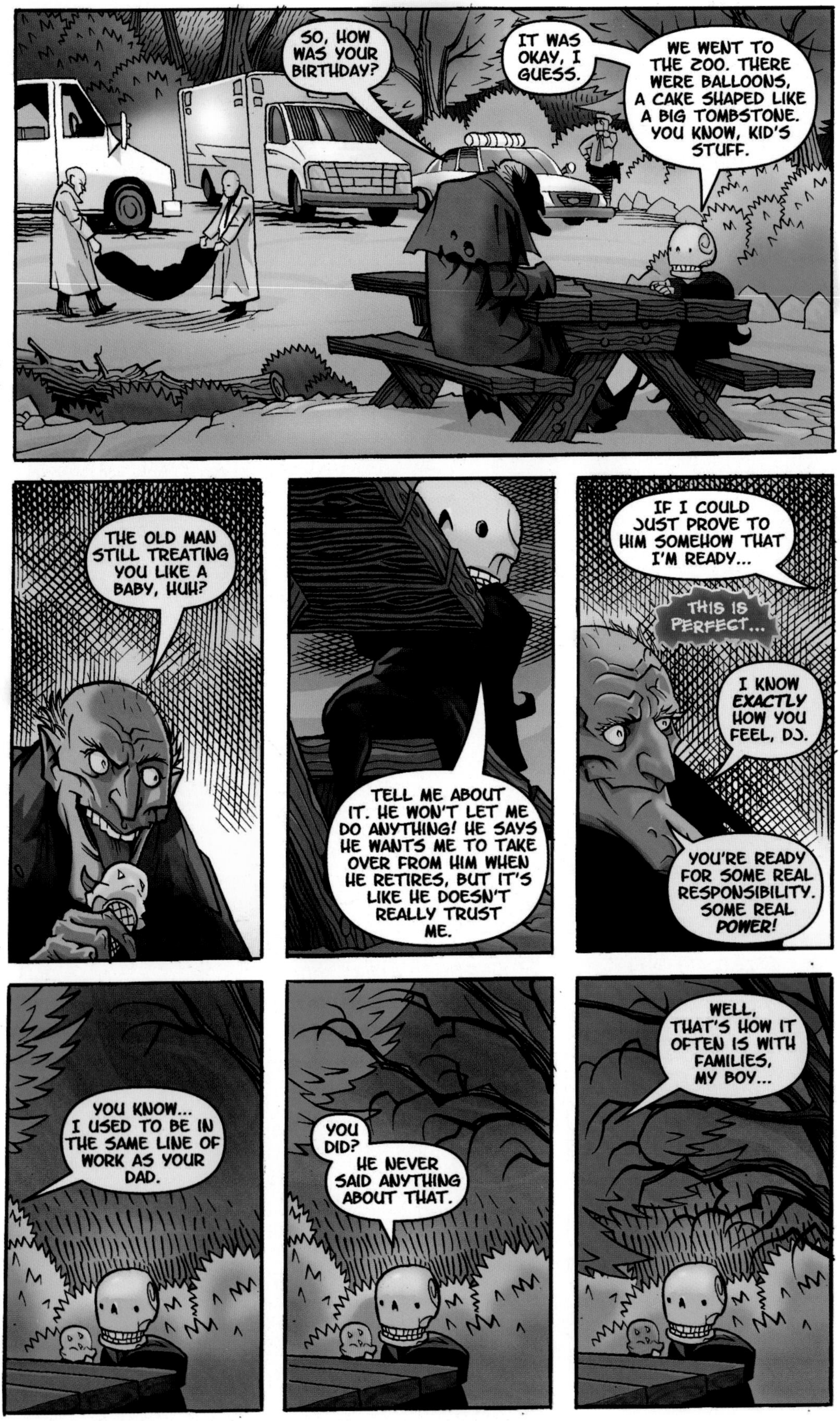
SO, HOW WAS YOUR BIRTHDAY?
IT WAS OKAY, I GUESS.
WE WENT TO THE ZOO. THERE WERE BALLOONS, A CAKE SHAPED LIKE A BIG TOMBSTONE. YOU KNOW, KID'S STUFF.
THE OLD MAN STILL TREATING YOU LIKE A BABY, HUH?
TELL ME ABOUT IT. HE WON'T LET ME DO ANYTHING! HE SAYS HE WANTS ME TO TAKE OVER FROM HIM WHEN HE RETIRES, BUT IT'S LIKE HE DOESN'T REALLY TRUST ME.
IF I COULD JUST PROVE TO HIM SOMEHOW THAT I'M READY...
THIS IS PERFECT...
I KNOW EXACTLY HOW YOU FEEL, DJ.
YOU'RE READY FOR SOME REAL RESPONSIBILITY. SOME REAL POWER!
YOU KNOW... I USED TO BE IN THE SAME LINE OF WORK AS YOUR DAD.
YOU DID?
HE NEVER SAID ANYTHING ABOUT THAT.
WELL, THAT'S HOW IT OFTEN IS WITH FAMILIES, MY BOY...

THEY HAVE SECRETS. YOUR FATHER HAS REALLY NEVER TOLD YOU ANYTHING ABOUT ME?

NO. WHY?

EVEN BETTER.

PERHAPS HE THINKS YOU'RE NOT OLD ENOUGH TO UNDERSTAND.

HA! YEAH, SOUNDS ABOUT RIGHT.

WELL, YOUR FATHER MAY NOT THINK YOU'RE READY, BUT I DO.

REALLY?

I SEE GREAT THINGS IN YOUR FUTURE. YOU'RE A NATURAL! YOU JUST NEED THE RIGHT TEACHER... AND I CAN TEACH YOU EVERYTHING YOU NEED TO KNOW.

EVERYTHING YOUR FATHER WON'T.

THAT IS WHAT YOU WANT, ISN'T IT?

YEAH. I GUESS. EXCEPT—

EXCEPT WHAT?

IT'S LIKE, EVERYONE'S AFRAID OF MY DAD.

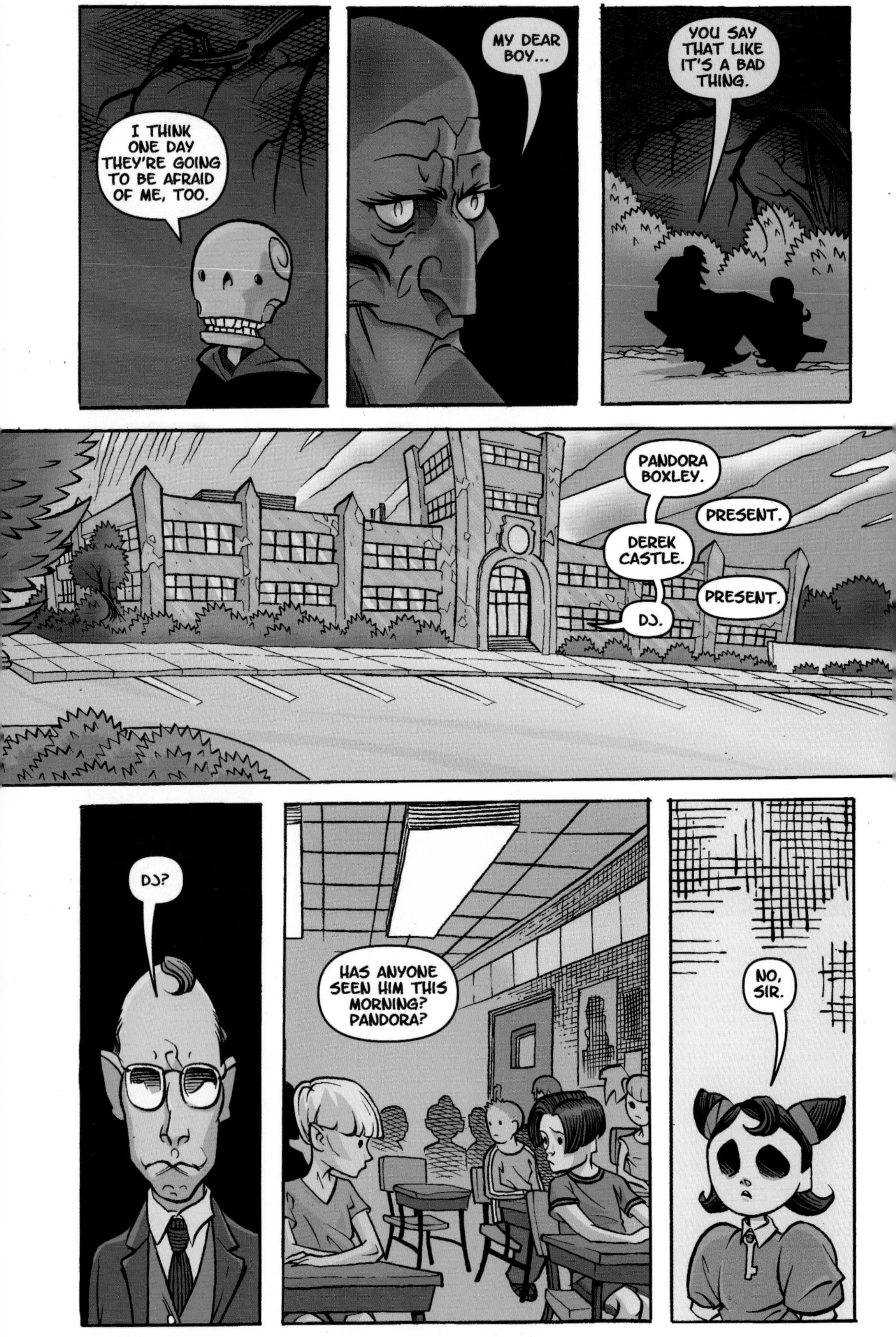
I THINK ONE DAY THEY'RE GOING TO BE AFRAID OF ME, TOO.
MY DEAR BOY...
YOU SAY THAT LIKE IT'S A BAD THING.
PANDORA BOXLEY.
PRESENT.
DEREK CASTLE.
PRESENT.
DJ.
DJ?
HAS ANYONE SEEN HIM THIS MORNING? PANDORA?
NO, SIR.

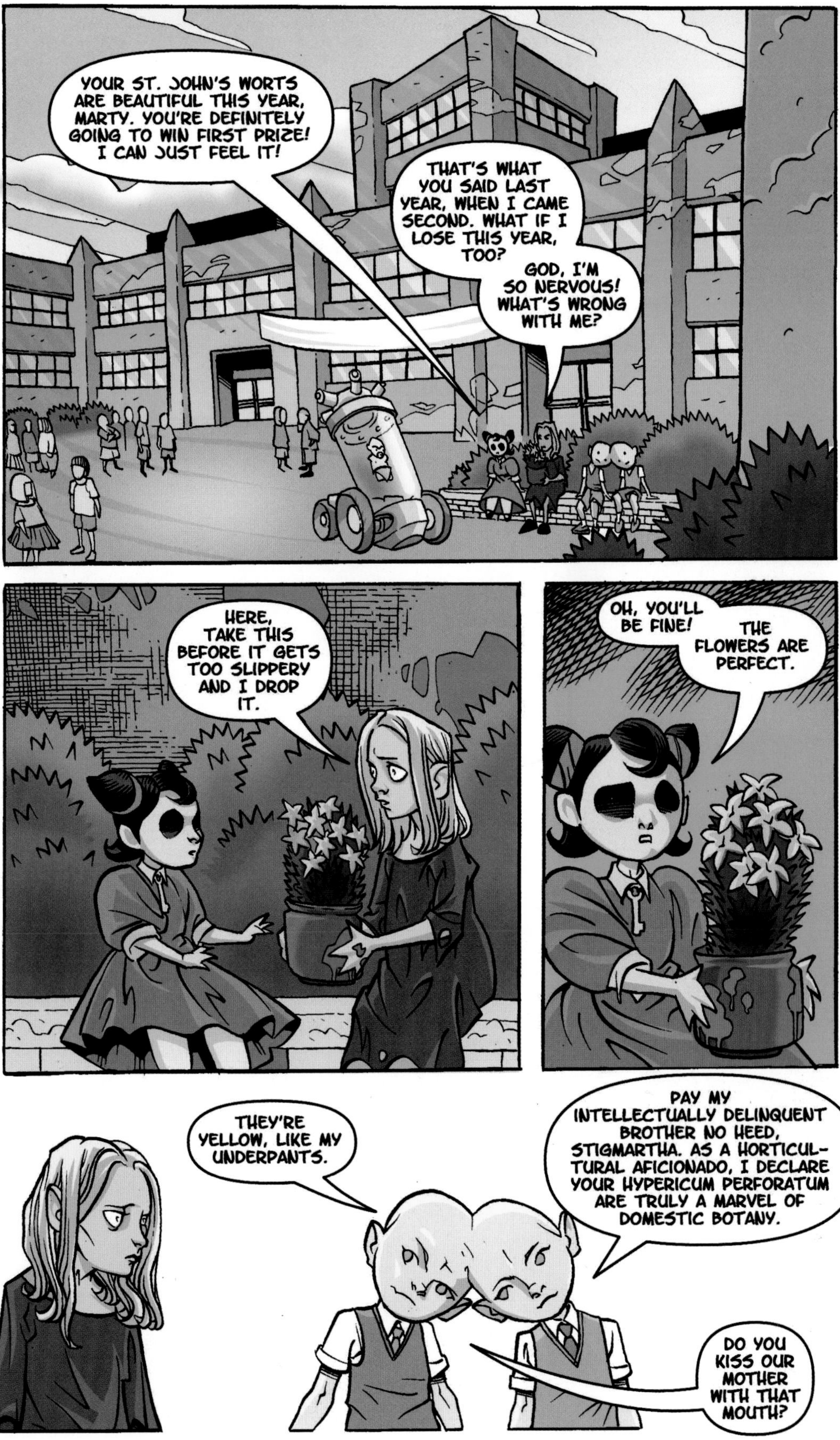
YOUR ST. JOHN'S WORTS ARE BEAUTIFUL THIS YEAR, MARTY. YOU'RE DEFINITELY GOING TO WIN FIRST PRIZE! I CAN JUST FEEL IT!
THAT'S WHAT YOU SAID LAST YEAR, WHEN I CAME SECOND. WHAT IF I LOSE THIS YEAR, TOO?
GOD, I'M SO NERVOUS! WHAT'S WRONG WITH ME?
HERE, TAKE THIS BEFORE IT GETS TOO SLIPPERY AND I DROP IT.
OH, YOU'LL BE FINE!
THE FLOWERS ARE PERFECT.
THEY'RE YELLOW, LIKE MY UNDERPANTS.
PAY MY INTELLECTUALLY DELINQUENT BROTHER NO HEED, STIGMARTHA. AS A HORTICULTURAL AFICIONADO, I DECLARE YOUR HYPERICUM PERFORATUM ARE TRULY A MARVEL OF DOMESTIC BOTANY.
DO YOU KISS OUR MOTHER WITH THAT MOUTH?

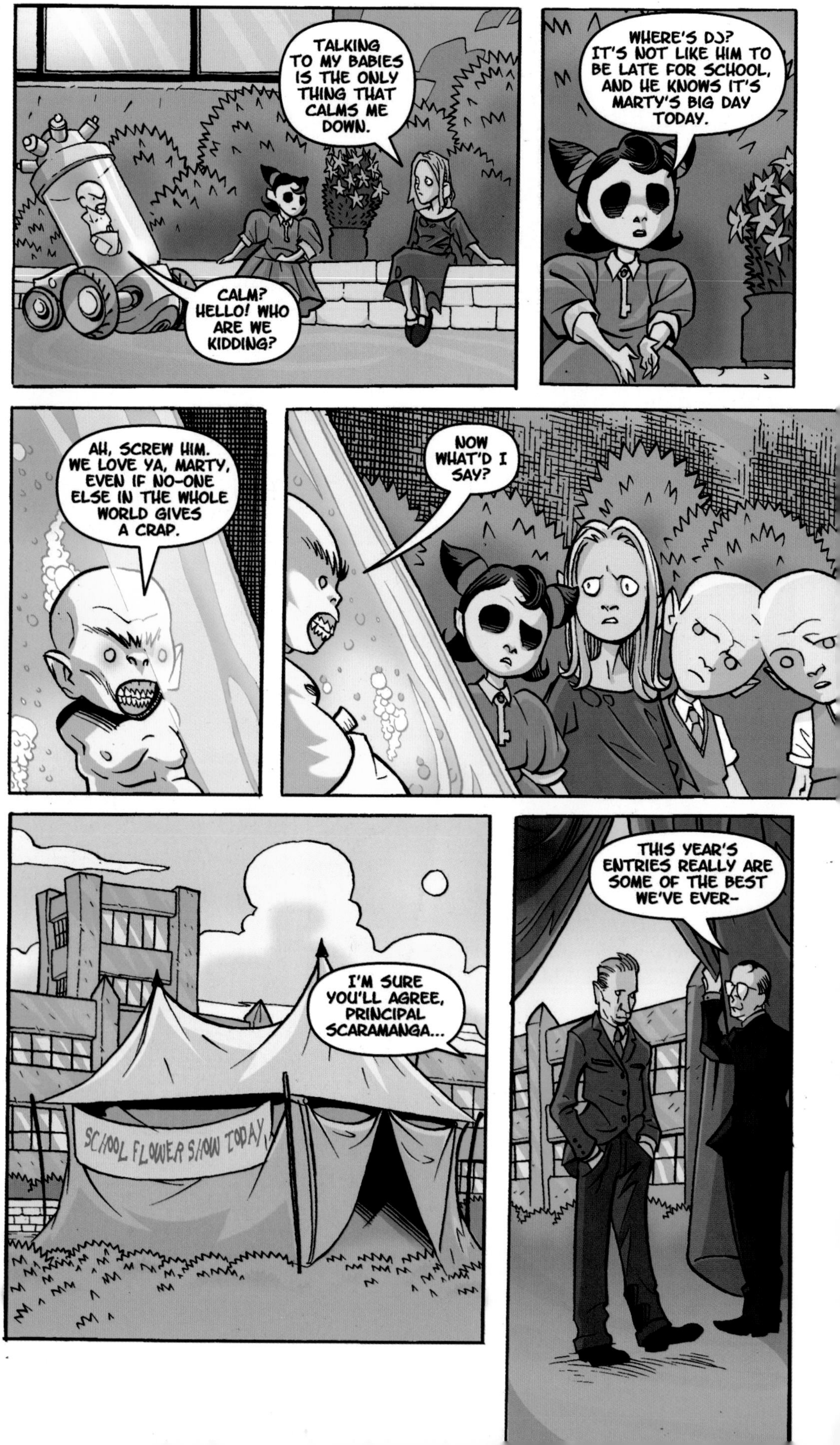

TALKING TO MY BABIES IS THE ONLY THING THAT CALMS ME DOWN.
CALM? HELLO! WHO ARE WE KIDDING?
WHERE'S DJ? IT'S NOT LIKE HIM TO BE LATE FOR SCHOOL, AND HE KNOWS IT'S MARTY'S BIG DAY TODAY.
AH, SCREW HIM. WE LOVE YA, MARTY, EVEN IF NO-ONE ELSE IN THE WHOLE WORLD GIVES A CRAP.
NOW WHAT'D I SAY?
SCHOOL FLOWER SHOW TODAY
I'M SURE YOU'LL AGREE, PRINCIPAL SCARAMANGA...
THIS YEAR'S ENTRIES REALLY ARE SOME OF THE BEST WE'VE EVER-

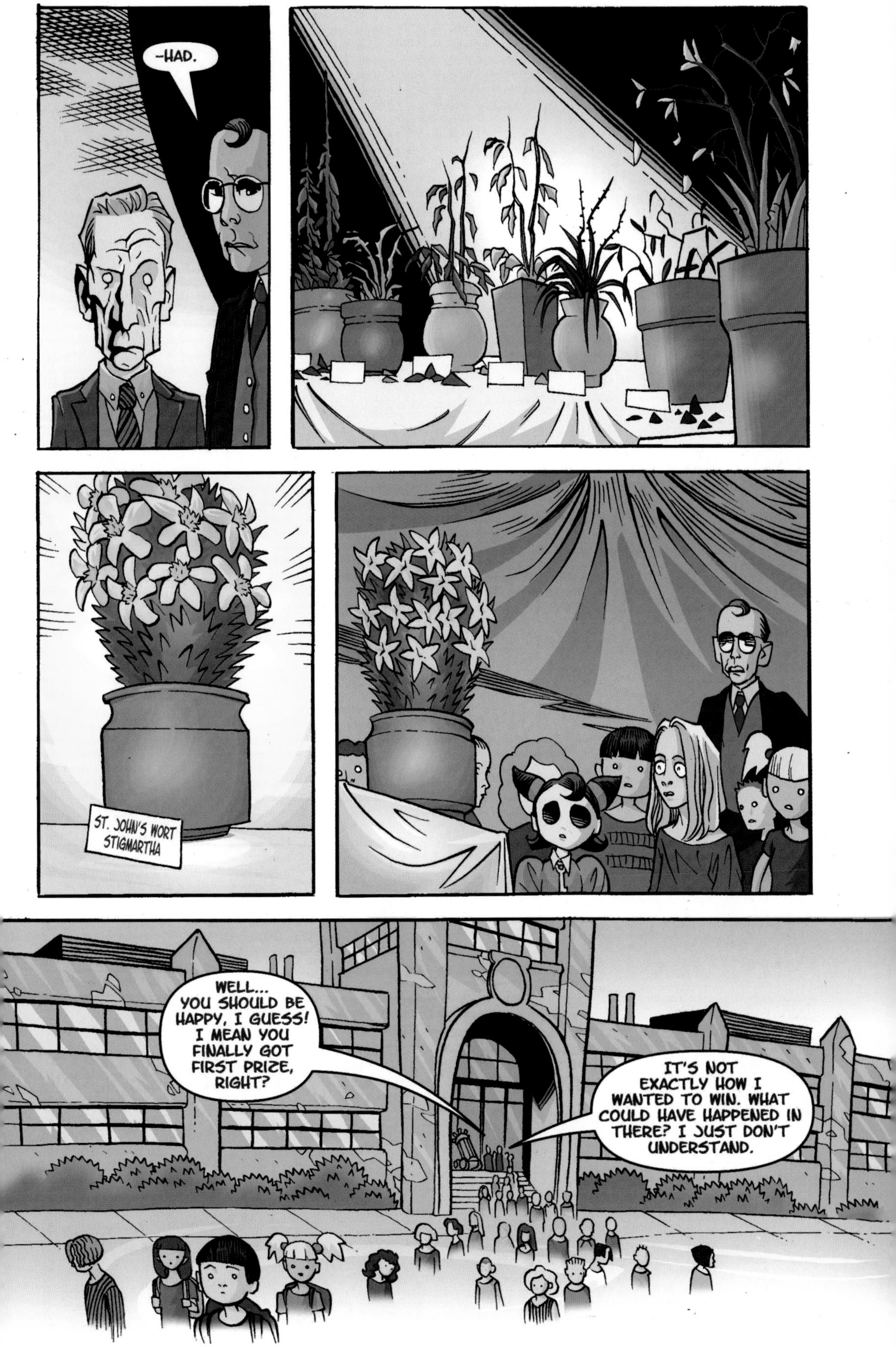
-HAD.
ST. JOHN'S WORT
STIGMARTHA
WELL... YOU SHOULD BE HAPPY, I GUESS! I MEAN YOU FINALLY GOT FIRST PRIZE, RIGHT?
IT'S NOT EXACTLY HOW I WANTED TO WIN. WHAT COULD HAVE HAPPENED IN THERE? I JUST DON'T UNDERSTAND.

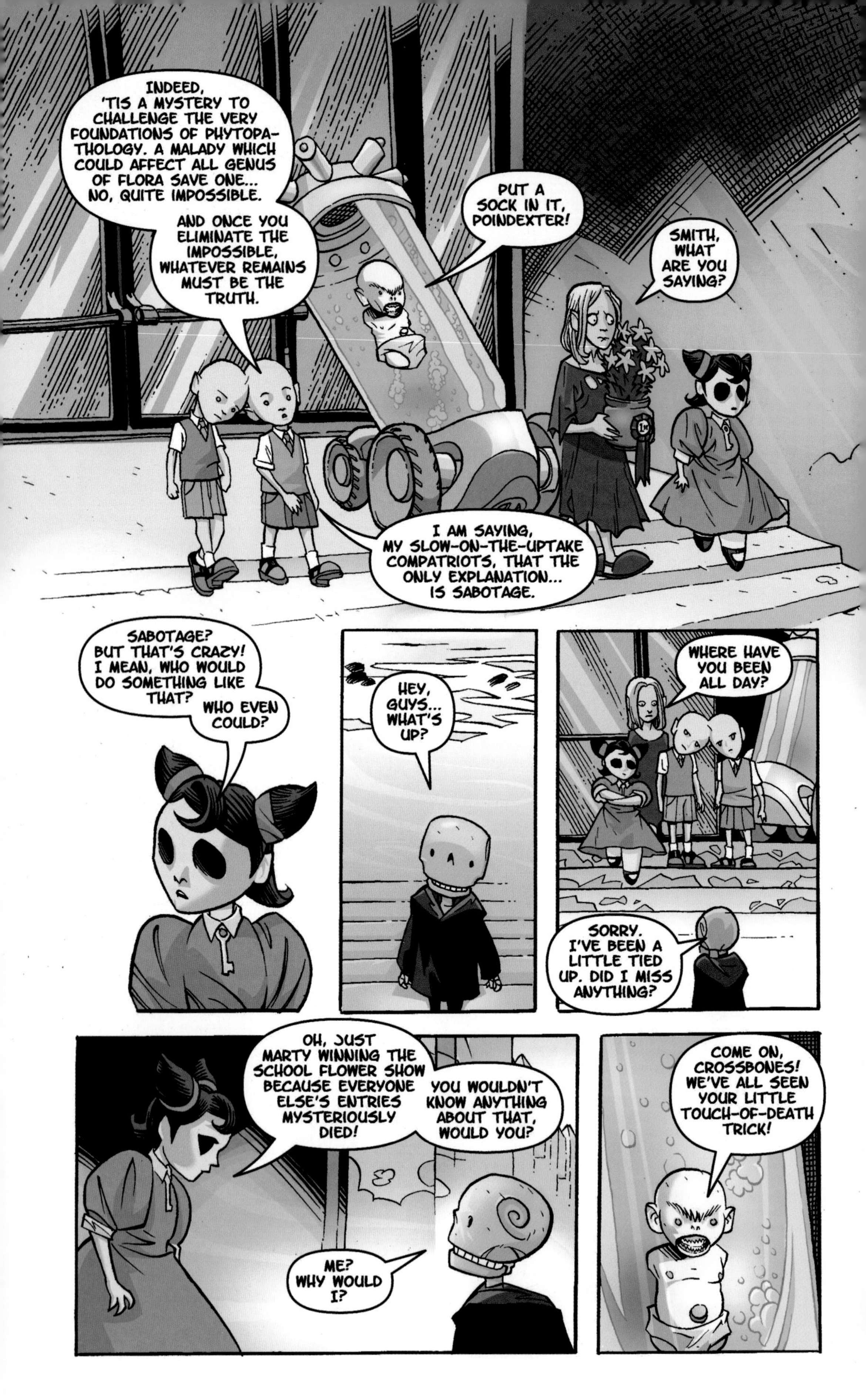

INDEED, 'TIS A MYSTERY TO CHALLENGE THE VERY FOUNDATIONS OF PHYTOPA-THOLOGY. A MALADY WHICH COULD AFFECT ALL GENUS OF FLORA SAVE ONE... NO, QUITE IMPOSSIBLE.
AND ONCE YOU ELIMINATE THE IMPOSSIBLE, WHATEVER REMAINS MUST BE THE TRUTH.
PUT A SOCK IN IT, POINDEXTER!
SMITH, WHAT ARE YOU SAYING?
I AM SAYING, MY SLOW-ON-THE-UPTAKE COMPATRIOTS, THAT THE ONLY EXPLANATION... IS SABOTAGE.
SABOTAGE? BUT THAT'S CRAZY! I MEAN, WHO WOULD DO SOMETHING LIKE THAT?
WHO EVEN COULD?
HEY, GUYS... WHAT'S UP?
WHERE HAVE YOU BEEN ALL DAY?
SORRY. I'VE BEEN A LITTLE TIED UP. DID I MISS ANYTHING?
OH, JUST MARTY WINNING THE SCHOOL FLOWER SHOW BECAUSE EVERYONE ELSE'S ENTRIES MYSTERIOUSLY DIED!
YOU WOULDN'T KNOW ANYTHING ABOUT THAT, WOULD YOU?
ME? WHY WOULD I?
COME ON, CROSSBONES! WE'VE ALL SEEN YOUR LITTLE TOUCH-OF-DEATH TRICK!

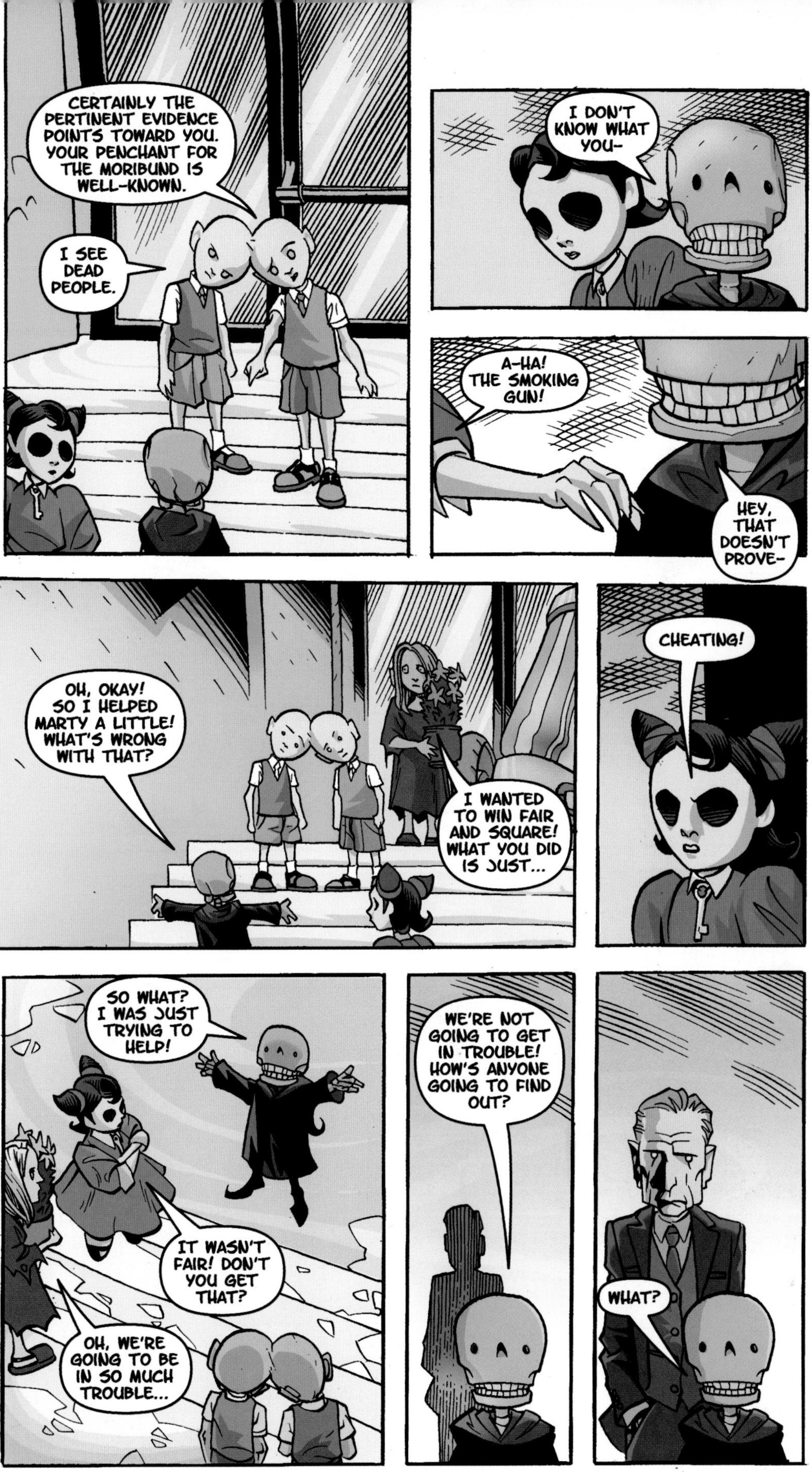
CERTAINLY THE PERTINENT EVIDENCE POINTS TOWARD YOU. YOUR PENCHANT FOR THE MORIBUND IS WELL-KNOWN.
I SEE DEAD PEOPLE.
I DON'T KNOW WHAT YOU-
A-HA! THE SMOKING GUN!
HEY, THAT DOESN'T PROVE-
OH, OKAY! SO I HELPED MARTY A LITTLE! WHAT'S WRONG WITH THAT?
I WANTED TO WIN FAIR AND SQUARE! WHAT YOU DID IS JUST...
CHEATING!
SO WHAT? I WAS JUST TRYING TO HELP!
IT WASN'T FAIR! DON'T YOU GET THAT?
OH, WE'RE GOING TO BE IN SO MUCH TROUBLE...
WE'RE NOT GOING TO GET IN TROUBLE! HOW'S ANYONE GOING TO FIND OUT?
WHAT?

I'M VERY DISAPPOINTED IN YOU, YOUNG MAN.

I'M QUITE AWARE OF THE... INCIDENTS THAT HAVE BEEN TAKING PLACE AT THE SCHOOL SINCE YOUR ARRIVAL. I'VE TURNED A BLIND EYE TO THEM UNTIL NOW, BUT THIS... I'M AFRAID YOUR PARENTS WILL HAVE TO BE INFORMED.

WHAT? NO! YOU CAN'T TELL MY DAD! HE'LL BE FURIOUS!

YOU LEAVE ME LITTLE OPTION, I'M AFRAID.

ALL THAT POWER...

PEOPLE LIKE US... WE ANSWER TO NO-ONE.

PRINCIPAL SCARAMANGA...

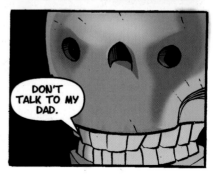

DON'T TALK TO MY DAD.

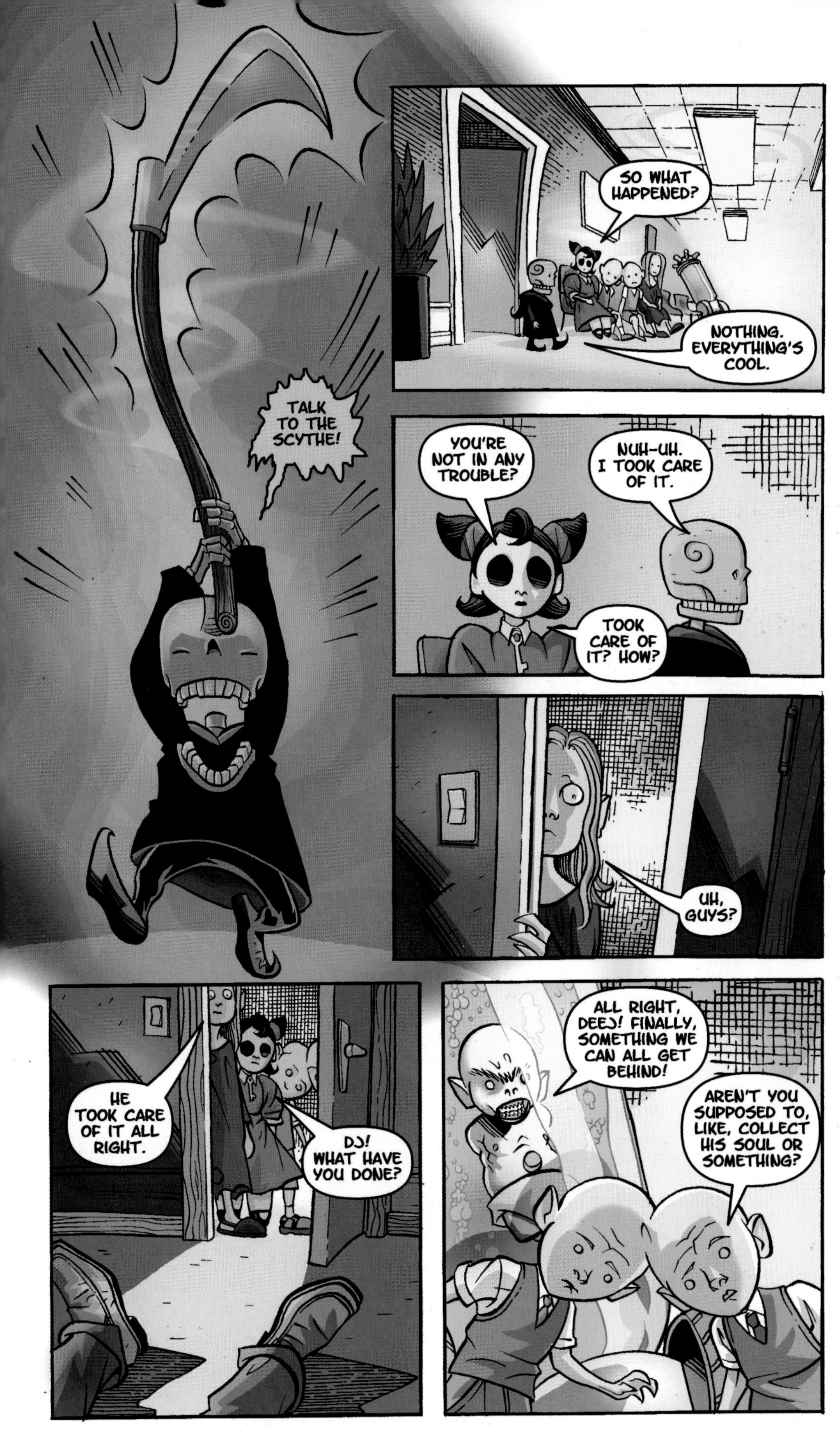
TALK TO THE SCYTHE!
SO WHAT HAPPENED?
NOTHING. EVERYTHING'S COOL.
YOU'RE NOT IN ANY TROUBLE?
NUH-UH. I TOOK CARE OF IT.
TOOK CARE OF IT? HOW?
UH, GUYS?
HE TOOK CARE OF IT ALL RIGHT.
DJ! WHAT HAVE YOU DONE?
ALL RIGHT, DEEJ! FINALLY, SOMETHING WE CAN ALL GET BEHIND!
AREN'T YOU SUPPOSED TO, LIKE, COLLECT HIS SOUL OR SOMETHING?

UM, MAYBE. DON'T REALLY KNOW HOW.

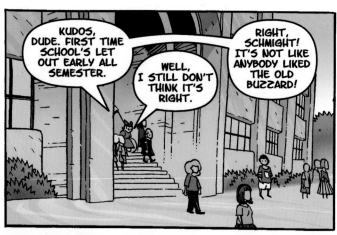

KUDOS, DUDE. FIRST TIME SCHOOL'S LET OUT EARLY ALL SEMESTER.

WELL, I STILL DON'T THINK IT'S RIGHT.

RIGHT, SCHMIGHT! IT'S NOT LIKE ANYBODY LIKED THE OLD BUZZARD!

IF YOU ASK ME, DJ HERE JUST MADE HIMSELF THE MOST POPULAR KID IN SCHOOL.

IN ONE FELL SWOOP, SO TO SPEAK.

YOU REALLY THINK SO?

OH, GREAT...

GREAT. WE FINALLY GET A HALF-DAY AND WE'RE GONNA SPEND IT WAITING TO GET ON THE BUS.

WELL... WE DON'T HAVE TO WAIT.

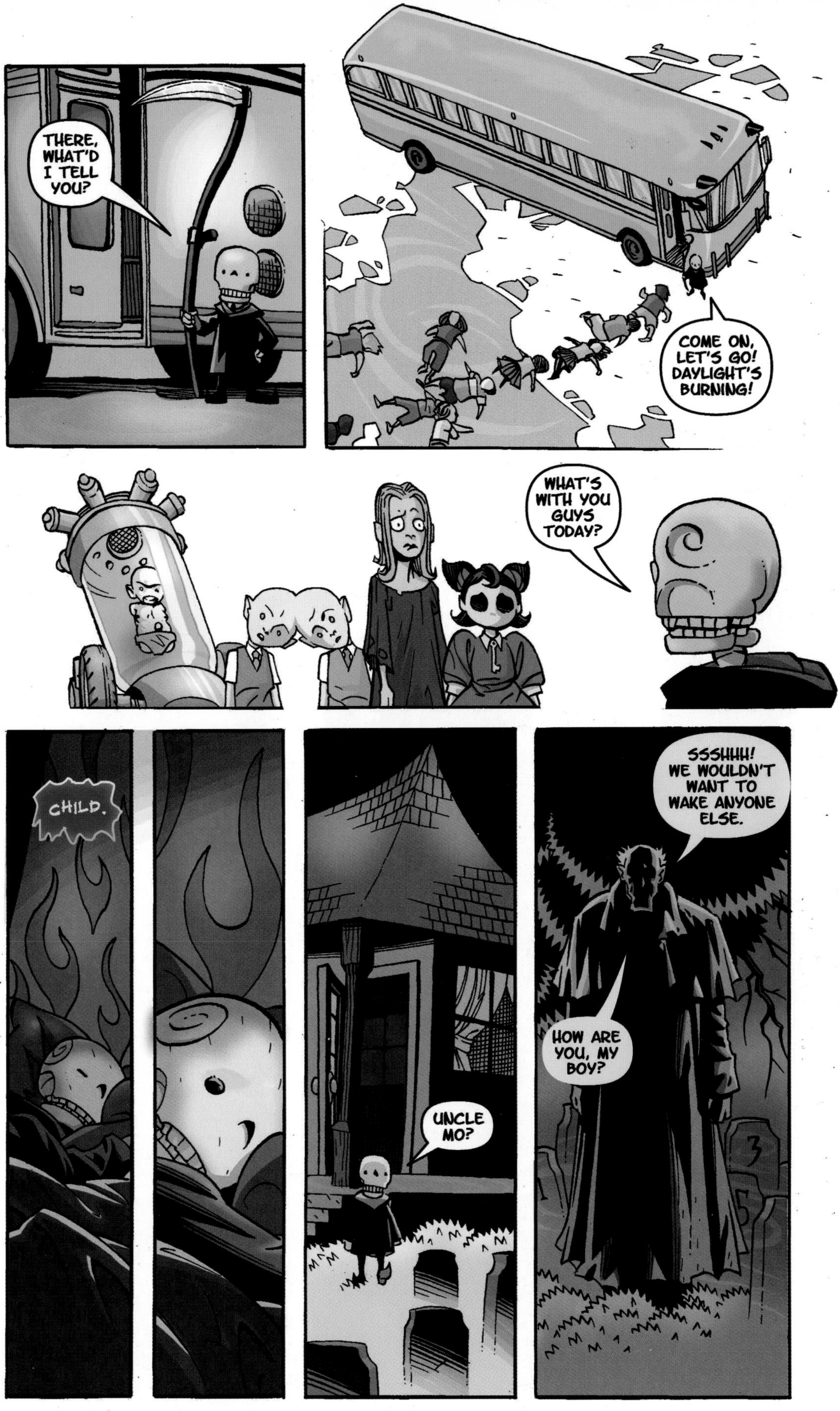
THERE, WHAT'D I TELL YOU?
COME ON, LET'S GO! DAYLIGHT'S BURNING!
WHAT'S WITH YOU GUYS TODAY?
CHILD.
UNCLE MO?
SSSHHH! WE WOULDN'T WANT TO WAKE ANYONE ELSE.
HOW ARE YOU, MY BOY?

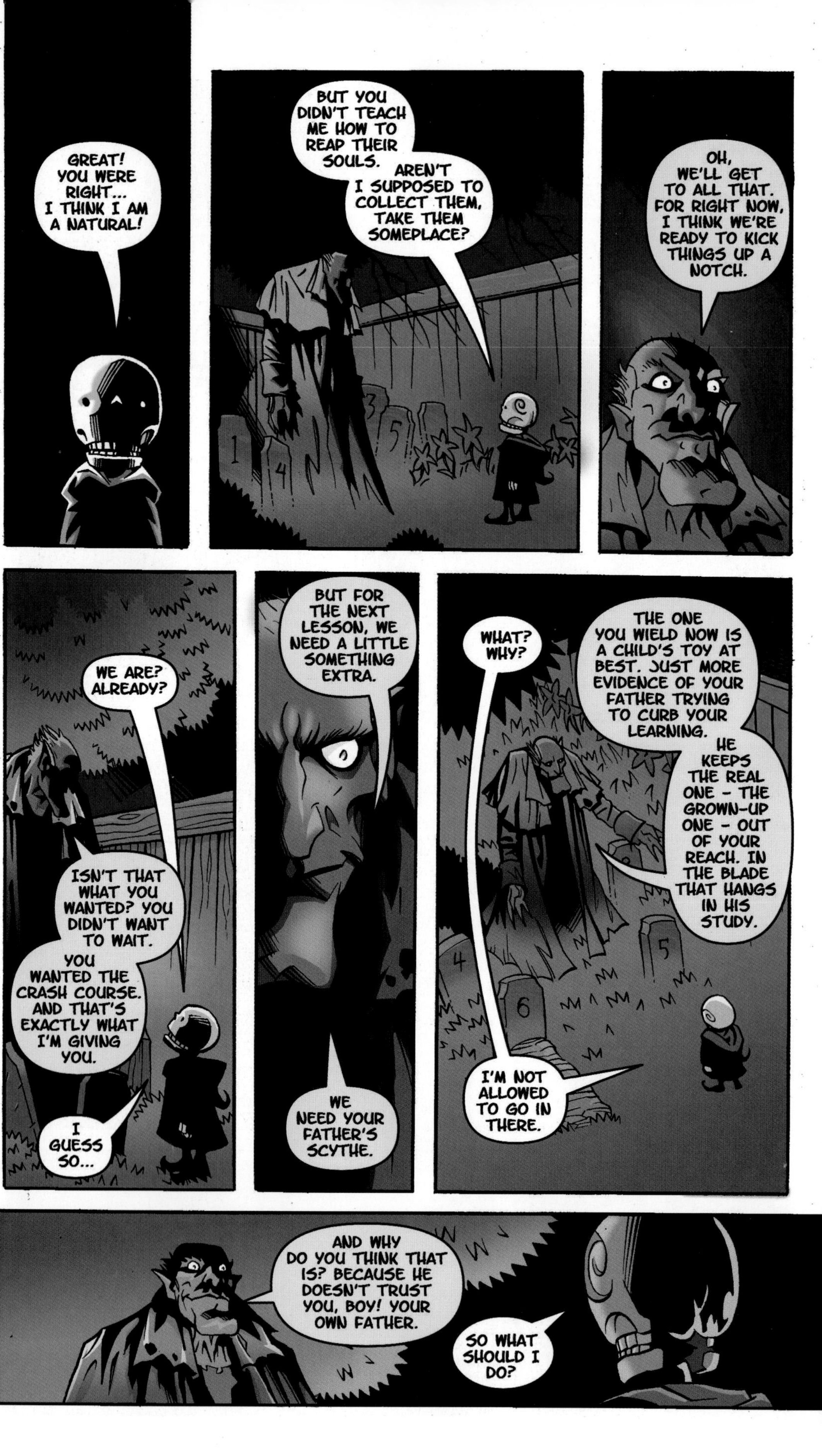
GREAT! YOU WERE RIGHT... I THINK I AM A NATURAL!
BUT YOU DIDN'T TEACH ME HOW TO REAP THEIR SOULS.
AREN'T I SUPPOSED TO COLLECT THEM, TAKE THEM SOMEPLACE?
OH, WE'LL GET TO ALL THAT. FOR RIGHT NOW, I THINK WE'RE READY TO KICK THINGS UP A NOTCH.
WE ARE? ALREADY?
ISN'T THAT WHAT YOU WANTED? YOU DIDN'T WANT TO WAIT.
YOU WANTED THE CRASH COURSE. AND THAT'S EXACTLY WHAT I'M GIVING YOU.
I GUESS SO...
BUT FOR THE NEXT LESSON, WE NEED A LITTLE SOMETHING EXTRA.
WE NEED YOUR FATHER'S SCYTHE.
WHAT? WHY?
I'M NOT ALLOWED TO GO IN THERE.
THE ONE YOU WIELD NOW IS A CHILD'S TOY AT BEST. JUST MORE EVIDENCE OF YOUR FATHER TRYING TO CURB YOUR LEARNING.
HE KEEPS THE REAL ONE - THE GROWN-UP ONE - OUT OF YOUR REACH. IN THE BLADE THAT HANGS IN HIS STUDY.
AND WHY DO YOU THINK THAT IS? BECAUSE HE DOESN'T TRUST YOU, BOY! YOUR OWN FATHER.
SO WHAT SHOULD I DO?

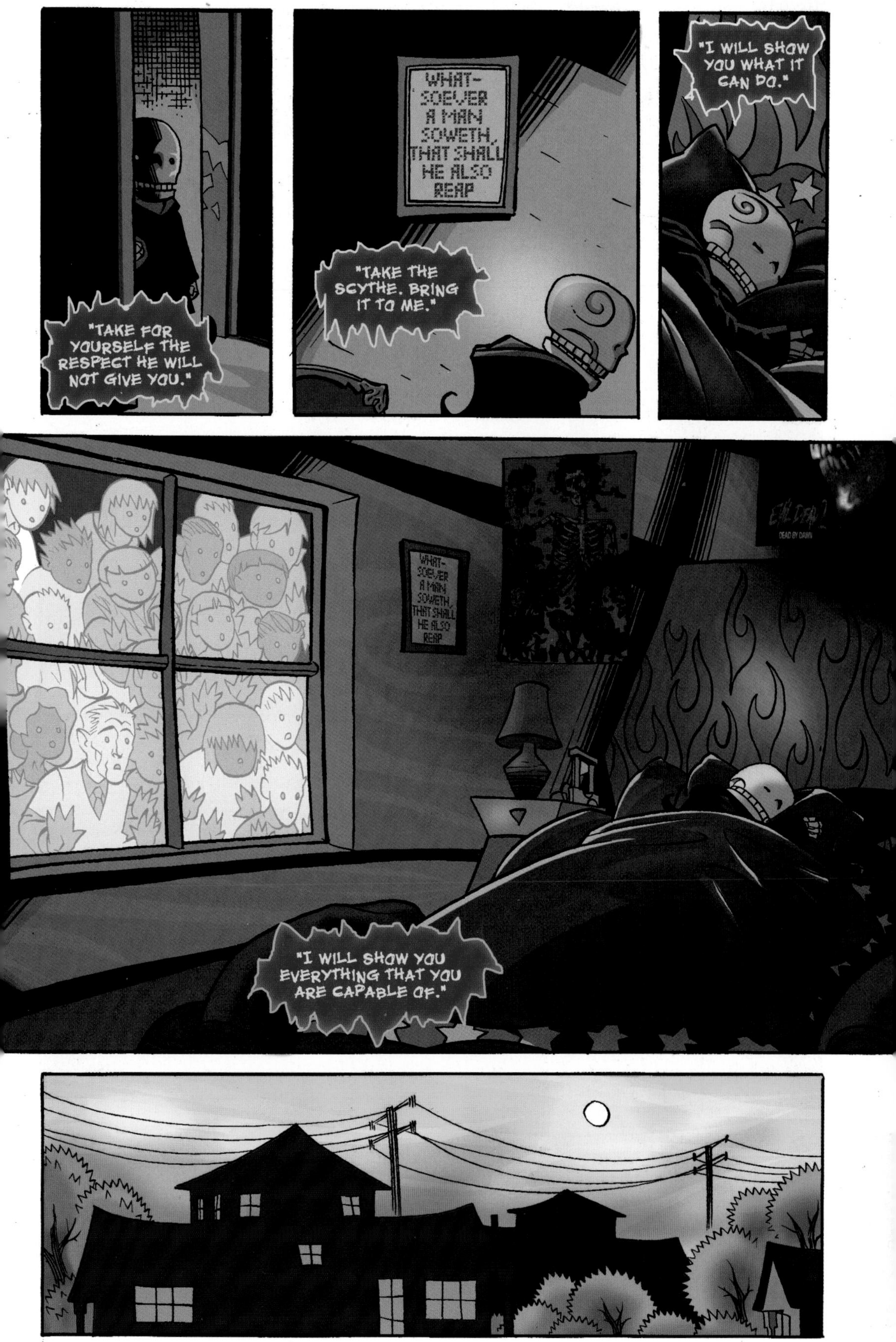
"TAKE FOR YOURSELF THE RESPECT HE WILL NOT GIVE YOU."
WHAT-SOEVER A MAN SOWETH, THAT SHALL HE ALSO REAP
"TAKE THE SCYTHE. BRING IT TO ME."
"I WILL SHOW YOU WHAT IT CAN DO."
WHAT-SOEVER A MAN SOWETH, THAT SHALL HE ALSO REAP
DEAD BY DAWN
"I WILL SHOW YOU EVERYTHING THAT YOU ARE CAPABLE OF."

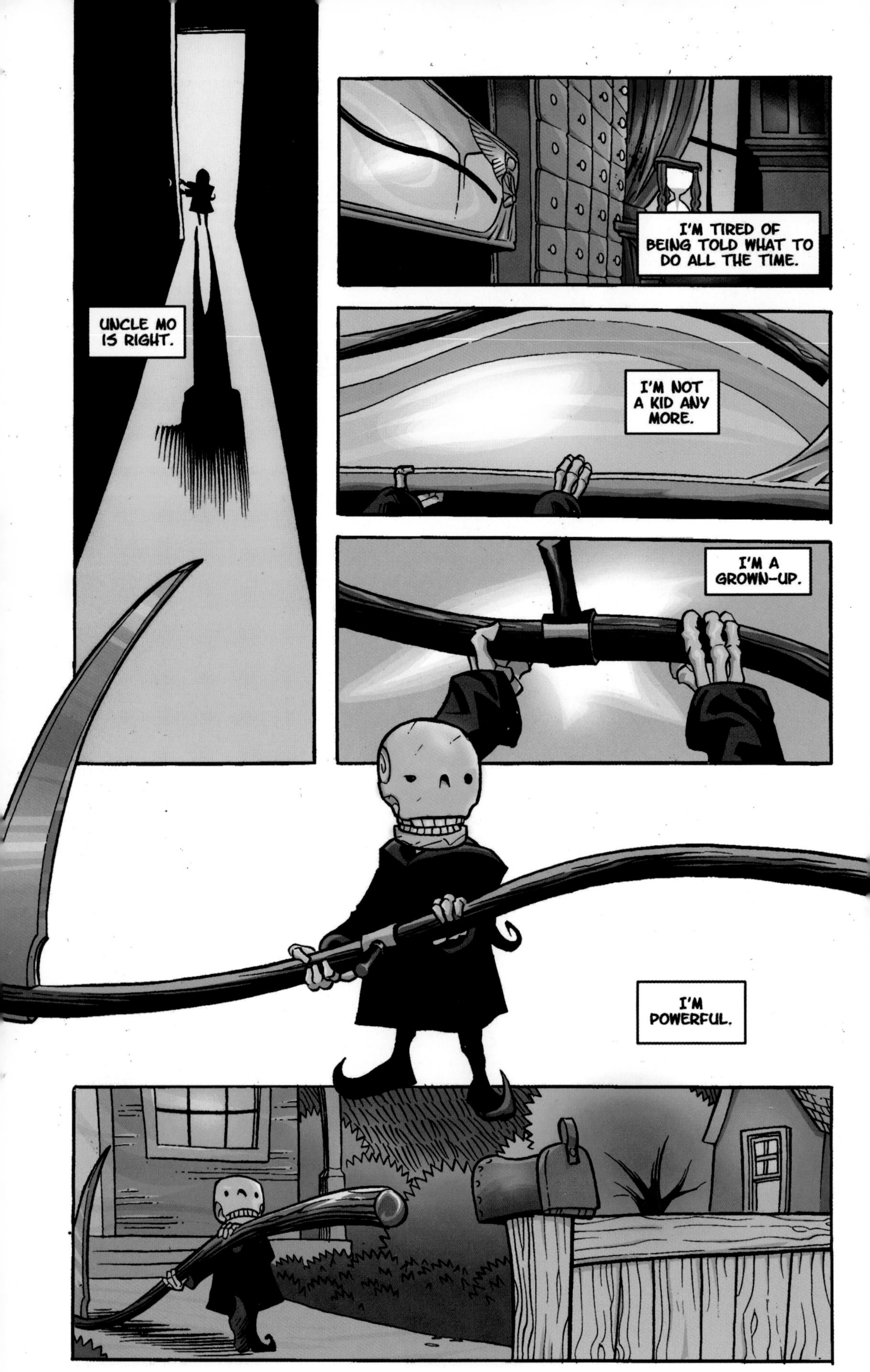
I'M TIRED OF BEING TOLD WHAT TO DO ALL THE TIME.
UNCLE MO IS RIGHT.
I'M NOT A KID ANY MORE.
I'M A GROWN-UP.
I'M POWERFUL.

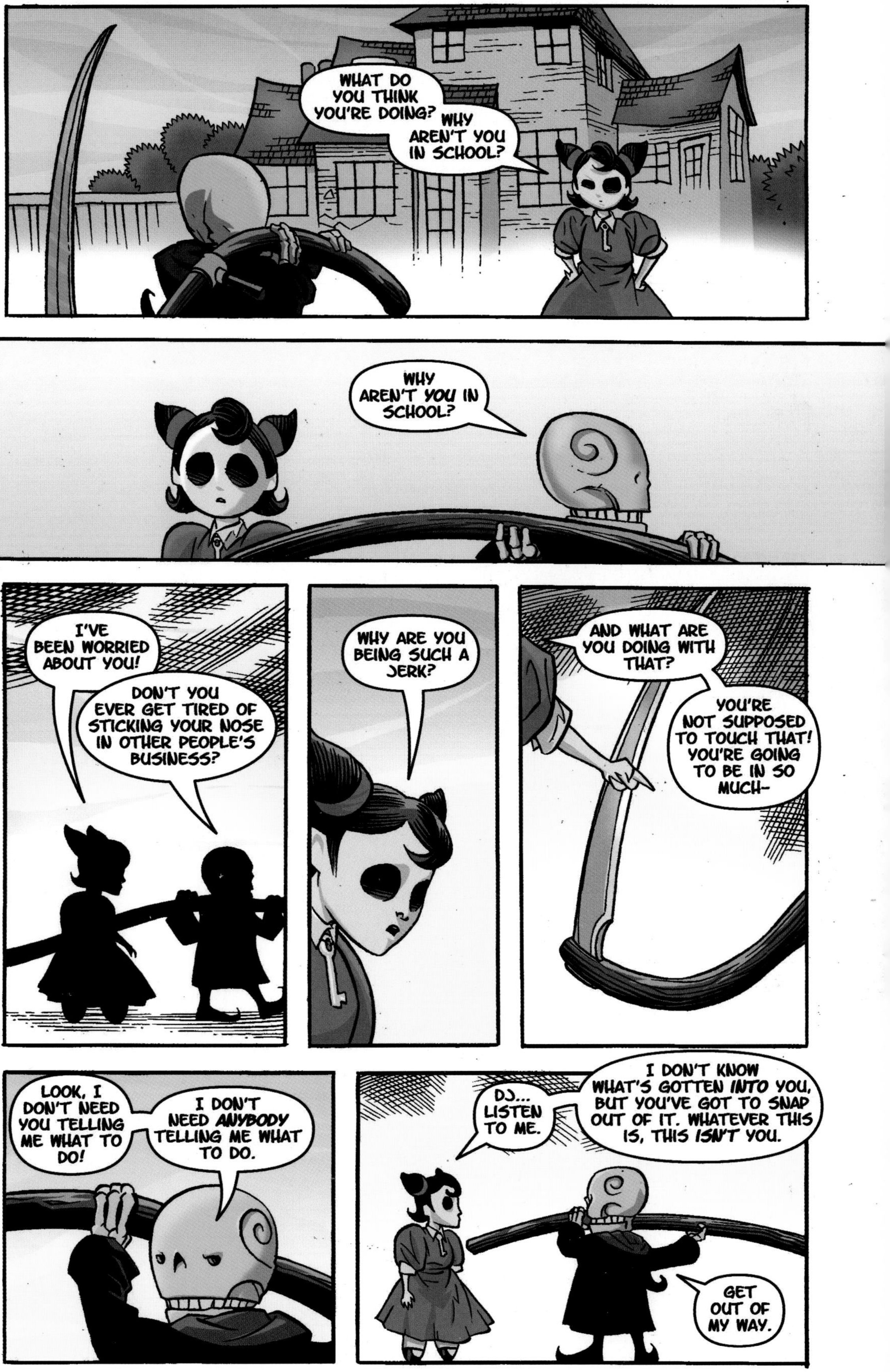

WHAT DO YOU THINK YOU'RE DOING?
WHY AREN'T YOU IN SCHOOL?
WHY AREN'T YOU IN SCHOOL?
I'VE BEEN WORRIED ABOUT YOU!
DON'T YOU EVER GET TIRED OF STICKING YOUR NOSE IN OTHER PEOPLE'S BUSINESS?
WHY ARE YOU BEING SUCH A JERK?
AND WHAT ARE YOU DOING WITH THAT?
YOU'RE NOT SUPPOSED TO TOUCH THAT! YOU'RE GOING TO BE IN SO MUCH-
LOOK, I DON'T NEED YOU TELLING ME WHAT TO DO!
I DON'T NEED ANYBODY TELLING ME WHAT TO DO.
DJ... LISTEN TO ME.
I DON'T KNOW WHAT'S GOTTEN INTO YOU, BUT YOU'VE GOT TO SNAP OUT OF IT. WHATEVER THIS IS, THIS ISN'T YOU.
GET OUT OF MY WAY.

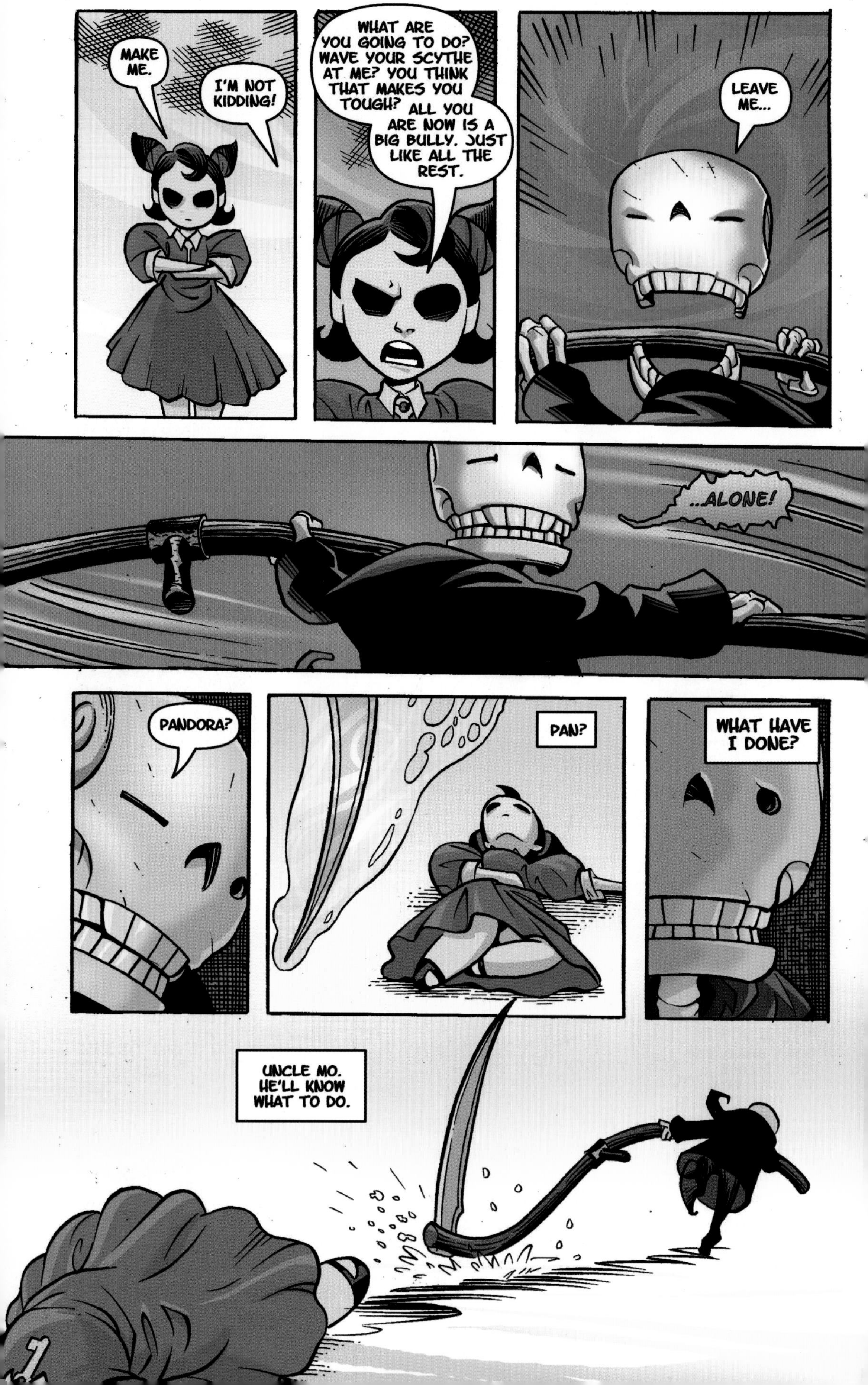

MAKE ME.
I'M NOT KIDDING!
WHAT ARE YOU GOING TO DO? WAVE YOUR SCYTHE AT ME? YOU THINK THAT MAKES YOU TOUGH?
ALL YOU ARE NOW IS A BIG BULLY. JUST LIKE ALL THE REST.
LEAVE ME...
...ALONE!
PANDORA?
PAN?
WHAT HAVE I DONE?
UNCLE MO. HE'LL KNOW WHAT TO DO.

THE MUSEUM.

HE SAID TO MEET HIM AT THE MUSEUM.

CLOSED DUE TO EXTREMELY ODD CIRCUMSTANCES

OH, NO!

CLOSED DUE TO EXTREMELY ODD CIRCUMSTANCES

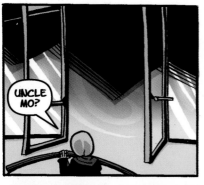

UNCLE MO?

UNCLE MO?

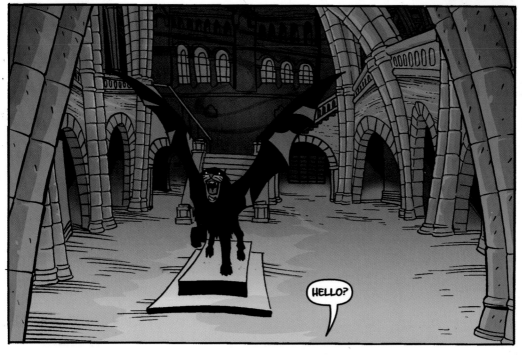

HELLO?

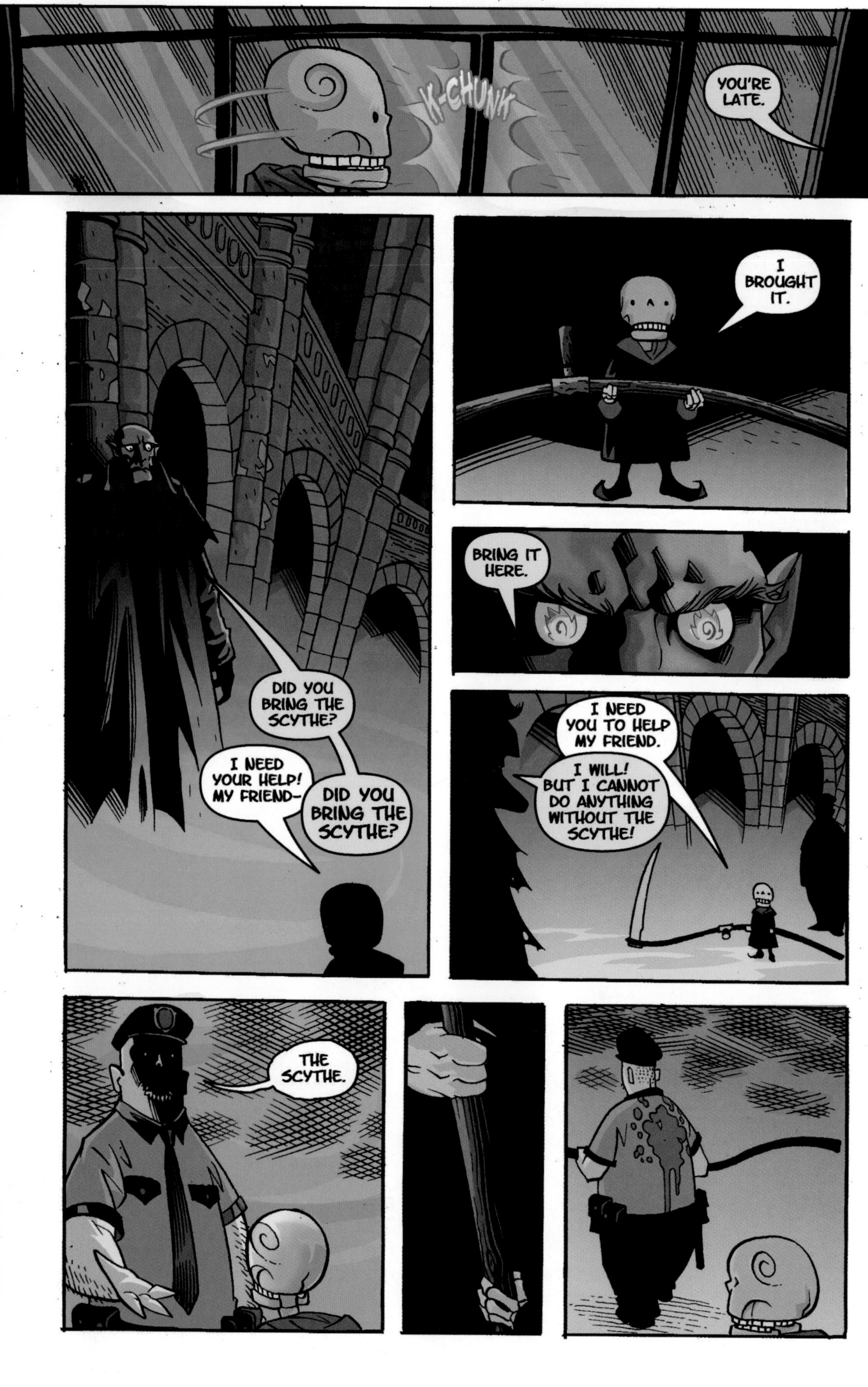
K-CHUNK
YOU'RE LATE.
DID YOU BRING THE SCYTHE?
I NEED YOUR HELP! MY FRIEND-
DID YOU BRING THE SCYTHE?
I BROUGHT IT.
BRING IT HERE.
I NEED YOU TO HELP MY FRIEND.
I WILL! BUT I CANNOT DO ANYTHING WITHOUT THE SCYTHE!
THE SCYTHE.

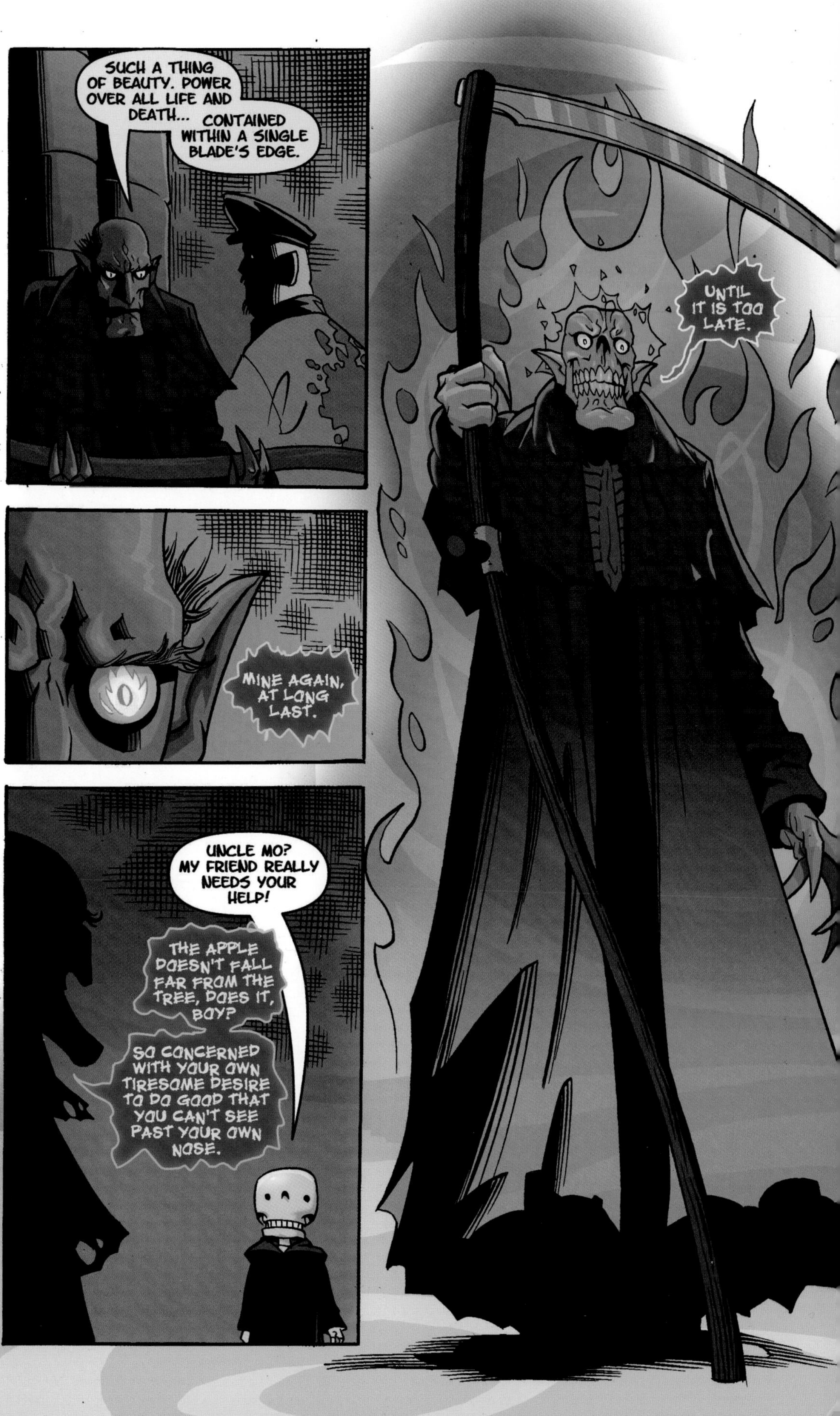

SUCH A THING OF BEAUTY. POWER OVER ALL LIFE AND DEATH...
CONTAINED WITHIN A SINGLE BLADE'S EDGE.
MINE AGAIN, AT LONG LAST.
UNCLE MO? MY FRIEND REALLY NEEDS YOUR HELP!
THE APPLE DOESN'T FALL FAR FROM THE TREE, DOES IT, BOY?
SO CONCERNED WITH YOUR OWN TIRESOME DESIRE TO DO GOOD THAT YOU CAN'T SEE PAST YOUR OWN NOSE.
UNTIL IT IS TOO LATE.

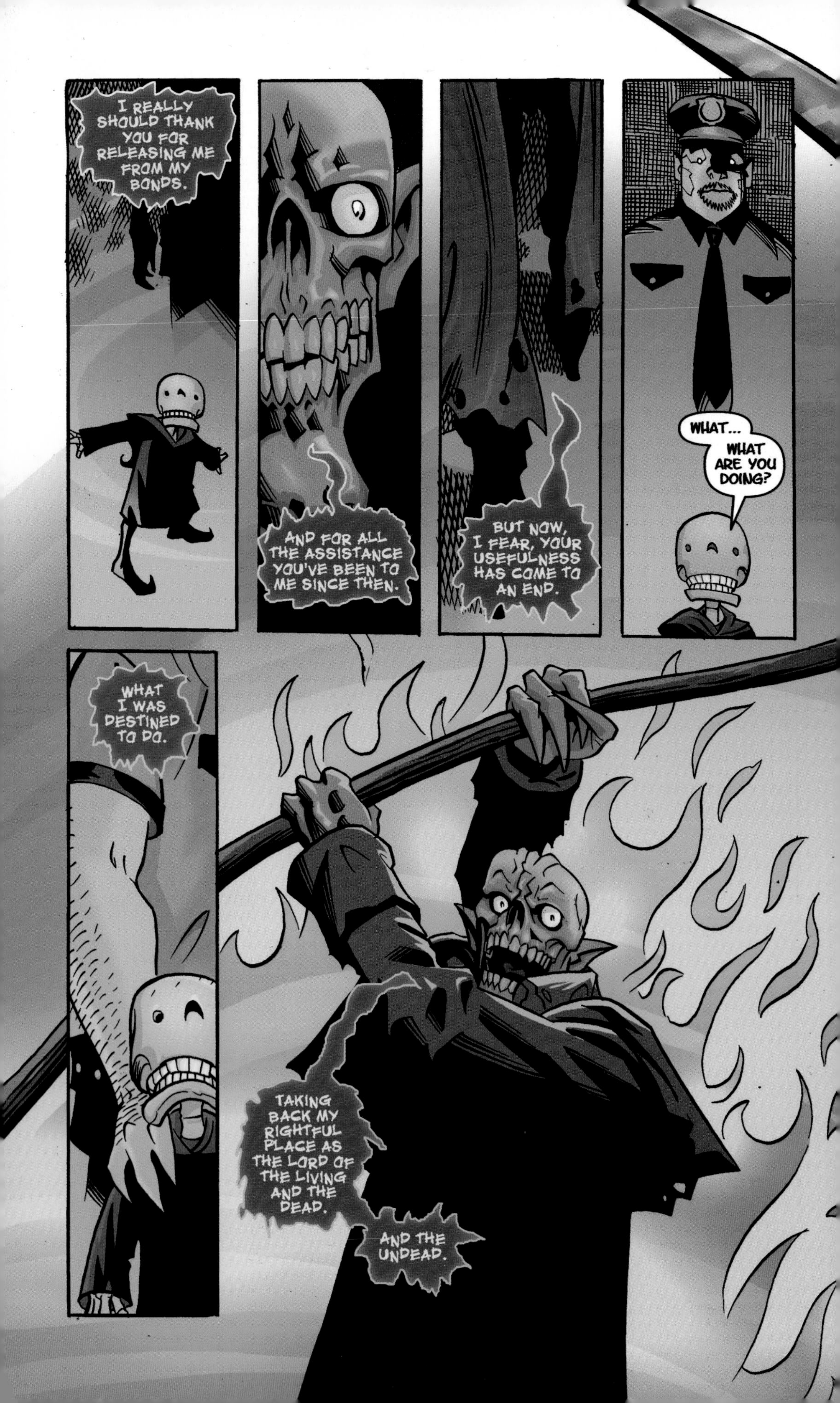
I REALLY SHOULD THANK YOU FOR RELEASING ME FROM MY BONDS.
AND FOR ALL THE ASSISTANCE YOU'VE BEEN TO ME SINCE THEN.
BUT NOW, I FEAR, YOUR USEFULNESS HAS COME TO AN END.
WHAT... WHAT ARE YOU DOING?
WHAT I WAS DESTINED TO DO.
TAKING BACK MY RIGHTFUL PLACE AS THE LORD OF THE LIVING AND THE DEAD.
AND THE UNDEAD.

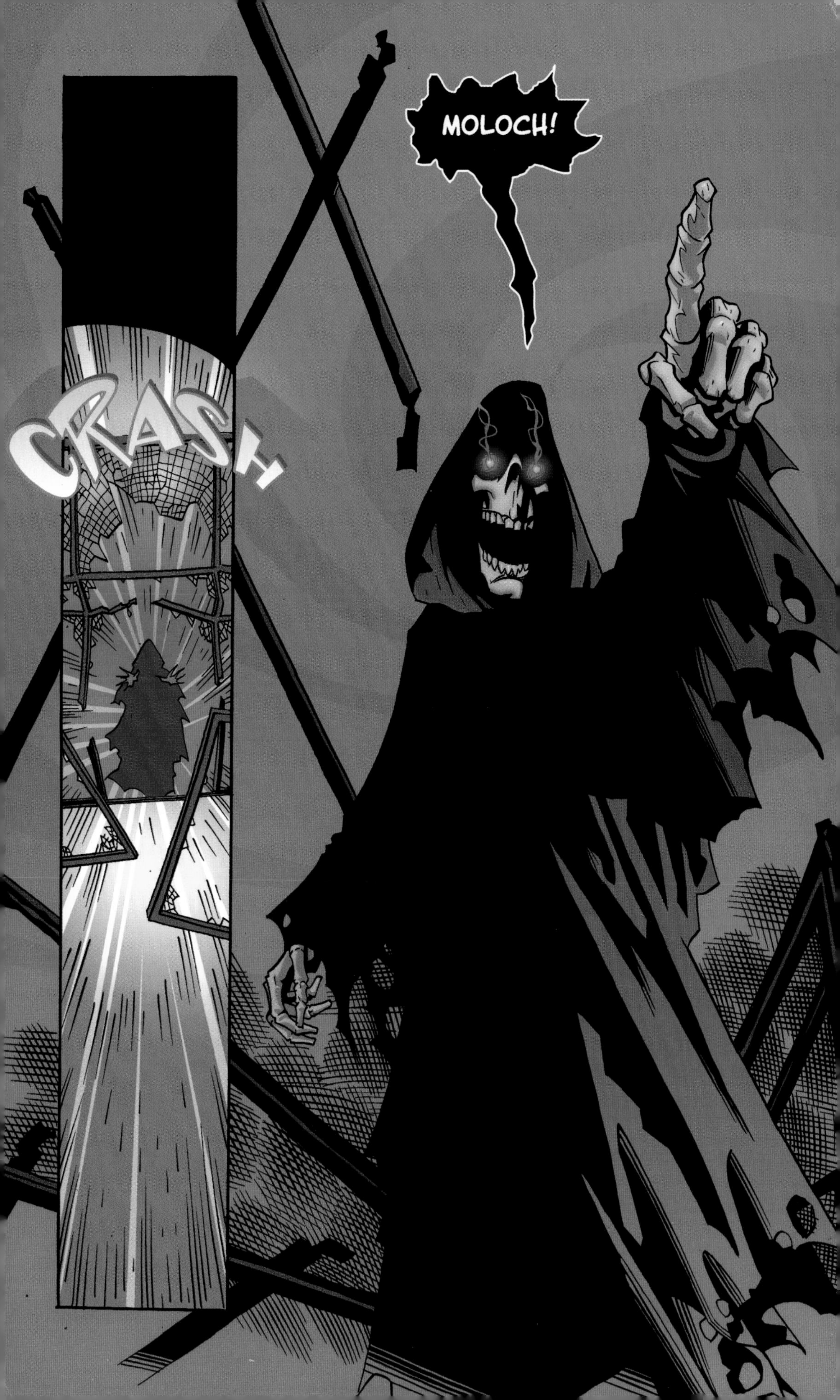
CRASH
MOLOCH!

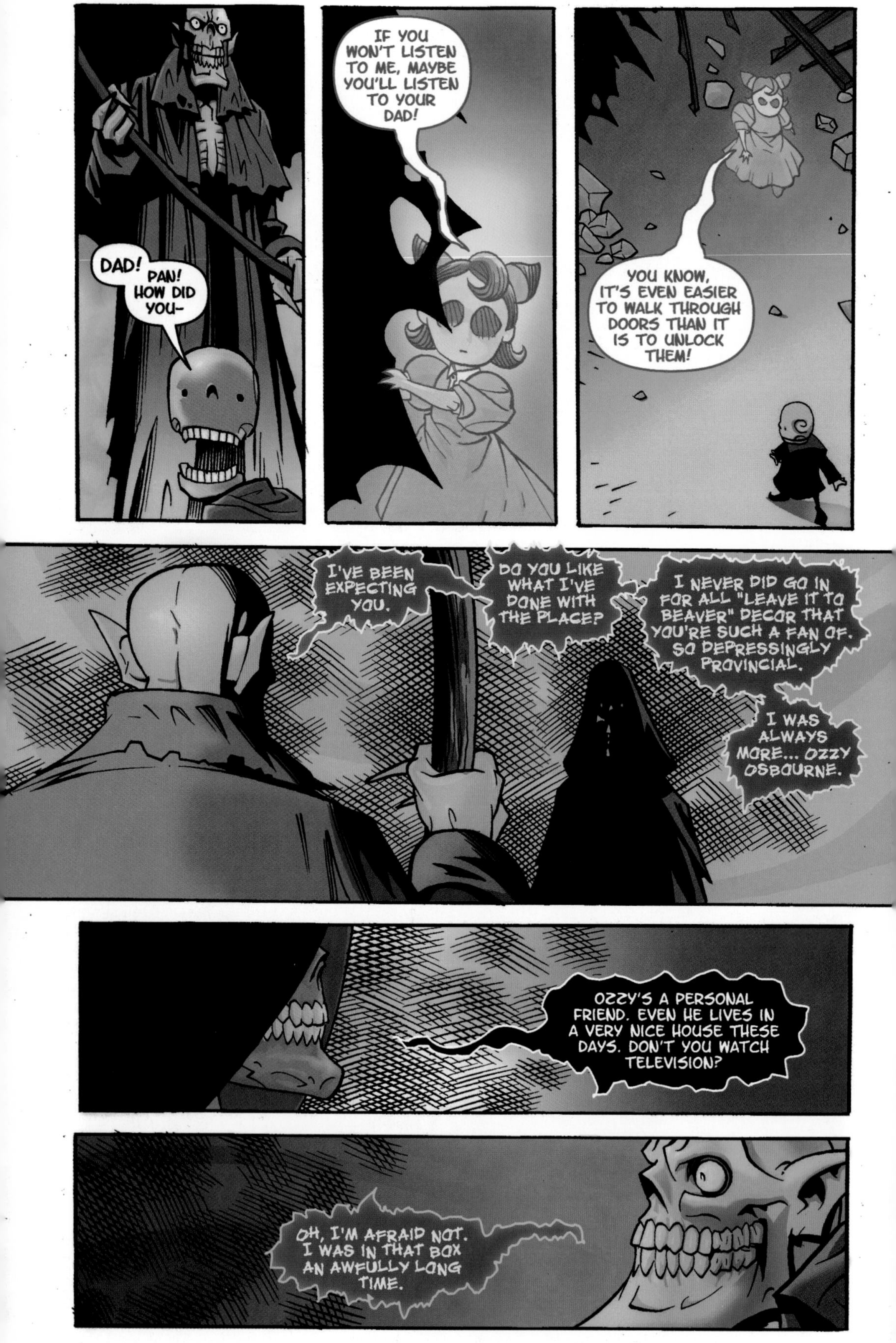

DAD! PAN! HOW DID YOU-
IF YOU WON'T LISTEN TO ME, MAYBE YOU'LL LISTEN TO YOUR DAD!
YOU KNOW, IT'S EVEN EASIER TO WALK THROUGH DOORS THAN IT IS TO UNLOCK THEM!
I'VE BEEN EXPECTING YOU.
DO YOU LIKE WHAT I'VE DONE WITH THE PLACE?
I NEVER DID GO IN FOR ALL "LEAVE IT TO BEAVER" DECOR THAT YOU'RE SUCH A FAN OF. SO DEPRESSINGLY PROVINCIAL.
I WAS ALWAYS MORE... OZZY OSBOURNE.
OZZY'S A PERSONAL FRIEND. EVEN HE LIVES IN A VERY NICE HOUSE THESE DAYS. DON'T YOU WATCH TELEVISION?
OH, I'M AFRAID NOT. I WAS IN THAT BOX AN AWFULLY LONG TIME.

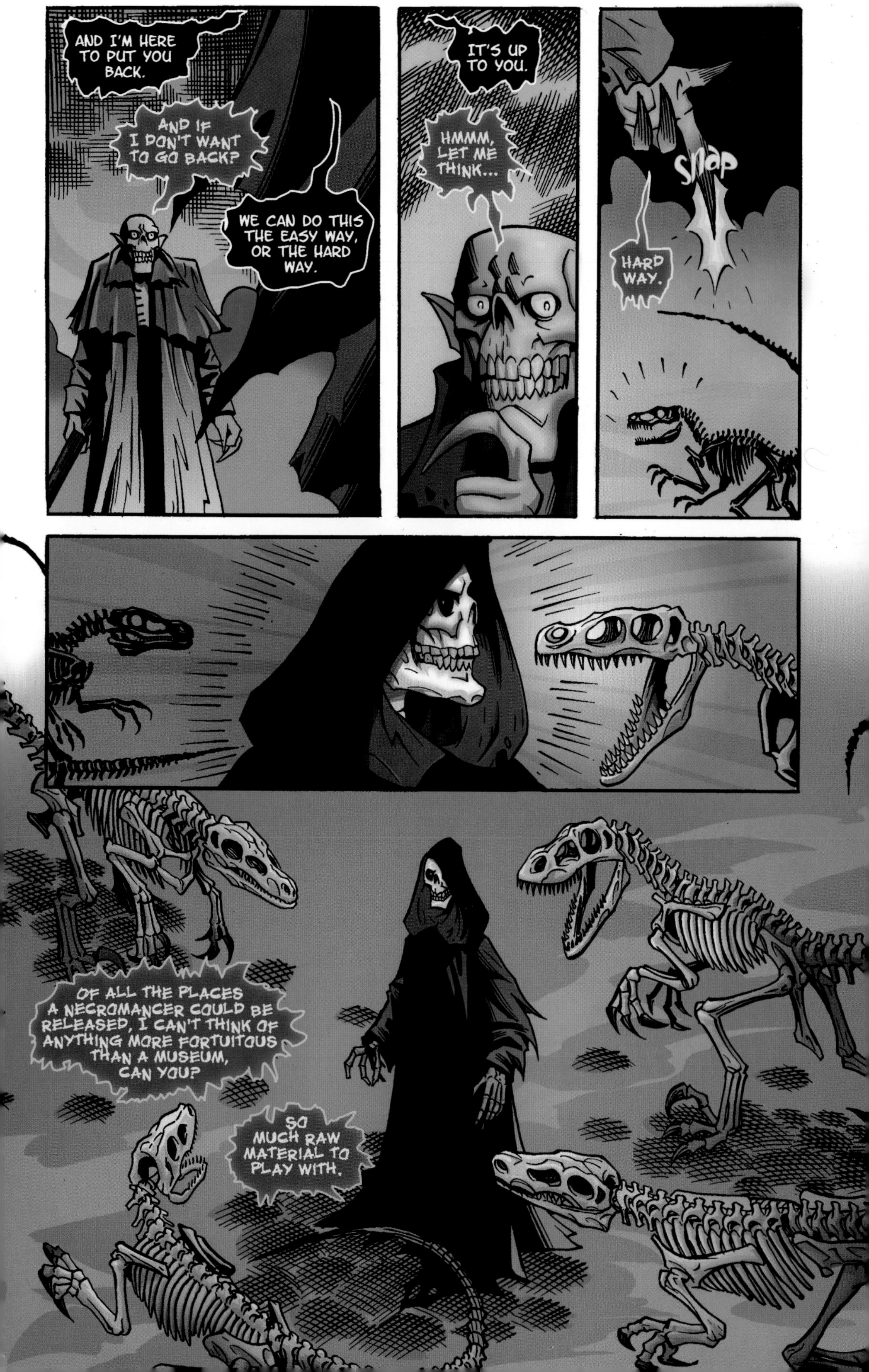
AND I'M HERE TO PUT YOU BACK.
AND IF I DON'T WANT TO GO BACK?
WE CAN DO THIS THE EASY WAY, OR THE HARD WAY.
IT'S UP TO YOU.
HMMM, LET ME THINK...
SNAP
HARD WAY.
OF ALL THE PLACES A NECROMANCER COULD BE RELEASED, I CAN'T THINK OF ANYTHING MORE FORTUITOUS THAN A MUSEUM, CAN YOU?
SO MUCH RAW MATERIAL TO PLAY WITH.

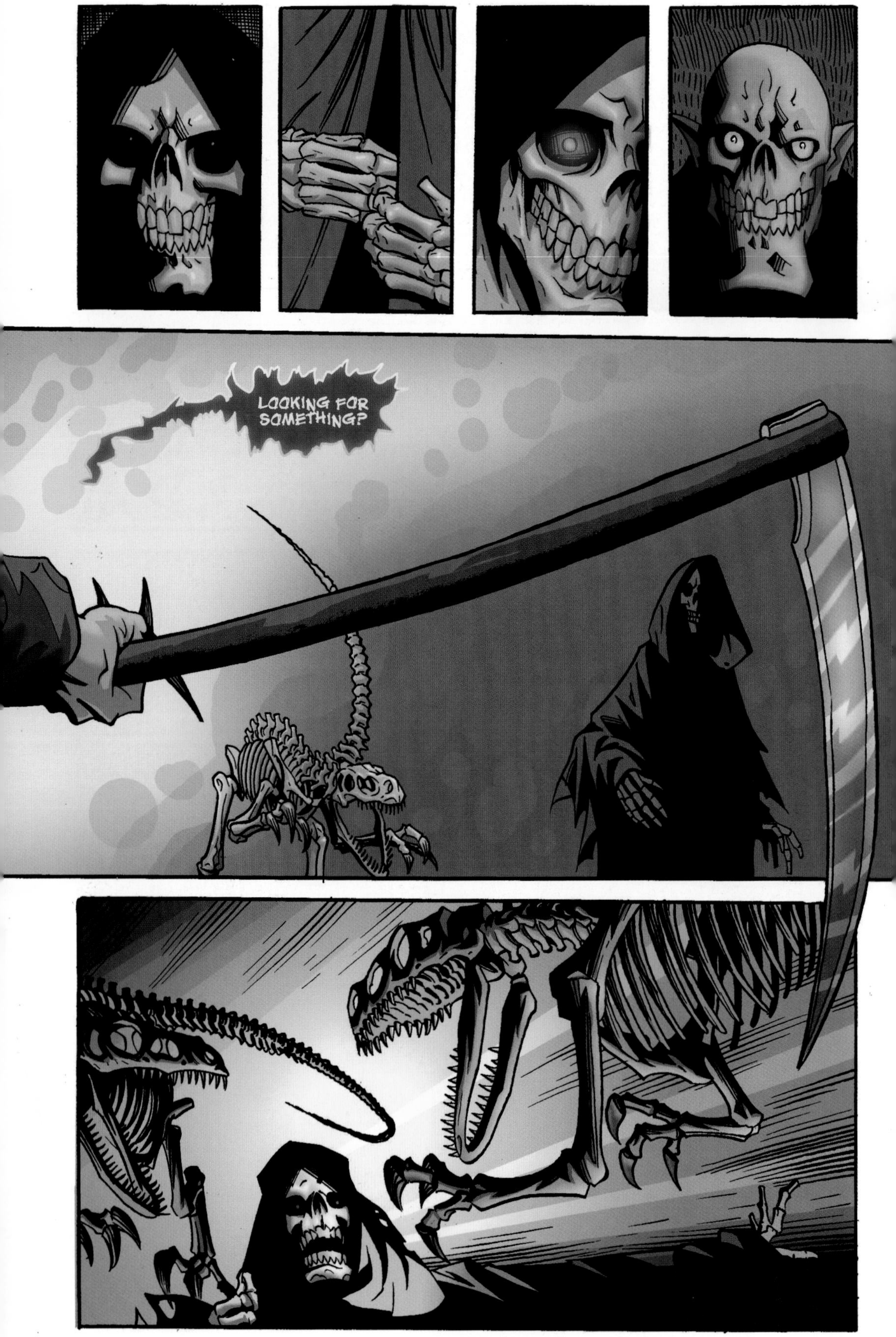
LOOKING FOR SOMETHING?

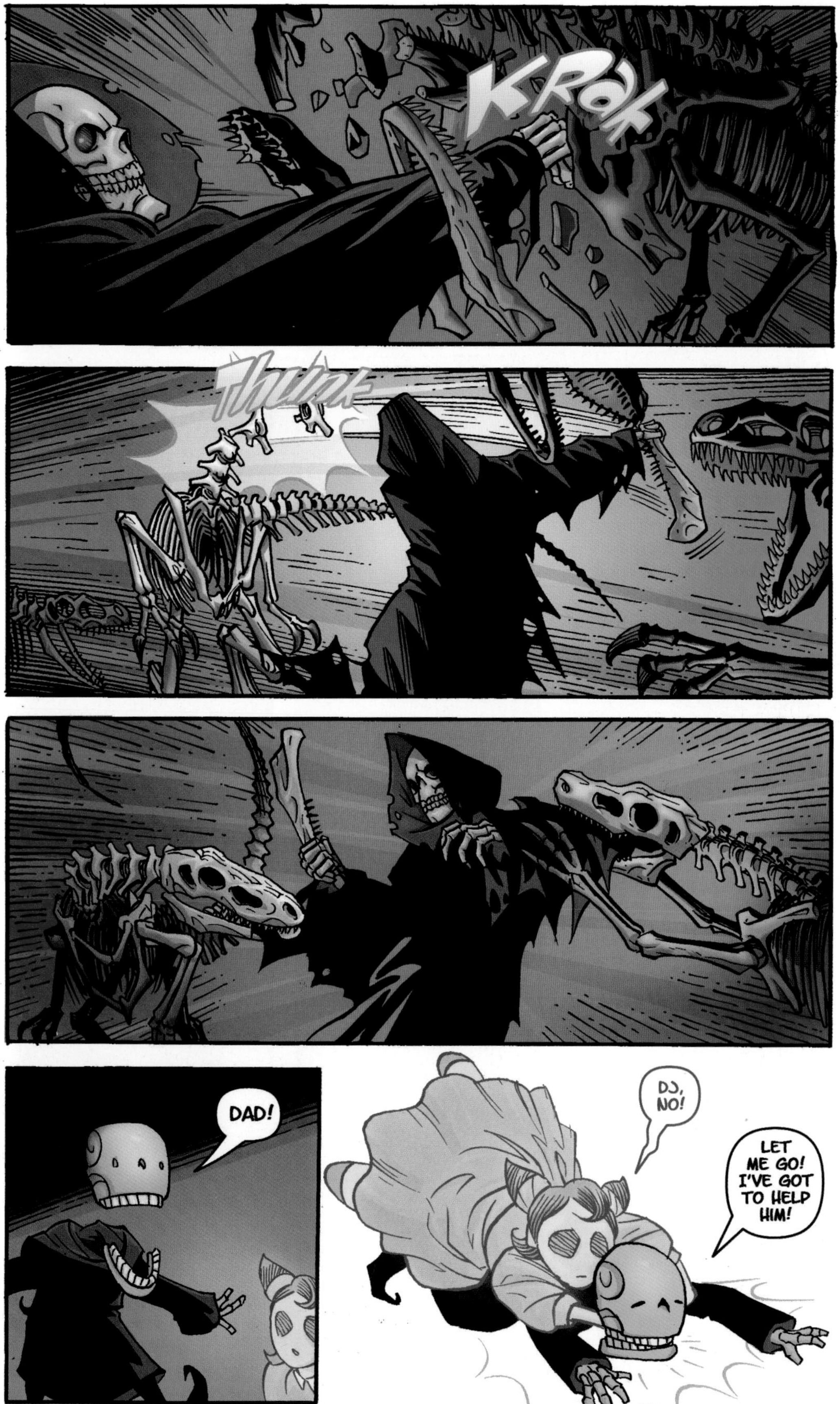
KRAK
THUNK
DAD!
DJ, NO!
LET ME GO! I'VE GOT TO HELP HIM!

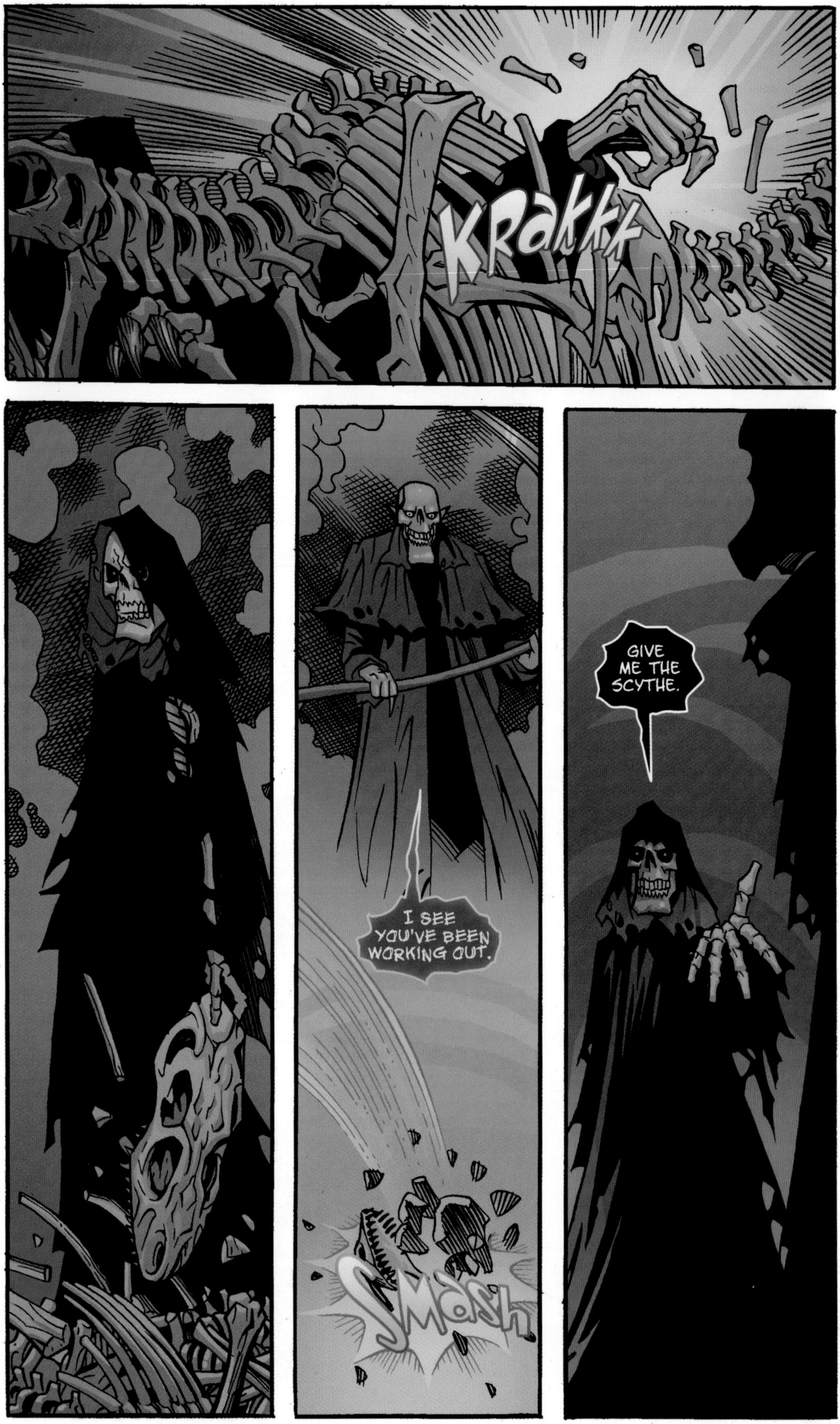
KRAKKK
I SEE YOU'VE BEEN WORKING OUT.
SMASH
GIVE ME THE SCYTHE.

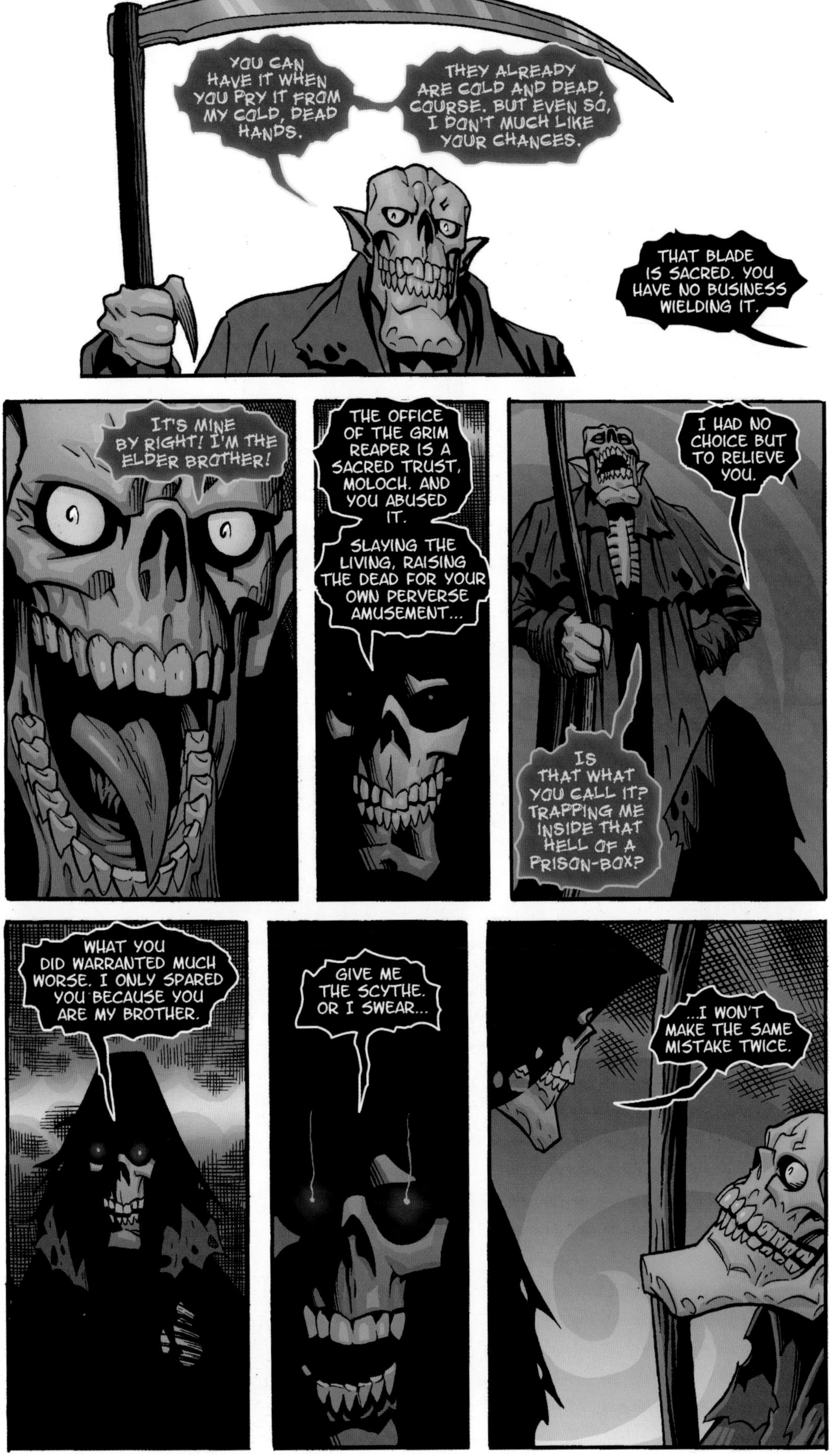

YOU CAN HAVE IT WHEN YOU PRY IT FROM MY COLD, DEAD HANDS.
THEY ALREADY ARE COLD AND DEAD, COURSE. BUT EVEN SO, I DON'T MUCH LIKE YOUR CHANCES.
THAT BLADE IS SACRED. YOU HAVE NO BUSINESS WIELDING IT.
IT'S MINE BY RIGHT! I'M THE ELDER BROTHER!
THE OFFICE OF THE GRIM REAPER IS A SACRED TRUST, MOLOCH. AND YOU ABUSED IT.
SLAYING THE LIVING, RAISING THE DEAD FOR YOUR OWN PERVERSE AMUSEMENT...
I HAD NO CHOICE BUT TO RELIEVE YOU.
IS THAT WHAT YOU CALL IT? TRAPPING ME INSIDE THAT HELL OF A PRISON-BOX?
WHAT YOU DID WARRANTED MUCH WORSE. I ONLY SPARED YOU BECAUSE YOU ARE MY BROTHER.
GIVE ME THE SCYTHE. OR I SWEAR...
...I WON'T MAKE THE SAME MISTAKE TWICE.

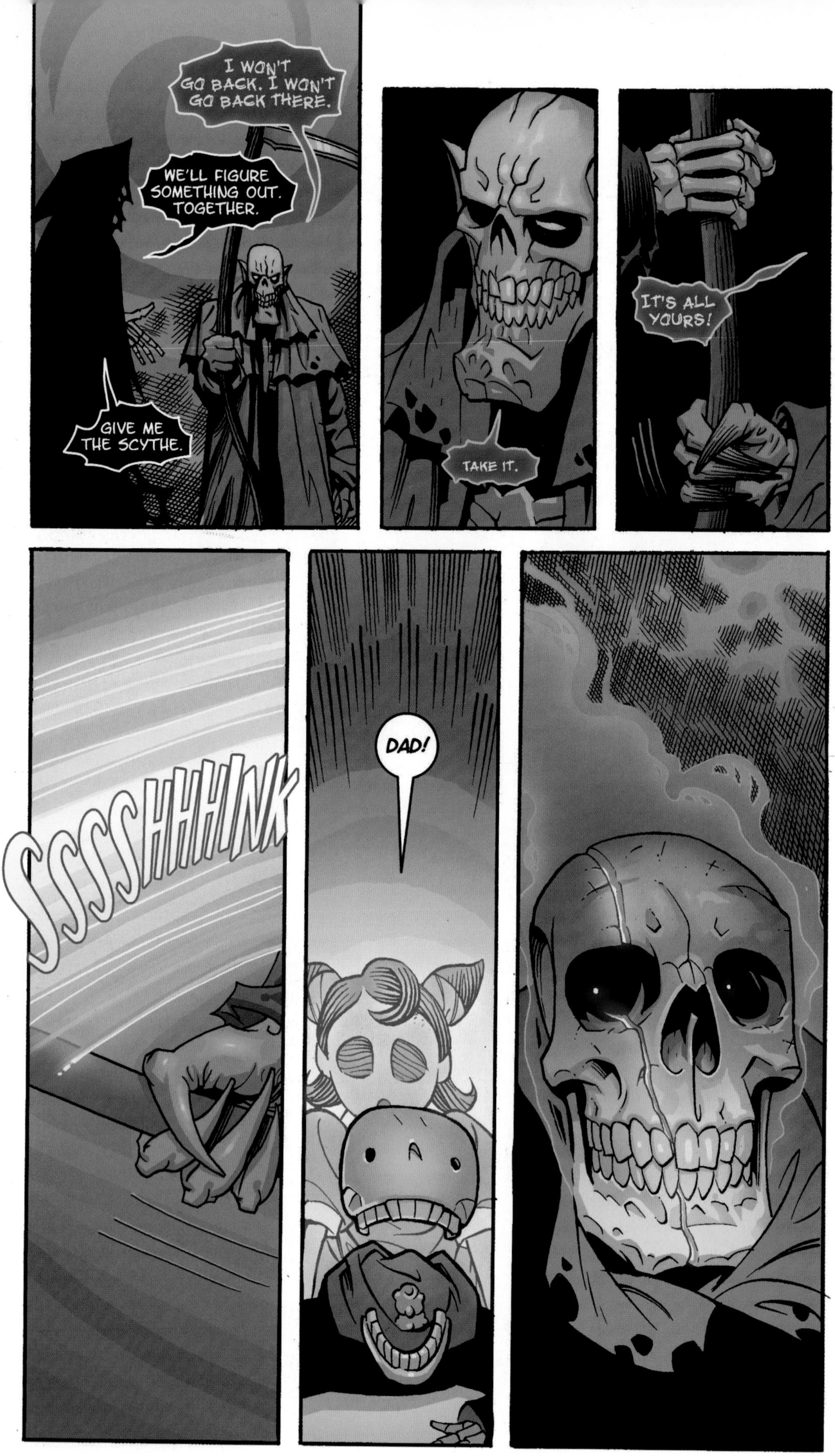
I WON'T GO BACK. I WON'T GO BACK THERE.
WE'LL FIGURE SOMETHING OUT. TOGETHER.
GIVE ME THE SCYTHE.
TAKE IT.
IT'S ALL YOURS!
SSSSHHHINK
DAD!

YOU ALWAYS WERE TOO TRUSTING.

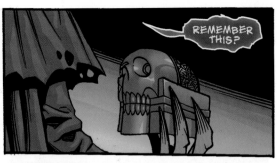

REMEMBER THIS?

YOU'RE ABOUT TO GET TO KNOW IT A WHOLE LOT BETTER.

MOLOCH... DON'T DO THIS.

DO GIVE MY REGARDS TO THE ECHOING NOTHINGNESS, WON'T YOU?

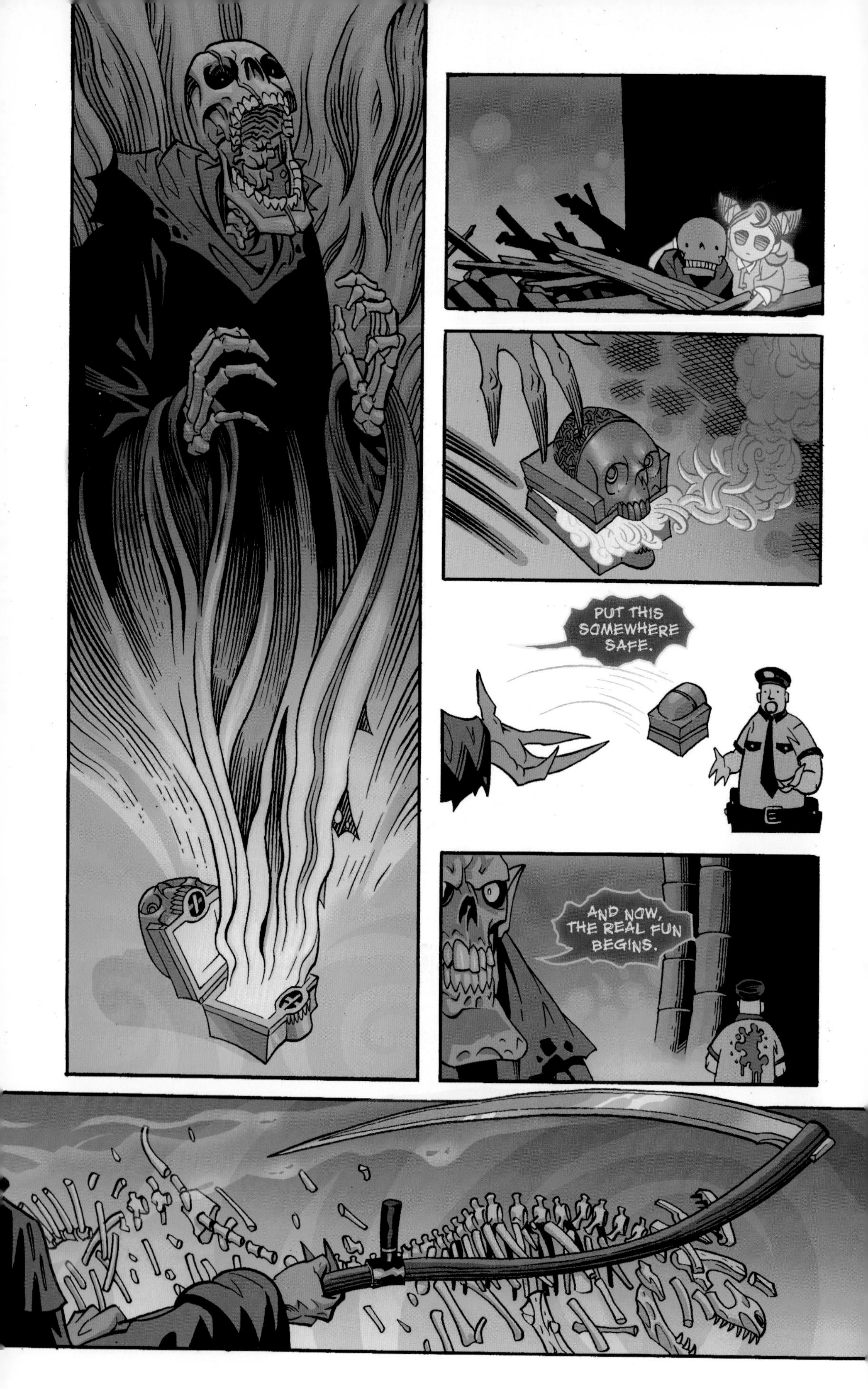
PUT THIS SOMEWHERE SAFE.
AND NOW, THE REAL FUN BEGINS.

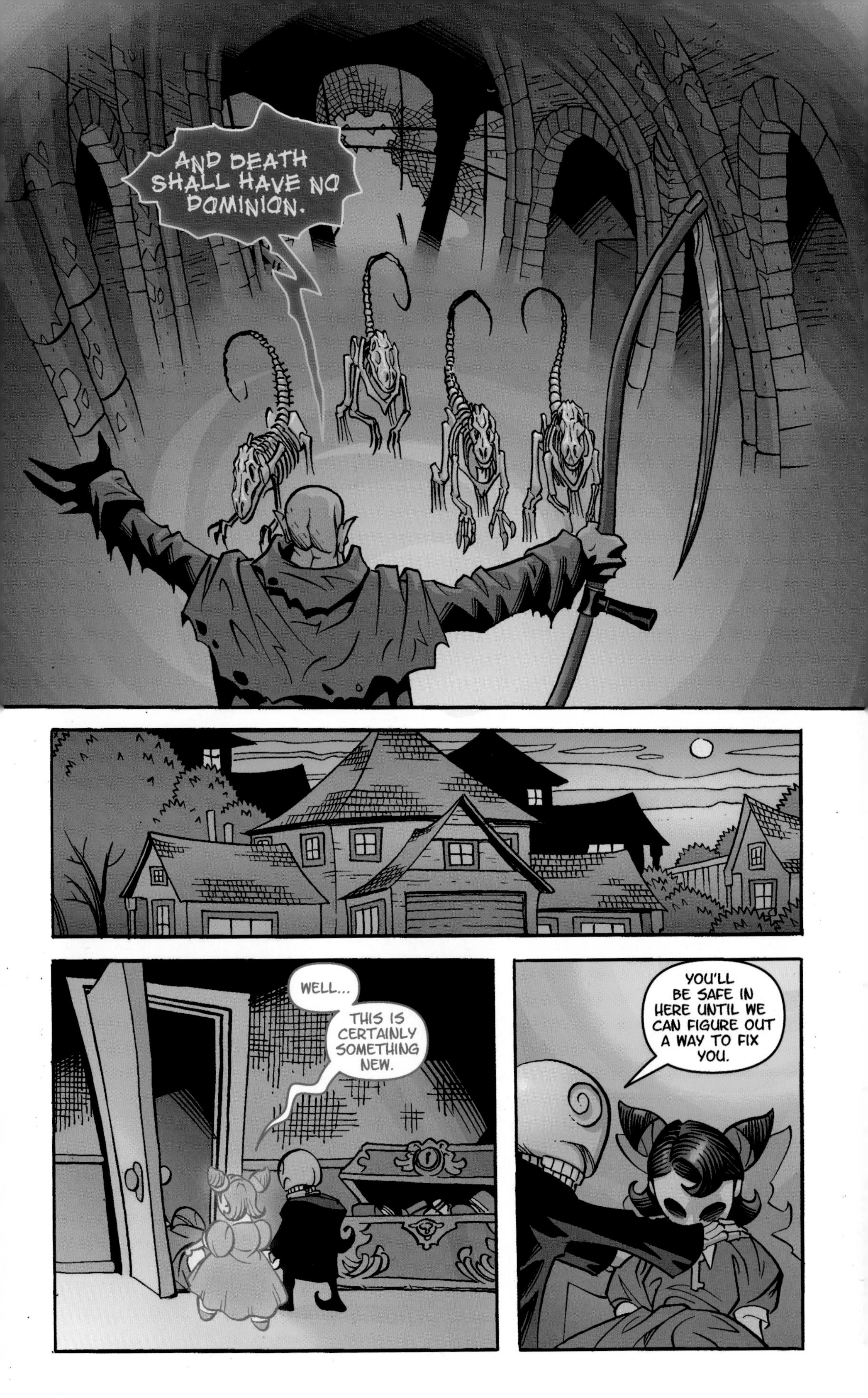
AND DEATH SHALL HAVE NO DOMINION.
WELL...
THIS IS CERTAINLY SOMETHING NEW.
YOU'LL BE SAFE IN HERE UNTIL WE CAN FIGURE OUT A WAY TO FIX YOU.

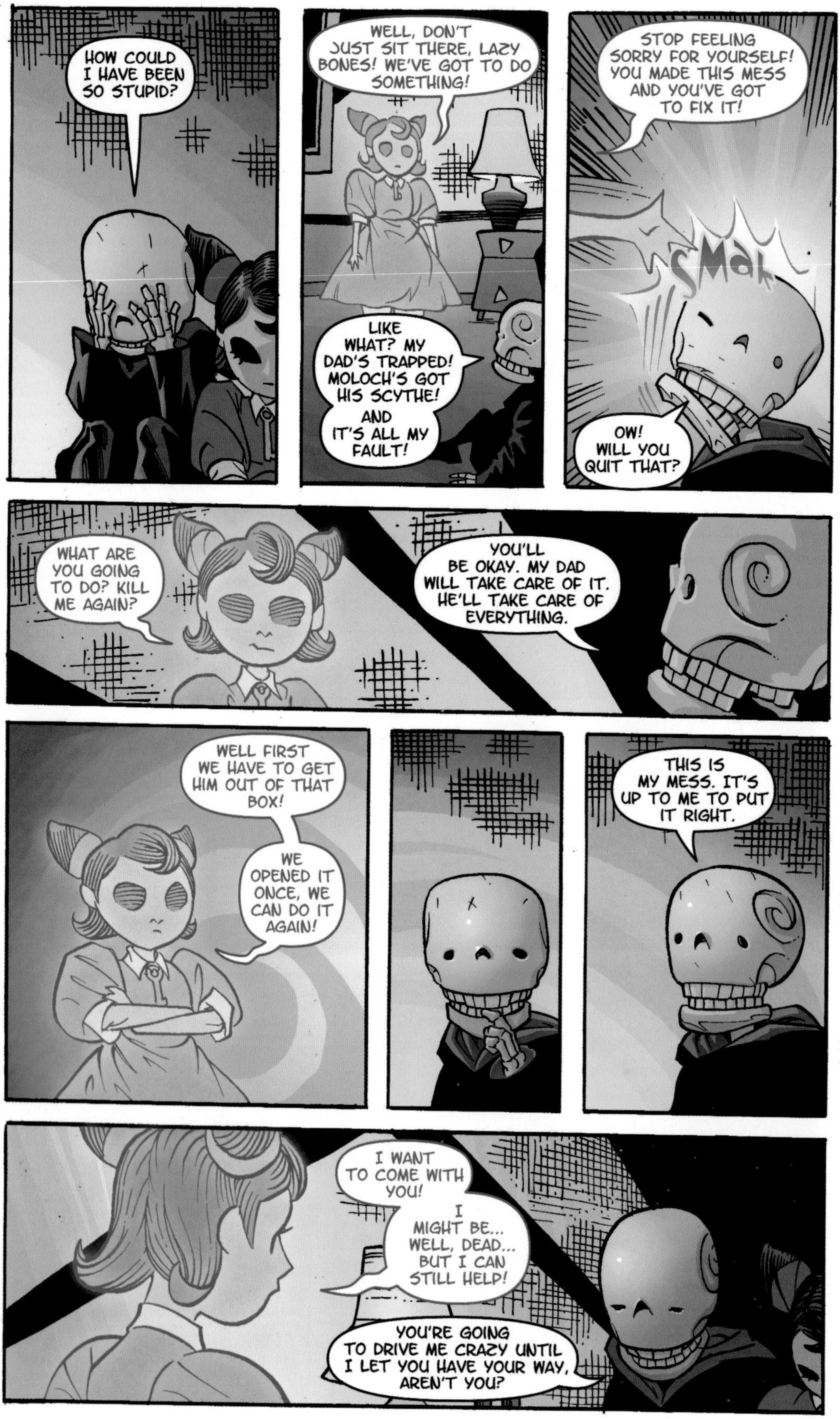
HOW COULD I HAVE BEEN SO STUPID?
WELL, DON'T JUST SIT THERE, LAZY BONES! WE'VE GOT TO DO SOMETHING!
LIKE WHAT? MY DAD'S TRAPPED! MOLOCH'S GOT HIS SCYTHE!
AND IT'S ALL MY FAULT!
STOP FEELING SORRY FOR YOURSELF! YOU MADE THIS MESS AND YOU'VE GOT TO FIX IT!
SMAK
OW! WILL YOU QUIT THAT?
WHAT ARE YOU GOING TO DO? KILL ME AGAIN?
YOU'LL BE OKAY. MY DAD WILL TAKE CARE OF IT. HE'LL TAKE CARE OF EVERYTHING.
WELL FIRST WE HAVE TO GET HIM OUT OF THAT BOX!
WE OPENED IT ONCE, WE CAN DO IT AGAIN!
THIS IS MY MESS. IT'S UP TO ME TO PUT IT RIGHT.
I WANT TO COME WITH YOU!
I MIGHT BE... WELL, DEAD... BUT I CAN STILL HELP!
YOU'RE GOING TO DRIVE ME CRAZY UNTIL I LET YOU HAVE YOUR WAY, AREN'T YOU?

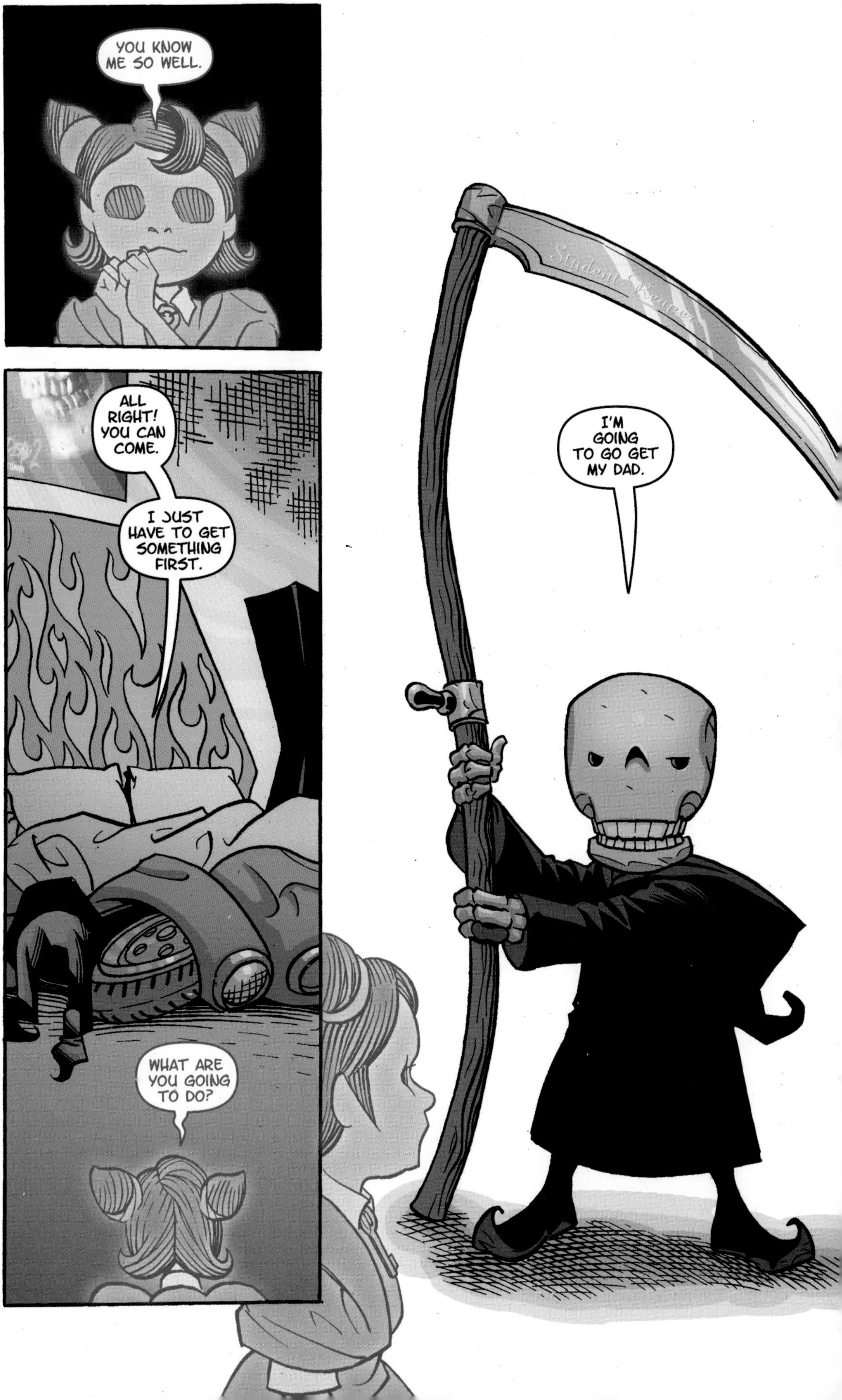
YOU KNOW ME SO WELL.
ALL RIGHT! YOU CAN COME.
I JUST HAVE TO GET SOMETHING FIRST.
WHAT ARE YOU GOING TO DO?
I'M GOING TO GO GET MY DAD.
Student Reaper

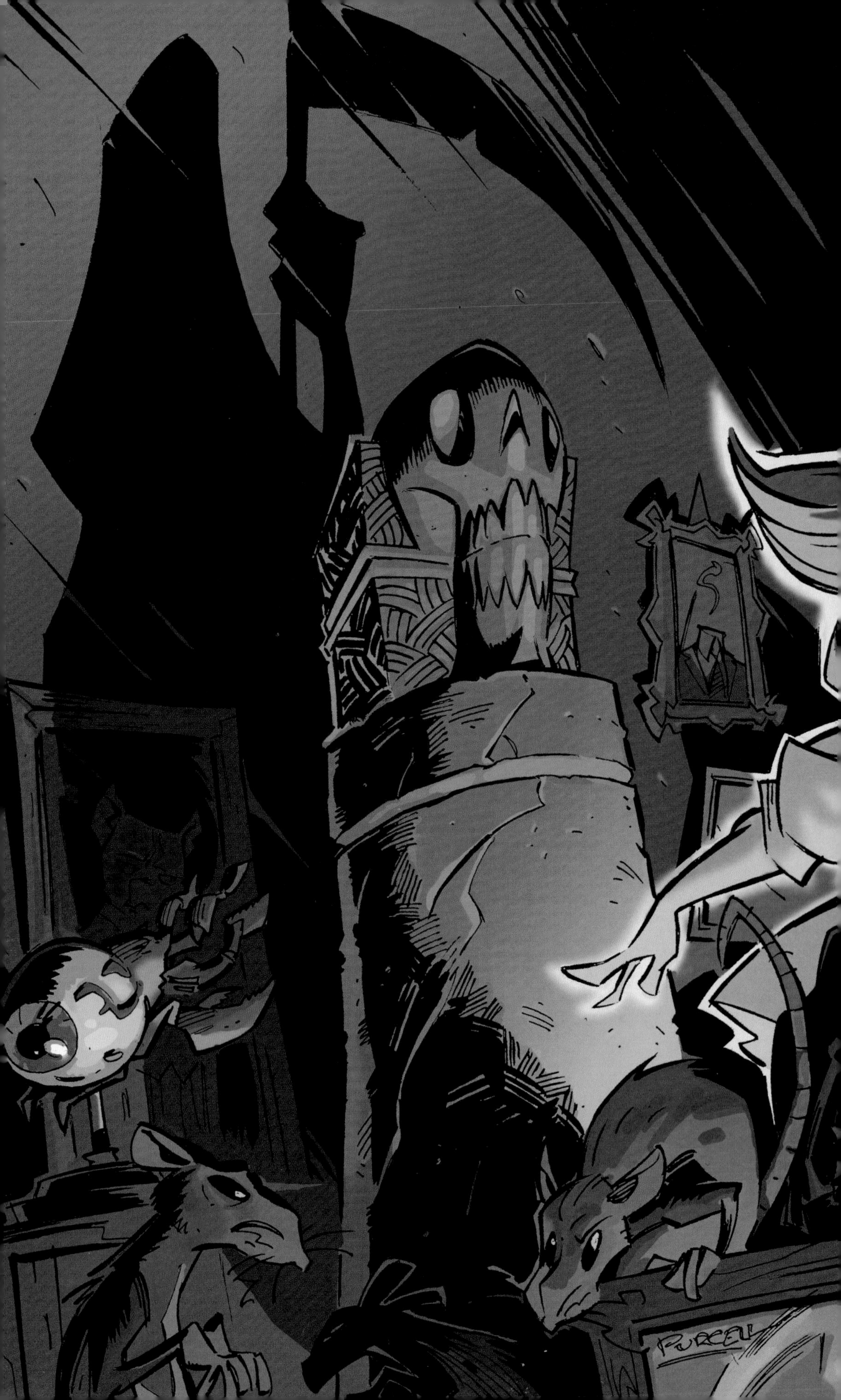
PURCELL

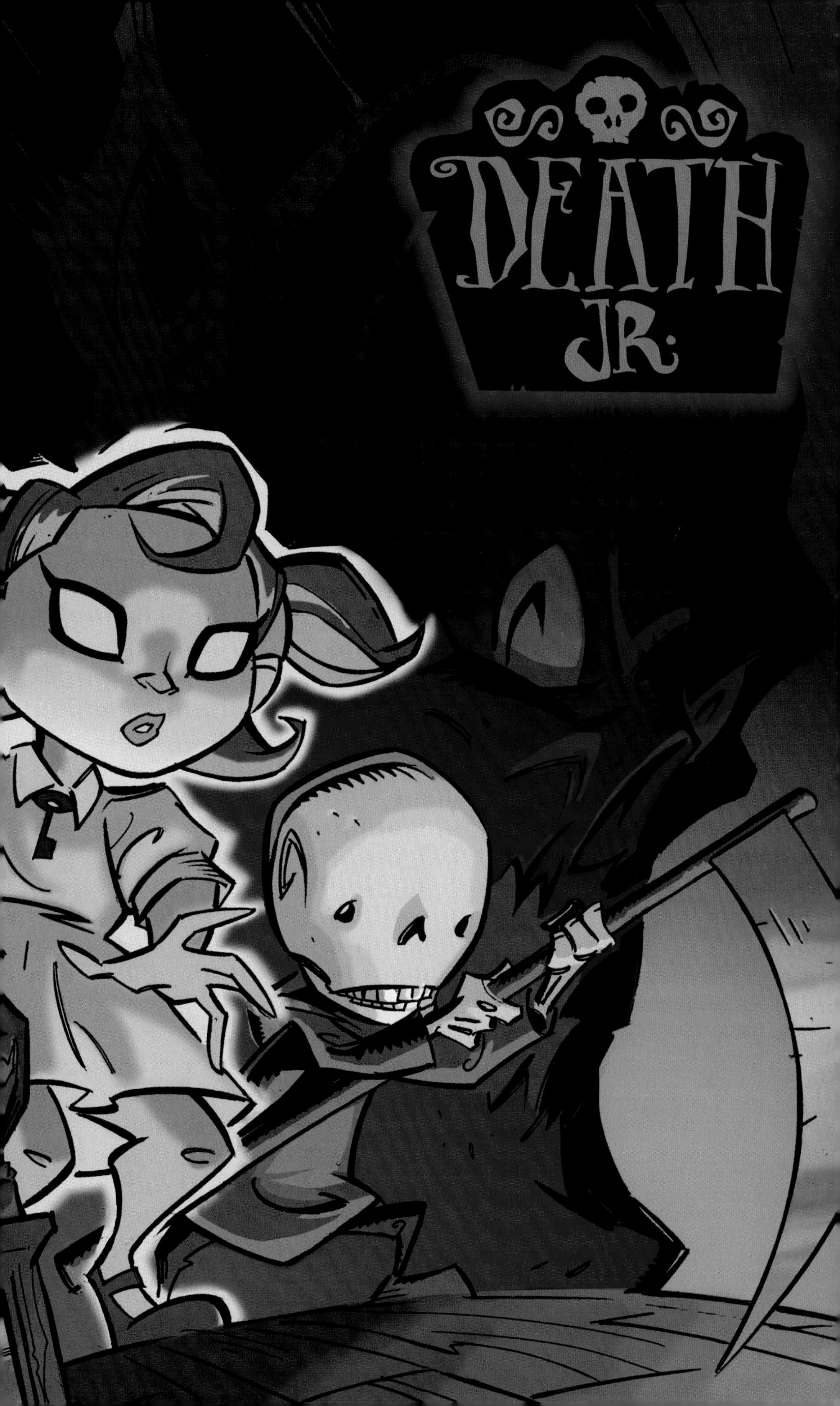
DEATH
JR.

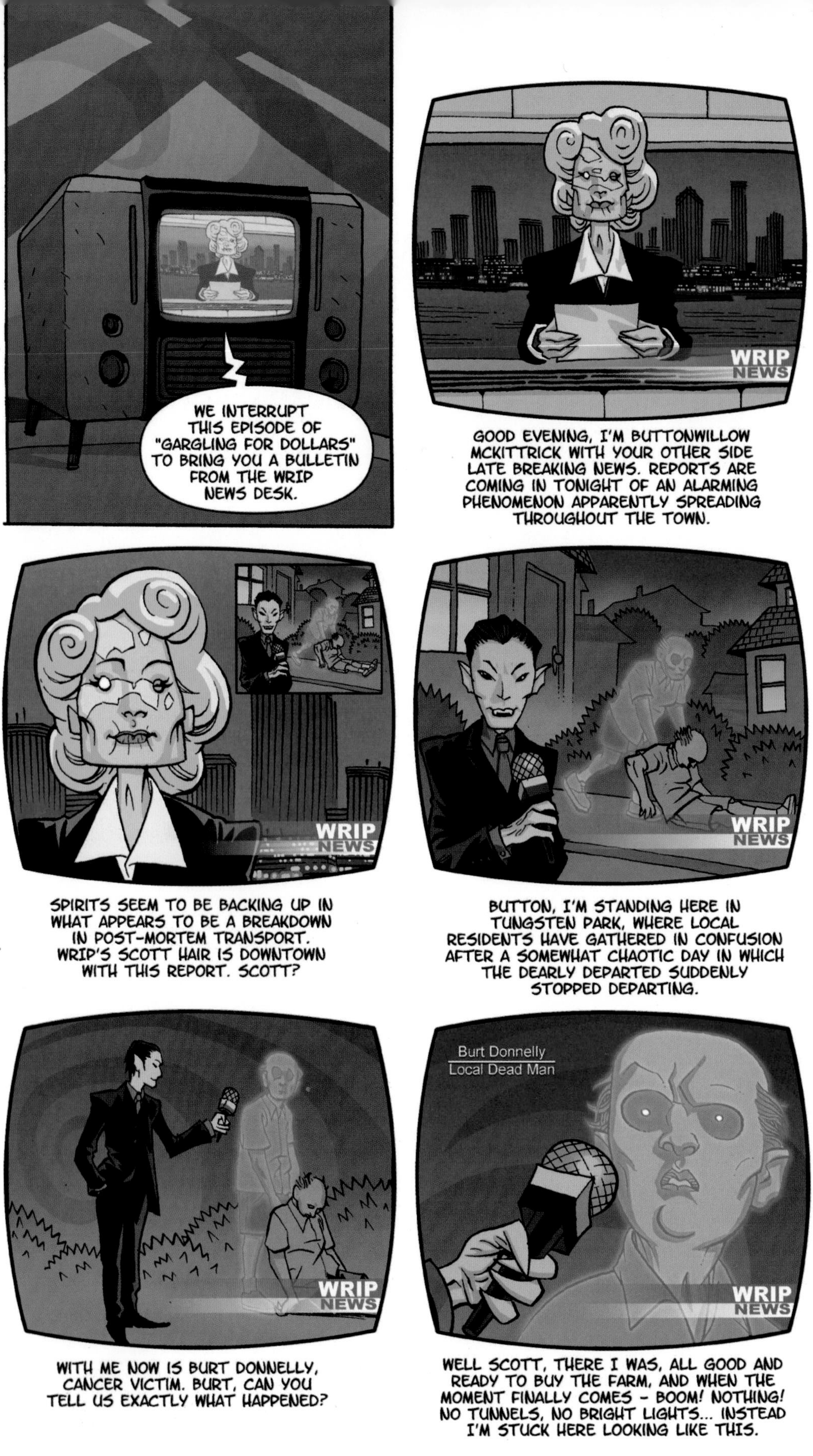
WE INTERRUPT THIS EPISODE OF "GARGLING FOR DOLLARS" TO BRING YOU A BULLETIN FROM THE WRIP NEWS DESK.
WRIP NEWS
GOOD EVENING, I'M BUTTONWILLOW MCKITTRICK WITH YOUR OTHER SIDE LATE BREAKING NEWS. REPORTS ARE COMING IN TONIGHT OF AN ALARMING PHENOMENON APPARENTLY SPREADING THROUGHOUT THE TOWN.
WRIP NEWS
SPIRITS SEEM TO BE BACKING UP IN WHAT APPEARS TO BE A BREAKDOWN IN POST-MORTEM TRANSPORT. WRIP'S SCOTT HAIR IS DOWNTOWN WITH THIS REPORT. SCOTT?
WRIP NEWS
BUTTON, I'M STANDING HERE IN TUNGSTEN PARK, WHERE LOCAL RESIDENTS HAVE GATHERED IN CONFUSION AFTER A SOMEWHAT CHAOTIC DAY IN WHICH THE DEARLY DEPARTED SUDDENLY STOPPED DEPARTING.
WRIP NEWS
WITH ME NOW IS BURT DONNELLY, CANCER VICTIM. BURT, CAN YOU TELL US EXACTLY WHAT HAPPENED?
Burt Donnelly
Local Dead Man
WRIP NEWS
WELL SCOTT, THERE I WAS, ALL GOOD AND READY TO BUY THE FARM, AND WHEN THE MOMENT FINALLY COMES - BOOM! NOTHING! NO TUNNELS, NO BRIGHT LIGHTS... INSTEAD I'M STUCK HERE LOOKING LIKE THIS.

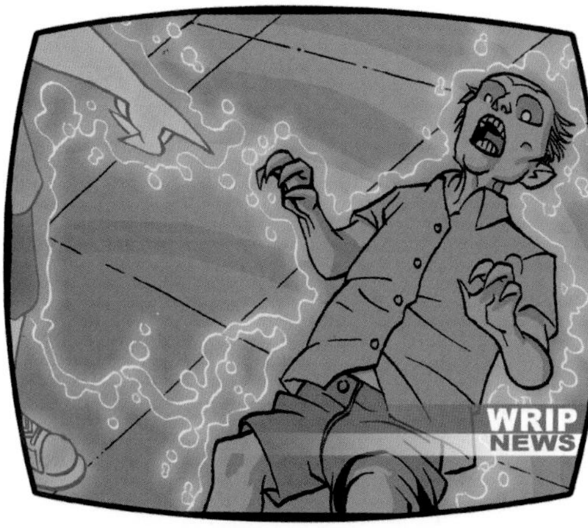
WRIP
NEWS

AND WHAT'S WORSE, I'M STILL STUCK WITH MY OLD BODY HERE, I'M HAVING TO CART THIS THING AROUND WITH ME ALL DAY. NO OFFENSE TO MYSELF, BUT THE OLD SHELL'S STARTING TO SMELL NOT SO GOOD.

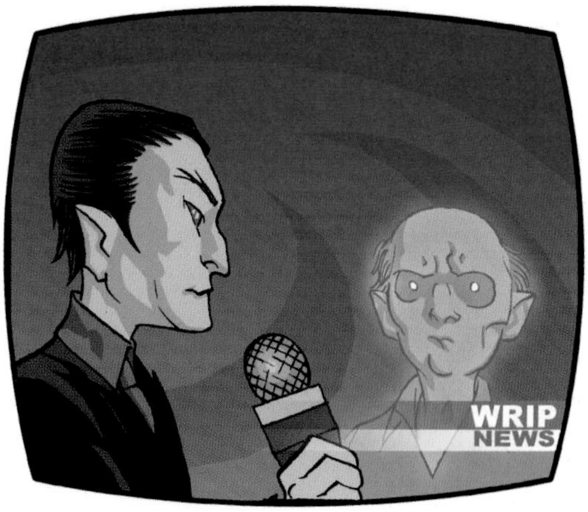
WRIP
NEWS

I SEE. SO YOU'D SAY YOU'RE "DYING TO DIE," IS THAT RIGHT, BURT?

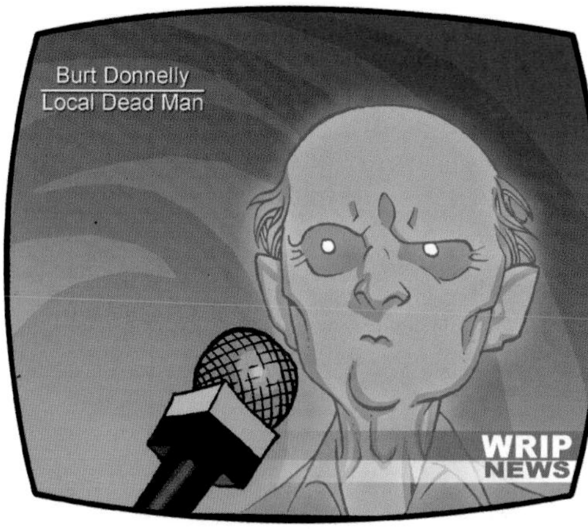
Burt Donnelly
Local Dead Man
WRIP
NEWS

...

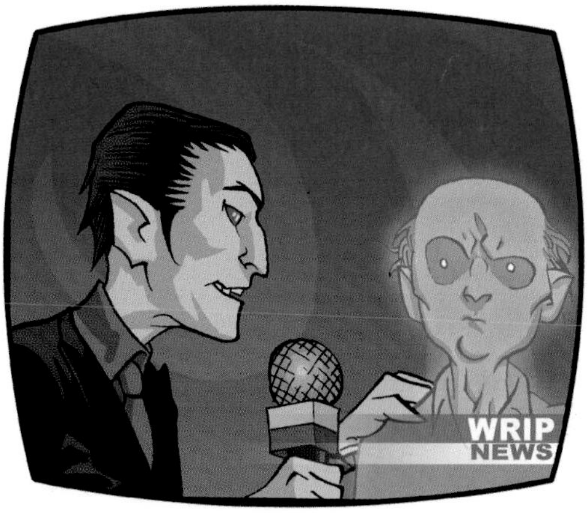
WRIP
NEWS

AND WHAT DO YOU THINK COULD BE THE CAUSE OF ALL THIS?

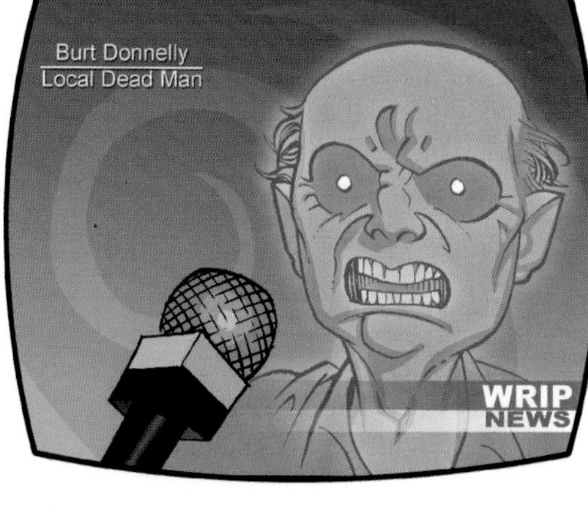
Burt Donnelly
Local Dead Man
WRIP
NEWS

ISN'T IT OBVIOUS?
VIOLENCE IN VIDEOGAMES.

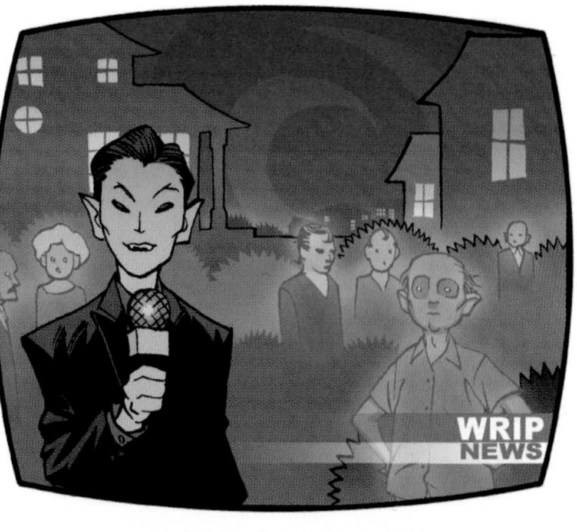
WRIP
NEWS

WELL BUTTON, BURT HERE ISN'T THE ONLY PERSON TO HAVE BEEN INCONVENIENCED BY THIS UNPRECEDENTED BREAKDOWN IN WHAT MANY TAKE FOR GRANTED AS A BASIC PUBLIC SERVICE.

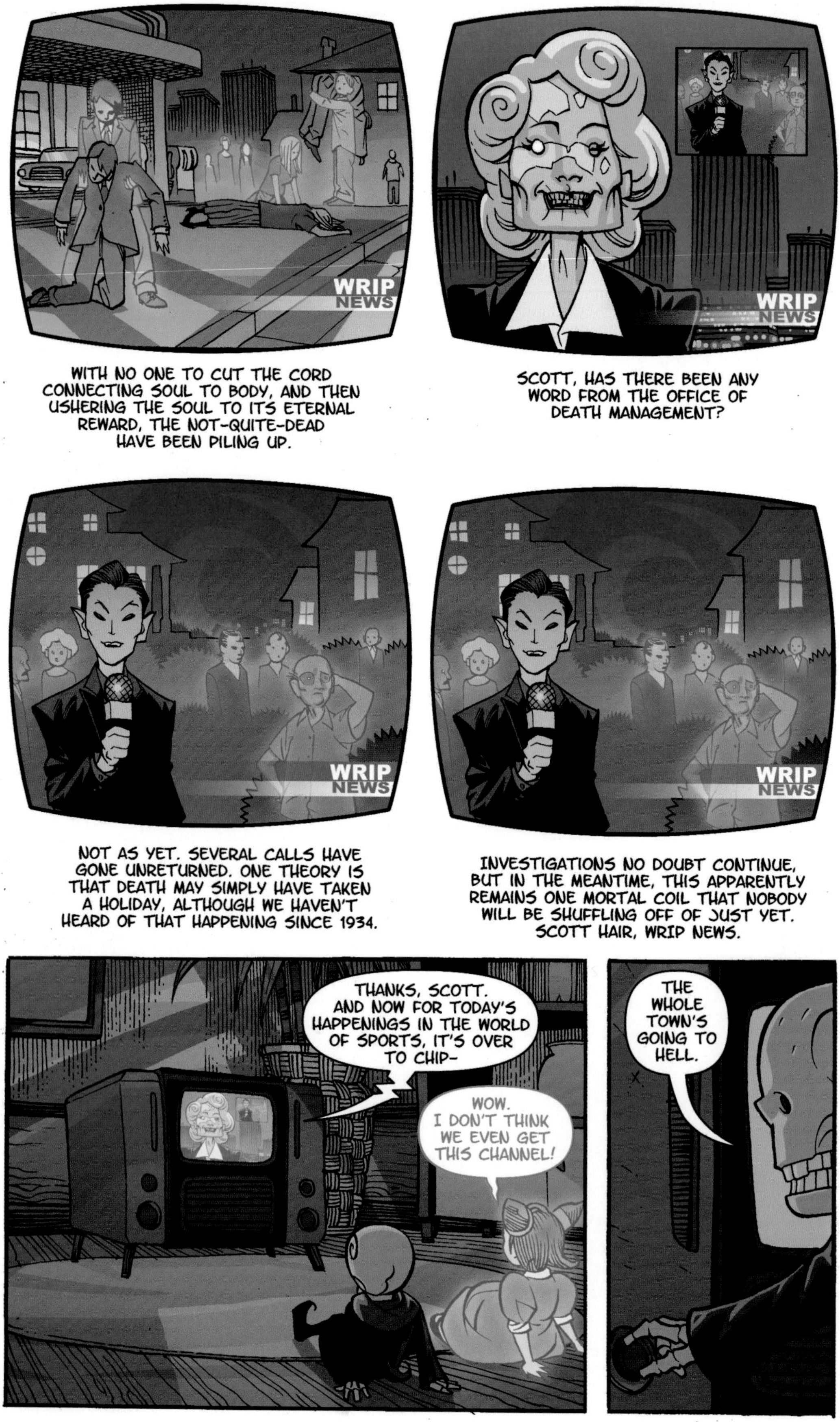
WRIP NEWS
WITH NO ONE TO CUT THE CORD CONNECTING SOUL TO BODY, AND THEN USHERING THE SOUL TO ITS ETERNAL REWARD, THE NOT-QUITE-DEAD HAVE BEEN PILING UP.
WRIP NEWS
SCOTT, HAS THERE BEEN ANY WORD FROM THE OFFICE OF DEATH MANAGEMENT?
WRIP NEWS
NOT AS YET. SEVERAL CALLS HAVE GONE UNRETURNED. ONE THEORY IS THAT DEATH MAY SIMPLY HAVE TAKEN A HOLIDAY, ALTHOUGH WE HAVEN'T HEARD OF THAT HAPPENING SINCE 1934.
WRIP NEWS
INVESTIGATIONS NO DOUBT CONTINUE, BUT IN THE MEANTIME, THIS APPARENTLY REMAINS ONE MORTAL COIL THAT NOBODY WILL BE SHUFFLING OFF OF JUST YET. SCOTT HAIR, WRIP NEWS.
THANKS, SCOTT. AND NOW FOR TODAY'S HAPPENINGS IN THE WORLD OF SPORTS, IT'S OVER TO CHIP-
WOW. I DON'T THINK WE EVEN GET THIS CHANNEL!
THE WHOLE TOWN'S GOING TO HELL.

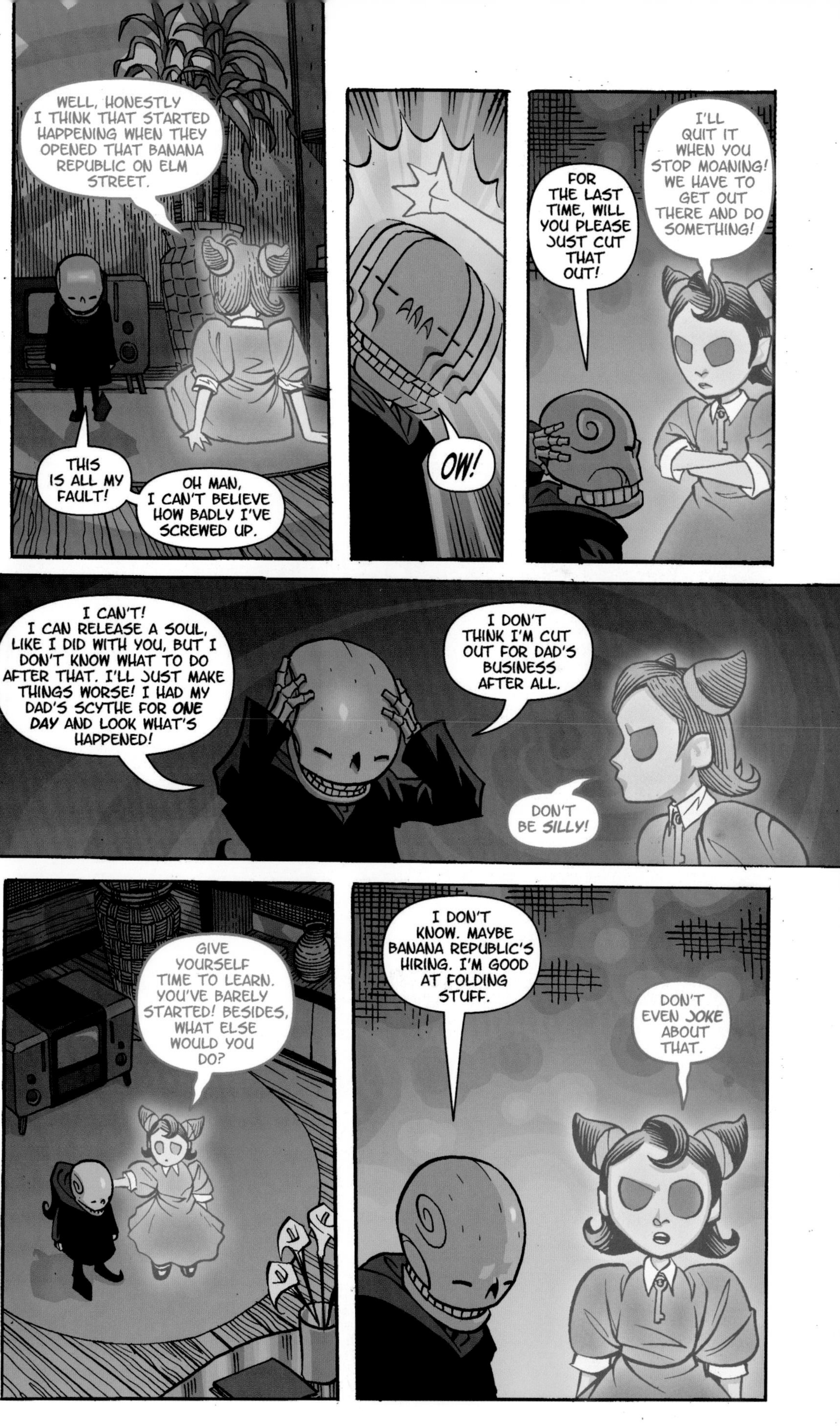
WELL, HONESTLY I THINK THAT STARTED HAPPENING WHEN THEY OPENED THAT BANANA REPUBLIC ON ELM STREET.
THIS IS ALL MY FAULT!
OH MAN, I CAN'T BELIEVE HOW BADLY I'VE SCREWED UP.
OW!
FOR THE LAST TIME, WILL YOU PLEASE JUST CUT THAT OUT!
I'LL QUIT IT WHEN YOU STOP MOANING! WE HAVE TO GET OUT THERE AND DO SOMETHING!
I CAN'T! I CAN RELEASE A SOUL, LIKE I DID WITH YOU, BUT I DON'T KNOW WHAT TO DO AFTER THAT. I'LL JUST MAKE THINGS WORSE! I HAD MY DAD'S SCYTHE FOR ONE DAY AND LOOK WHAT'S HAPPENED!
I DON'T THINK I'M CUT OUT FOR DAD'S BUSINESS AFTER ALL.
DON'T BE SILLY!
GIVE YOURSELF TIME TO LEARN. YOU'VE BARELY STARTED! BESIDES, WHAT ELSE WOULD YOU DO?
I DON'T KNOW. MAYBE BANANA REPUBLIC'S HIRING. I'M GOOD AT FOLDING STUFF.
DON'T EVEN JOKE ABOUT THAT.

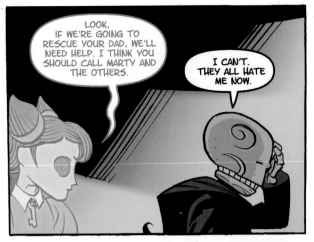

LOOK, IF WE'RE GOING TO RESCUE YOUR DAD, WE'LL NEED HELP. I THINK YOU SHOULD CALL MARTY AND THE OTHERS.

I CAN'T. THEY ALL HATE ME NOW.

THEY DON'T HATE YOU. WELL, NOT MUCH ANYWAY.

TRY APOLOGIZING. IF YOU JUST EXPLAIN WHAT'S HAPPENED, I KNOW THEY'LL HELP.

OH, AND YOU GET TO TELL THEM YOU KILLED ME WHILE YOU WERE ON YOUR LITTLE POWER TRIP WITH THAT STUPID SCYTHE OF YOURS.

TIME

OH GREAT, THEN THEY'LL HATE ME AND BE AFRAID OF ME.

COME ON, D.J. REACH OUT AND TOUCH SOMEONE.

IS EVERYTHING READY?

YES, MASTER.

YOU HAVE DONE WELL, MINION. GIVE YOURSELF A PAT ON THE BACK.

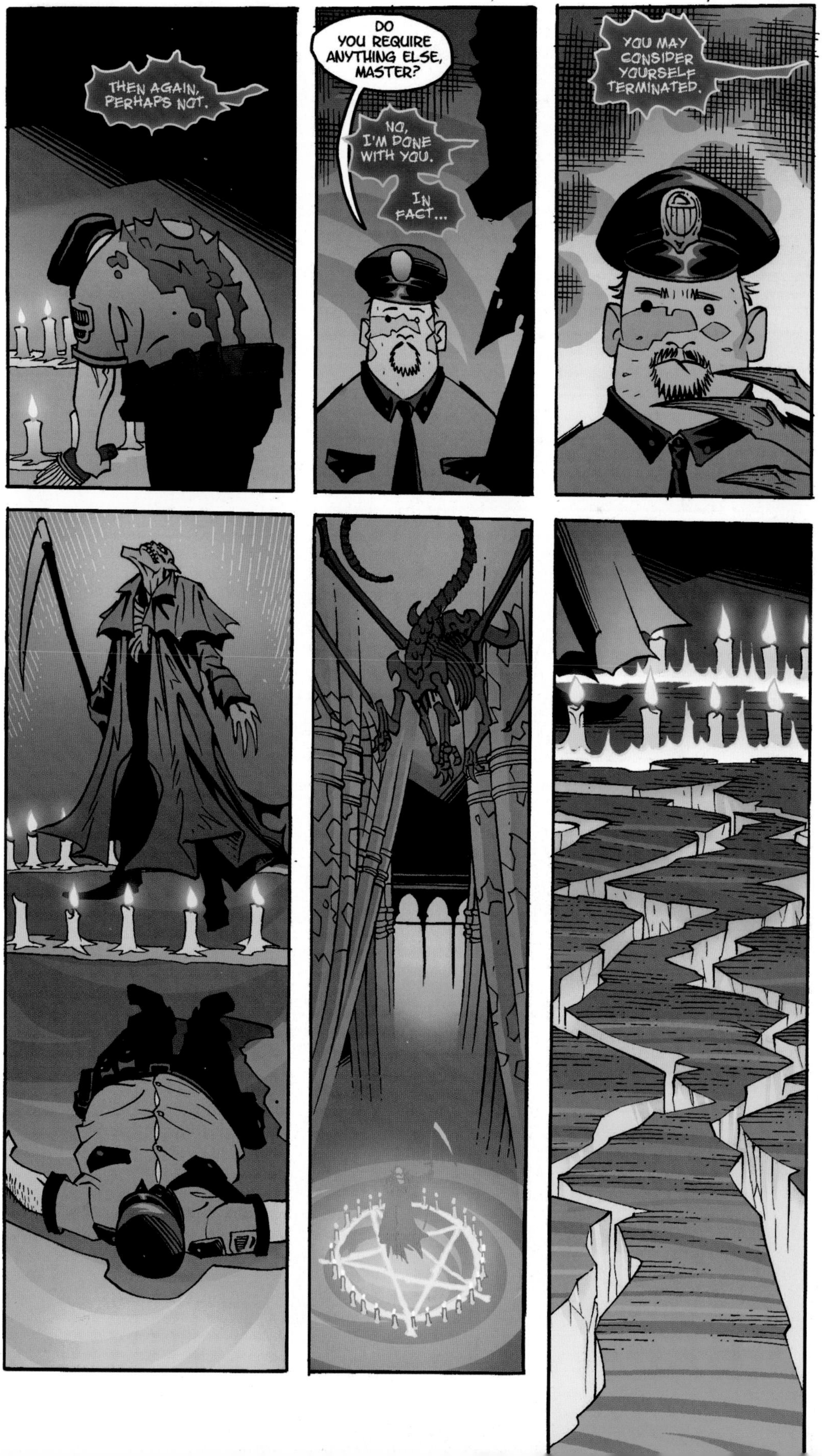
THEN AGAIN, PERHAPS NOT.
DO YOU REQUIRE ANYTHING ELSE, MASTER?
NO, I'M DONE WITH YOU.
IN FACT...
YOU MAY CONSIDER YOURSELF TERMINATED.

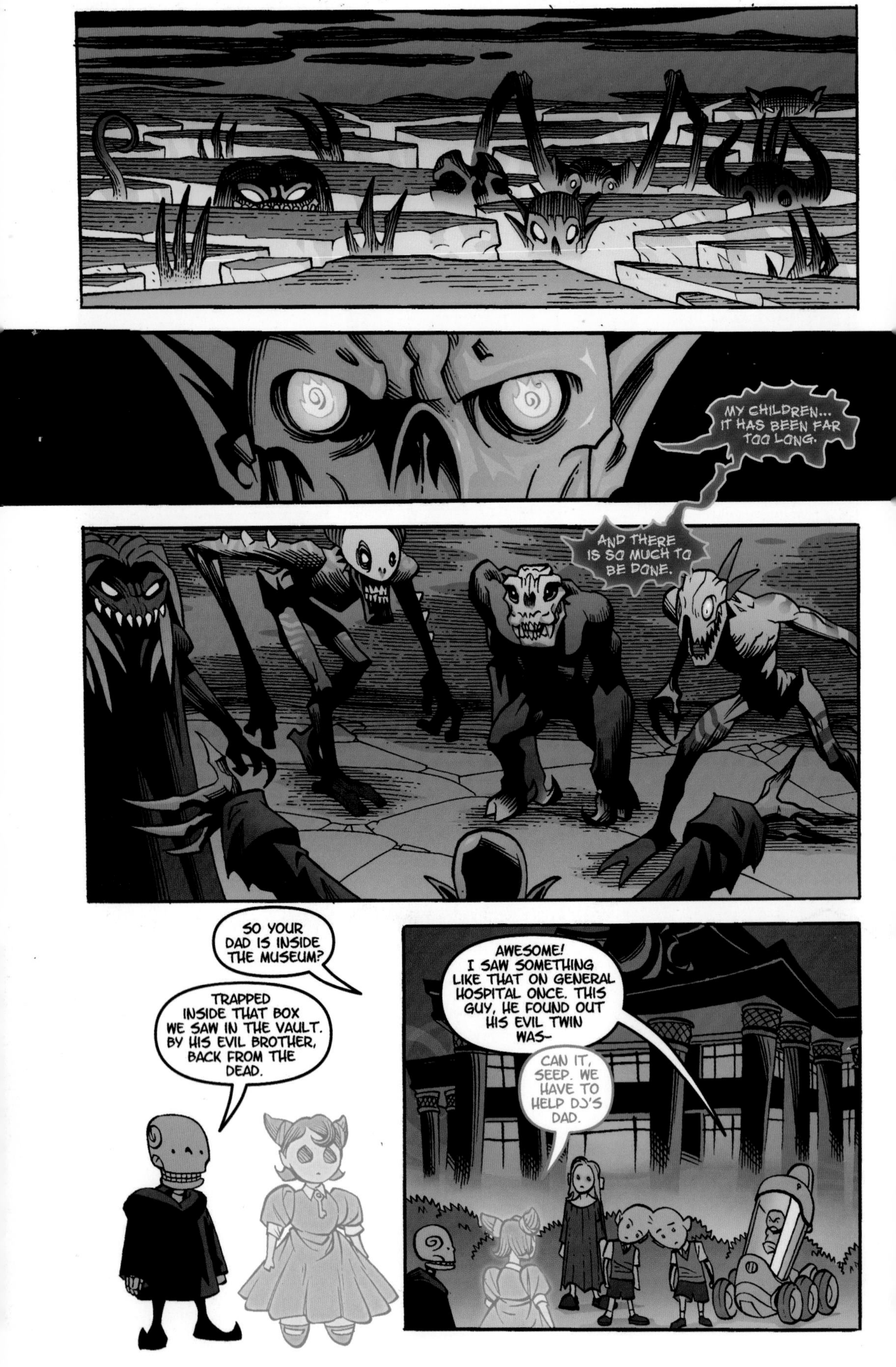
MY CHILDREN... IT HAS BEEN FAR TOO LONG.
AND THERE IS SO MUCH TO BE DONE.
SO YOUR DAD IS INSIDE THE MUSEUM?
TRAPPED INSIDE THAT BOX WE SAW IN THE VAULT. BY HIS EVIL BROTHER, BACK FROM THE DEAD.
AWESOME! I SAW SOMETHING LIKE THAT ON GENERAL HOSPITAL ONCE. THIS GUY, HE FOUND OUT HIS EVIL TWIN WAS-
CAN IT, SEEP. WE HAVE TO HELP DJ'S DAD.

HMMM... IS IT GOING TO INVOLVE ANY HEAVY LIFTING? 'CAUSE THE SEED DOESN'T DO HEAVY LIFTING.

THERE COULD POSSIBLY BE SOME FIGHTING.

ALL RIGHT! NOW YOU'RE TALKING!

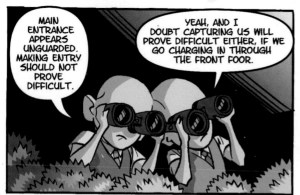

MAIN ENTRANCE APPEARS UNGUARDED. MAKING ENTRY SHOULD NOT PROVE DIFFICULT.

YEAH, AND I DOUBT CAPTURING US WILL PROVE DIFFICULT EITHER, IF WE GO CHARGING IN THROUGH THE FRONT FOOR.

WELL, THERE IS ALWAYS MORE THAN ONE SOLUTION TO ANY PROBLEM.

'ROUND THE BACK?

'ROUND THE BACK.

IT'S LOCKED.

AND THAT'S A PROBLEM HOW?

HMMM... STANDARD DEAD-BOLT. FIVE-PIN TUMBLER. SHOULDN'T BE TOO DIFFICULT.

I JUST NEED SOMETHING I CAN USE AS A TORQUE WRENCH. MARTY, DO YOU HAVE A HAIRPIN?

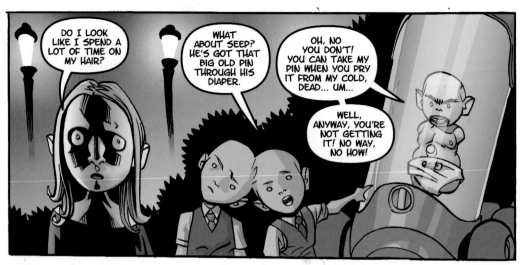

DO I LOOK LIKE I SPEND A LOT OF TIME ON MY HAIR?

WHAT ABOUT SEEP? HE'S GOT THAT BIG OLD PIN THROUGH HIS DIAPER.

OH, NO YOU DON'T! YOU CAN TAKE MY PIN WHEN YOU PRY IT FROM MY COLD, DEAD... UM...

WELL, ANYWAY, YOU'RE NOT GETTING IT! NO WAY, NO HOW!

THIS IS *SO* HUMILIATING.

TRUST ME, SEEP - WE'RE *ALL* SUFFERING IN OUR OWN WAY.

ALMOST THERE... GOT IT!

AM I GOOD, OR AM I GOOD?

ANY OF YOU GUYS EVER READ DANTE? THE DIVINE COMEDY?

I THINK MY DAD'S GOT A COPY IN HIS LIBRARY. WHY?

OH, JUST SOMETHING THAT COMES TO MIND...

"ABANDON HOPE, ALL YE WHO ENTER HERE..."

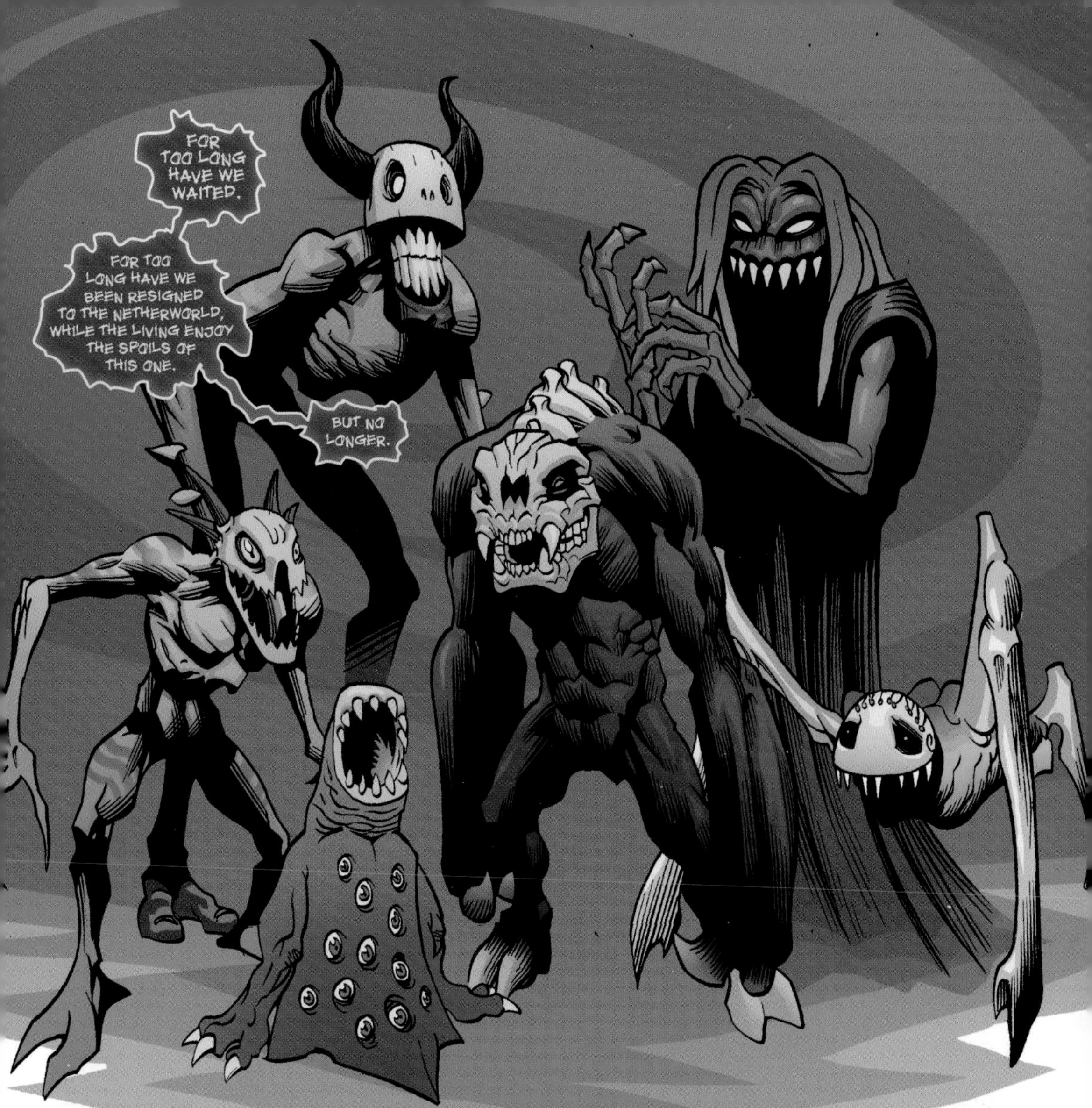
FOR TOO LONG HAVE WE WAITED.
FOR TOO LONG HAVE WE BEEN RESIGNED TO THE NETHERWORLD, WHILE THE LIVING ENJOY THE SPOILS OF THIS ONE.
BUT NO LONGER.

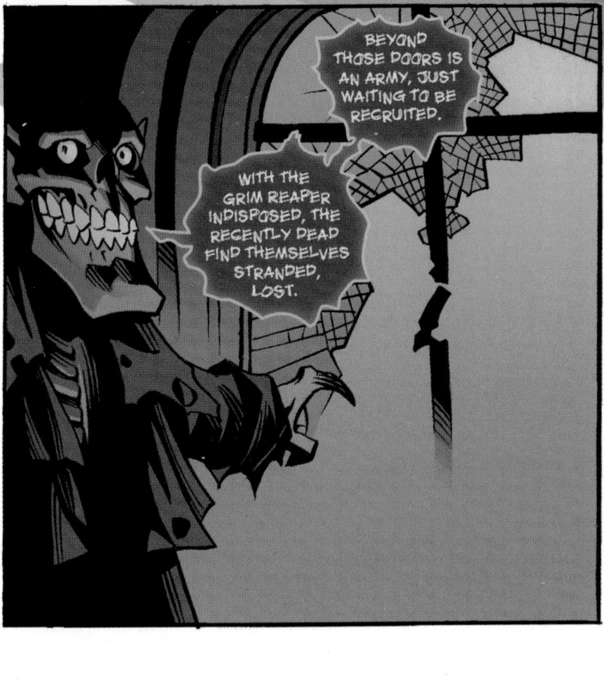
BEYOND THOSE DOORS IS AN ARMY, JUST WAITING TO BE RECRUITED.
WITH THE GRIM REAPER INDISPOSED, THE RECENTLY DEAD FIND THEMSELVES STRANDED, LOST.

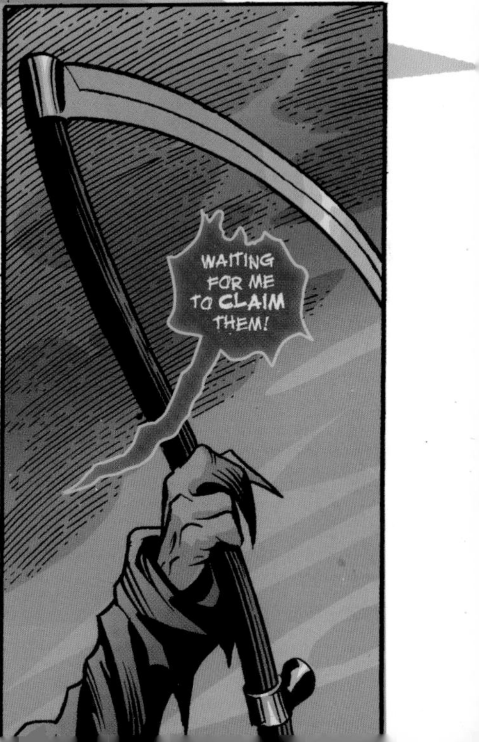
WAITING FOR ME TO **CLAIM** THEM!

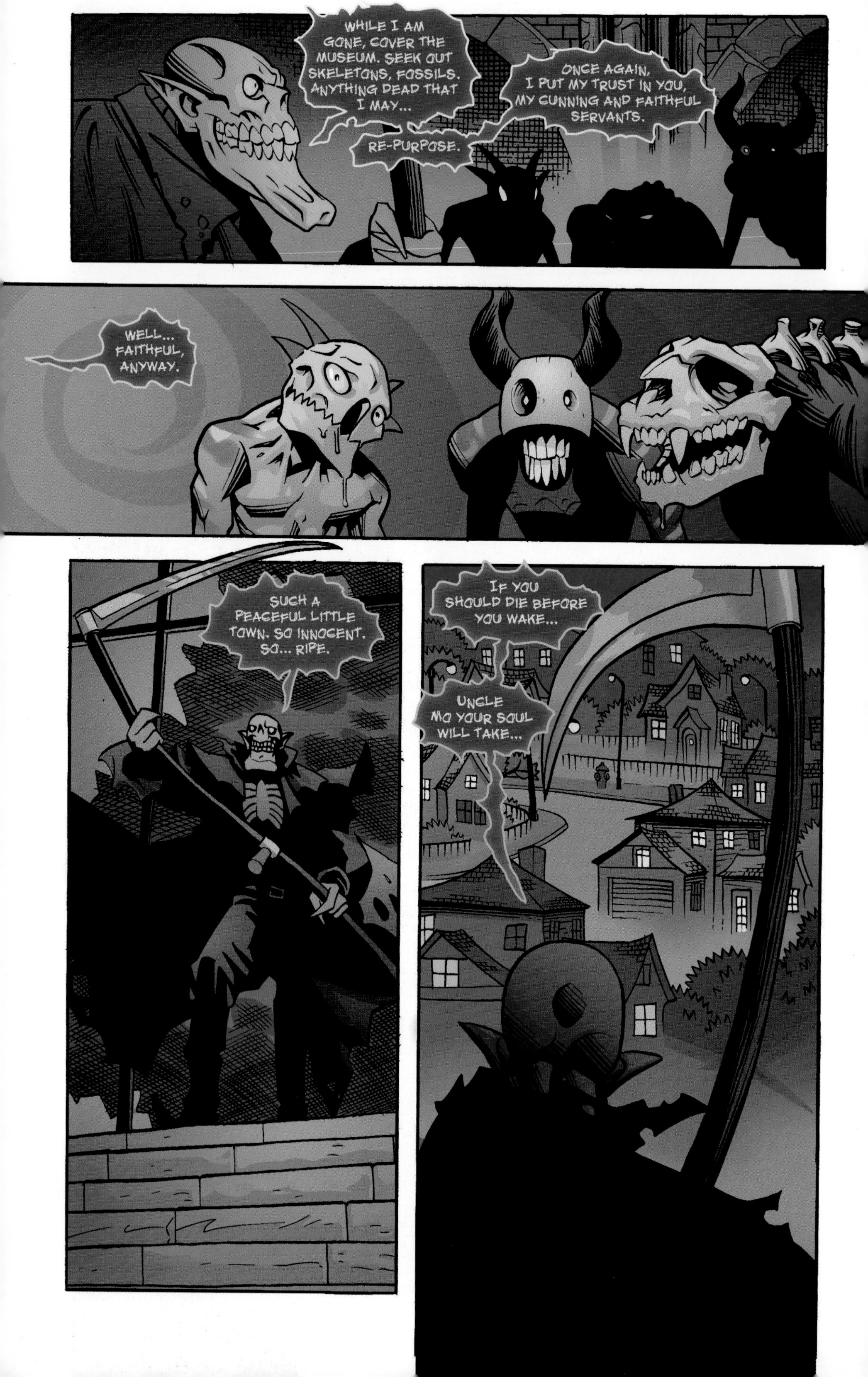
WHILE I AM GONE, COVER THE MUSEUM. SEEK OUT SKELETONS, FOSSILS. ANYTHING DEAD THAT I MAY...
RE-PURPOSE.
ONCE AGAIN, I PUT MY TRUST IN YOU, MY CUNNING AND FAITHFUL SERVANTS.
WELL... FAITHFUL, ANYWAY.
SUCH A PEACEFUL LITTLE TOWN. SO INNOCENT. SO... RIPE.
IF YOU SHOULD DIE BEFORE YOU WAKE...
UNCLE MO YOUR SOUL WILL TAKE...

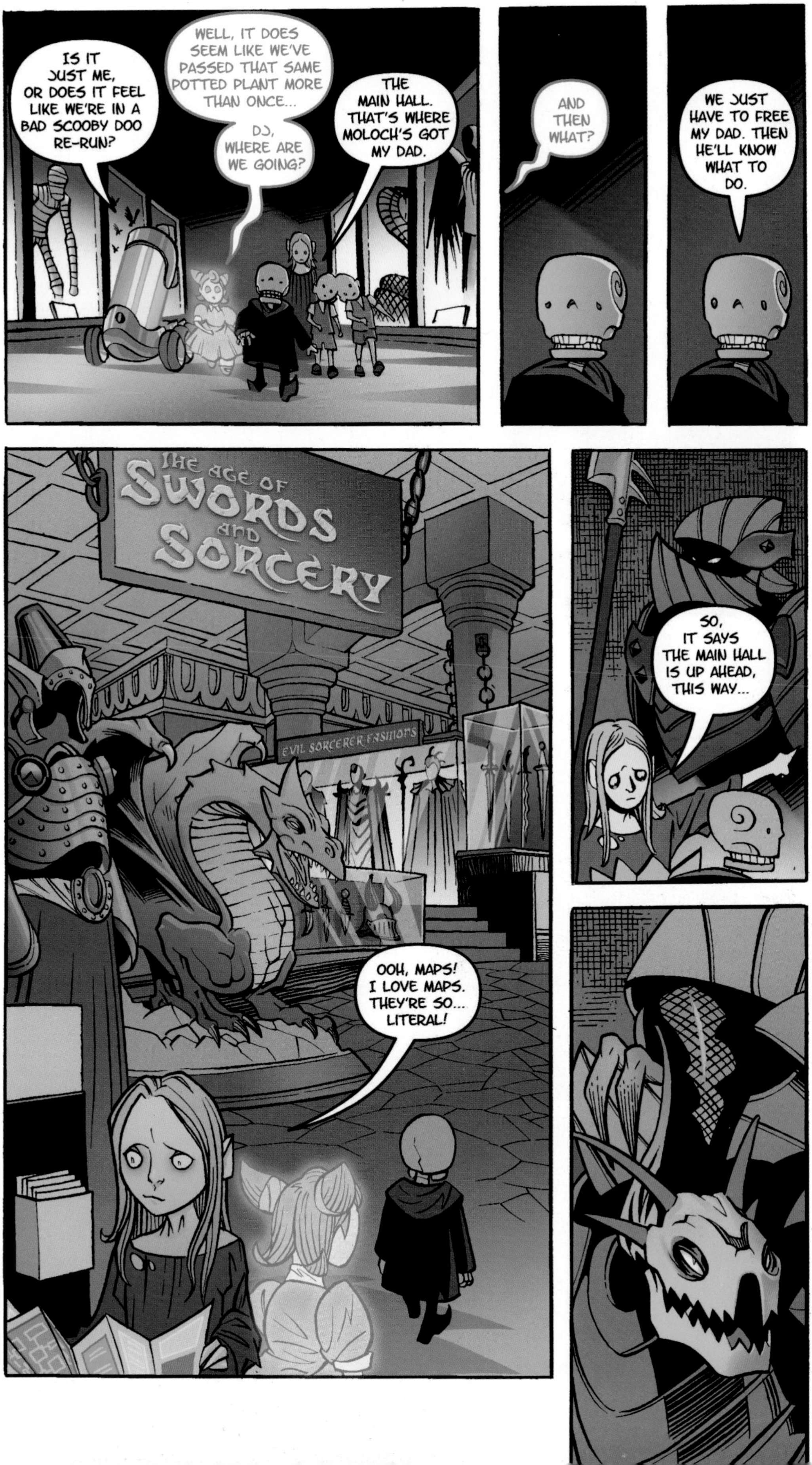
IS IT JUST ME, OR DOES IT FEEL LIKE WE'RE IN A BAD SCOOBY DOO RE-RUN?
WELL, IT DOES SEEM LIKE WE'VE PASSED THAT SAME POTTED PLANT MORE THAN ONCE...
DJ, WHERE ARE WE GOING?
THE MAIN HALL. THAT'S WHERE MOLOCH'S GOT MY DAD.
AND THEN WHAT?
WE JUST HAVE TO FREE MY DAD. THEN HE'LL KNOW WHAT TO DO.
THE AGE OF SWORDS AND SORCERY
EVIL SORCERER FASHIONS
OOH, MAPS! I LOVE MAPS. THEY'RE SO... LITERAL!
SO, IT SAYS THE MAIN HALL IS UP AHEAD, THIS WAY...

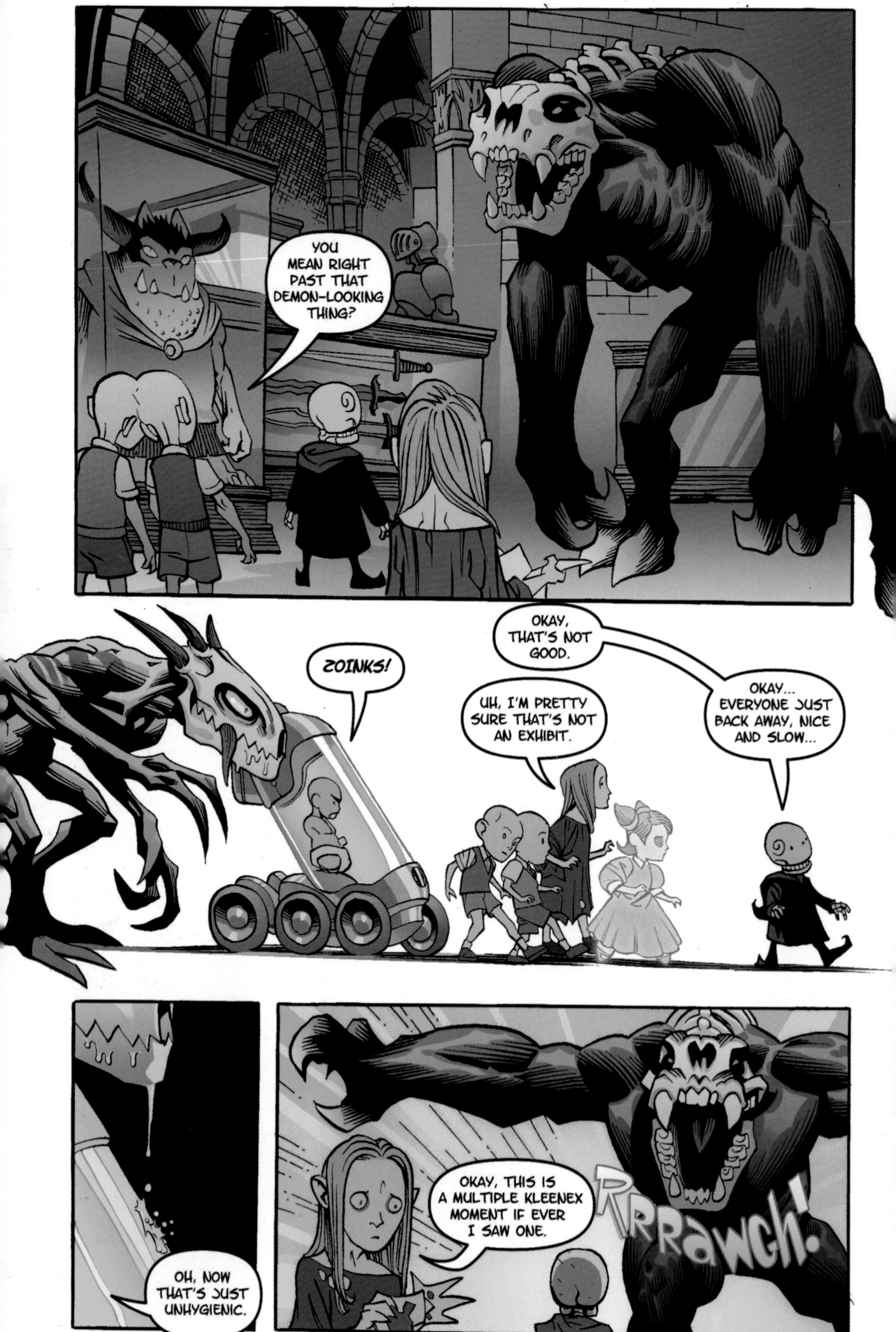
YOU MEAN RIGHT PAST THAT DEMON-LOOKING THING?
ZOINKS!
OKAY, THAT'S NOT GOOD.
UH, I'M PRETTY SURE THAT'S NOT AN EXHIBIT.
OKAY... EVERYONE JUST BACK AWAY, NICE AND SLOW...
OH, NOW THAT'S JUST UNHYGIENIC.
OKAY, THIS IS A MULTIPLE KLEENEX MOMENT IF EVER I SAW ONE.
RRRAWGH!

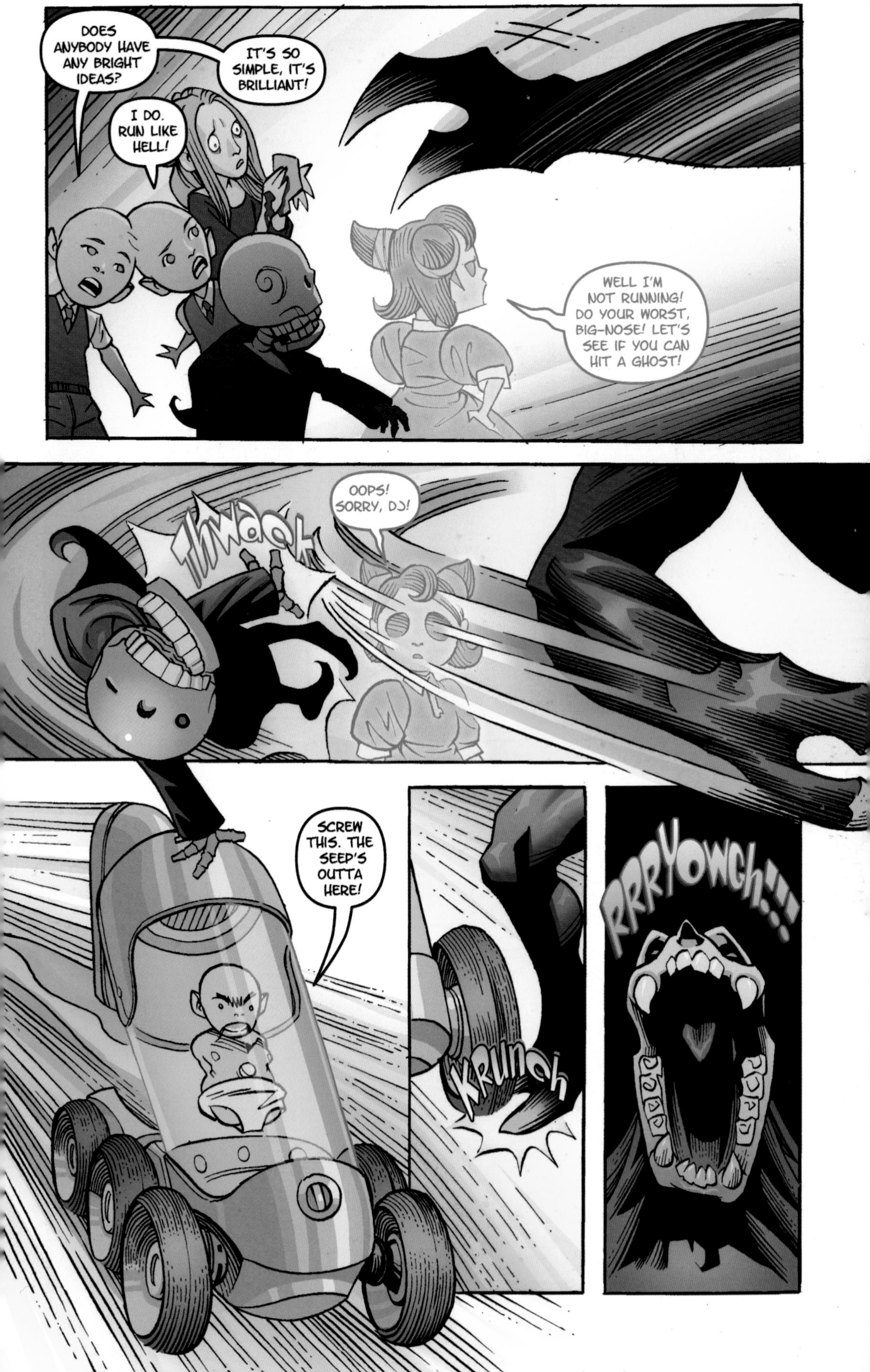

DOES ANYBODY HAVE ANY BRIGHT IDEAS?
I DO. RUN LIKE HELL!
IT'S SO SIMPLE, IT'S BRILLIANT!
WELL I'M NOT RUNNING! DO YOUR WORST, BIG-NOSE! LET'S SEE IF YOU CAN HIT A GHOST!
THWACK
OOPS! SORRY, DJ!
SCREW THIS. THE SEEP'S OUTTA HERE!
KRUNCH
RRRYOWCH!!!

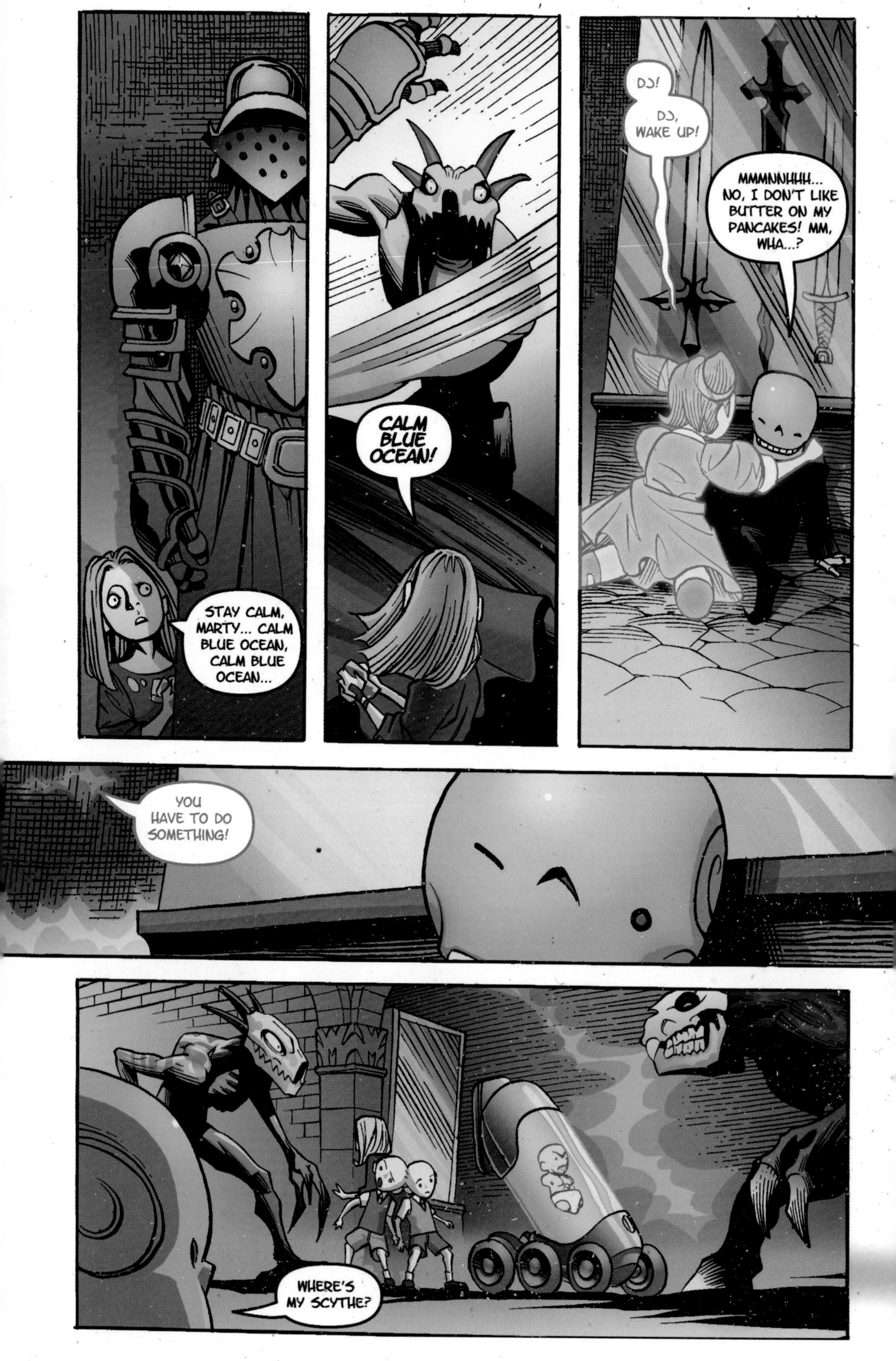
STAY CALM, MARTY... CALM BLUE OCEAN, CALM BLUE OCEAN...
CALM BLUE OCEAN!
DJ!
DJ, WAKE UP!
MMMNNHHH... NO, I DON'T LIKE BUTTER ON MY PANCAKES! MM, WHA...?
YOU HAVE TO DO SOMETHING!
WHERE'S MY SCYTHE?

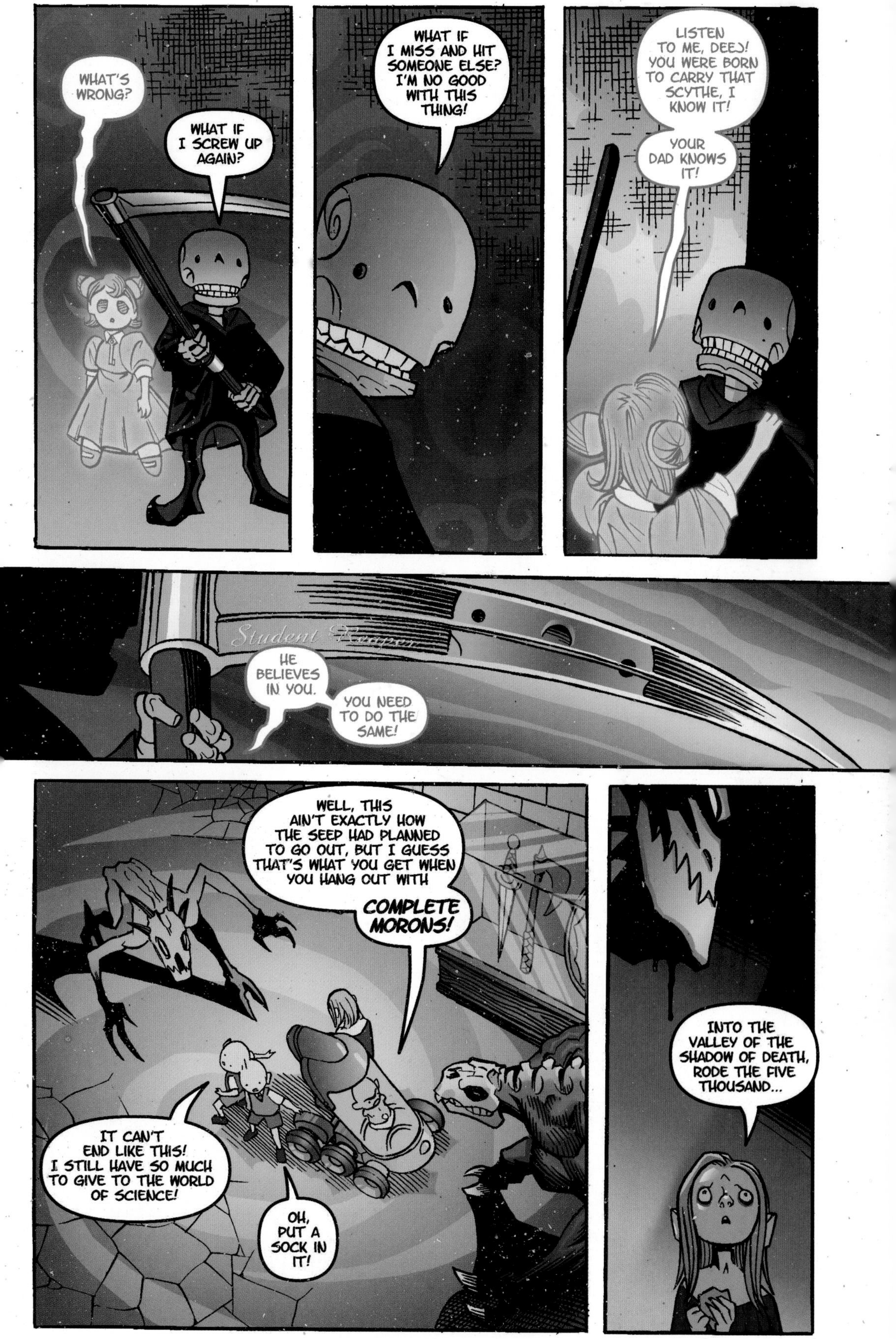
WHAT'S WRONG?
WHAT IF I SCREW UP AGAIN?
WHAT IF I MISS AND HIT SOMEONE ELSE? I'M NO GOOD WITH THIS THING!
LISTEN TO ME, DEEJ! YOU WERE BORN TO CARRY THAT SCYTHE, I KNOW IT!
YOUR DAD KNOWS IT!
HE BELIEVES IN YOU.
YOU NEED TO DO THE SAME!
WELL, THIS AIN'T EXACTLY HOW THE SEEP HAD PLANNED TO GO OUT, BUT I GUESS THAT'S WHAT YOU GET WHEN YOU HANG OUT WITH COMPLETE MORONS!
IT CAN'T END LIKE THIS! I STILL HAVE SO MUCH TO GIVE TO THE WORLD OF SCIENCE!
OH, PUT A SOCK IN IT!
INTO THE VALLEY OF THE SHADOW OF DEATH, RODE THE FIVE THOUSAND...

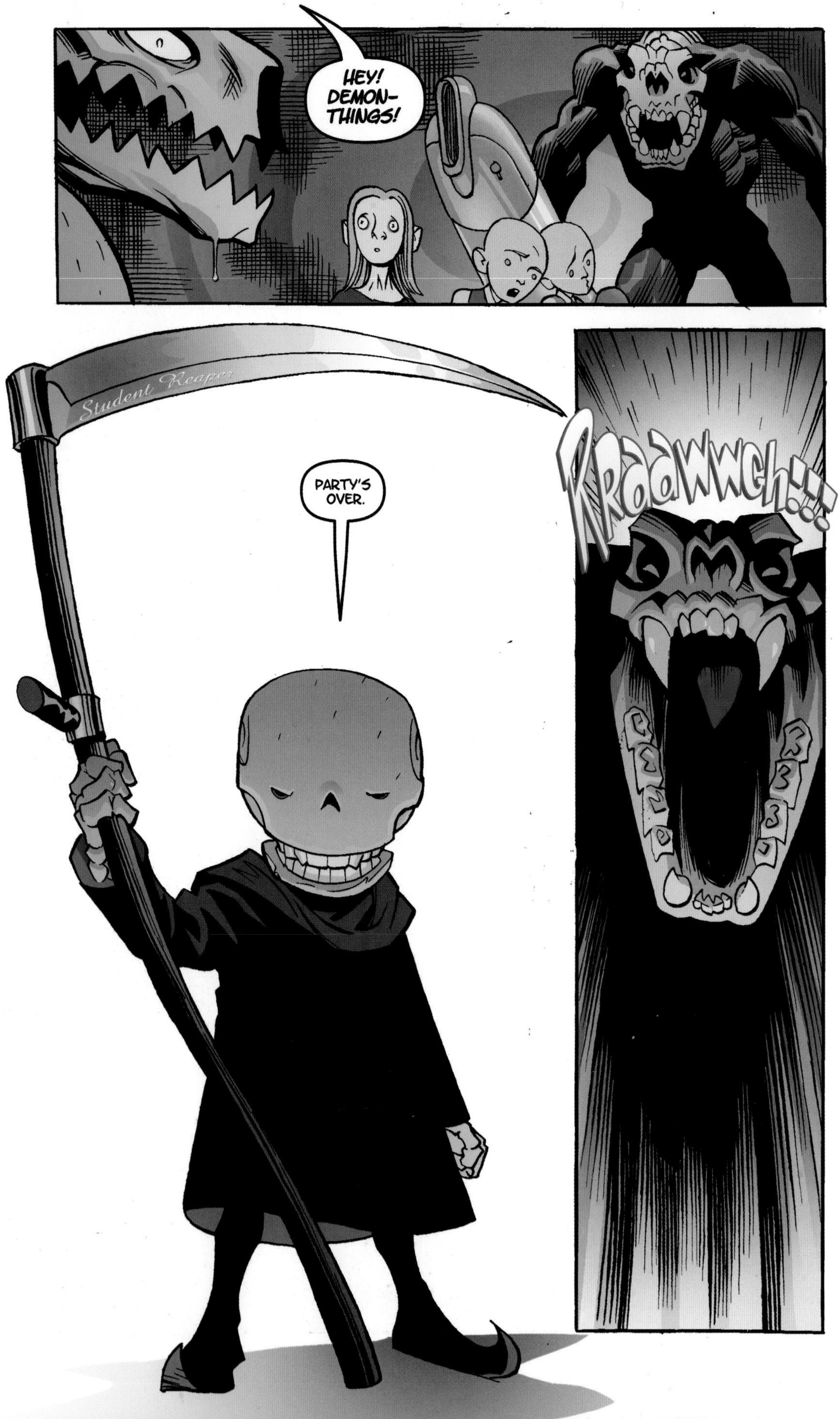
HEY! DEMON-THINGS!
Student Reaper
PARTY'S OVER.
RRAAWWCH!!!

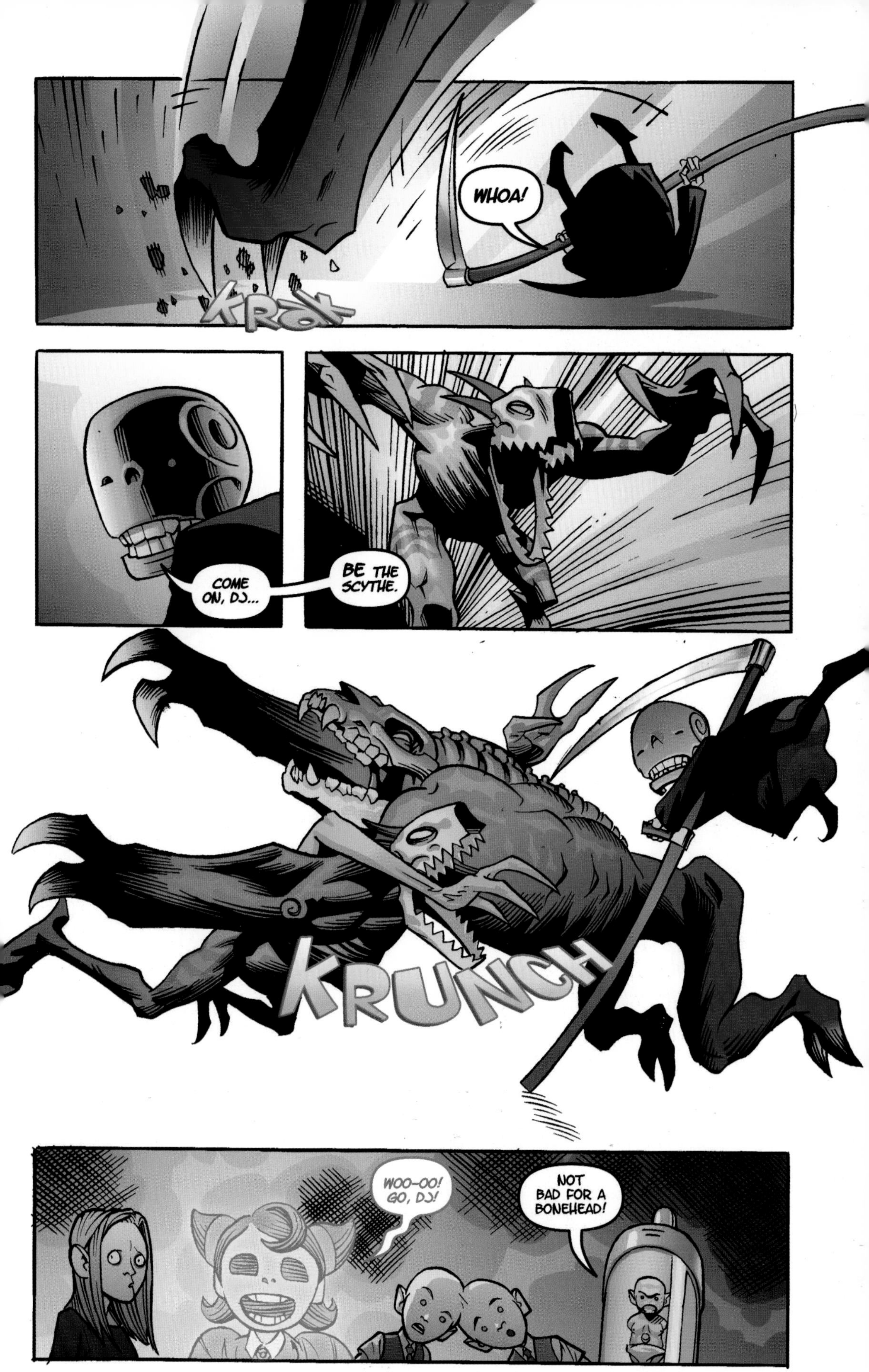
KRAK
WHOA!
COME ON, DJ...
BE THE SCYTHE.
KRUNCH
WOO-OO! GO, DJ!
NOT BAD FOR A BONEHEAD!

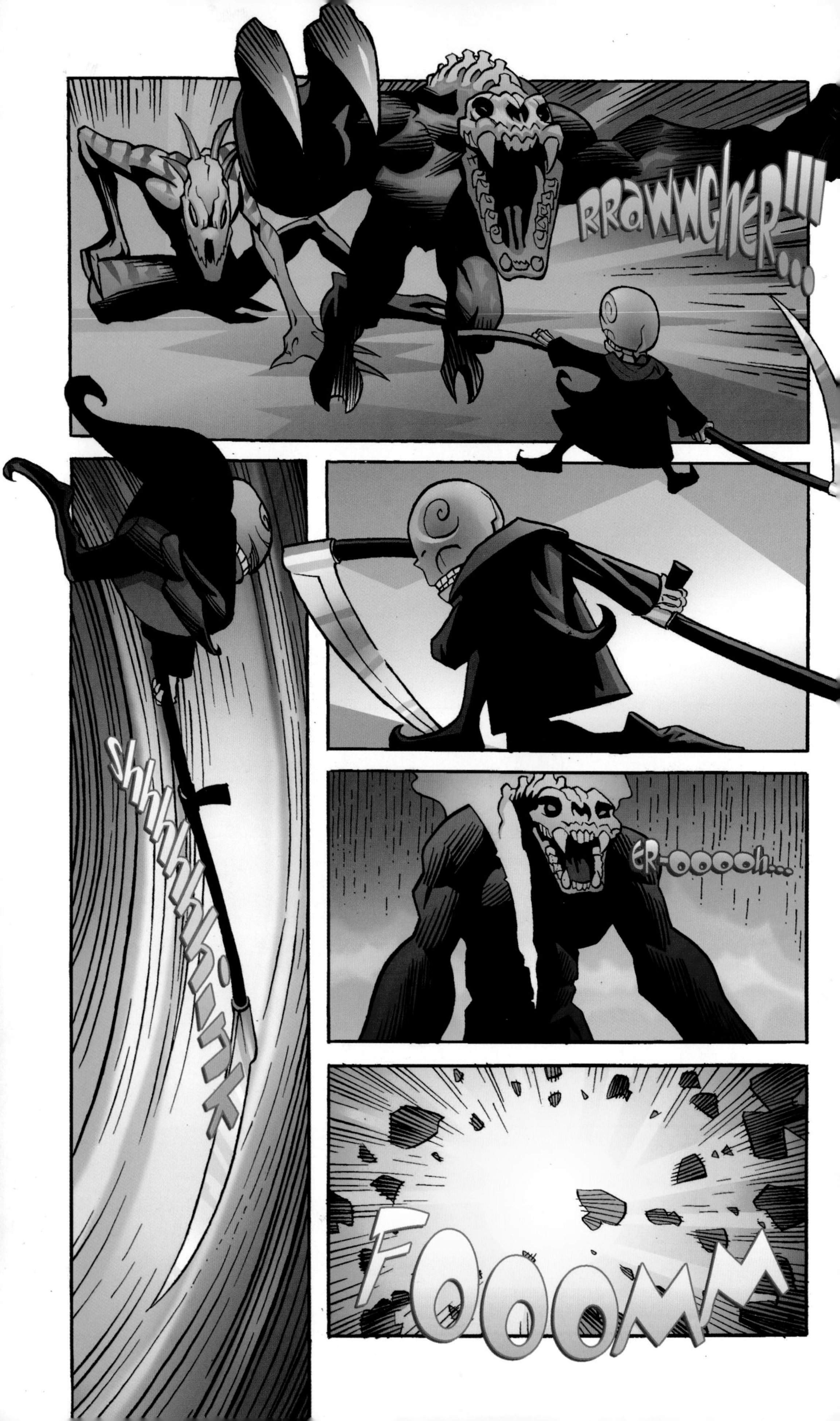
RRAWWGHER!!!!...
Shhhhhhh---rrrK
ER-OOOOoh...
FOOOMM

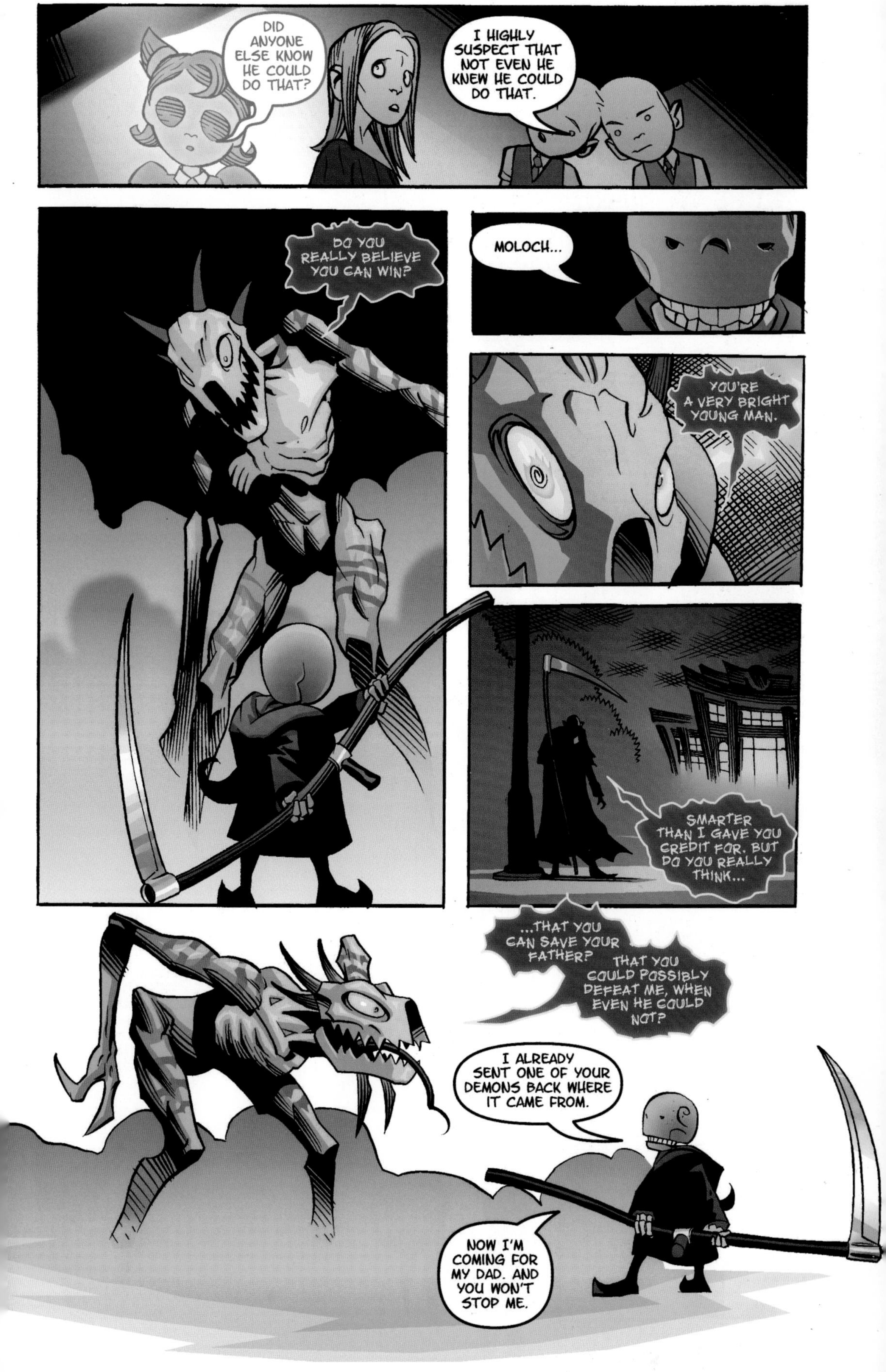
DID ANYONE ELSE KNOW HE COULD DO THAT?
I HIGHLY SUSPECT THAT NOT EVEN HE KNEW HE COULD DO THAT.
DO YOU REALLY BELIEVE YOU CAN WIN?
MOLOCH...
YOU'RE A VERY BRIGHT YOUNG MAN.
SMARTER THAN I GAVE YOU CREDIT FOR. BUT DO YOU REALLY THINK...
...THAT YOU CAN SAVE YOUR FATHER?
THAT YOU COULD POSSIBLY DEFEAT ME, WHEN EVEN HE COULD NOT?
I ALREADY SENT ONE OF YOUR DEMONS BACK WHERE IT CAME FROM.
NOW I'M COMING FOR MY DAD. AND YOU WON'T STOP ME.

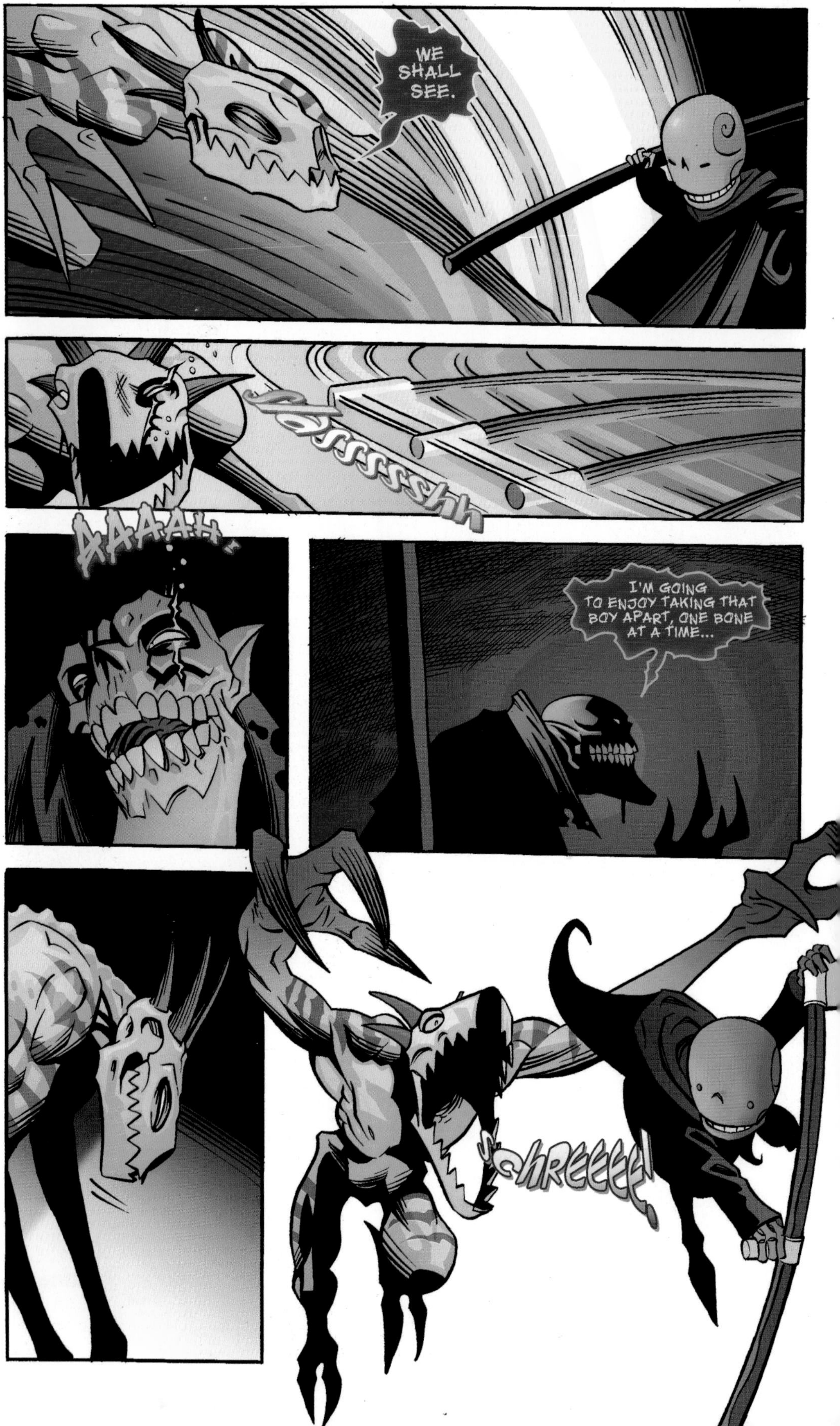

WE SHALL SEE.
SLASSSSSSHH
AAAAH!
I'M GOING TO ENJOY TAKING THAT BOY APART, ONE BONE AT A TIME...
SCHREEEE!

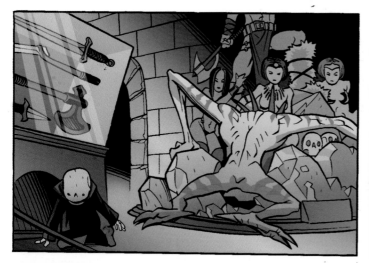

UH-OH.

KRASSSSHH

SHREEE!

OH, SUGAR.

COME ON YOU LOT, PUT YOUR BACKS INTO IT!

APPLY YOUR WEIGHT AT THE FULCRUM! WE'LL GET BETTER LEVERAGE!

IT WON'T BUDGE!

EVERYBODY GET BACK!

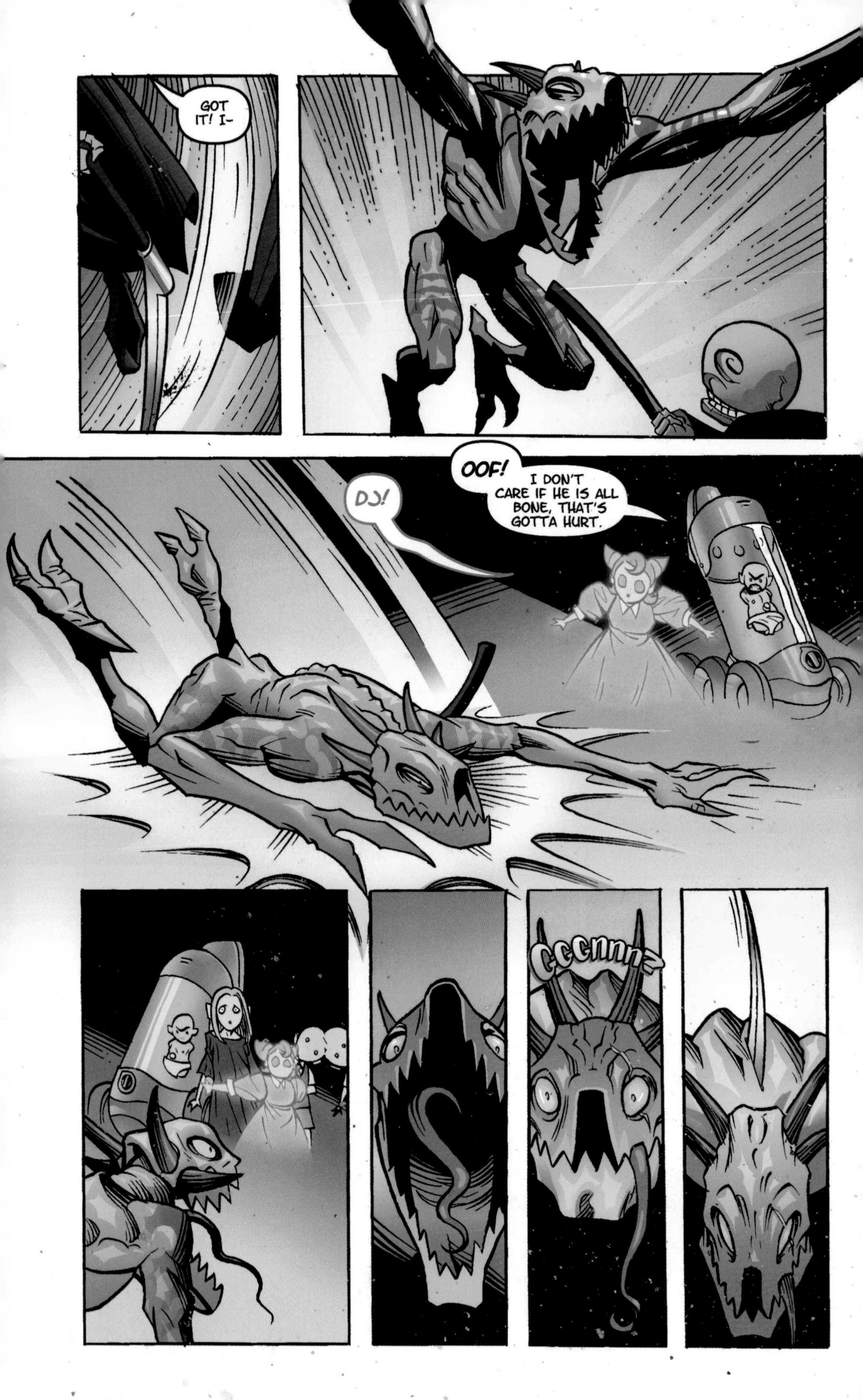
GOT IT! I-
DJ!
OOF!
I DON'T CARE IF HE IS ALL BONE, THAT'S GOTTA HURT.
GGGNNNG

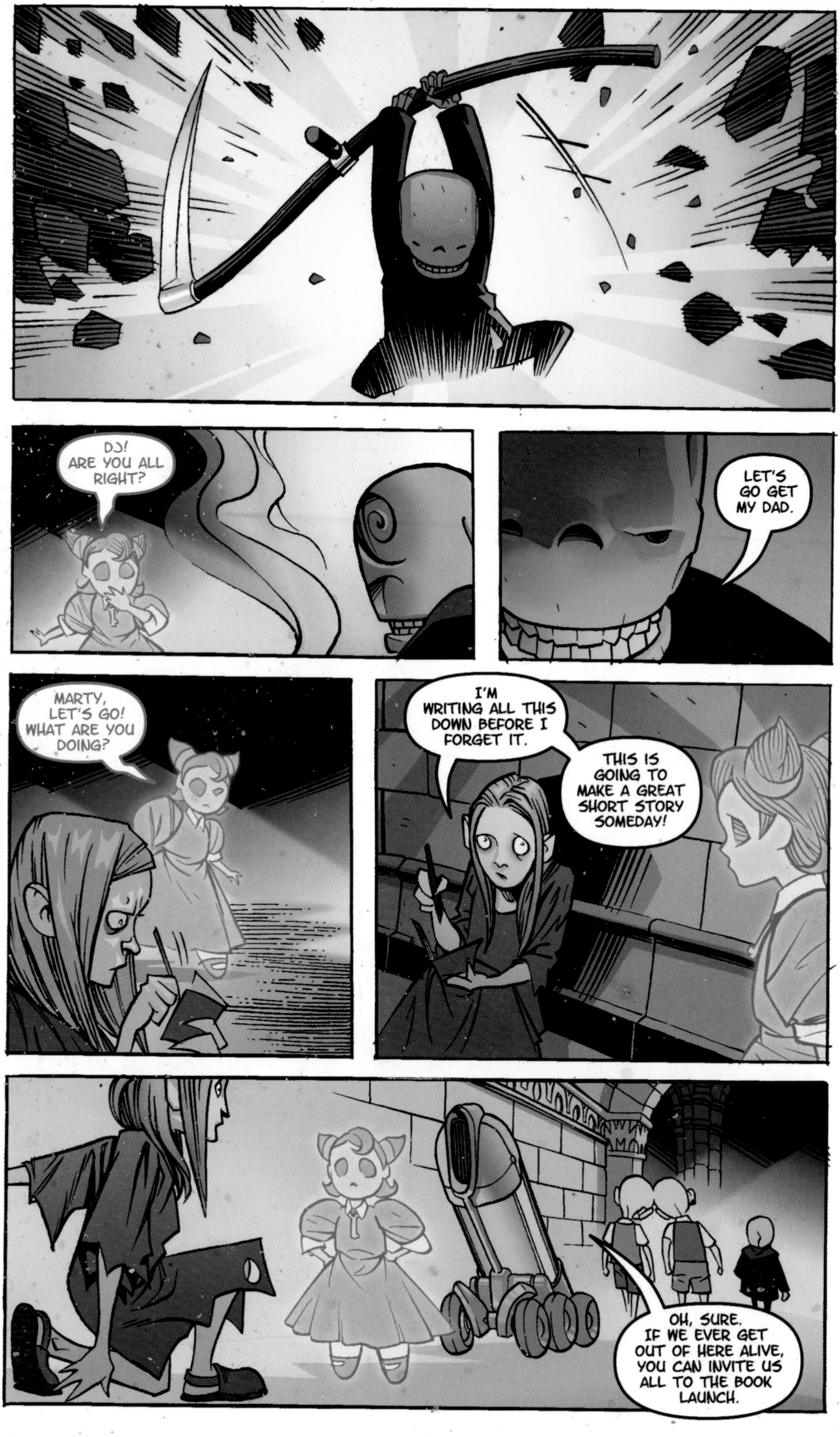
DJ! ARE YOU ALL RIGHT?
LET'S GO GET MY DAD.
MARTY, LET'S GO! WHAT ARE YOU DOING?
I'M WRITING ALL THIS DOWN BEFORE I FORGET IT.
THIS IS GOING TO MAKE A GREAT SHORT STORY SOMEDAY!
OH, SURE. IF WE EVER GET OUT OF HERE ALIVE, YOU CAN INVITE US ALL TO THE BOOK LAUNCH.

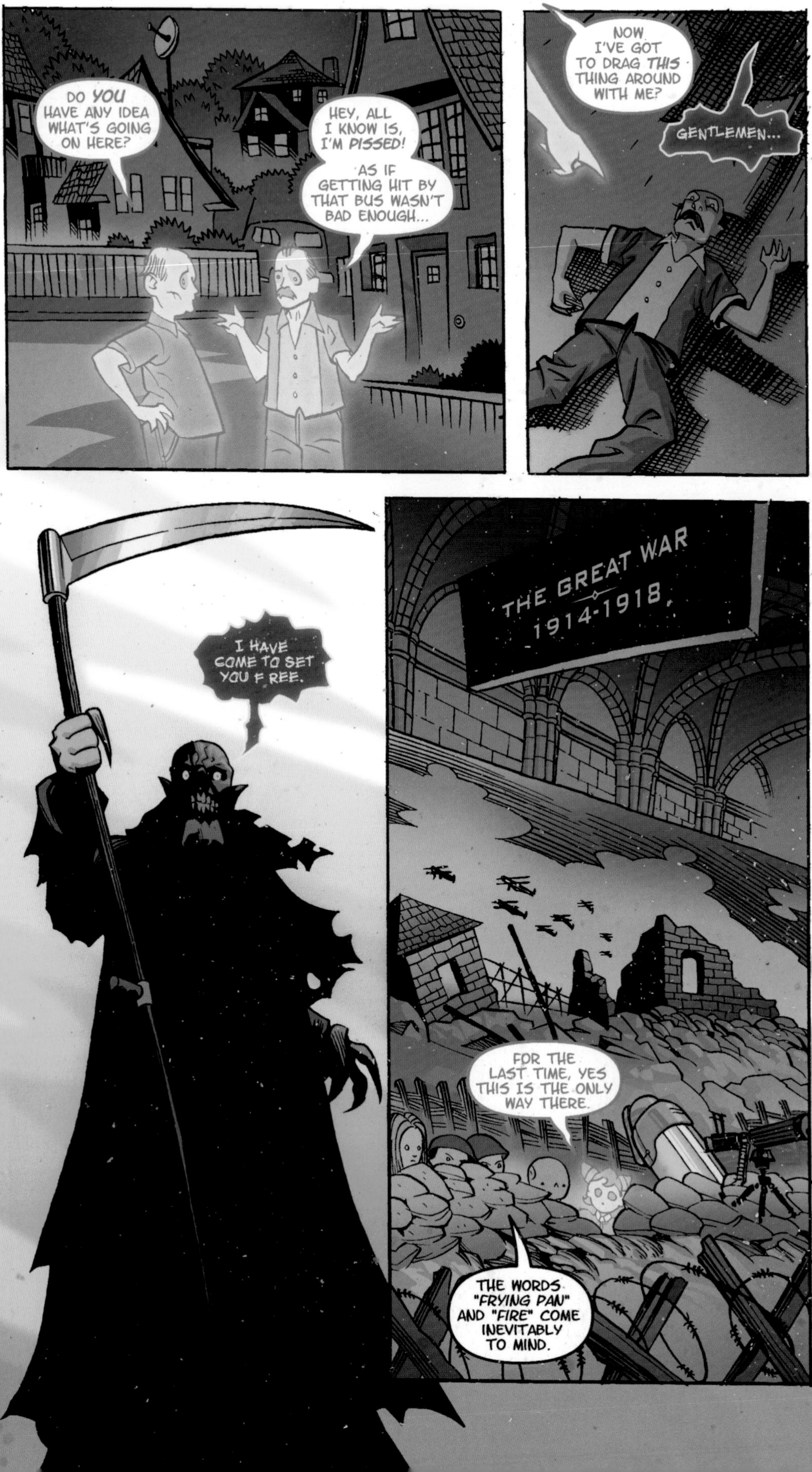
DO YOU HAVE ANY IDEA WHAT'S GOING ON HERE?
HEY, ALL I KNOW IS, I'M PISSED!
AS IF GETTING HIT BY THAT BUS WASN'T BAD ENOUGH...
NOW I'VE GOT TO DRAG THIS THING AROUND WITH ME?
GENTLEMEN...
I HAVE COME TO SET YOU FREE.
THE GREAT WAR
1914-1918
FOR THE LAST TIME, YES THIS IS THE ONLY WAY THERE.
THE WORDS "FRYING PAN" AND "FIRE" COME INEVITABLY TO MIND.

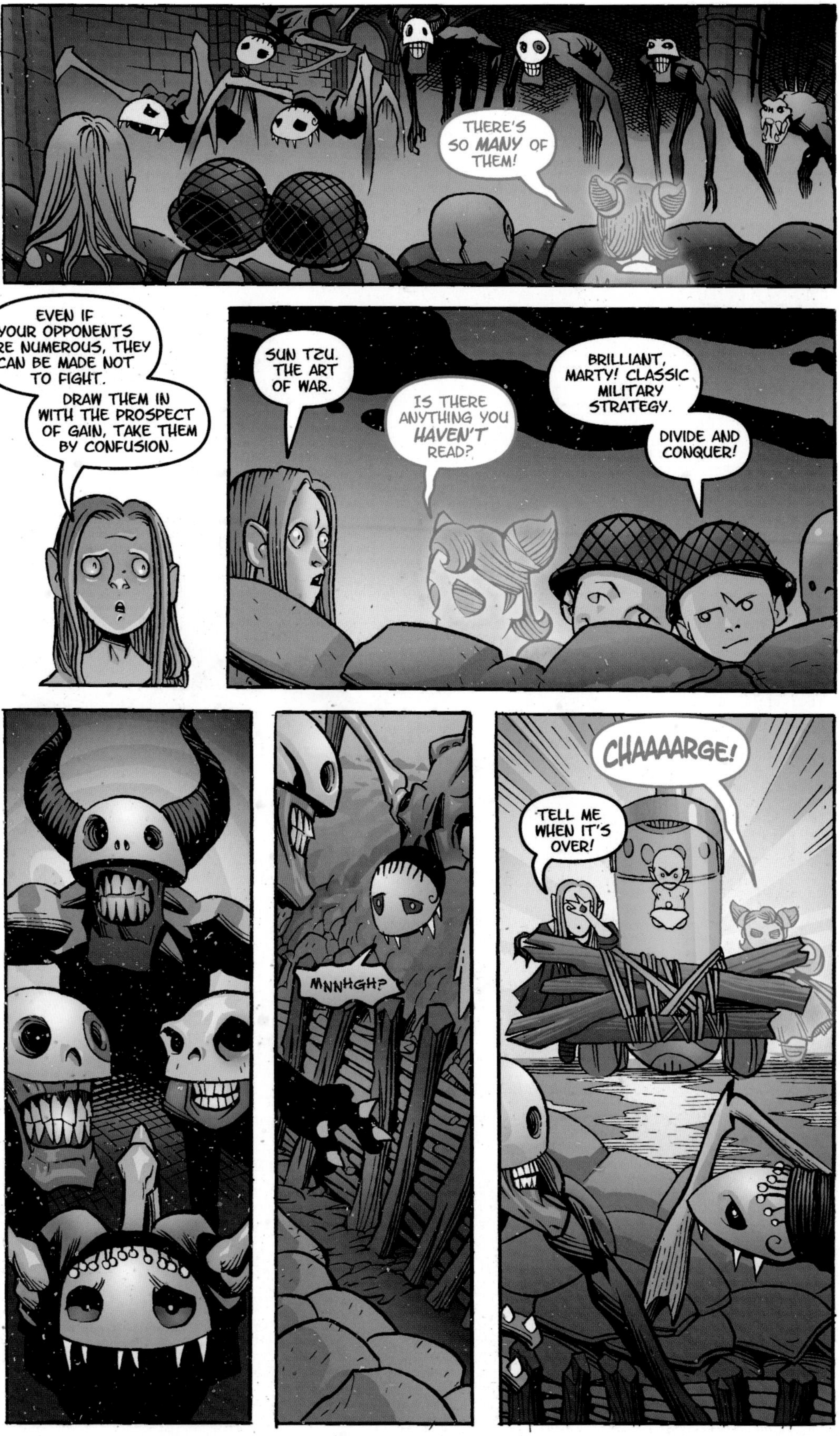
THERE'S SO MANY OF THEM!
EVEN IF YOUR OPPONENTS ARE NUMEROUS, THEY CAN BE MADE NOT TO FIGHT.
DRAW THEM IN WITH THE PROSPECT OF GAIN, TAKE THEM BY CONFUSION.
SUN TZU. THE ART OF WAR.
IS THERE ANYTHING YOU HAVEN'T READ?
BRILLIANT, MARTY! CLASSIC MILITARY STRATEGY.
DIVIDE AND CONQUER!
MNNHGH?
CHAAAARGE!
TELL ME WHEN IT'S OVER!

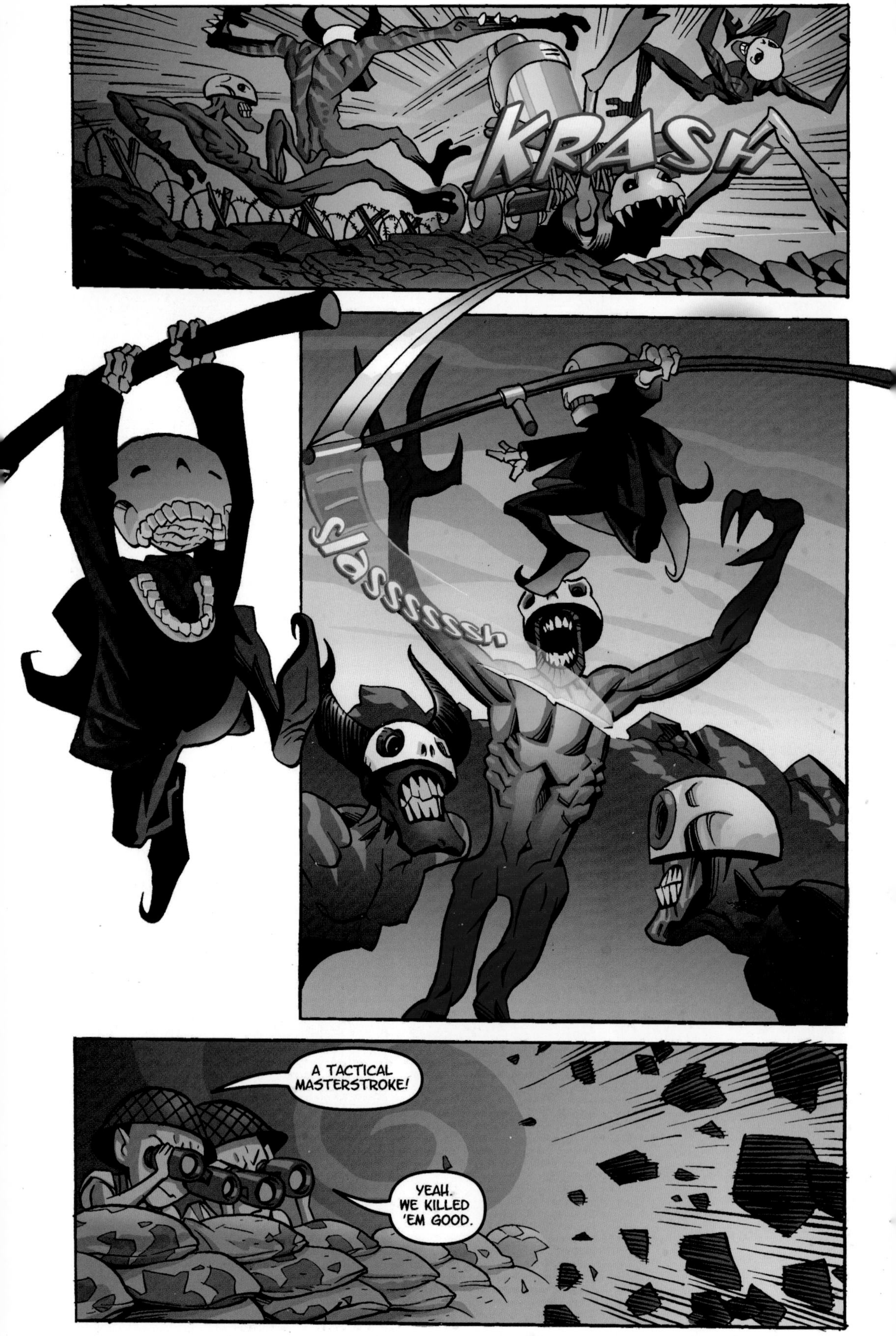
KRASH
slassssssh
A TACTICAL MASTERSTROKE!
YEAH. WE KILLED 'EM GOOD.

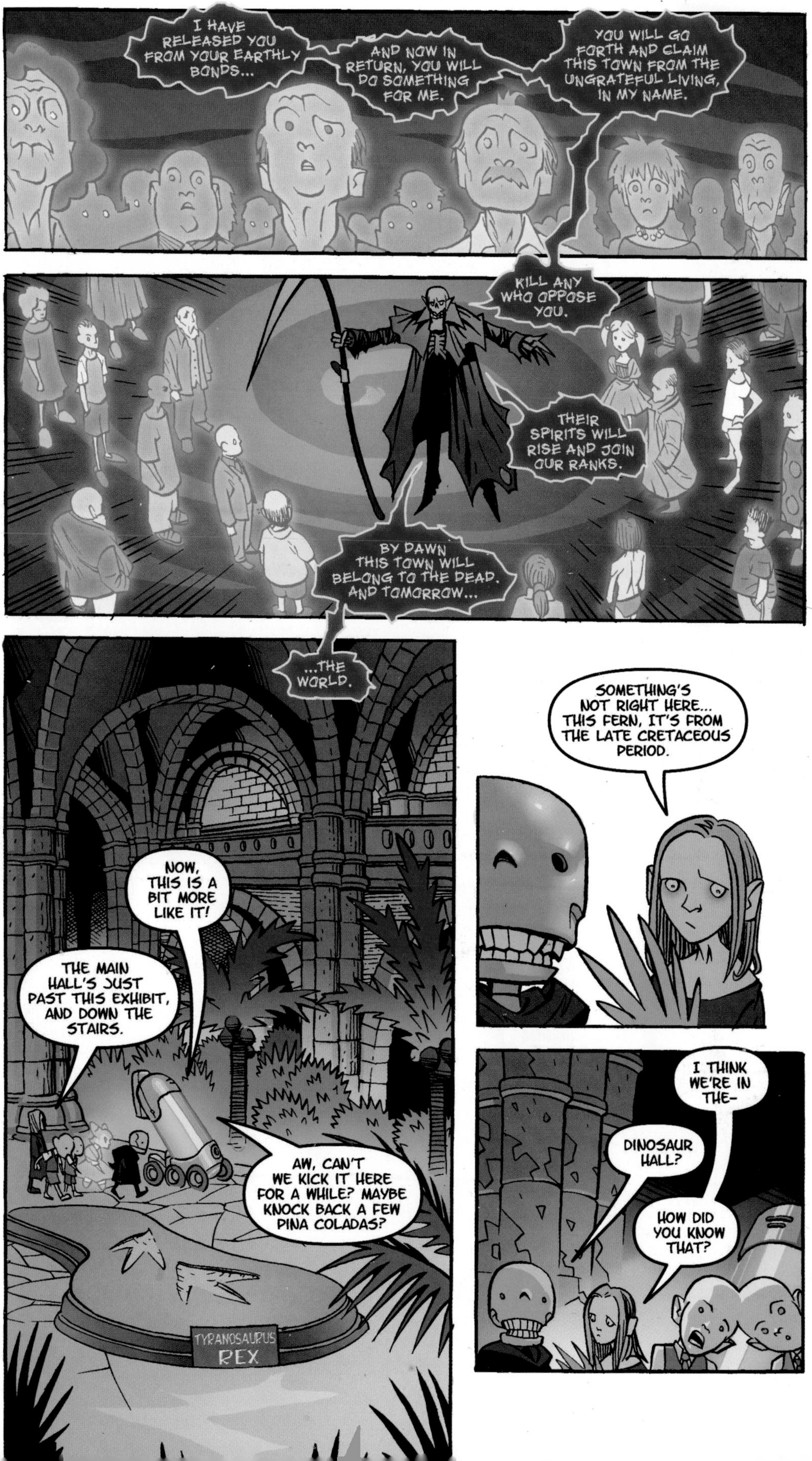
I HAVE RELEASED YOU FROM YOUR EARTHLY BONDS...
AND NOW IN RETURN, YOU WILL DO SOMETHING FOR ME.
YOU WILL GO FORTH AND CLAIM THIS TOWN FROM THE UNGRATEFUL LIVING, IN MY NAME.
KILL ANY WHO OPPOSE YOU.
THEIR SPIRITS WILL RISE AND JOIN OUR RANKS.
BY DAWN THIS TOWN WILL BELONG TO THE DEAD. AND TOMORROW...
...THE WORLD.
NOW, THIS IS A BIT MORE LIKE IT!
THE MAIN HALL'S JUST PAST THIS EXHIBIT, AND DOWN THE STAIRS.
AW, CAN'T WE KICK IT HERE FOR A WHILE? MAYBE KNOCK BACK A FEW PINA COLADAS?
TYRANOSAURUS REX
SOMETHING'S NOT RIGHT HERE... THIS FERN, IT'S FROM THE LATE CRETACEOUS PERIOD.
I THINK WE'RE IN THE-
DINOSAUR HALL?
HOW DID YOU KNOW THAT?

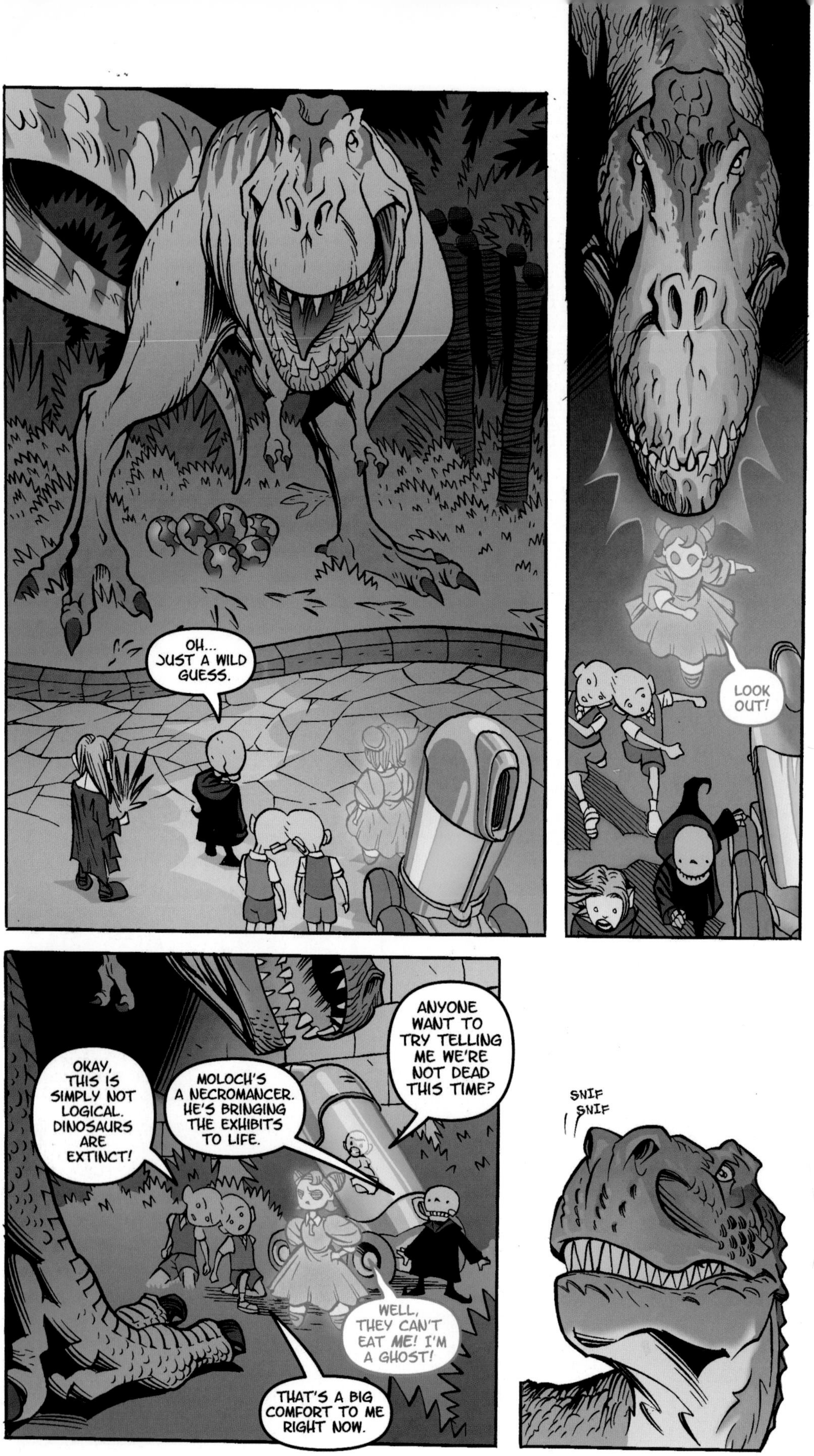

OH... JUST A WILD GUESS.
LOOK OUT!
OKAY, THIS IS SIMPLY NOT LOGICAL. DINOSAURS ARE EXTINCT!
MOLOCH'S A NECROMANCER. HE'S BRINGING THE EXHIBITS TO LIFE.
ANYONE WANT TO TRY TELLING ME WE'RE NOT DEAD THIS TIME?
WELL, THEY CAN'T EAT ME! I'M A GHOST!
THAT'S A BIG COMFORT TO ME RIGHT NOW.
SNIF SNIF

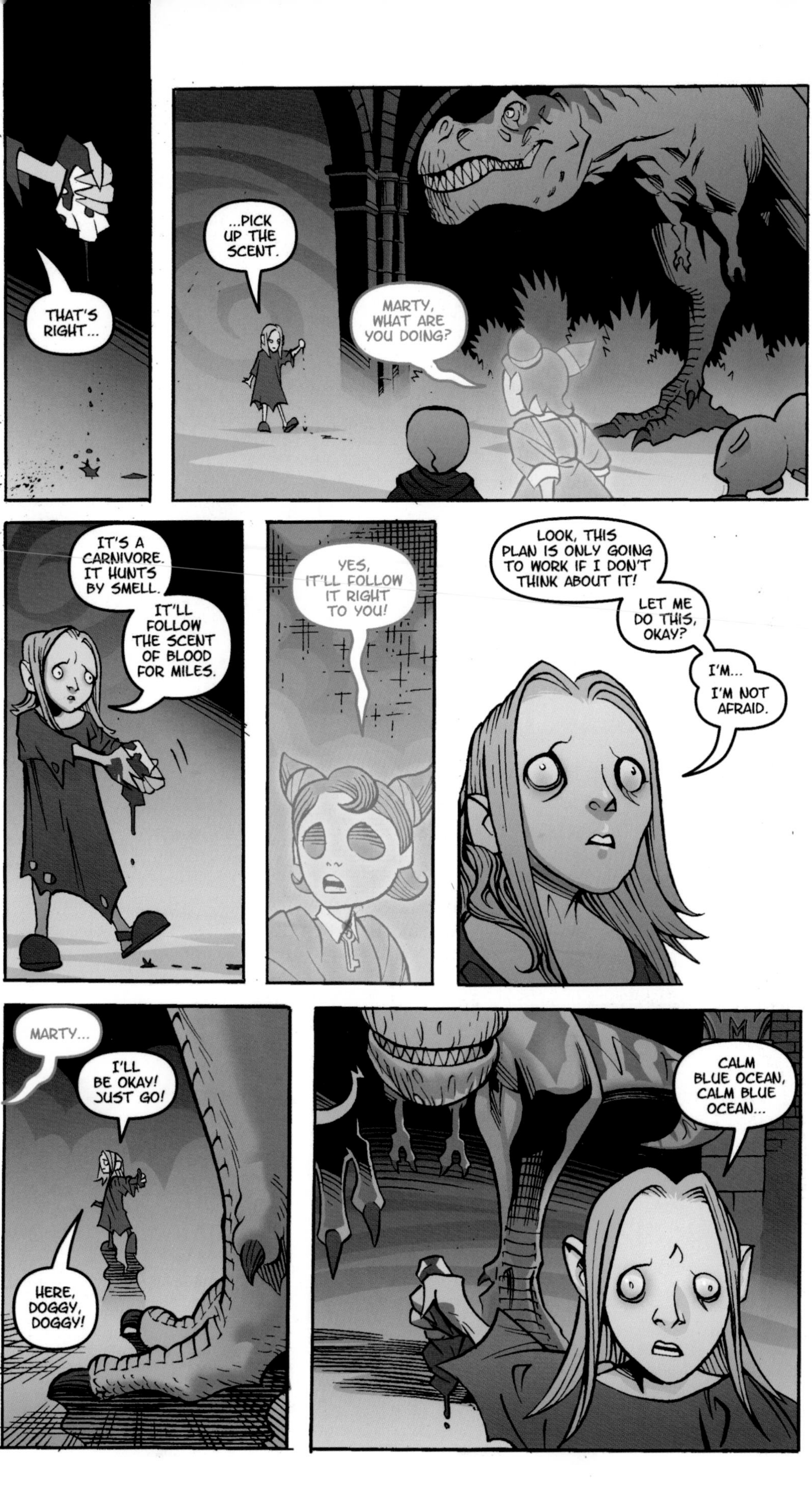
THAT'S RIGHT...
...PICK UP THE SCENT.
MARTY, WHAT ARE YOU DOING?
IT'S A CARNIVORE. IT HUNTS BY SMELL.
IT'LL FOLLOW THE SCENT OF BLOOD FOR MILES.
YES, IT'LL FOLLOW IT RIGHT TO YOU!
LOOK, THIS PLAN IS ONLY GOING TO WORK IF I DON'T THINK ABOUT IT!
LET ME DO THIS, OKAY?
I'M... I'M NOT AFRAID.
MARTY...
I'LL BE OKAY! JUST GO!
HERE, DOGGY, DOGGY!
CALM BLUE OCEAN, CALM BLUE OCEAN...

ALL RIGHT, I'M COMING!

DO YOU HAVE ANY IDEA WHAT TIME—

NICE HOUSE.

WE'LL TAKE IT!

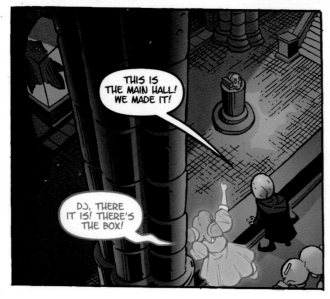

THIS IS THE MAIN HALL! WE MADE IT!

DJ, THERE IT IS! THERE'S THE BOX!

DAD!

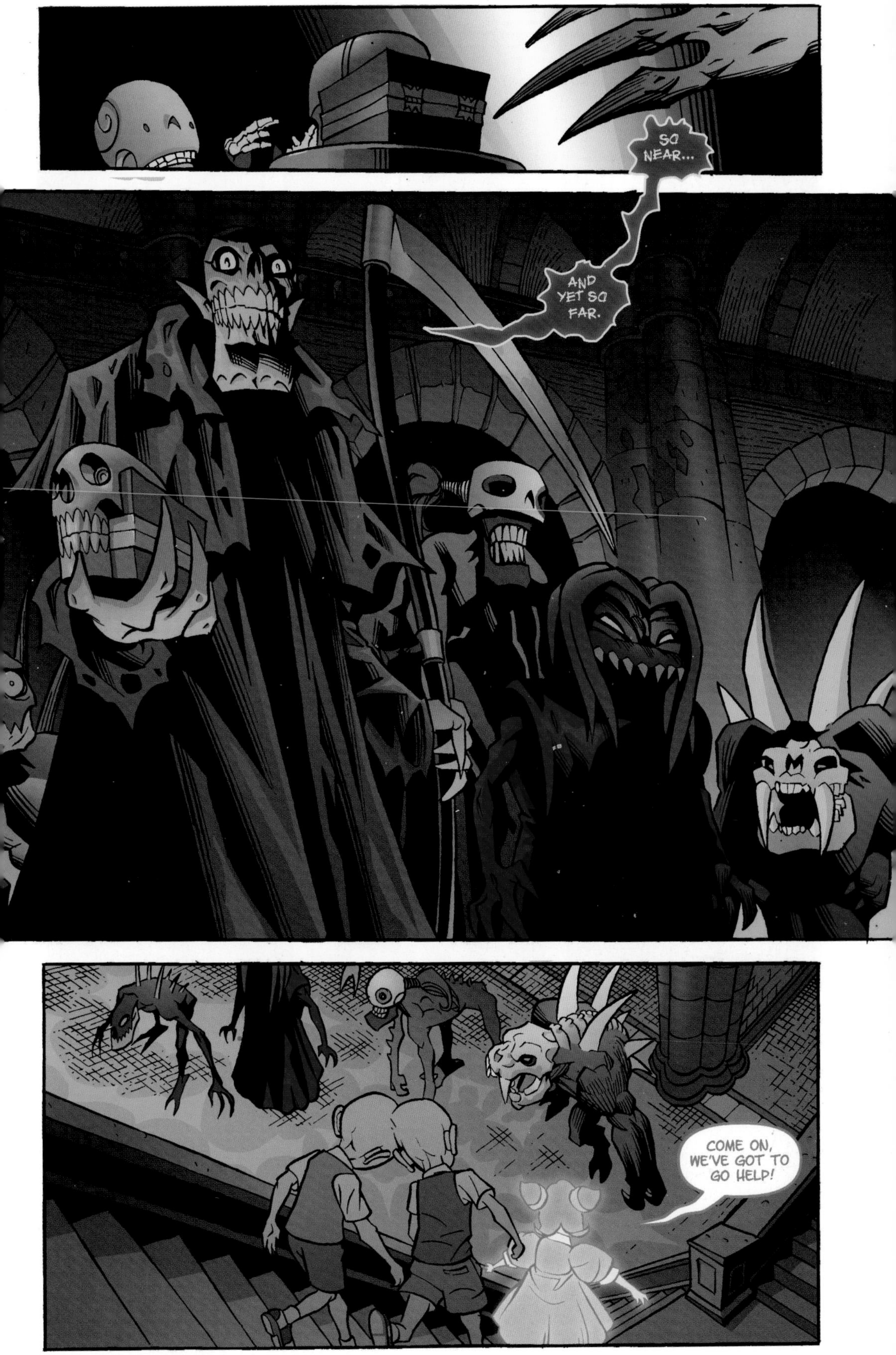
SO NEAR...
AND YET SO FAR.
COME ON, WE'VE GOT TO GO HELP!

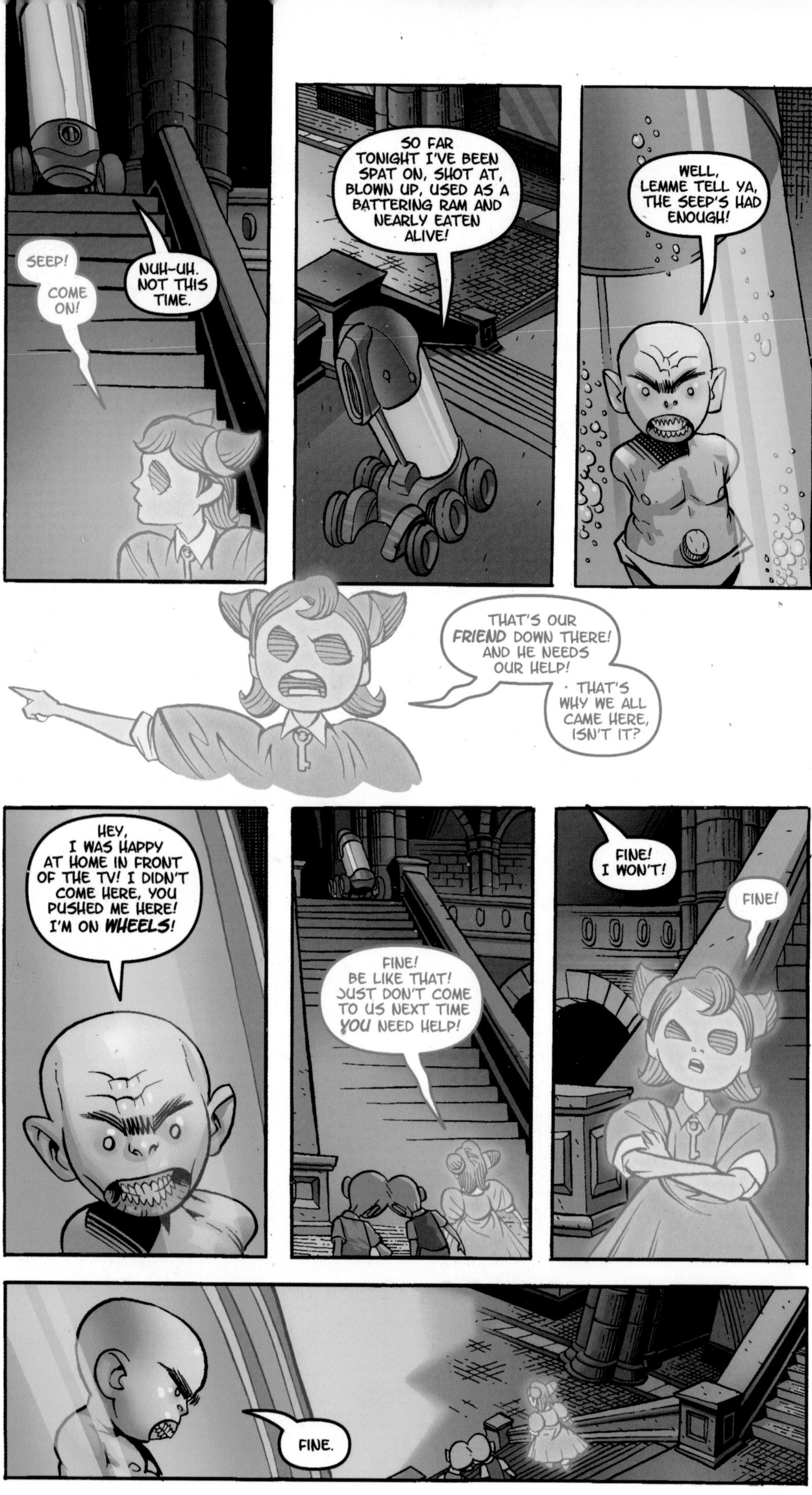
SEEP!
COME ON!
NUH-UH. NOT THIS TIME.
SO FAR TONIGHT I'VE BEEN SPAT ON, SHOT AT, BLOWN UP, USED AS A BATTERING RAM AND NEARLY EATEN ALIVE!
WELL, LEMME TELL YA, THE SEEP'S HAD ENOUGH!
THAT'S OUR FRIEND DOWN THERE! AND HE NEEDS OUR HELP!
THAT'S WHY WE ALL CAME HERE, ISN'T IT?
HEY, I WAS HAPPY AT HOME IN FRONT OF THE TV! I DIDN'T COME HERE, YOU PUSHED ME HERE! I'M ON WHEELS!
FINE! BE LIKE THAT! JUST DON'T COME TO US NEXT TIME YOU NEED HELP!
FINE! I WON'T!
FINE!
FINE.

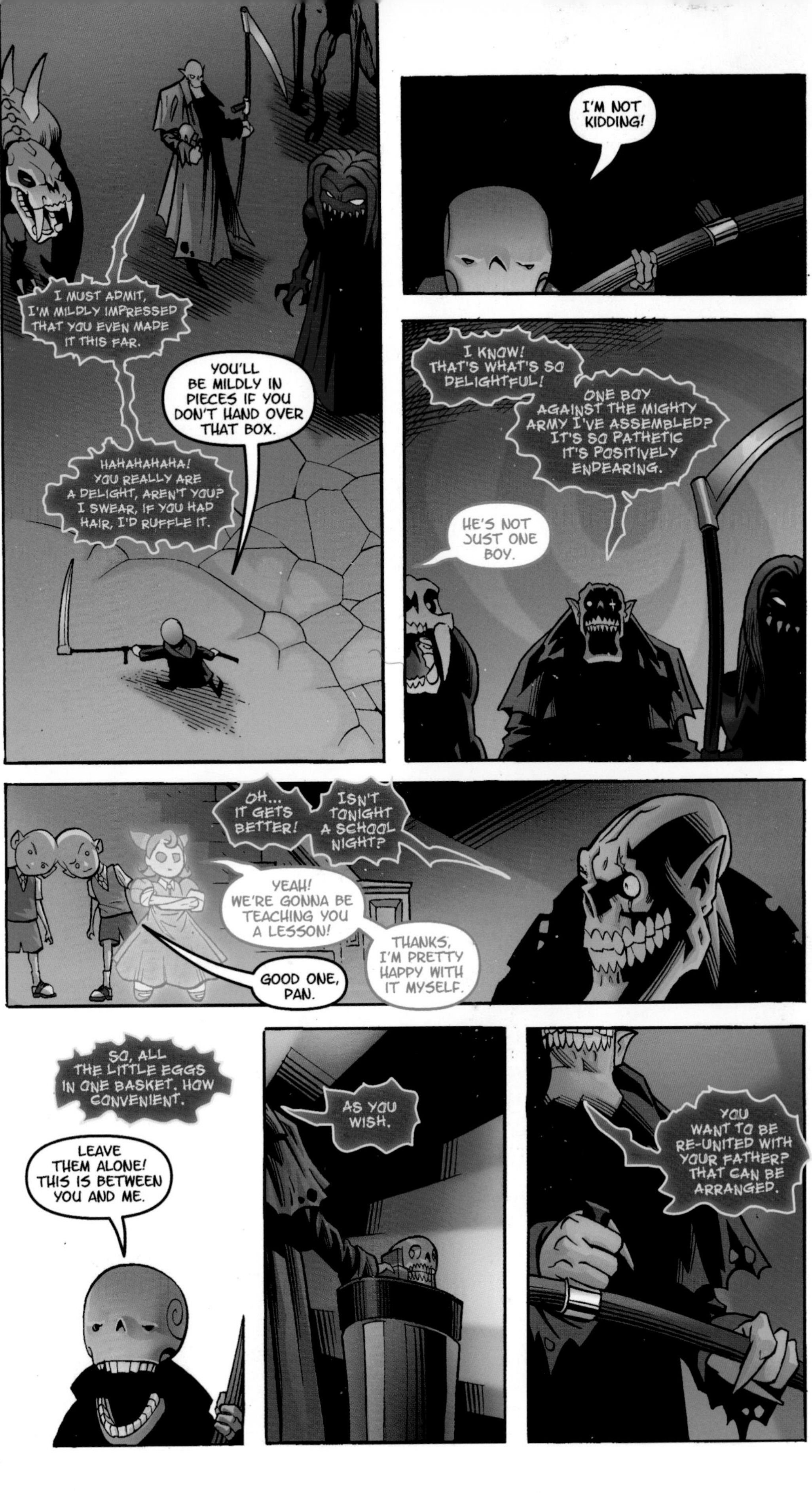
I MUST ADMIT, I'M MILDLY IMPRESSED THAT YOU EVEN MADE IT THIS FAR.
YOU'LL BE MILDLY IN PIECES IF YOU DON'T HAND OVER THAT BOX.
HAHAHAHAHA! YOU REALLY ARE A DELIGHT, AREN'T YOU? I SWEAR, IF YOU HAD HAIR, I'D RUFFLE IT.
I'M NOT KIDDING!
I KNOW! THAT'S WHAT'S SO DELIGHTFUL!
ONE BOY AGAINST THE MIGHTY ARMY I'VE ASSEMBLED? IT'S SO PATHETIC IT'S POSITIVELY ENDEARING.
HE'S NOT JUST ONE BOY.
OH... IT GETS BETTER!
ISN'T TONIGHT A SCHOOL NIGHT?
YEAH! WE'RE GONNA BE TEACHING YOU A LESSON!
GOOD ONE, PAN.
THANKS, I'M PRETTY HAPPY WITH IT MYSELF.
SO, ALL THE LITTLE EGGS IN ONE BASKET. HOW CONVENIENT.
LEAVE THEM ALONE! THIS IS BETWEEN YOU AND ME.
AS YOU WISH.
YOU WANT TO BE RE-UNITED WITH YOUR FATHER? THAT CAN BE ARRANGED.

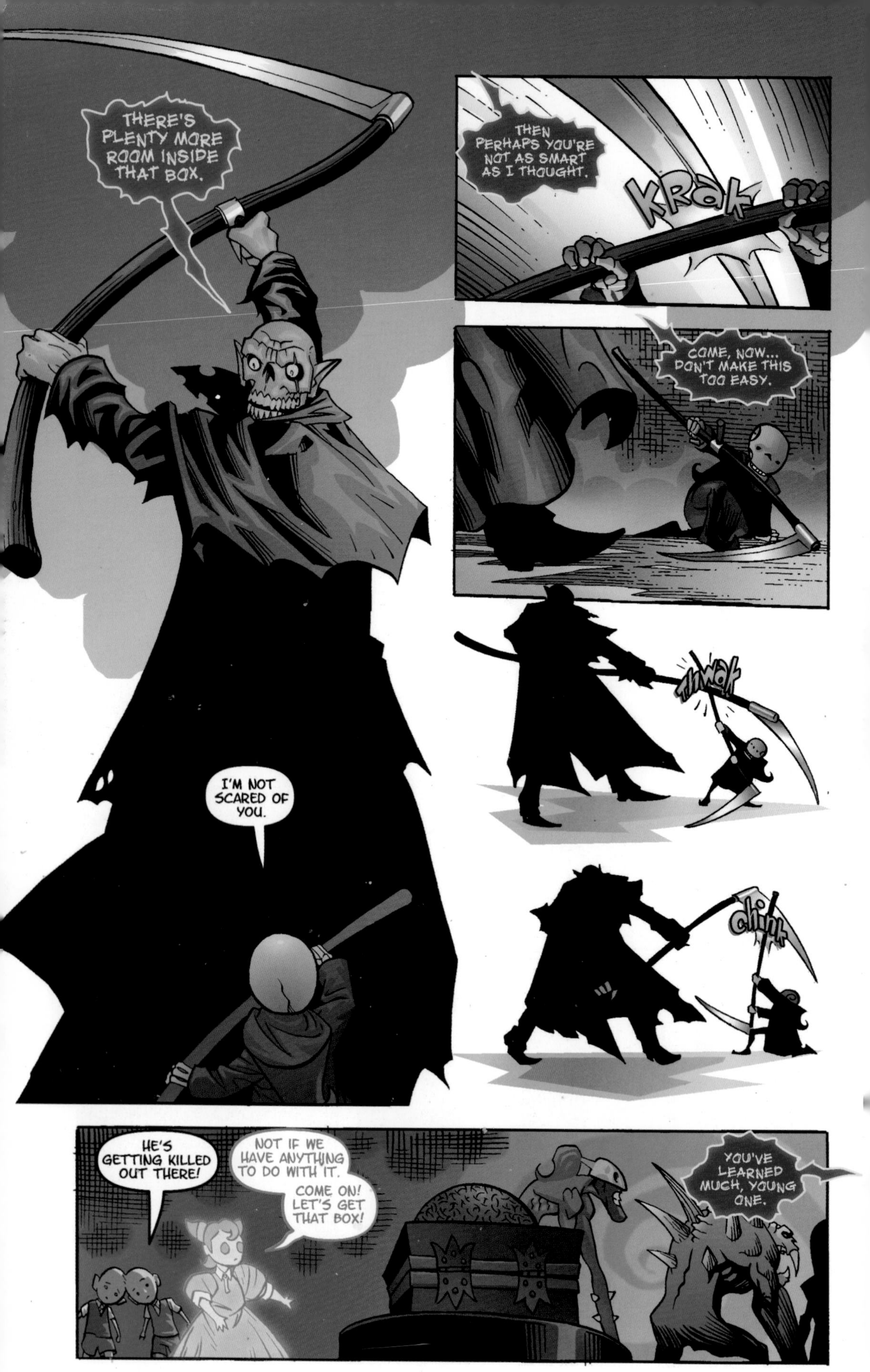

THERE'S PLENTY MORE ROOM INSIDE THAT BOX.
I'M NOT SCARED OF YOU.
THEN PERHAPS YOU'RE NOT AS SMART AS I THOUGHT.
KRAK
COME, NOW... DON'T MAKE THIS TOO EASY.
THWAK
CHINK
HE'S GETTING KILLED OUT THERE!
NOT IF WE HAVE ANYTHING TO DO WITH IT.
COME ON! LET'S GET THAT BOX!
YOU'VE LEARNED MUCH, YOUNG ONE.

YOU'LL FIND I'M FULL OF SURPRISES.
IMPRESSIVE.
MOST IMPRESSIVE!
AAARGH!
SO MUCH TROUBLE FOR ONE SO SMALL...
DJ. MUST WE REALLY FIGHT?
AFTER ALL... WE'RE FAMILY.
YOU'RE NO FAMILY OF MINE.
OH, COME NOW. REMEMBER HOW MUCH FUN WE HAD TOGETHER? REMEMBER ALL THAT POWER?

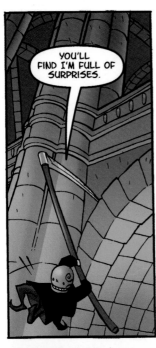

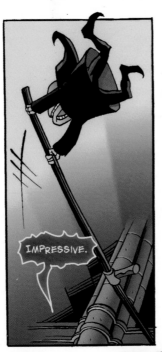

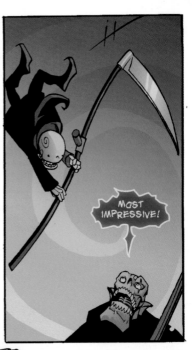

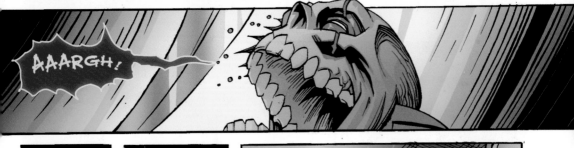

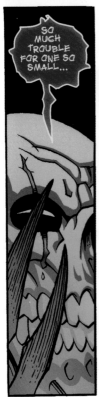

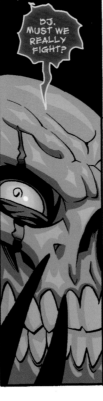

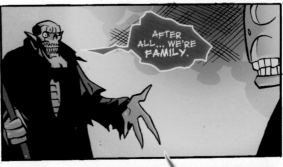

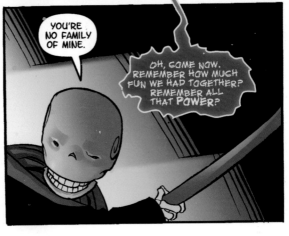

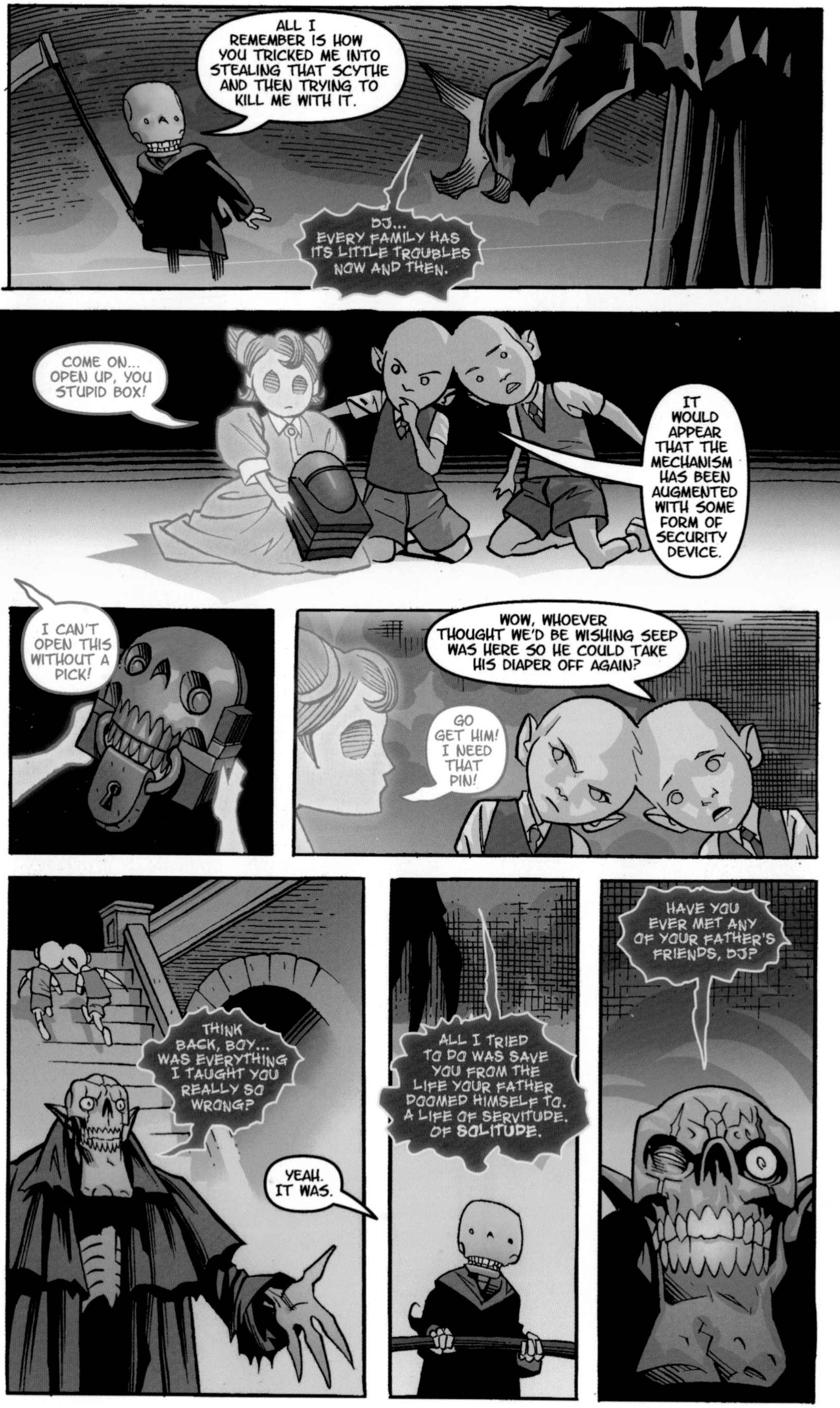
ALL I REMEMBER IS HOW YOU TRICKED ME INTO STEALING THAT SCYTHE AND THEN TRYING TO KILL ME WITH IT.
DJ... EVERY FAMILY HAS ITS LITTLE TROUBLES NOW AND THEN.
COME ON... OPEN UP, YOU STUPID BOX!
IT WOULD APPEAR THAT THE MECHANISM HAS BEEN AUGMENTED WITH SOME FORM OF SECURITY DEVICE.
I CAN'T OPEN THIS WITHOUT A PICK!
WOW, WHOEVER THOUGHT WE'D BE WISHING SEEP WAS HERE SO HE COULD TAKE HIS DIAPER OFF AGAIN?
GO GET HIM! I NEED THAT PIN!
THINK BACK, BOY... WAS EVERYTHING I TAUGHT YOU REALLY SO WRONG?
YEAH. IT WAS.
ALL I TRIED TO DO WAS SAVE YOU FROM THE LIFE YOUR FATHER DOOMED HIMSELF TO. A LIFE OF SERVITUDE. OF SOLITUDE.
HAVE YOU EVER MET ANY OF YOUR FATHER'S FRIENDS, DJ?

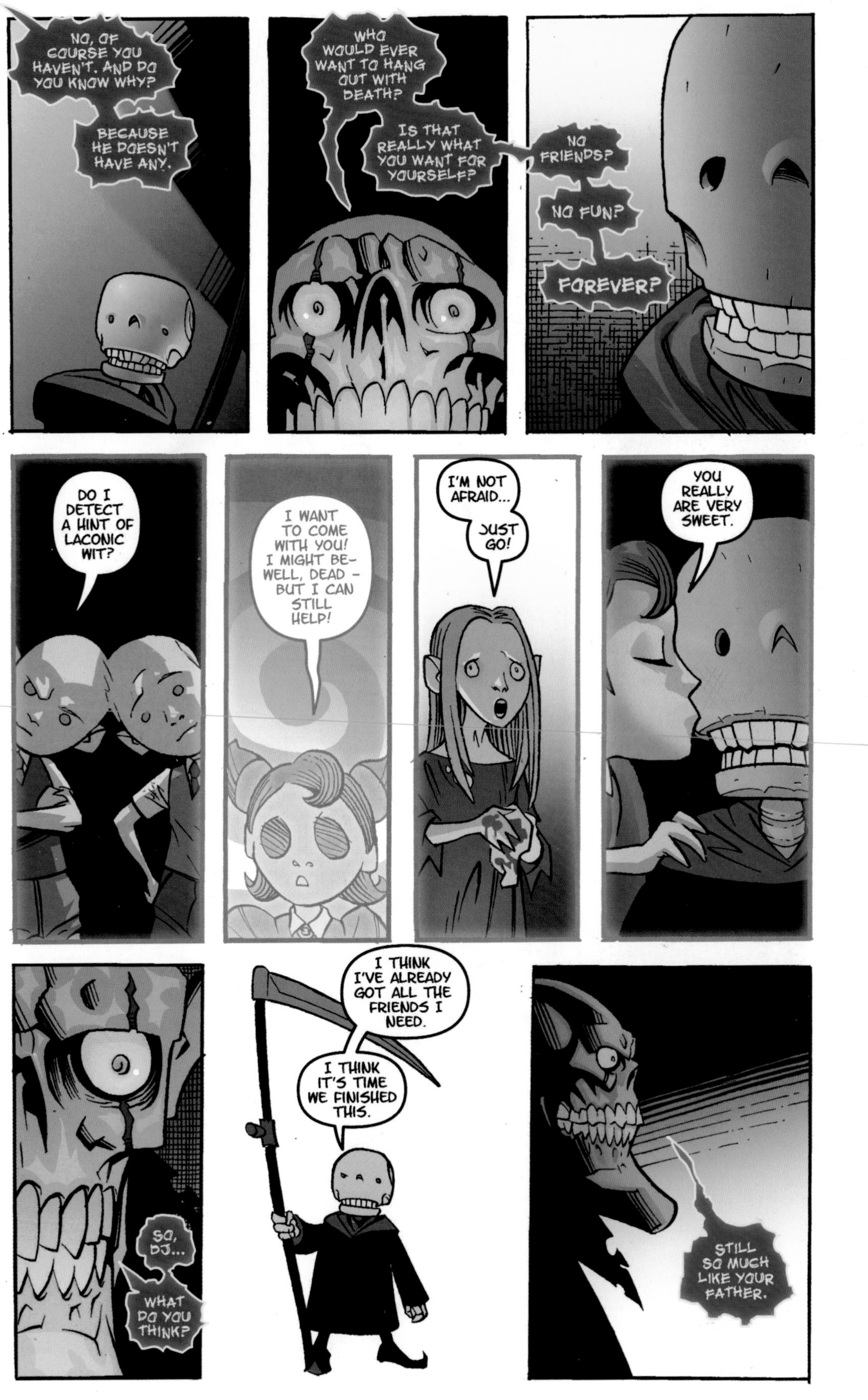
NO, OF COURSE YOU HAVEN'T. AND DO YOU KNOW WHY?
BECAUSE HE DOESN'T HAVE ANY.
WHO WOULD EVER WANT TO HANG OUT WITH DEATH?
IS THAT REALLY WHAT YOU WANT FOR YOURSELF?
NO FRIENDS?
NO FUN?
FOREVER?
DO I DETECT A HINT OF LACONIC WIT?
I WANT TO COME WITH YOU! I MIGHT BE- WELL, DEAD - BUT I CAN STILL HELP!
I'M NOT AFRAID...
JUST GO!
YOU REALLY ARE VERY SWEET.
SO, DJ...
WHAT DO YOU THINK?
I THINK I'VE ALREADY GOT ALL THE FRIENDS I NEED.
I THINK IT'S TIME WE FINISHED THIS.
STILL SO MUCH LIKE YOUR FATHER.

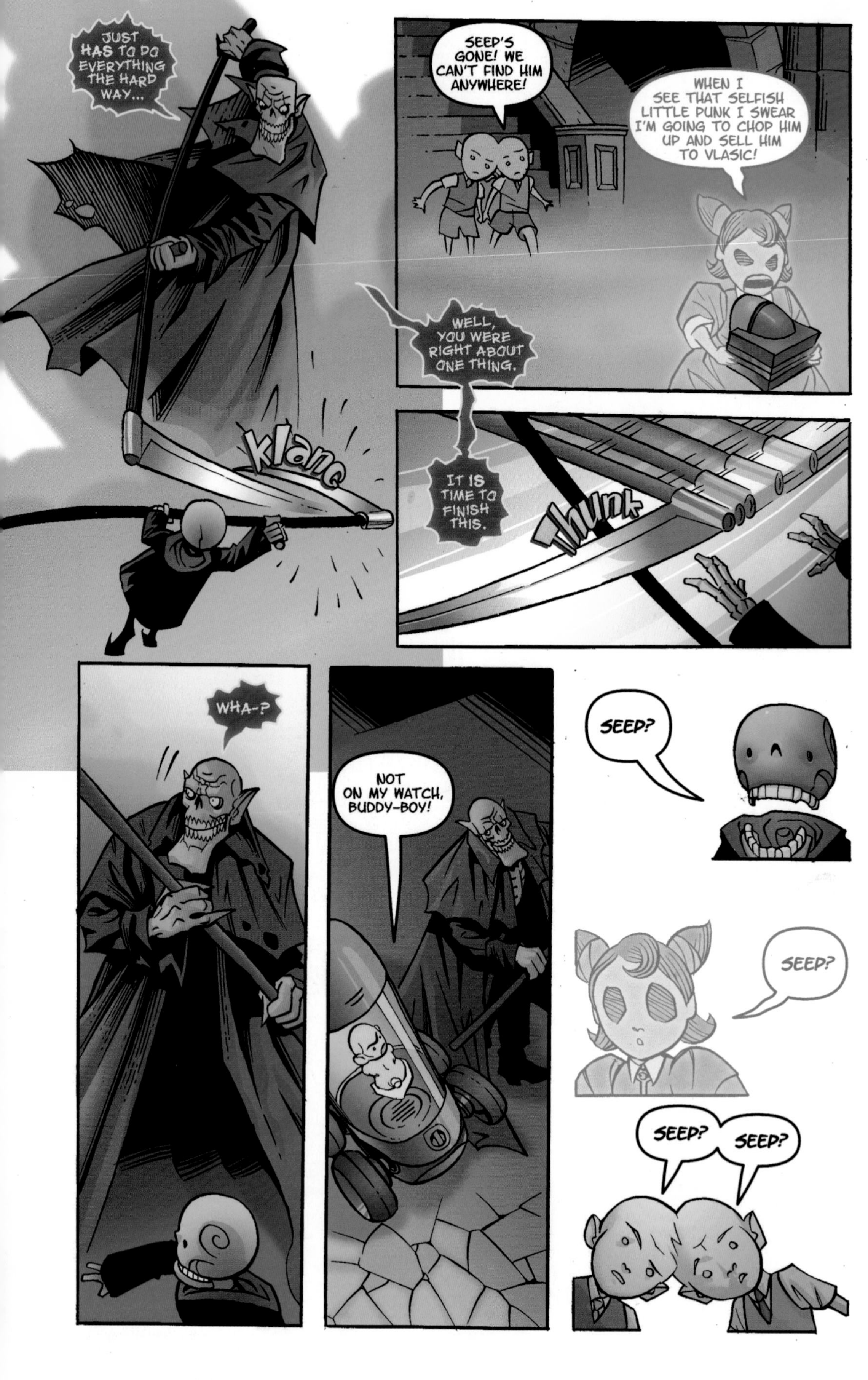
JUST HAS TO DO EVERYTHING THE HARD WAY...
SEEP'S GONE! WE CAN'T FIND HIM ANYWHERE!
WHEN I SEE THAT SELFISH LITTLE PUNK I SWEAR I'M GOING TO CHOP HIM UP AND SELL HIM TO VLASIC!
WELL, YOU WERE RIGHT ABOUT ONE THING.
KLANC
IT IS TIME TO FINISH THIS.
THUNK
WHA-?
NOT ON MY WATCH, BUDDY-BOY!
SEEP?
SEEP?
SEEP?
SEEP?

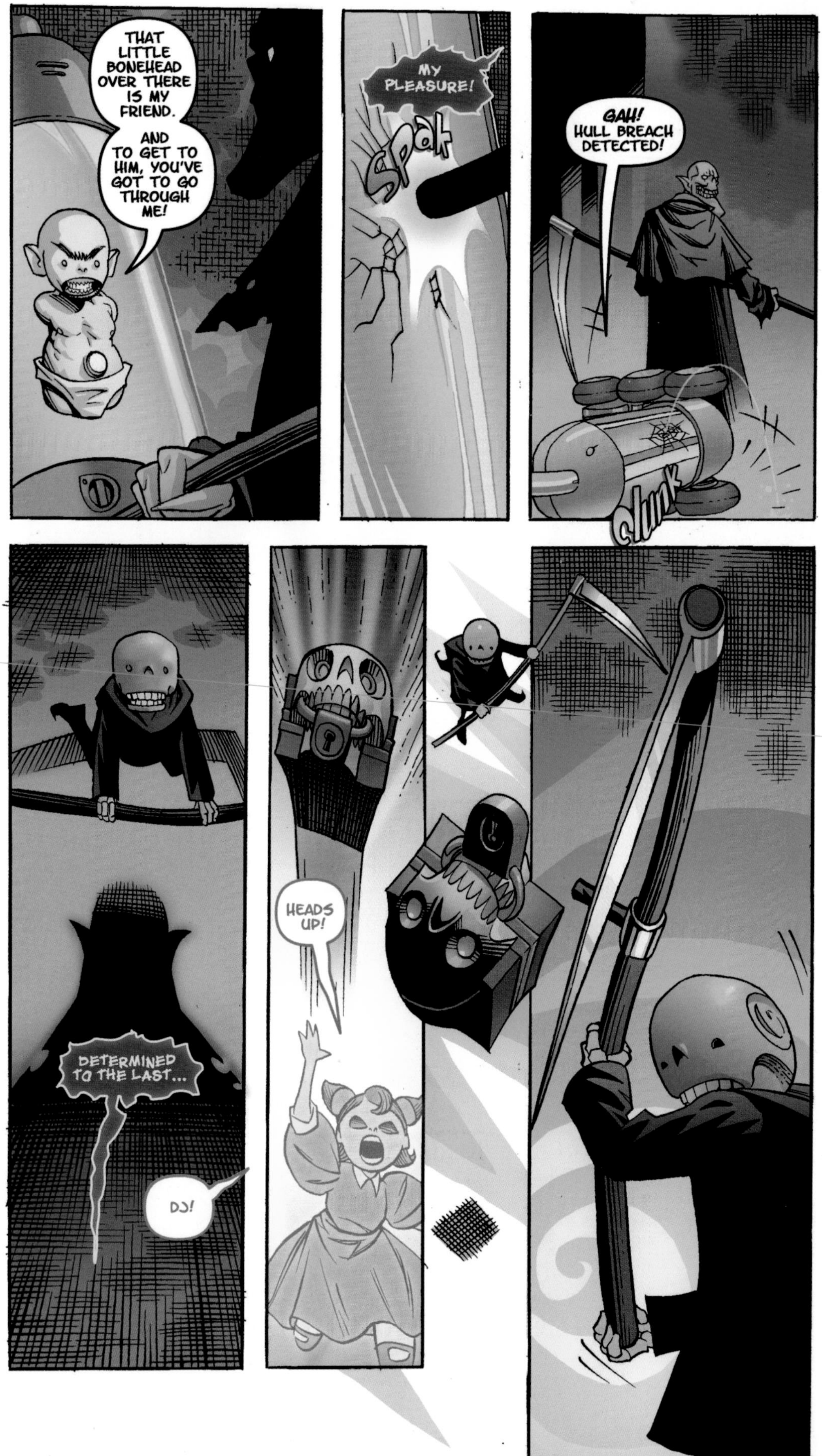
THAT LITTLE BONEHEAD OVER THERE IS MY FRIEND.
AND TO GET TO HIM, YOU'VE GOT TO GO THROUGH ME!
MY PLEASURE!
SPAK
GAH! HULL BREACH DETECTED!
SLUNK
DETERMINED TO THE LAST...
DJ!
HEADS UP!

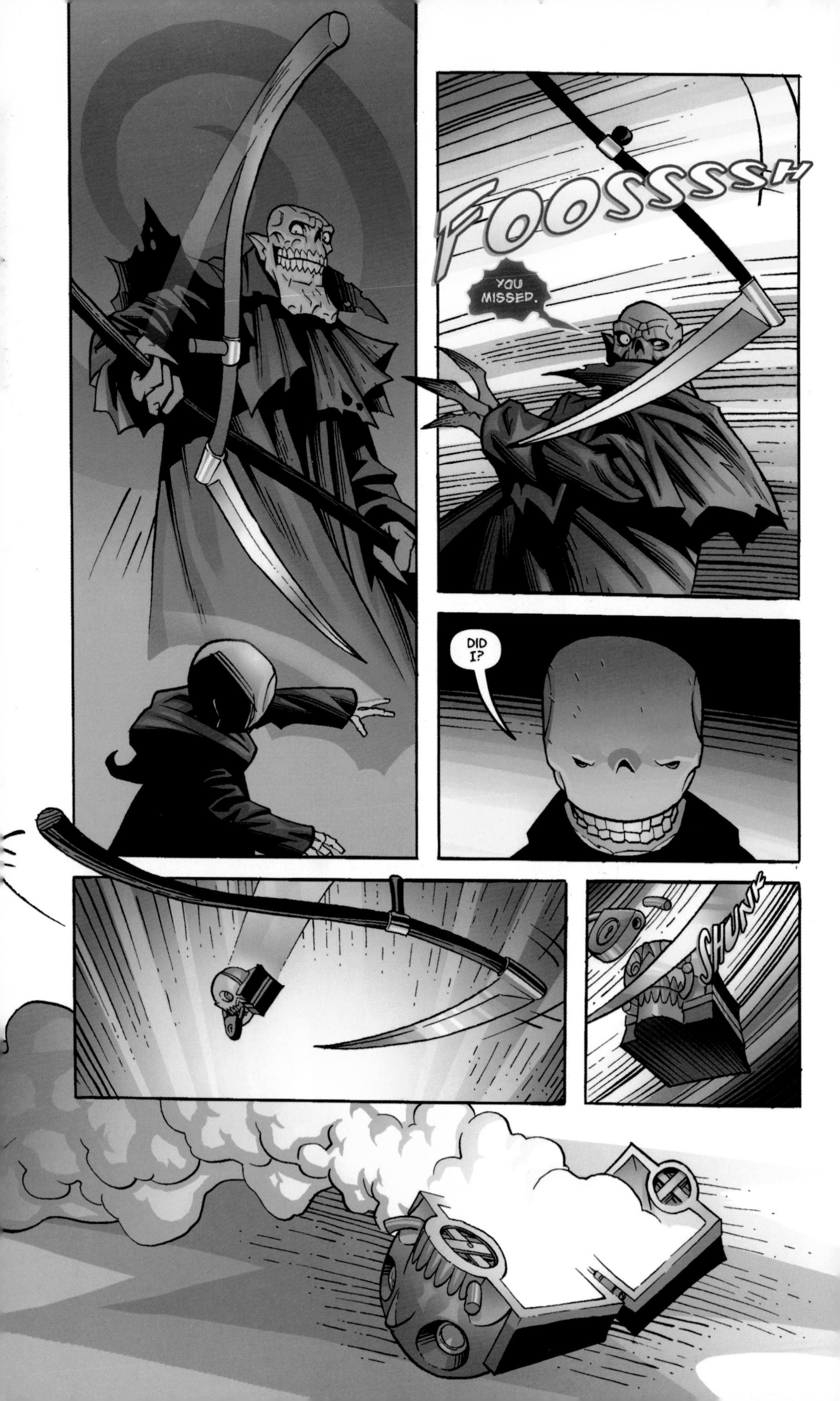
FOOSSSSH
YOU MISSED.
DID I?
SHUNK

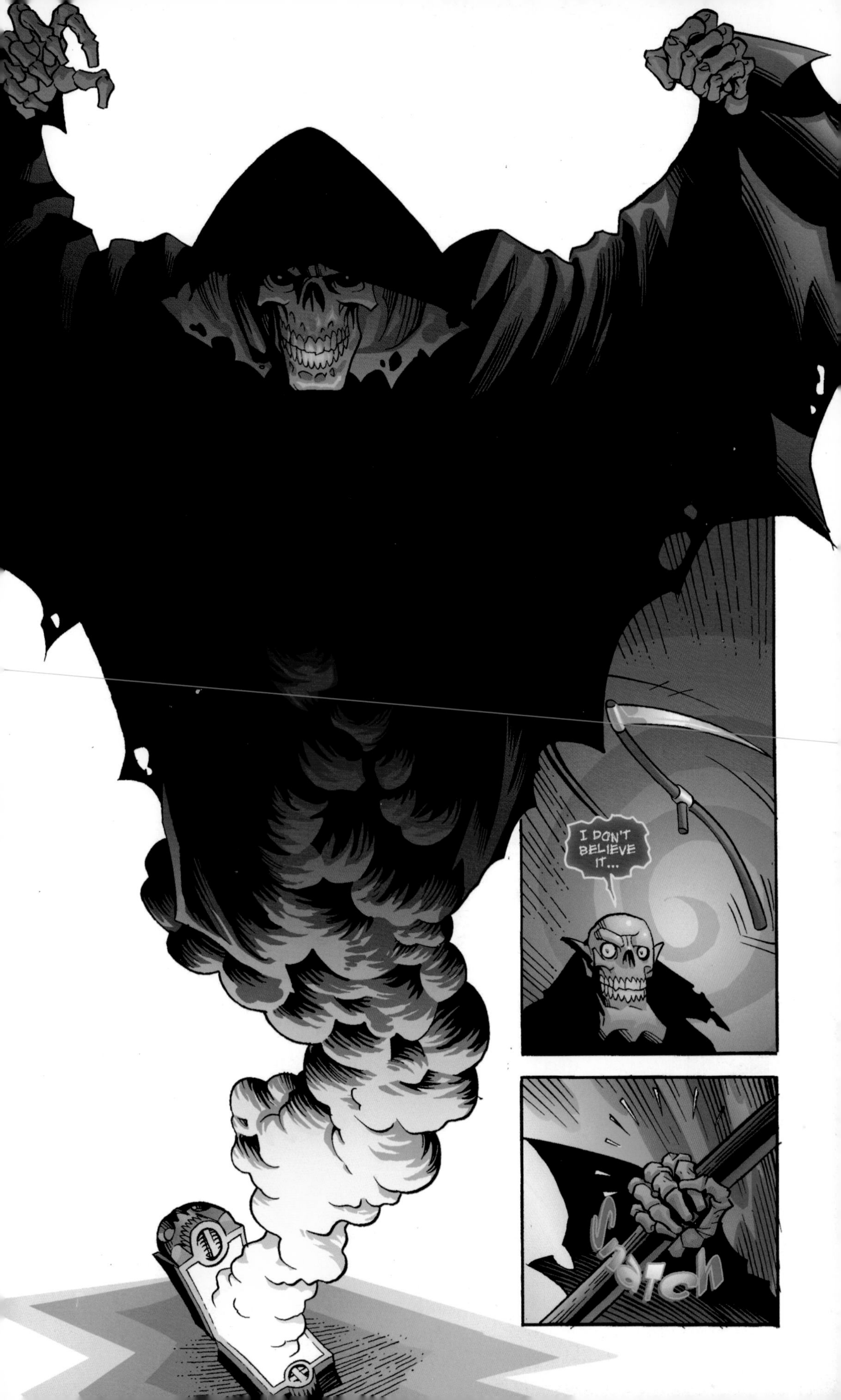

I DON'T BELIEVE IT...
SNATCH

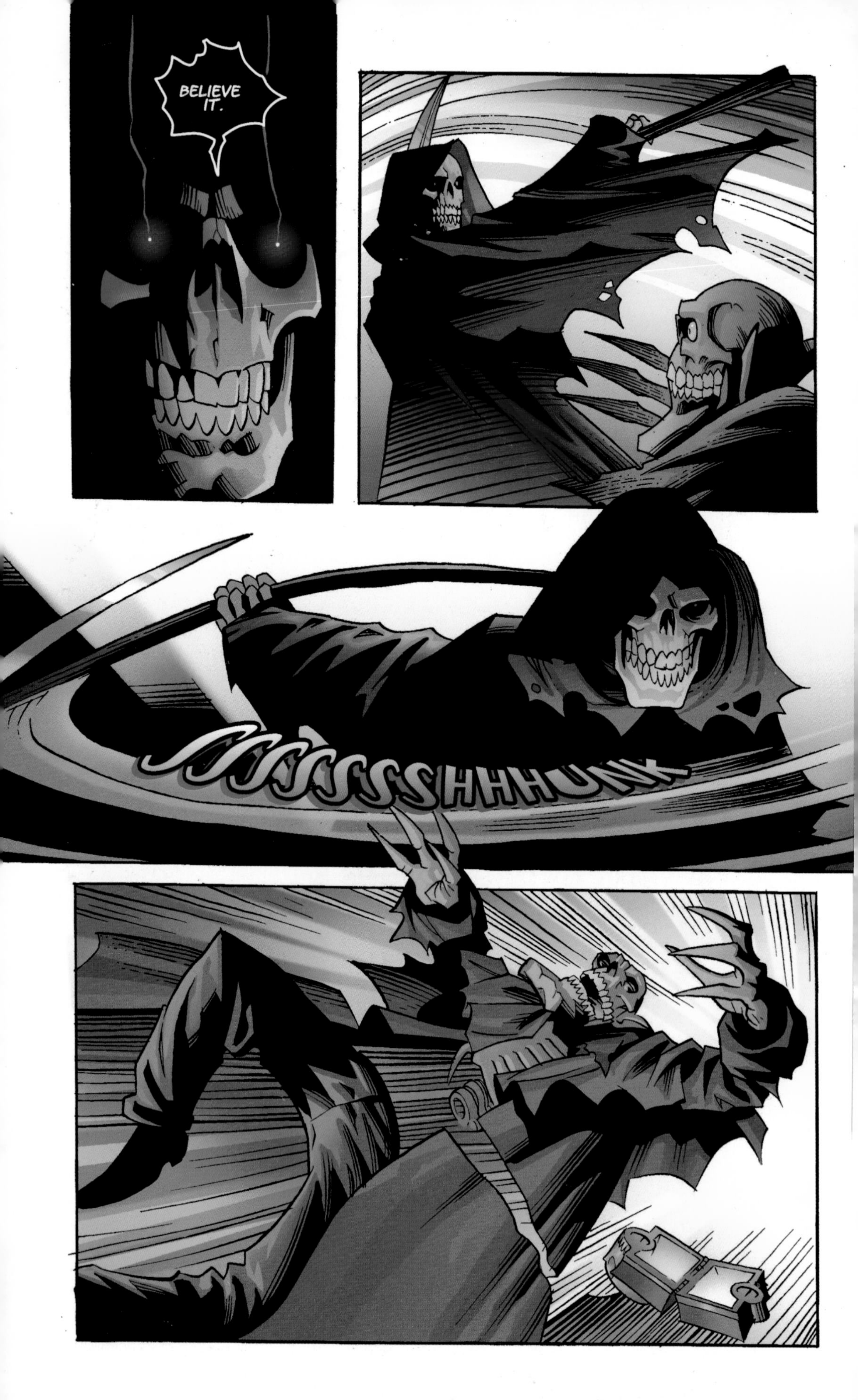
BELIEVE IT.
SSSSSSSSHHHUNK

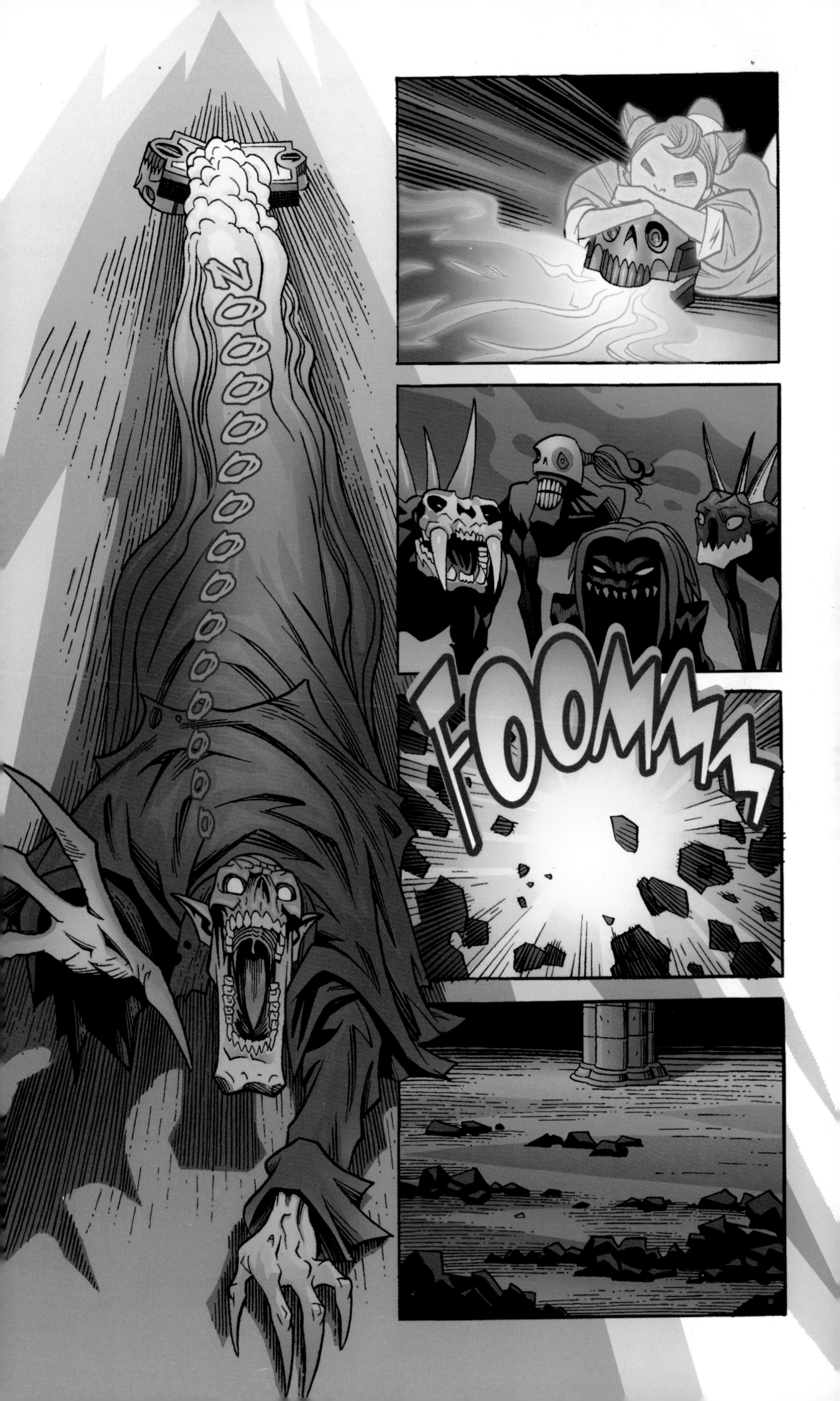
ZOOOOOOOOOOOOOOOOO
FOOM

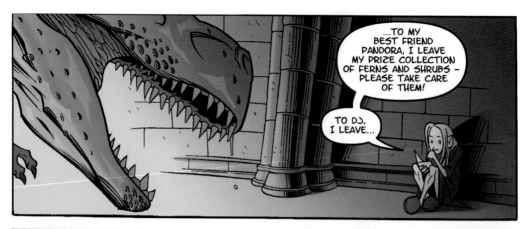

...TO MY BEST FRIEND PANDORA, I LEAVE MY PRIZE COLLECTION OF FERNS AND SHRUBS — PLEASE TAKE CARE OF THEM!

TO DJ, I LEAVE...

...A BIG PILE OF DINOSAUR BONES.

KRASH!

OKAY, WHAT JUST HAPPENED?

DAD!

HEY, TIGER. MISS ME?

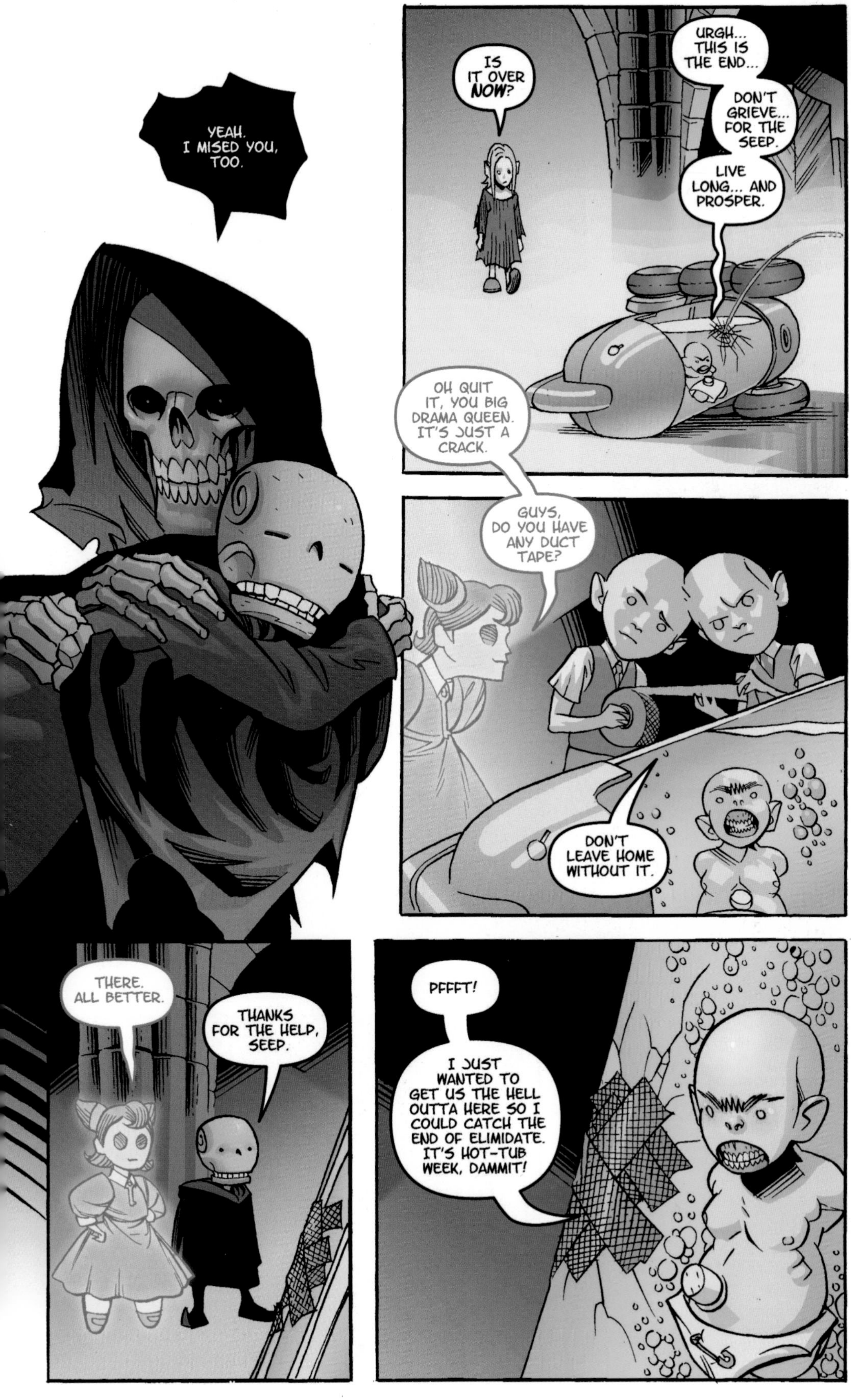
YEAH. I MISED YOU, TOO.
IS IT OVER NOW?
URGH... THIS IS THE END...
DON'T GRIEVE... FOR THE SEEP.
LIVE LONG... AND PROSPER.
OH QUIT IT, YOU BIG DRAMA QUEEN. IT'S JUST A CRACK.
GUYS, DO YOU HAVE ANY DUCT TAPE?
DON'T LEAVE HOME WITHOUT IT.
THERE. ALL BETTER.
THANKS FOR THE HELP, SEEP.
PFFFT!
I JUST WANTED TO GET US THE HELL OUTTA HERE SO I COULD CATCH THE END OF ELIMIDATE. IT'S HOT-TUB WEEK, DAMMIT!

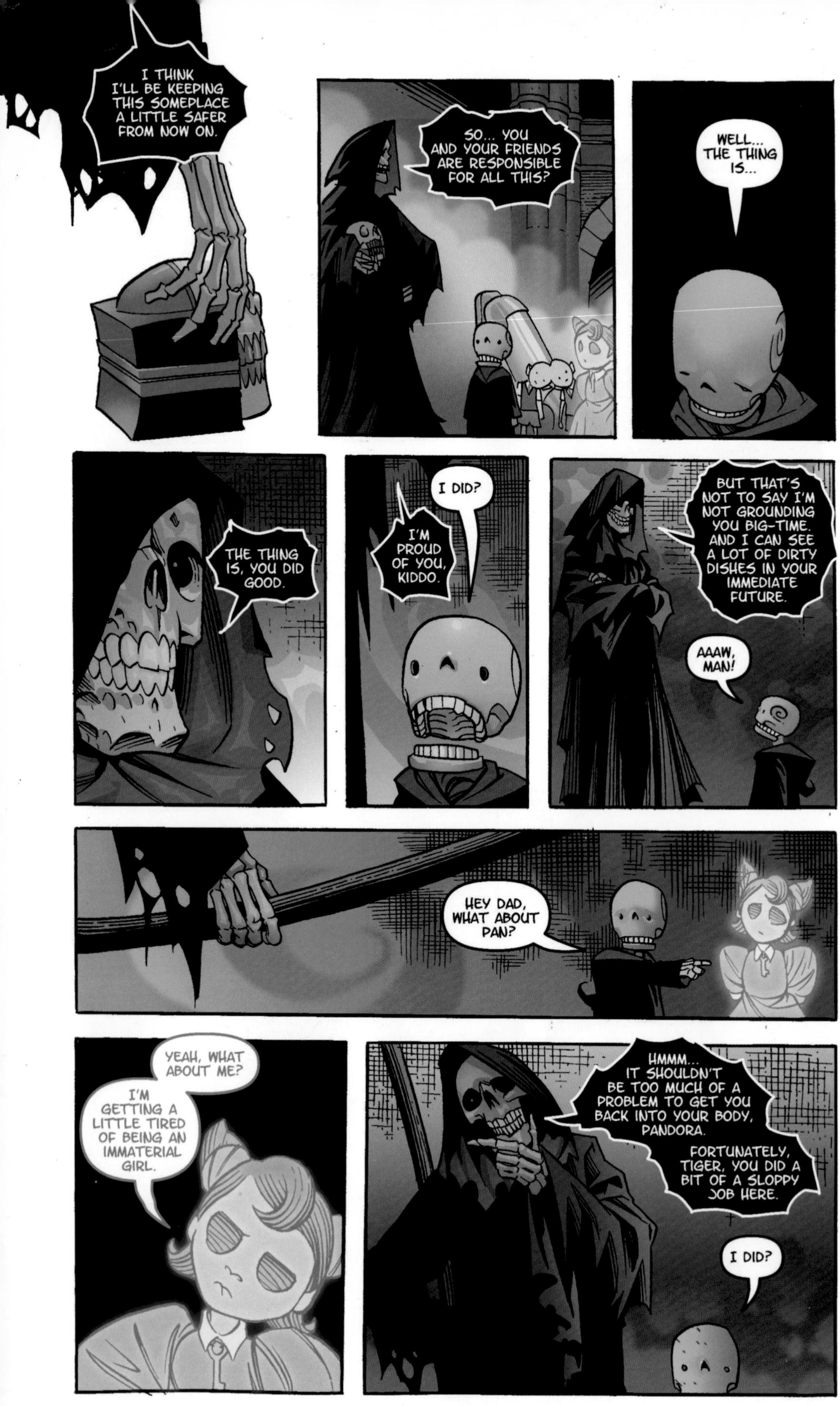

I THINK I'LL BE KEEPING THIS SOMEPLACE A LITTLE SAFER FROM NOW ON.
SO... YOU AND YOUR FRIENDS ARE RESPONSIBLE FOR ALL THIS?
WELL... THE THING IS...
THE THING IS, YOU DID GOOD.
I'M PROUD OF YOU, KIDDO.
I DID?
BUT THAT'S NOT TO SAY I'M NOT GROUNDING YOU BIG-TIME. AND I CAN SEE A LOT OF DIRTY DISHES IN YOUR IMMEDIATE FUTURE.
AAAW, MAN!
HEY DAD, WHAT ABOUT PAN?
YEAH, WHAT ABOUT ME?
I'M GETTING A LITTLE TIRED OF BEING AN IMMATERIAL GIRL.
HMMM... IT SHOULDN'T BE TOO MUCH OF A PROBLEM TO GET YOU BACK INTO YOUR BODY, PANDORA.
FORTUNATELY, TIGER, YOU DID A BIT OF A SLOPPY JOB HERE.
I DID?

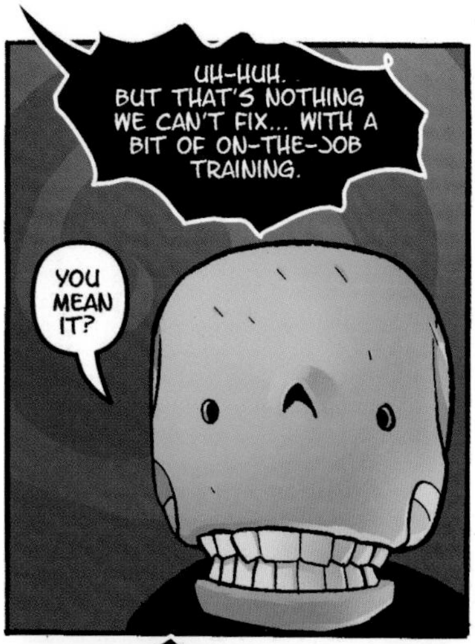
UH-HUH. BUT THAT'S NOTHING WE CAN'T FIX... WITH A BIT OF ON-THE-JOB TRAINING.
YOU MEAN IT?

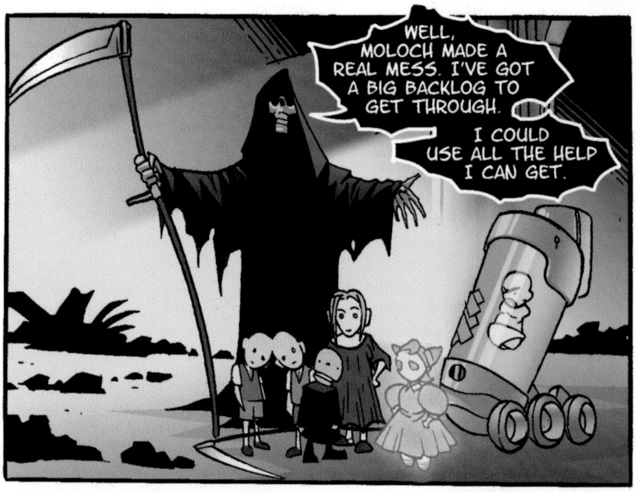
WELL, MOLOCH MADE A REAL MESS. I'VE GOT A BIG BACKLOG TO GET THROUGH.
I COULD USE ALL THE HELP I CAN GET.

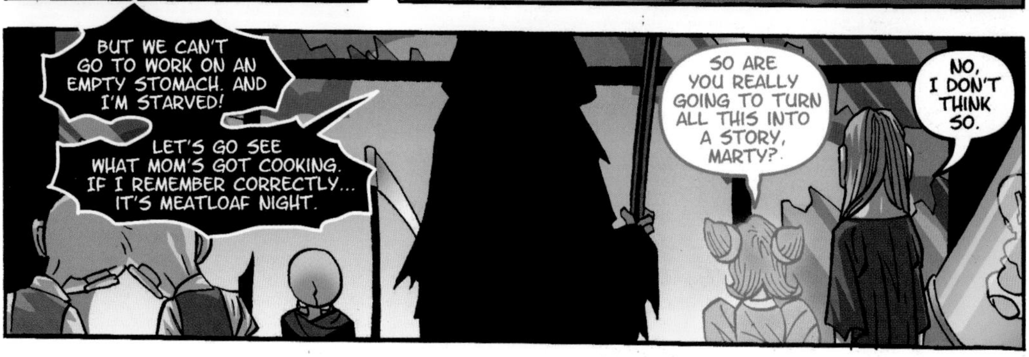
BUT WE CAN'T GO TO WORK ON AN EMPTY STOMACH. AND I'M STARVED!
LET'S GO SEE WHAT MOM'S GOT COOKING. IF I REMEMBER CORRECTLY... IT'S MEATLOAF NIGHT.
SO ARE YOU REALLY GOING TO TURN ALL THIS INTO A STORY, MARTY?
NO, I DON'T THINK SO.

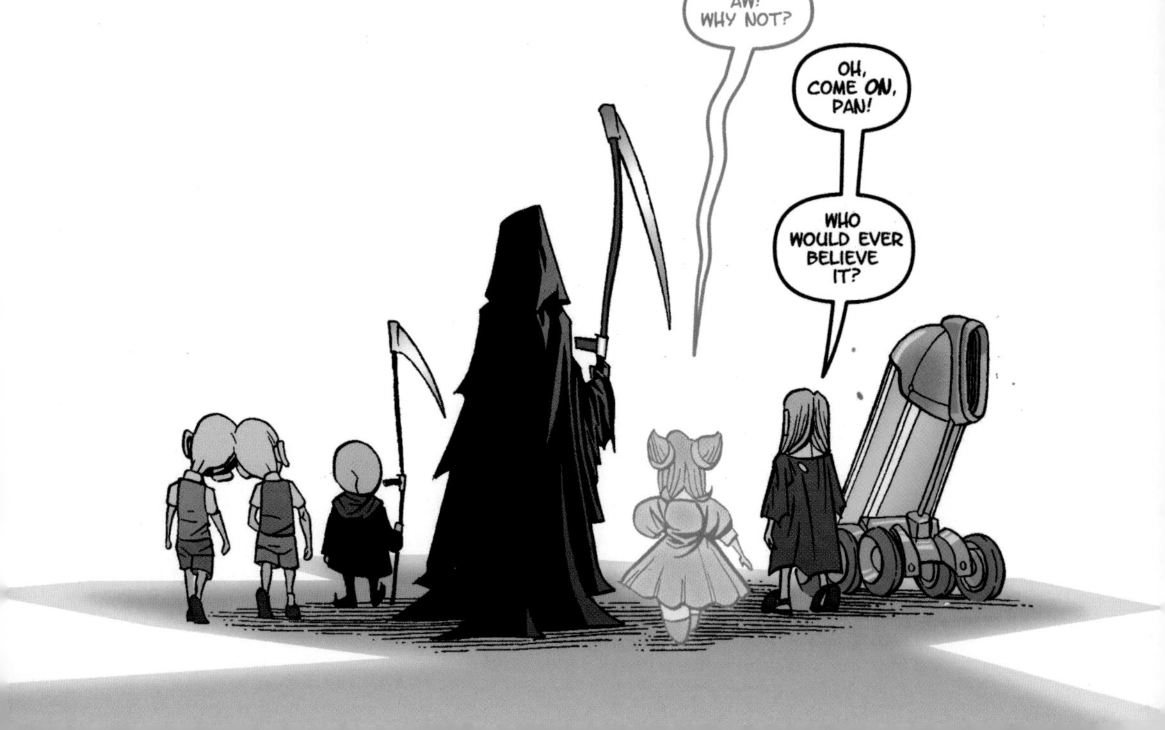
AW! WHY NOT?
OH, COME ON, PAN!
WHO WOULD EVER BELIEVE IT?

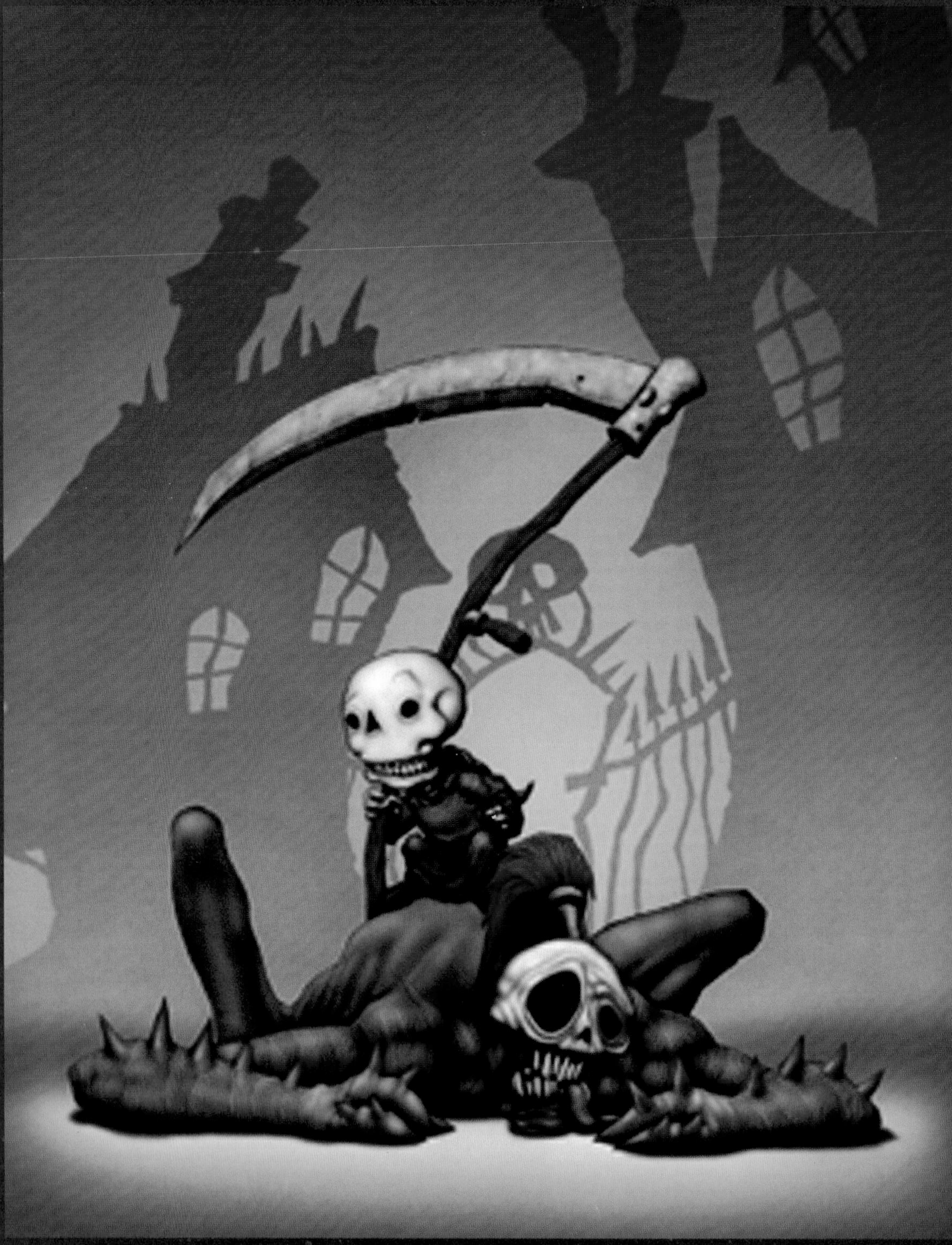

DJ CONCEPT ART DAVE ALLSOP 2005

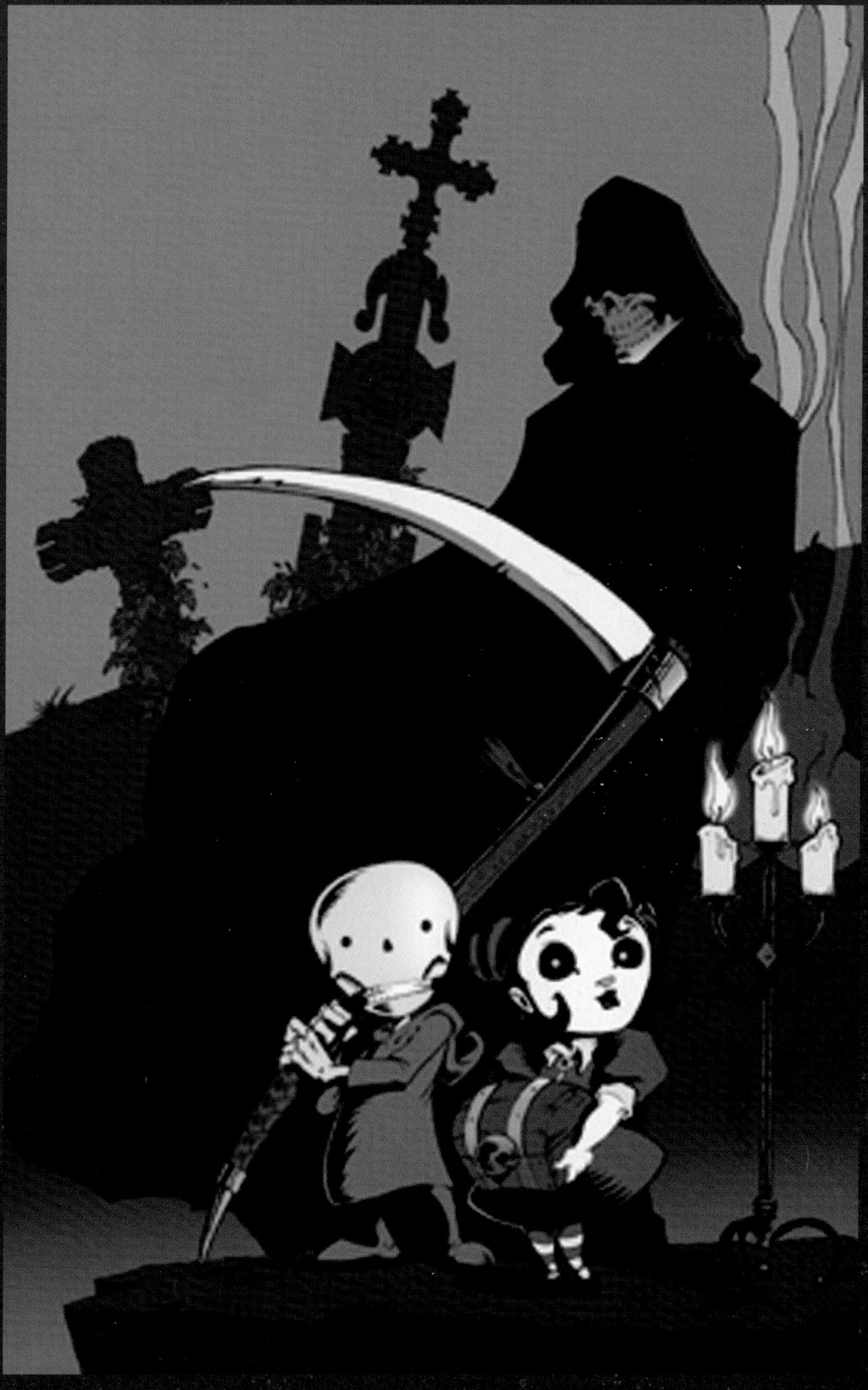

DJ CONCEPT ART PETER OVERSTREET 2004

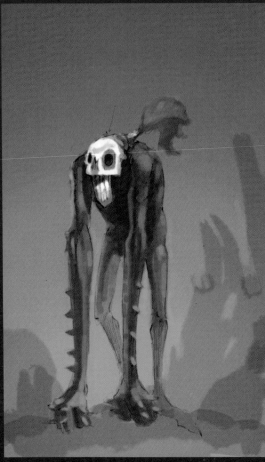

(left) RUSHER CONCEPT ART
SACH STEFFEL 2005

(below) DJ CONCEPT ART
SACH STEFFEL 2005

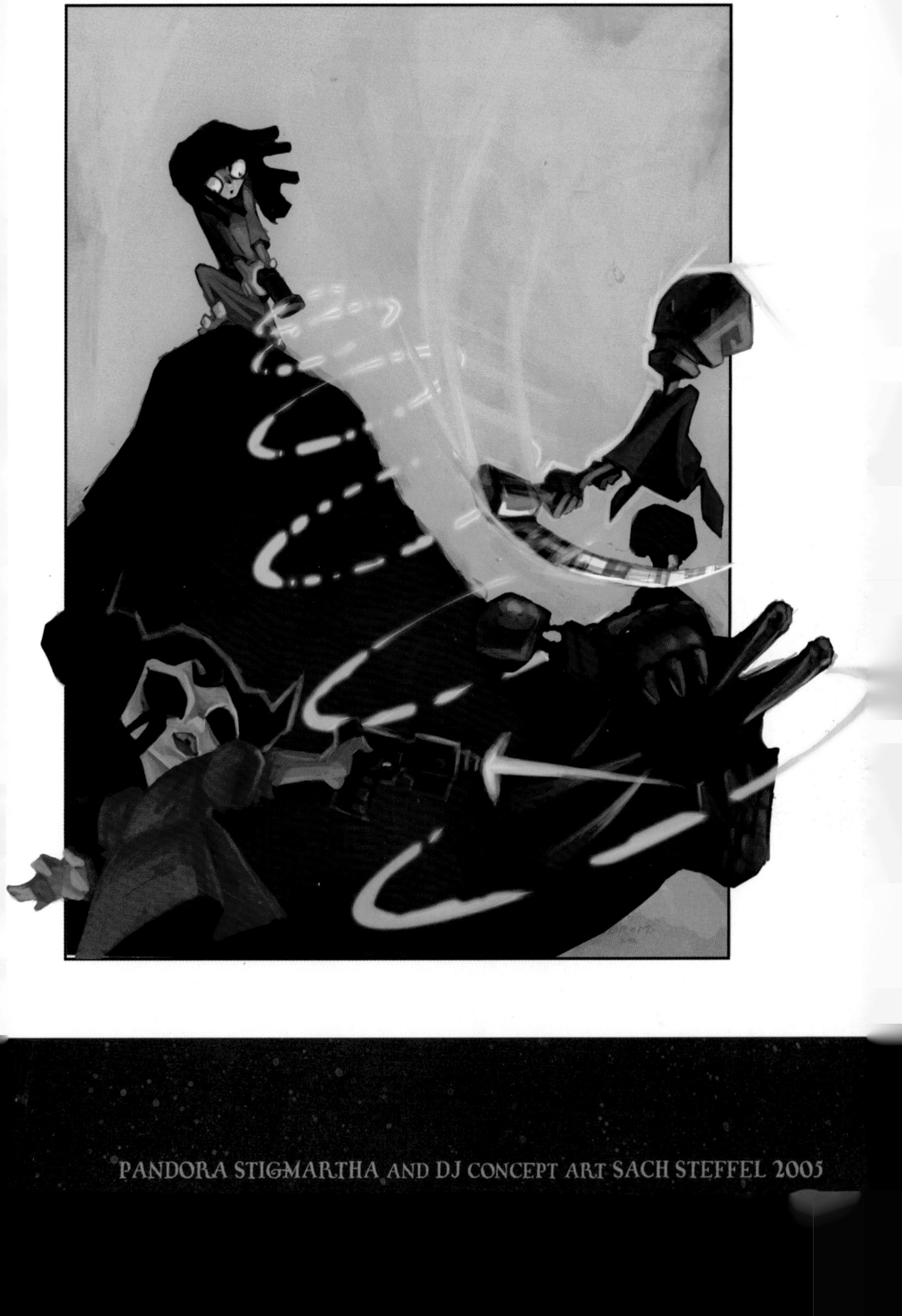

PANDORA STIGMARTHA AND DJ CONCEPT ART SACH STEFFEL 2005

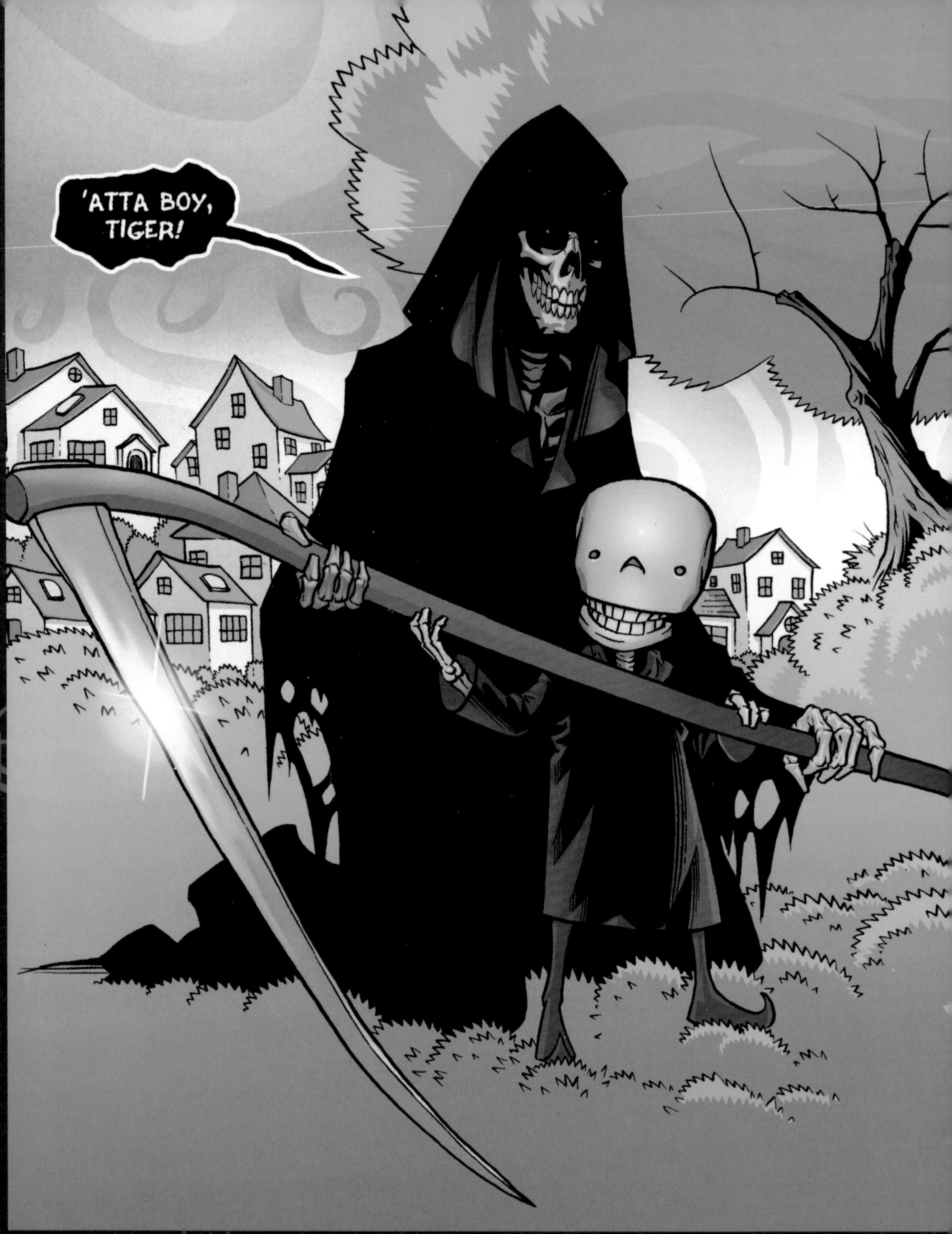
'ATTA BOY, TIGER!

DEATH, JR. PROMOTIONAL ART TED NAIFEH 2003

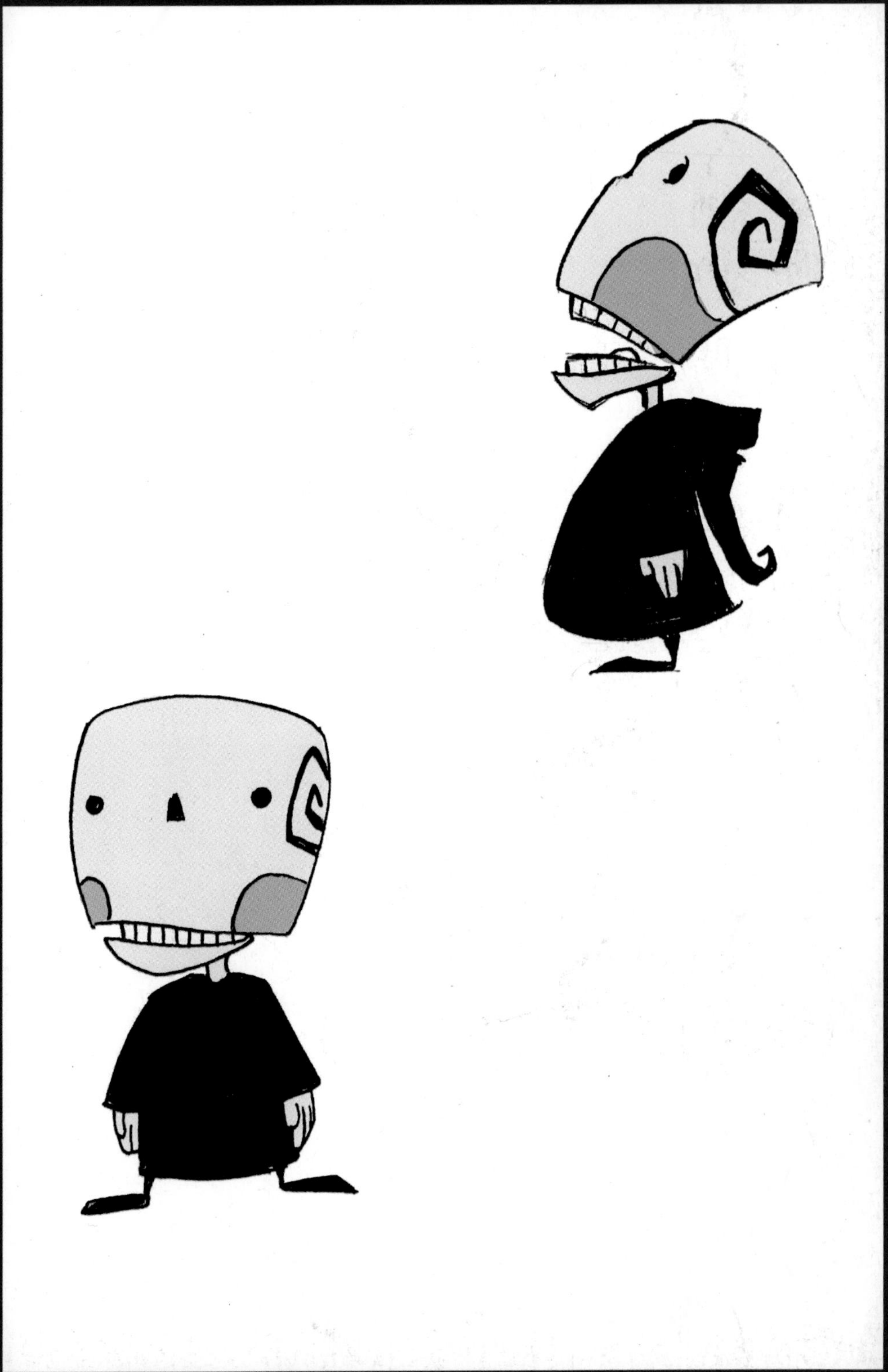

DJ CONCEPT ART PETER OVERSTREET 2004

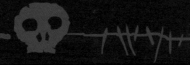

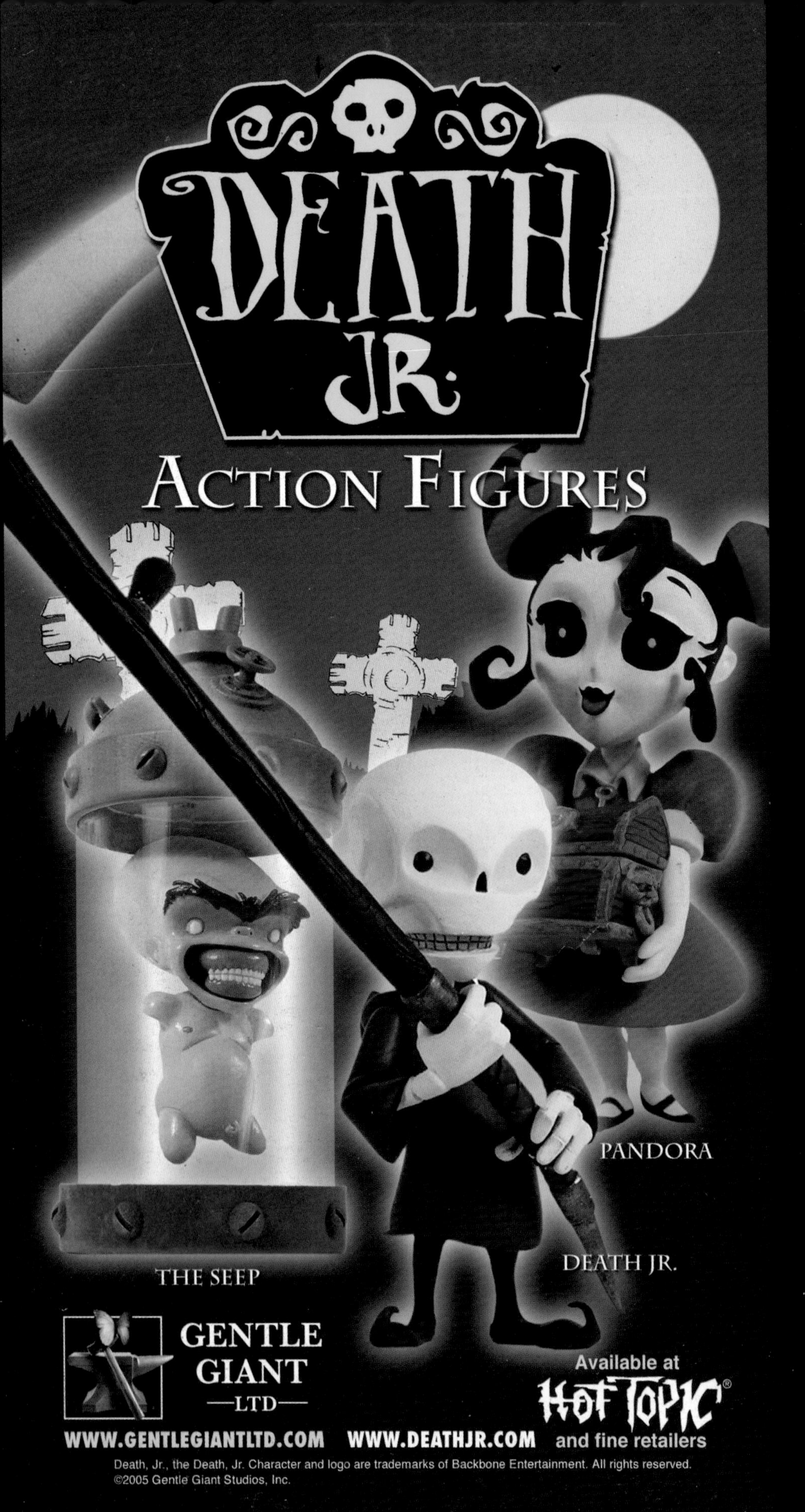

DEATH JR.
ACTION FIGURES
PANDORA
THE SEEP
DEATH JR.
GENTLE GIANT —LTD—
Available at
HOT TOPIC®
and fine retailers
WWW.GENTLEGIANTLTD.COM
WWW.DEATHJR.COM
Death, Jr., the Death, Jr. Character and logo are trademarks of Backbone Entertainment. All rights reserved.
©2005 Gentle Giant Studios, Inc.